LIVING FREE

Other Neil Anderson books published by Monarch Books.

A Way of Escape
The Bondage Breaker
The Bondage Breaker (Study Guide Edition)
The Common Made Holy
Daily In Christ (New Edition)
Living Free In Christ
Released From Bondage
Set Free (Omnibus Edition)
Victory Over the Darkness
Victory Over the Darkness (Study Guide Edition)
Walking In the Light

Available from Christian Bookshops or if difficulty, contact
Monarch Books, Concorde House, Grenville Place, Mill Hill,
London NW7 3SA.

LIVING FREE

Dr NEIL T. ANDERSON

MONARCH
BOOKS

British Library Cataloguing in Publication Data
A catalogue record for this book is available from the British Library.

Designed and produced by Bookprint Creative Services
P.O. Box 827, BN21 3YJ, England for
MONARCH BOOKS
in association with
ANGUS HUDSON LTD
Concorde House, Grenville Place, Mill Hill
London, NW7 3SA.
Printed in Great Britain.

CONTENTS

Book 2   Living Free in Christ

Part Three: Our Significance in Christ

In Christ…

Book 1

WALKING IN
THE LIGHT

Acknowledgements

For forty-nine years people have been building into my life. Books by authors I have never met and tapes by people I never knew have all contributed to my life. I'm grateful for all the teachers that I have had over the years. I'm sure each has contributed something to this book.

I want to thank Dr Robert Saucey, Dr Lloyd Kwast and my pastor, Reverend Byron McDonald, for reading through the rough draft and adding valuable insight and making needed suggestions. I carefully chose these three because I respect them and know of their love for the Lord and commitment to the truth. Together they represent theology, missions and pastoral ministry.

I couldn't have finished this project if it weren't for my wife, Joanne, who typed the rough draft. As always I'm thankful for a faithful companion who supports me and loves me enough to give me honest feedback. I appreciate so much the patience of my children, Heidi and Karl, who lost a little of their dad during some long days.

I'm deeply grateful for Dr Bill Bright and Campus Crusade for Christ. It was through the early days of this ministry that I found the Lord. Years later, I was one of the hundreds who stood up for full-time Christian ministry at Explo '72 in response to a message by Dr Bright. I was an aerospace engineer at the time. The foundation that was laid by Campus Crusade material provided solid guidance during my early Christian years. I especially appreciate the staff at Here's Life Publishers who have been so supportive.

Joanne and I want to dedicate this book to our parents, Marvin and Bertha Anderson, Chauncey and Alice Espe.

Thank you for staying together and standing at the top of our two families. You provided the love and moral foundation that made easy our entrance into the kingdom of God. You met our needs and provided the guidance we needed when we were young. Now that we have our own family, we look to the Lord for our guidance. You made that transition easy. We love you and we thank you for all the good memories.

1
Can We Really Know?

Does God communicate His will to us? If so, how?

In a telephone conversation a lady asked, 'Dr Anderson, my pastor says my favourite television evangelist is a false teacher. Is he right?'

At a ministerial retreat, a pastor stopped me and said, 'Neil, I've been at this church three years, and here's the situation...' After finishing his description he asked, 'Do you think God is calling me out of there?'

A seminary student stopped by my office and asked, 'You've met with my girlfriend and me twice now. Do you think we should get married?'

Good questions. Important questions for those asking them. They all hinge on the answer to a much larger question:

Does God communicate His will to us? If so, how?

Each of these fine Christians was coming to me because of personal confusion about how God reveals His will today. Specifically, they did not have the assurance that He had given them the spiritual discernment to make the right decision. They were thinking that I, like the referee in a game, would make the right 'call' for them.

A reliable guide
If what the Bible teaches is true, and I believe it is, then you don't need me or any other more 'spiritual' person to help you discern the spirits of the age or to find guidance in the

darkness we are living in. In the first place, we have the Bible, God's Word, which the Holy Spirit will enlighten for us as we meditate on it, providing us with remarkably clear guidance in most areas of our life. And secondly, we usually can experience the direct guidance of the Holy Spirit in areas not covered by God's Word — if we meet His conditions.

That kind of personal guidance occasionally becomes apparent to us very early in life. I remember as a young child sitting in church, listening to the minister and thinking, *I can do that*. Years later, at one of the church services I attended in the military, I left with the sense that God was calling me into ministry. I even informed my parents in a letter that I was considering becoming a pastor.

God prepares hearts

It is not uncommon to sense a call into ministry at an early age. Yet in my case, the unusual part is that I did not become a Christian until four years *after* my military service. This raises the question, 'Does God prepare hearts even before we belong to Him?' Again, if we accept God as sovereign and actively at work in the lives of people, we really must believe that. The apostle Paul alludes to it in Ephesians 2:10: 'We are His workmanship, created in Christ Jesus for good works, which God prepared *beforehand*, that we should walk in them.'

So where did I end up after the military? Despite my sense of His call to ministry I became an aerospace engineer. Was I now outside the will of God, or was God using that preparation to make me a better minister later on? I'll let you ask one of my students for an answer to that.

After four years in the aerospace industry, I again clearly heard God's call. I left a successful career and attended seminary. Along the way I had the privilege of serving as a club director for a campus outreach ministry, then as a youth pastor, an associate pastor, a senior pastor and now a seminary professor.

I never applied for, sent a résumé to or personally sought after any of those positions. In each case, I believe God clearly led me. When I started my walk with God, I had no desire to be a senior pastor and certainly not a seminary professor. My own sense of giftedness and direction became evident as I grew in the Lord.

A matter of shaping

You see, when I left engineering school, I was sure that my education was finished. I had no desire to pursue any more formal education. As I began to mature in the Lord, my desire to read and learn increased. The Lord was shaping my life in ways that I never would have anticipated. Since then I have finished two masters degrees and two doctoral programmes. Anybody who knew me in high school would have to acknowledge that as a miracle.

As a result of my experience, and from my contact with many Christians, I have come to believe deeply that God does sovereignly govern the affairs of mankind. He gently guides our steps as we choose to walk with Him. I believe in divine guidance. I believe that God wants to make His presence known in our lives and in our ministries.

Discerning deceiving spirits

Yet I also know that there are false teachers and false prophets in the world. People are paying attention to deceiving spirits. This should not surprise us, of course, for the apostle Paul wrote to Timothy: 'The Spirit clearly says that in later times some will abandon the faith and follow deceiving spirits and things taught by demons' (1 Timothy 4:1, NIV).

Does this deception happen in Christian circles, or is it only the experience of the unbeliever? Unfortunately, I have abundant evidence that today we have an extraordinary level of deception going on even among believers. I have been helping people find freedom in Christ for several years, and hardly a day goes by that I do not talk to a believer who has been deceived. Many, believe it or not, are in full-time ministry or preparing for it. They are all Christians desiring to know and do God's will.

While my ministry was developing, I watched several of my Christian friends (some were actually under my teaching) drift from the faith and fall prey to the deception of false teachers. I saw their character erode and their morality deteriorate.

At a conference, a pastor handed this note to me: 'This may be an unreasonable request, but would it be possible to talk to you privately? I am a pastor, yet I struggle with bizarre thoughts that I used to think were from God, and I'm consumed by lust.'

I have listened to hundreds of parents tell of their children falling away. Others have told me about their spouses, relatives and friends being deceived. That's the kind of world we live in since Satan deceived Eve, though it seems the intensity of the enemy's attacks are increasing as the day of the Lord draws near.

New Age influence

Though New Age religion is not new, what is new is how it has penetrated every level of society in the Western world. You think you are going to a helpful seminar on resolving conflict in the workplace, when instead you are introduced to New Age meditation techniques. Without spiritual discernment, even the best-intentioned Christian can be deceived.

Your teenage son or daughter may have to take a class in health, only to find the teacher is espousing New Age medicine. Your primary school child is frightened by an appearance in his or her room or terrorised by nightmares that you cannot explain. Later you learn of your child's exposure to the game of Dungeons and Dragons, opening the door to demonic activity.

That's why we need to expose counterfeits before we are able to come to grips fully with the subject of God's direct guidance in our lives.

Thus in Part One of this book, we'll see how many of us are being led astray by counterfeit guidance.

Counterfeits result in bondage

I have counselled people who were once heralded as great prophets, but now they find themselves in deep spiritual bondage to the lies of Satan. Others believed they were guided by God but were actually paying attention to a deceiving spirit.

A pastor wrote: 'I discovered that one of the older members of our deacon board along with two other long-standing members of my church practise a form of spirit contact that sounds something like a séance. They told me that not all of the spirits one can contact are necessarily bad and that one had to consider the enduring nature of the "good things" they brought, such as healings and messages from the other side.'

At the same time, in our technological age, many misguided people are so orientated to knowledge and are so anti-supernatural, that they have reduced our walk with God to nothing more than an intellectual exercise. Thus we will explore the balance between Western humanistic rationalism and Eastern mysticism.

I will also analyse fear, since fear is a great strategy of Satan. Through his lies he paralyses his prey in fear so that they cannot do the will of God. Fear and faith are mutually exclusive — they cannot both be guiding a believer at the same time. With the rise of Satanism and the advance of the

New Age philosophies, we in the church must know the truth and exercise discernment as never before.

Seven standards for divine guidance

Once we have established how counterfeit discernment and guidance operates in our day, we will look at seven standards of divine guidance in Part Two. I will attempt to address such questions as: What is God's will for our lives? How can we tell the difference between the 'voice of God' and deceiving spirits? How do we walk by faith, and how does the Holy Spirit enable us to discern the true from the false?

One of the elements of the Christian faith I have had to learn is that, at times, God seems to veil His face. We cannot seem to get any answers to our most important questions. It is then, I have discovered, that we need simply to walk with God through the darkness, trusting in His sovereign will for us. Thus in Part Three we will focus on 'Walking With God'.

No easy answers

I did not write this book simply to set forth some easy-to-follow guidelines for knowing God's will. My purpose is to help you walk closely with God, which does require an understanding of how He guides. I will do my best to draw a fine line on issues that are clearly black and white in Scripture, but I will cover grey issues only in broad strokes. Some things will remain unanswered and seem ambiguous until the Lord returns. It is not God's will for us to know everything or to be omniscient, but to be truly dependent upon Him.

I cannot answer all the questions that I have in my own mind, much less yours. I am deeply sensitive to the possibility of leading one of God's lambs down a wrong path. After all, it is a bit presumptuous for any mortal to say how God guides. But my prayer is that you will keep an open mind and search the Scriptures with me.

Be discerning of what I have to say. The Bible is the only infallible source, not Neil Anderson or any other pastor or seminary professor. How presumptuous to think otherwise. That's why I have committed myself to God's Word, since it is the only reliable source of absolute truth.

I encourage you to 'be diligent to present yourself approved to God as a workman who does not need to be ashamed, handling accurately the word of truth' (2 Timothy 2:15). If I help some of you stay on the narrow path of truth in your walk with God, I will be satisfied. If I help others to get back on the path, I will be thrilled.

2
Rationalism Versus Mysticism

We'll find truth somewhere between the extremes of
Western rationalism and Eastern mysticism

While sharing with a university group, I could sense that
one of the local heroes wasn't buying what I was saying.
Rather than try and ignore him, since he was distracting the
group, I asked what he believed in. He said, 'I believe in
this,' putting his arm around his girlfriend. 'I only believe in
what I can see, feel, hear and touch.'

I asked him if he had a brain. 'You better believe it,' he
responded.

'Have you ever seen it, felt it, heard it or touched it?' I
asked.

'I know it's there because I can sense its effect,' he said
with confidence.

I said, 'Look around, and you will see the effect of God's
hand everywhere.'

A timid soul from another corner of the room entered
into our discussion, 'I think it's silly to argue about what is
true,' he began. 'I believe in all religions. I just close my eyes
and God reveals Himself to me. We can all be one with God
if we will just let our minds be enlightened.'

Same classroom, opposite ends of the spectrum. Eastern
mysticism was squaring off with Western rationalism. Two

opposing ways of looking at life, both contrary to the Word of God.

To understand these diverse ways of thinking today, we need to see how they have developed. It shouldn't be difficult to see the god of this world in action as we trace the move away from a God-centred faith.

The shift from God

Secular humanism grew out of the Renaissance when people began to focus more and more on the glory of humanity to the exclusion of the glory of God. Human reason and scientific innovation became the final authority of life, replacing God's revelation. Man decided he could live independent of God. This is the same old lie from the Garden.

Humanism's goal was to gain freedom from religious superstition and the authority of the church, but it contained fatal flaws. With God out of the picture, the universe lost its purpose, meaning and value. People like you and me were no longer seen as being made in the image of God but merely as the product of evolutionary forces.

The Western mind

How did this translate into Western culture? In search of truth, the Western world resorts to observation and experimentation, a process known as *empiricism*. The Western world's educational system says that all that needs to be known can be learned through a scientific method of investigation. Then once that knowledge is gained, rationalism steps in. The information must be analysed by a rational person in order to be of value.

Having been an aerospace engineer and having completed a research doctorate, I certainly can relate to this process. To the scientific mind, empiricism and rationalism are two sides of the same coin. Do the research, then make the analysis. To accept something as true, it must be systematic and fit the facts.

An example of Western thinking would be the belief that if A equals B, and B equals C, then A must equal C. It's hard for a person educated in the West to accept the fact that there are many educated people in the world who think differently. A person raised with a Hindu mindset would say maybe A equals C and maybe it doesn't.

Empiricism and revelation

Now let's take this a step further into the Christian world. Many Christians feel that the general revelation of God in nature justifies looking at the world through the eyes of empiricism. They would point to such passages as, 'The heavens are telling the glory of God; and their expanse is declaring the work of His hands' (Ps 19:1). And, 'For since the creation of the world His invisible attributes, His eternal power and divine nature, have been clearly seen, being understood through what has been made, so that they are without excuse' (Rom 1:20). Since all truth is God's truth, whatever we discover empirically by observation and experimentation must be true.

It sounds good, but I have serious reservations. In and of itself, nature doesn't provide any answers concerning purpose and meaning in life; it must be explained by special revelation, the Word of God. Second, the scientific method of investigation, by nature and design, does not take into account the spiritual world.

The scientific method was developed in the natural sciences, which are, generally speaking, precise sciences. By that I mean that all physical substances can be reduced to one atom categorised in the periodic table of the elements. Given enough time and experimentation, almost every chemical combination could be analysed and explained.

The social sciences, however, are not precise sciences. We

cannot accurately predict how man will react in any given situation. What we research is man operating in the flesh. How can this provide definitive truth to the child of God designed to walk by the Spirit? Obviously, it cannot. It can only verify statistically what is, not what can or should be.

Limitations of our society

Without the authority of the Bible, our society treats the social sciences as precise sciences. For instance, a judge may appoint a court-ordered psychiatrist to determine a person's competence. I would ask, 'What psychology does the psychiatrist adhere to?' He or she may not have a biblical view of man, and 'science' varies greatly concerning the nature of man. There are scores of psychological theories. Each has some truth, but none are capable of an infallible judgement.

There's another limitation. The laws of nature don't apply to the spiritual world. You may be able to get full cooperation from people for research, but don't expect the kingdom of darkness to comply. Even God doesn't submit to our methods of investigation. We can't put Him in a box. This doesn't mean that the scientific method is wrong; it's just incomplete and insufficient to be a reliable basis for our faith.

Finally, our best reasoning is always biased because of our culture, education and personal experience. None of us is a totally objective observer. We all look at reality through our own knowledge and experience. Wisdom, on the other hand, is seeing truth from God's perspective.

We need to interpret research through the eyes of revelation. Research does not validate revelation; revelation validates research. Research sheds light on what is; revelation sheds light on why it is, what it should be and what it will be.

Our ability to reason is limited on three counts. First, we can never be sure we have all the facts. Second, we can never be sure we are perfectly interpreting the facts. And third, we can never be sure what the consequences will be after any decided course of action. Consequently, we need divine guidance. There is only one who is all-knowing. We will never know so much that we will no longer need God. In fact, I have found that the more I know God and His Word, the more dependent I have become. I believe Paul's words illustrate this great need:

> Where is the wise man? Where is the scribe? Where is the debater of this age? Has not God made foolish the wisdom of this world? For since in the wisdom of God the world through its wisdom did not come to know God, God was well-pleased through the foolishness of the message preached to save those who believe (1 Cor 1:20,21).

Eastern mysticism

The Eastern world takes an opposite approach from the Western world, looking at truth more from intuition than from reason. Hinduism and Taoism are metaphysical, relying on mysticism from divine guidance. The Eastern Mystic sees the mind as the problem. If truth is to be known, the mind must be bypassed. Listen to the words of Guru Maharaj-Ji:

> Ignorance is only created by the mind, and the mind keeps the secret that you are something divine away from you. This is why you have to tame the mind first. The mind is a snake, and the treasure is behind it. The snake lies over the treasure, so if you want the treasure, you will have to kill the snake. And killing the snake is not an easy job.

Mystic sects talk of a 'new organ of perception' in man, another way of 'knowing'. Yoga refers to the development of a third eye which gives spiritual sight to the advanced yogi.

Other sects refer to 'intuition', the 'psychic self' or the 'unconscious mind' as the means of perception. They say that the first step toward spiritual growth is to train oneself to ignore all messages from the mind. Next comes the tuning of one's 'second organ of perception' to the 'universal mind' or the impersonal 'god of mysticism'. Once attuned, the psychic self can bypass the mind and thus perceive reality directly. Attempts to erase the mind range from transcendental meditation to Silva mind control.

Most Westerners, however, are uncomfortable with throwing their minds into neutral, and Hinduism is too ascetic for the materialistic Westerner. So this is where the New Age steps in. It takes this unpalatable Eastern approach and makes it appealing to Westerners.

The New Age movement modifies this mindless approach by claiming that the mind is not being bypassed; it is actually the mind that is achieving 'cosmic consciousness.' They say that the mind creates reality. This is the basic teaching behind the Church of Religious Science. Ernest Holmes and other proponents of science of mind teaching believe that the supreme, creative power of the universe is a cosmic principle which is present throughout the universe and in every one of us. Science of the mind teaches that we are creating our own day-to-day experiences by the form and procession of our thoughts. They teach that man, by the way he thinks, can bring whatever he desires into his experience. And so we begin to see the popular appeal of New Age thinking to the undiscerning person.

The unifying factors of the New Age

Recently I was preparing for a conference designed to reach New Agers. After reading several volumes, I was struck by the fact that differing religious and philosophical groups which previously had very little in common were suddenly finding unity under the New Age banner.

The New Age movement is not seen as a religion but a new way to think and understand reality. It's very attractive to the natural man who has become disillusioned with organised religion and Western rationalism. He desires spiritual reality but doesn't want to give up materialism, deal with his moral problems or come under authority.

Do you remember the snake Maharaj-Ji mentioned earlier? Well, there was another snake in the Garden. And all false religions of the world are nothing more than different humps of that same snake. It would only make sense that they would hold some things in common. I've discovered six unifying factors in New Age thinking.

The first is *monism* — the belief that all is one and one is all. It says we all swim in one great cosmic ocean. All human ills stem from an inability to perceive this unity. History is not the story of humanity's fall into sin and its restoration by God's saving grace. Rather, it is humanity's fall into ignorance and the gradual ascent into enlightenment.

Clearly, this is not the case. There is a definite boundary between the finite and the infinite. Monism is a counterfeit to the unity Jesus prayed for in John 17:21. That unity is possible only as we are united together in Christian fellowship. New Agers would seek unity without the Holy Spirit. We are to be diligent to preserve the unity of the Spirit (Eph 4:3).

Second, *all is God*. If all is one, including God, then one must conclude that all is God. Pantheism would have us believe that trees, snails, books and people are all of one divine essence. A personal God is abandoned in favour of an impersonal energy force or consciousness, and if God is no longer personal, He doesn't have to be served. God is an 'it', not a 'He'.

Hinduism says, 'Atman is Brahman' (The individual self is really the universal self). Occultists say, 'As above, so below' (God and humanity are one). Satan says, 'You will be like God' (Gen 3:5).

How revealing it is, therefore, for New Agers to say, 'We are gods, and we might as well get good at it.' Their thought is, 'When I was a little child, I believed in God. When I began to mature, I stopped believing in God. Then I grew up and realised I was God.' That's like me saying, 'When I was a boy I believed in Santa Claus. Then I grew up and didn't believe in Santa Claus. Then I grew up some more and found I was Santa Claus!'

A third unifying factor refers to *a change in consciousness*. If we are God, we need to know we are God. We must become cosmically conscious, also called 'at-one-ment' (a counterfeit of atonement), self-realisation, god-realisation, enlightenment or attune-ment. Some who reach this enlightenment status will claim to be 'born-again'. This is counterfeit conversion. Their faith has no object, neither does their meditation, so it becomes an inward journey. To us, the essential issue is not whether we believe or meditate, but who we believe in and what we meditate upon. We believe God and meditate upon His law day and night. These seekers contemplate their navels.

The fourth unifying factor is *a cosmic evolutionary optimism*. There is a New Age coming. There will be a new world order with a one-world government. New Agers believe in a progressive unification of world consciousness eventually reaching the 'omega point'. This is a counterfeit kingdom and we know who its prince is. It's not hard now to identify the head attached to the hump of this snake.

Fifth, New Agers *create their own reality*. They believe they can determine reality by what they believe, so by changing what they believe, they can change reality. All moral boundaries have been erased by the metaphysical influence of Taoism's *yin* and *yang*, the ebb and flow of competing and complementary forces. There are no moral absolutes because there is no distinction between good and evil.

Sixth, New Agers *make contact with the kingdom of darkness*. Calling a medium a 'channeller', and a demon a 'spirit guide' has not changed the reality of what they are. This is the head of the snake, and they don't know it. They are in contact with the god of this world instead of the God of Abraham, Isaac and Jacob.

Recently I received a call from a lady who was concerned about the turn of events in a small group she was attending. It had started out as a rebirthing class attended by a group of supposedly Christian women. A woman in the group began to function as a medium, and they thought they were hearing from God. They recorded six hours of videotape and manuscripted the words into almost a hundred pages. In the six hours of taping, five different personalities can be identified in the medium. The group was convinced they were hearing from God, Jesus, the Holy Spirit and two angels.

The lady functioning as a medium was later identified as not being a Christian. In the tape her eyes rolled back in a trance-like state. At one point a voice says through her, 'It's going to snow here tomorrow.' I'm surprised that when it didn't snow the next day, they couldn't see the snow job being done on them!

How can a thinking person professing to be a Christian consider this as anything other than demonisation? But it isn't just lonely homemakers who are being deceived. We shall see as we proceed with our study of knowing God's will how this deception invades every area of society today.

The middle ground of truth
The truth is somewhere between the extremes of Western rationalism and Eastern mysticism. I believe truth lies at the apex of a bell-shaped curve, between these two extremes as shown opposite.

Colossians 3:15-17	**Truth**		Ephesians 5:15-20
Word of God			Filled With the Spirit
	right	real	
	wisdom	power	
Kingdom of Light	knowledge	zeal	Kingdom of Light
Kingdom of Darkness	**Left Brain**	**Right Brain**	Kingdom of Darkness
	reason	intuition	
"Always learning	cognitive	subjective	"Led by various
but never able to	task	personal	Impulses"
come to the	verbal	visual	(2 Tim 3:6).
knowledge of	facts	feelings	
the truth"	language	art	
(2 Tim 3:7).	maths	music	
	linear	spatial	
Rationalism			**Mysticism**

The Western world has a hard time with the fact that we can know all things and be nothing more than 'a noisy gong and a clanging symbol' (1 Cor 13:1). We have a tendency to extol the virtues of theologians and apologists over lovers and soul-winners. Because of my engineering background, I entered seminary with one goal: I just wanted the facts. My approach to evangelism was to win arguments. I finally admitted, though, that I wasn't winning many converts that way. Later I learned, 'Knowledge makes arrogant, but love edifies' (1 Cor 8:1).

When I became a Christian, I charged up the Western slopes of rationalism. But as the truth became more real, I slowed to a crawl, like many (if not most) of my evangelical associates who had either stopped maturing or were progressing at a snail's pace. I didn't want to let go of my intellectual approach; I wanted to stay in control. Besides, I didn't want to be too real. Being vulnerable is risky.

When I taught evangelism, I asked my students three things to help them break down the barrier of Western rationalism. One, have you ever met God? (The question was a little more subjective than what they were used to.) Two, can you describe the experience? Three, how did you know it was God you met? At least ninety per cent had a subjective answer to the last question: 'I just knew it!' Is that wrong? Not if ninety per cent of my students found assurance that way. It sounds like a confirmation of Romans 8:16, 'The Spirit Himself bears witness with our spirit that we are children of God.'

Our whole-hemisphere God

Some researchers have suggested that our brains have two hemispheres. We are led to believe that each hemisphere functions slightly differently from the other as follows:

Left Brain	Right Brain
reason	intuition
cognitive	subjective
task orientated	relationship orientated
verbal	visual
facts	feelings
language	arts
maths	music
linear	spatial

When God works through the church, He doesn't bypass our minds. And neither does He bypass one hemisphere for the sake of the other. We only have one brain and one mind. We have a whole-hemisphere God. Without Christ, the cognitive people are 'always learning, but never able to come to the knowledge of the truth' (2 Tim 3:7). Without Christ, the intuitive people are 'led on by various impulses' (2 Tim 3:6).

Neither the rationalist nor the mystic will ever come to Christ by reason or intuition. Jesus said:

And I, if I be lifted up from the earth, will draw all men to Myself (Jn 12:32).

No one can come to Me, unless the Father who sent Me draws him, and I will raise him up on the last day (Jn 6:44).

When you lift up the Son of Man, then you will know that I am He (Jn 8:28).

Jesus is the ultimate revelation of God. He is the truth. He draws both the rationalist and the mystic to Himself when neither lean on their own understanding.

When we receive Christ by faith, we are transferred out of the kingdom of darkness into the kingdom of light. Cognitive-oriented Christians strive to be right and search for wisdom and knowledge. The intuitive-oriented Christians are looking for reality and power and want to express themselves with zeal. When fact-oriented people start desiring reality and feeling-oriented people start searching for biblical truth, we will probably strike the balance that our churches need.

The sister epistles, Colossians and Ephesians, reflect this balance. According to Ephesians 5:15-20, in order to stop being foolish and know what the will of God is, a Christian is to be filled with the Spirit. The Spirit-filled person will sing and make melody in his heart to the Lord. But according to Colossians 3:15-17, the way to know the will of God is to let the Word of Christ richly dwell within us. The result is the same — singing and making melody in our hearts. It's not either/or, but both/and! Being filled with the Spirit and letting the Word richly dwell within us are really two sides of the same coin.

Lifeless orthodoxy is dead. The Holy Spirit doesn't just work in the right brain and the Word doesn't dwell only in the left brain. There is only one brain and one mind and only one God. The Holy Spirit will lead us into all truth, and the Word is a living reality. We must strive to be both real and wise, or we will not live balanced lives.

That balance is our goal — not just knowing about it, but experiencing it in our daily lives. If this truly is your desire, then would you pray with me?

Dear Heavenly Father, You are more than a good idea to me. You are my heavenly Father. I desire for my walk with You to be real. But, dear Lord, don't let my desire to be real ever shove aside my need to think. I acknowledge that You have told us to think so as to have sound judgement. I choose to think the truth and Your Word is truth. As I grow in grace, enable me to be a good witness to those who are lost in rationalism and mysticism. I choose to be sanctified in Christ so I can give an answer for the hope that lies within me. I shall not fear their intimidation, but as I sanctify Christ as the Lord of my life, may my walk with You always be made evident by the fruit of the Spirit. Amen.

Issue Comparison

Issues	Rationalism	Christianity	Mysticism
Identity:	product of evolution	child of God	god
Truth:	empirical	revelation	intuition
Guidance:	reason	Word and Holy Spirit	psychic
Eternity:	nihilism	resurrection	reincarnation

3
Deceiving Spirits

We can win the battle for our minds

A seminary student stopped by my office to tell me he was having difficulty getting to school on time. What should have been a five-minute drive lengthened to forty-five minutes because a voice in his mind kept telling him to turn at intersections. Not wanting to disobey what he perceived to be the 'still, small voice of God,' he was treated to a tour of the city almost every morning.

A pastor's wife, desperately needing the comfort of the Holy Spirit and desiring His leading, passively believed that whatever entered her mind was from God. She soon found herself bound by fear and plagued by condemning thoughts.

These examples underscore the wisdom of John Wesley's words:

> Do not hastily ascribe things to God. Do not easily suppose dreams, voices, impressions, visions or revelations to be from God. They may be from Him. They may be from nature. They may be from the devil. Therefore, do not believe every spirit, but try the spirits, whether they be from God.[1]

Satan lies, the Spirit leads

Martin Wells Knapp, co-founder of the Wesleyan Church, wrote the book *Impressions: From God or Satan, How to Know the Difference*.[2] Writing at the end of the last century, Knapp attempts to distinguish between the lies of Satan and the leading of the Holy Spirit. By quoting Hannah W. Smith, he offers this insight:

> There are voices of evil and deceiving spirits who lie in wait to entrap every traveller entering the higher regions of spiritual life. In the same epistle that tells us we are seated in heavenly places in Christ, we are also told that we will have to fight with spiritual enemies. These spiritual enemies, whoever or whatever they may be, must necessarily communicate with us by means of our spiritual faculties. And their voices, as the voice of God, are an inward impression made upon our spirit. Therefore, just as the Holy Spirit may tell us by impressions what the will of God is concerning us, so also will these spiritual enemies tell us by impression what is their will concerning us, though not of course giving it their name.[3]

In that same work, Knapp also makes one major point clear: 'Oh, that I could write one message with the point of a diamond upon the heart of every Christian. It should be this: Be sure that the slightest impression upon your heart disposing you to do Christian work has a divine stamp, and then obey it at whatever cost.'

We have this tension. We do need to be aware of deceiving spirits, but we also need to heed the leading of God. There is a battle going on for our minds: 'The Spirit explicitly says that in later times some will fall away from the faith, paying attention to deceitful spirits and doctrines [teachings] of demons' (1 Tim 4:1).

This is graphically revealed by the research for our book, *The Seduction of Our Children*. Steve Russo and I surveyed thousands of junior high and senior high students. One of southern California's better Christian schools returned the following results from 286 high school students:

- 45 per cent have experienced some presence (seen or heard) in their room that scared them;
- 59 per cent said that they have had bad thoughts about God;
- 43 per cent said that it is mentally hard to pray and read their Bibles;
- 69 per cent have heard voices in their head, like there was a subconscious self talking to them;
- 22 per cent said they frequently had thoughts of suicide;
- 29 per cent have had impulsive thoughts to kill somebody, like 'grab that knife and kill that person.'

I realise that interpretation of this data will vary according to our world view. If we don't believe in a kingdom of darkness, then a neutral explanation would have to be given for the battle going on in these children's minds. In our culture, if a person is hearing voices or struggling with his thought life, it is assumed to be a psychological or neurological problem. But I have personally counselled hundreds of people who are hearing voices and most situations, if not all, have been demonic.

As I share with these tormented people that they aren't going crazy but they are under attack, they usually respond, 'Praise the Lord, someone understands.' It's freeing to know this truth, because if people are mentally ill for some neurological reason, the prognosis is not very good. But if there is a battle going on for their minds, we can win that war.

Who's well and who isn't?

Mental health experts define a mentally healthy person as someone who is in touch with reality and relatively free of anxiety. From a secular perspective, every person harassed by deceiving spirits would be mentally ill. The secular counsellor would conclude that the voices people hear or the images they see are only hallucinations. From God's perspective, it is the secular person who isn't in touch with reality. The spiritual world is very real.

I'm so glad that the greatest determinant of mental health is a true knowledge of God and a proper understanding of who we are as children of God. This means we don't have to fear anything; we have an eternal relationship with the creator of everything. We are free from condemnation since our sins are forgiven. Above all, we know that we are loved. So we, of all people, should be mentally healthy.

But let me quickly add that the opposite is also true. The greatest determinant of mental illness is a distorted perception of God and who we are. That's why you'll find that most secular counsellors don't like religion. Their clients claim to be religious, but they have a sick understanding of God and their relationship with Him.

Whilst I would disagree that God could ever be the cause of mental illness, I do believe that we should avoid being one-sided in our approach. In treating our mental problems, we have a tendency to polarise — psychotherapeutic ministries ignore spiritual realities while deliverance ministries ignore developmental experiences and human responsibilities. Either extreme cannot adequately address mental illness. Our problems are never not psychological. There is no time when our minds, wills and emotions are not all involved. At the same time, though, our problems are never not spiritual. There is no time when God isn't present. We need a biblical view of reality. We have to contend with the world, the flesh and the devil. We are both physical and spiritual beings.

Because our culture has ignored the reality of the spiritual world, it is set up to be deceived. The secular world is turning to spirit guides for guidance and channellers for advice. The gullible public doesn't realise that they are dealing with demons and mediums, and the church is only slightly more informed. Ignorant of Satan's schemes, many are paying attention to a deceiving spirit thinking it is God. We need to understand how Satan works in order to know how to defend ourselves against him.

Satan's strategies to break the believer

Most people don't understand the true nature of one of Satan's primary strategies: *temptation*. Though Satan used a piece of fruit to tempt Eve, it was merely an object of deception. Every temptation Satan uses is an attempt to get us to live our lives independently of God. Satan attacks in the area of our legitimate needs. Then we have to decide whether those needs will be met by living independently of God or by living in the will of the Lord Jesus Christ. Paul answers the question for us: 'My God shall supply all your needs according to His riches in glory in Christ Jesus' (Phil 4:19). Satan, the deceiver, tries to destroy this lifestyle of Christ-dependency and rob us of our peace.

Another misunderstood attack of Satan comes from his role as *accuser of the brethren*. The accuser of the brethren is determined to undermine our understanding of who we are in Christ. Everyone entertains thoughts like, 'I'm stupid,' 'I can't,' 'I'm no good,' or 'God doesn't love me.' If we believe these accusations, we will live defeated lives even though victory is assured in Christ. Satan can't do anything about our position in Christ, but if he is successful in getting us to believe we aren't complete in Christ, we will live as though we aren't. We can fight this ploy of Satan by reminding ourselves who has the ultimate victory:

Now the salvation, and the power, and the kingdom of our God and the authority of His Christ have come, for the accuser of the brethren has been thrown down, who accuses them before our God day and night. And they overcame him

because of the blood of the lamb and because of the word of
their testimony, and they did not love their life even to death
(Rev 12:10,11).

Neither temptation nor accusation is Satan's greatest
strategy, however. If I tempt you, you know it. If I accuse
you, you know it. But if I deceive you, you don't know it.
Thus the primary strategy of Satan is *deception*: '[Satan]
does not stand in the truth, because there is no truth in him.
Whenever he speaks a lie, he speaks from his own nature;
for he is a liar, and the father of lies' (Jn 8:44). Satan is
determined to undermine the work of the Holy Spirit who
leads us all into truth.

Over and over, Scripture teaches that we will be led in
truth:

> If you abide in My word, then you are truly disciples of
> Mine; and you shall know the truth, and the truth shall
> make you free (Jn 8:31,32).
>
> I am the way, the truth, and the life; no one comes to the
> Father, but through Me (Jn 14:6).
>
> I do not ask Thee to take them out of the world, but to
> keep them from the evil one. They are not of the world, even
> as I am not of the world. Sanctify them in the truth; Thy
> word is truth (Jn 17:15–17).

When we put on the armour of God, the first thing we
do is gird our loins with truth (Eph 6:14). The seriousness
of not walking in truth is seen when God intervened in the
early church by dramatically striking down Ananias and
Sapphira. Why the severity of the discipline? Because they
were living a lie. Peter asked, 'Why has Satan filled your
heart to lie to the Holy Spirit?' (Acts 5:3) It is crucial for
believers to live in truth.

Obviously, God knows what the primary strategy of

Satan is. He knows that if Satan can operate undetected in any home, church, family, committee or person, and get people to believe a lie, he can control their lives. That is the battle going on for our minds. That is why 'we are destroying speculations and every lofty thing raised up against the knowledge of God, and we are taking every thought captive to the obedience of Christ' (2 Cor 10:5).

The battleground

I believe that the greatest access Satan has to the church in waging his war for our minds is our unwillingness to forgive each other. We are so slow to surrender to Christ in this area, even though the consequences of unforgiveness are so great. Paul said:

> But whom you forgive anything, I forgive also; for indeed what I have forgiven, if I have forgiven anything, I did it for your sakes in the presence of Christ, in order that no advantage be taken of us by Satan; for we are not ignorant of his schemes (2 Cor 2:10,11).

Jesus admonished us to forgive them from our heart or He will hand us over to the torturers (Mt 18:34). The word for *torturer* is used throughout the New Testament for 'spiritual torment.' Bitter people set themselves up for personal torment. Paul and Jesus urge us to forgive. That's the pathway to peace.

Satan, the architect of torment, is also battling for the mind of the unbeliever:

> But their minds were hardened; for until this very day at the reading of the old covenant the same veil remains unlifted, because it is removed in Christ.... And even if our gospel is veiled, it is veiled to those who are perishing, in whose case the god of this world has blinded the minds of the unbeliev-

ing, that they might not see the light of the gospel of the
glory of Christ, who is the image of God (2 Cor 3:14; 4:3,4).

As I was counselling a deeply troubled young man, I
asked him about his personal relationship with God.
Realising he had none, I shared God's plan of salvation. I
asked him if he'd like to make a decision for Christ, and he
said he would.

When I started to pray, his mind blanked out and I could
feel the presence of evil in the room. I looked at him and
said, 'There's a battle going on for your mind. I'm going to
pray and read Scripture. As soon as you can, call upon the
name of the Lord.' After about five minutes, one word at a
time came out, 'Lord... Jesus... I... need... you.' The
moment he said it, he collapsed in his chair. Then he looked
up with tears in his eyes and said, 'I'm free.'

How are we going to see people come to Christ if Satan
has blinded their minds?

We need to exercise the authority that we have in Christ
and demand that Satan release those people whom he is
holding so they can see the light of the gospel. We need to
fix our eyes on Jesus, the author and perfecter of faith (Heb
12:2). We are deceived when our thoughts are led astray
from the only legitimate object of our faith.

Cults talk about historical Jesus, but they preach Him
another way. He's not the eternal Son of God; He's just a
good moral teacher. Those who believe that will not be led
by the Holy Spirit, but by a deceiving spirit. And they will
have a completely different gospel. It won't be a gospel of
grace but a gospel of works. Notice how Paul clearly
teaches this in 2 Corinthians 11:3,4:

But I am afraid, lest as the serpent deceived Eve by his
craftiness, your minds should be led astray from the simplicity and purity of devotion to Christ. For if one comes

and preaches another Jesus whom we have not preached, or you receive a different spirit which you have not received, or a different gospel which you have not accepted, you bear this beautifully.

Choosing truth

It is our responsibility to use our minds and to know the truth:

[We are] to think so as to have sound judgement (Rom 12:3).
   Brethren, do not be children in your thinking; yet in evil be babes, but in your thinking be mature (1 Cor 14:20).
   Therefore, gird our minds for action (1 Pet 1:13).

Passively putting our minds in neutral invites spiritual disaster. We are to choose truth aggressively and actively. The Magna Carta of this concept is found in Philippians 4:8,9:

Finally, brethren, whatever is true, whatever is honourable, whatever is right, whatever is pure, whatever is lovely, whatever is of good repute, if there is any excellence and if anything worthy of praise, let your mind dwell on these things. The things you have learned and received and heard and seen in me, practise these things; and the God of peace shall be with you.

Don't pay attention to deceiving spirits. If a thought comes to your mind, compare it with the list in Philippians 4:8 above. Don't entertain thoughts that are contrary to it. Then follow the admonition of the next verse (v 9), and put into practice what you know to be true. If we really believe the truth, we will do what we know to be right.

When I counsel people who are in deep spiritual conflict, I aim for two results. First, I want them to know who they are as children of God. Second, I want them to experience freedom and peace in their minds. With this desire, I sought to help a missionary who was struggling just to hold her life together. After our counselling session, she sent me this letter:

> The edge of tension and irritation is gone. I feel so free. The Bible has been really exciting, stimulating and more understandable than ever before. I am no longer bound by accusations, doubts, thoughts of suicide, murder or other harm that comes straight from hell into my head. There is a serenity in my mind and spirit, a clarity of consciousness that is profound. I've been set free. My ability to process things has increased many fold. Not only is my spirit more serene, my head is actually clearer. It's easier to make connections and integrate things now. It seems like everything is easier to understand now.
>
> My relationship with God has changed significantly. For eight years, I felt He was distant from me. I was desperately crying out to Him to set me free, to release me from the bondage I was in. I wanted so badly to meet with Him, to know His presence with me again. I needed to know Him as a friend and companion, not as the distant authority figure He had become to my mind and experience.
>
> Now that I am free in Christ, I have seen my ability to trust grow and my ability to be honest with Him increase greatly. I really am experiencing the spiritual growth I had been praying for.

I don't know of a person who would not want to know that kind of freedom, joy and closeness to God. Isn't this your desire? To put an end to Satan's deception and be freed from his battle for control of your life? Or maybe you just want to reaffirm your freedom in Christ. Then would you pray with me?

Dear Heavenly Father, I thank You for setting the captives free. I have accepted Your free gift of salvation, so I am now a child of God, seated with Christ in the heavenlies. I know that nothing can separate me from Your love or snatch me out of Your hand. Your Holy Spirit bears witness to me that I am Your child.

I bring my anxious thoughts before You and ask that Your peace will guard my heart and my mind. I now realise that it is my responsibility to take every thought captive to the obedience of Christ. I choose to believe the truth and I reject the lies of Satan. I will not pay attention to any thoughts that are contrary to what is true or lovely or right.

Forgive me for the times that I have ever doubted You. Forgive me for the times I paid attention to deceiving spirits. In the name of Christ, I resist the evil one, and I focus my mind on Jesus. You are the author and perfecter of my faith. Amen.

NOTES

1. Martin Wells Knapp, *Impressions* (Wheaton, IL: Tyndale House Publishers, 1984), p 32.

2. Knapp, *Impressions*, p 43.

3. Knapp, *Impressions*, p 14.

4
False Prophets

Does God use prophets today?

One late afternoon I was sitting in a coffee shop waiting for my son to finish football practice. A young man noticed I was reading my Bible and asked if I was studying to be a Christian. I told him I'd been a Christian for some time, and I asked him if he had ever made a decision for Christ. He said he had just become a Christian.

He told me that two friends had given a prophecy for him specifying what he should do with his life. He was troubled because the prophecies were not the same. 'Which one should I believe?' he asked. 'Neither one,' I suggested. I asked him if he believed in the priesthood of believers. He said he wasn't sure, so I explained to him that all of God's children have access to Him. I asked him, 'If God wanted you to do something, wouldn't He tell you?'

Understanding the gift of prophecy and distinguishing it from the role of a prophet may be the biggest battle for the church at the end of the twentieth century.[1] Certainly we don't want to limit the Lord from speaking to the church and His followers in these critical days. But if we don't ask hard questions and aren't open to other viewpoints, we may do just that or, even worse, end up paying attention to a false prophet. How can we tell the difference between the counterfeit and the real?

Differences of opinion
At one extreme we have Christians who believe that the miraculous presence of God is no longer evident, that God

speaks to His church only through the written Word of God as understood by elite theologians or pastors. They would deny that latter sentiment, but if you disagree with them, it comes through loud and clear that their faith is grounded in their perception and theological persuasion. These believers can be identified by their demand for loyalty and their need to be right as opposed to a sense of security in Christ and the need to be loving.

At the other end of the spectrum are Christians who deliberately try to get God to manifest Himself in every public worship. Their goal is to enter into the 'holy of holies' and have prophecies, words of knowledge, healings, tongues and every other manifestation hinted at or eluded to in the Bible present every time they assemble.

The first group sits outside the spiritual world and critiques it. They don't worship God — they evaluate the worship service. They are more concerned about platform procedure than divine presence. The second group enters into the spiritual world, but nobody is critiquing! It is 'holy' abandonment.

Where is the balance between dead orthodoxy and zeal without knowledge? While I can't draw an absolute line between these matters, I think we can agree on some broad concepts from the warnings of Scripture. Let's start by taking a look at biblical history.

The need for prophets
God created mankind to rule over the birds of the sky, the beasts of the fields and the fish of the sea. His dominion extended over the earth, its atmosphere and oceans. When Adam sinned, he lost his relationship with God and forfeited his rule over creation. Satan became the rebel holder of authority and is now the prince of the power of the air and the ruler of this world. God's redemptive plan is to defeat the god of this world and restore fallen humanity,

establishing His kingdom so the will of God will be done on earth as it is in heaven.

The Bible reveals God's plan. It includes historical accounts of the progress of His unfolding plan, the establishment and commissioning of the church, and the assurance that His eschatological plan for the future will be accomplished. Where we stand presently and how God has communicated to us is summarised in Ephesians 2:19–22:

> So then you are no longer strangers and aliens, but you are fellow citizens with the saints, and are of God's household, having been built upon the foundation of the apostles and prophets, Christ Jesus Himself being the cornerstone, in whom the whole building, being fitted together is growing into a holy temple in the Lord; in whom you also are being built together into a dwelling of God in the Spirit.

God has delivered us from the domain of darkness and transferred us to the kingdom of His Son (Col 1:13). We are no longer sinners, but saints who sin. We are securely in God's household, seated with Christ in the heavenlies. Based on the foundation that has been laid by the apostles and prophets, we are being built up into a holy temple. The church has been established as a dwelling of God in the Spirit.

The means by which God has communicated this redemptive plan of His so clearly revealed in the Bible is through the prophets and the apostles. In addition, the ultimate revelation of God was Jesus Himself, the cornerstone of the church.

So Old Testament prophets were messengers of God. They never spoke presumptuously. God said to Moses, 'Now then go, and I, even I, will be with your mouth, and teach you what you are to say' (Ex 4:12); 'I will raise up a prophet from among their countrymen like you, and I will put My words in his mouth, and he shall speak to them all that I command him' (Deut 18:18). God said to Jeremiah, 'Behold, I have put My words in your mouth' (Jer 1:9). And Ezekiel received this instruction: 'But you shall speak My words to them whether they listen or not, for they are rebellious' (Ezek 2:7).

When Old Testament prophets spoke, it was 'Thus saith the Lord.' They spoke with authority because it was God's message, not man's. The test of a true prophet was that he was never wrong (Deut 18:20–22). People needed to discern whether a prophet was a true or false prophet, but they were not left with the responsibility of deciding what part of a prophecy was right and what part was wrong. If any part was wrong, the man was a false prophet. Unfortunately, they listened to a lot of false prophets and stoned a lot of true prophets because they didn't want to hear what the true prophets had to say. The Old Testament is one account after another of rebellious kings, Baal worship and false prophets.

Old Testament history closes with a 400-year silence during which the world was without a prophetic voice. Then the Word became flesh and dwelt among us (Jn 1:14). God was about to speak again, but it's interesting to note that even Jesus didn't speak on His own initiative: 'For I did not speak on My own initiative, but the Father Himself who sent Me has given Me commandment, what to say, and what to speak' (Jn 12:49). Then after a year of public ministry, Jesus appointed twelve disciples who were identified as apostles after Pentecost. They carried God's message in the early days of the church.

Does God use prophets today?

Most biblical scholars believe there are no longer any prophets and apostles who speak with the absolute authority of 'Thus saith the Lord.' Yet one cannot exclude the possibility that God could send someone to function as a prophet or apostle again.

Some have suggested that there are two prophets in Revelation 11:3, but the passage says they are 'witnesses' who prophesy. What's the difference? They are identified as witnesses, but what they *do* is prophecy. In a similar fashion, some would call me a seminary professor who exhorts. A seminary professor is a person; exhortation is a gift. The first describes my position, the latter my gift.

Regarding today's prophets, are we to accept what they say as authoritative for the church in the same way we understand Scripture to be? Since the church pronounced that the canon of Scripture has been closed, many false teachers and false prophets, such as Joseph Smith (founder of the Mormons), have arisen claiming new revelation beyond the Scriptures. Islam claims divine revelation in addition to the Bible, and yet the message of the Koran is in conflict with the prophets and the apostles of the Bible. The same is true of the message of the Mormon church.

One cannot say with absolute authority that God can't add to His Word, although we are clearly warned not to do so. Scripture teaches that the foundation has already been laid (past tense) by the apostles and prophets. God's plan has already been declared, we have been commissioned, and the future has been assured.

Yet God is still working today as He has in the past, through people. Prophets like Isaiah and apostles like Paul were people. The church has gifted people, and the gift of prophecy functions like other gifts within the church. But the New Testament gift of prophecy is not the same as the Old Testament office of prophet. If you have the gift of administration you are enabled by God to help structure the church and organise its efforts, but you probably will not be known only as an administrator. If you have the gift of exhortation, do people identify you as the exhorter? You may have the gift of tongues, but I'm fairly safe in saying that nobody refers to you as the tongue! Neither does the gift of prophecy necessarily make you a prophet. We are all simply children of God, supernaturally gifted to help build up one another to live righteous lives.

God builds upon the foundation that has already been laid by the apostles and prophets by giving us evangelists and pastor/teachers (Eph 4:11,12). Evangelists and pastor/teachers are people ordained by God to equip the saints so they (the saints) may reach their communities for Christ and build up one another.

Although Satan is defeated, the kingdom of darkness is still present in the church age. Along with the true evangelists, pastors, teachers and others gifted by God for ministry, expect Satan to have his false prophets, teachers and messiahs. Such is the case, and we have been warned sufficiently in the Scriptures. So let's examine how to identify false prophets and teachers, first from the Old Testament and then from the New Testament.

Identifying Old Testament false prophets

The standard way of identifying an Old Testament prophet has already been mentioned. Deuteronomy 18:20–22 explains that if an alleged prophet spoke presumptuously (ie, his own thoughts, not God's), the prophet was to die. If what he said didn't come true, he was a false prophet. That test works only when the words of the prophet predict some future event. As we shall see shortly, that wasn't the primary function of a true prophet.

Deuteronomy 13:1–3 identifies an even more insidious nature of false prophets to be discerned:

> If a prophet or a dreamer of dreams arises among you and gives you a sign or a wonder, and the sign or the wonder comes true, concerning which he spoke to you, saying, 'Let

us go after other gods (whom you have not known) and let us serve them,' you shall not listen to the words of that prophet or that dreamer of dreams; for the Lord your God is testing you to find out if you love the Lord your God with all your heart and with all your soul.

In this case the signs and wonders come true, but their purpose is to lead people away from God to serve other gods. These dreamers of dreams are rebellious at heart (Deut 13:5). They use signs and wonders to lure people off the true path, and a gullible public follows blindly because they accept anything supernatural as being from God. The purpose is to get people dependent upon miraculous interventions, instead of the Word of God, as the means to know God's will. In Old Testament times God considered their evil so great that He required their life by the hands of their own family members (Deut 13:4–10).

Several years ago I had a university ministry near Long Beach, California. A nearby ministry created quite a controversy. Everybody was hearing about the great signs and wonders coming true at the hands of its young prophet. Several students under my ministry went to the Friday evening services which were held in a hired theatre. God seemed to be blessing that work far more than mine. Eventually, though, the 'prophet' moved his ministry and a few years later he died of AIDS as the result of his decadent lifestyle. A lot of people were led down the wrong path.

How can we identify a false prophet like that? Jeremiah 23:21–32 contains the most extensive discussion on this in the Old Testament:

I did not send these prophets, but they ran. I did not speak to them, but they prophesied. But if they had stood in My council, then they would have announced My words to My people, and would have turned them back from their evil way and from the evil of their deeds (vs 21,22).

Notice that there are two errors. They were doing evil deeds and they were going down the wrong path.

Prophets were only to announce God's words, and the primary purpose was to call people to turn away from sin. They called people back to the moral standards of the law. They were to declare the way of the Lord, exhorting people to turn from their evil ways and accept God's plan for their lives.

The false prophets Jeremiah speaks of have only dreams, and believing them to be from God, they prophesy in the name of the Lord (Jer 23:25). If you have a dream that you believe is from God, then understand the relative value of dreams. Jeremiah 23:28-29 explains:

'The prophet who has a dream may relate his dream, but let him who has My word speak My word in truth. What does straw have in common with grain?' declares the LORD, 'Is not My word like fire?' declares the LORD, 'and like a hammer which shatters a rock?'

Being an old farm boy, I know the relative value of straw. If you try to feed straw to cattle, they won't eat it because it has no nutritional value. It makes good bedding, but only grain has nutritional value. God says a dream is like straw, but His Word is like wheat, and we will only grow when we devour God's Word. When we substitute the chaff of dreams for the wheat of biblical truth, we will soon become spiritually starved.

God is also against prophets who 'steal [His] words from each other' (Jer 23:30). Notice they are God's words, but false prophets have stolen them from others, and share them as though God has given the words to them. That's called plagiarism.

In addition, God is against prophets 'who use their tongues and declare, "The Lord declares"' (Jer 23:31). This is subtly happening in our churches. I had a pulpit committee stop by my office for advice. The grandson of a former pastor had called the church and told them that God had revealed to him he was to be the new pastor. They were split as a committee.

Some reasoned that if God had spoken to this man, they'd better obey God and extend him an invitation. I asked what the young man was like. They said he seemed legitimate, but they were troubled by his request for absolute authority to carry out the plan God had given him.

I asked, 'Don't you think God will work through the group that is responsible?' In this case it was the pulpit committee. I wanted to suggest that stones may be the best response to this young 'prophet'! If God burdened my heart to pastor a congregation, I would wait for the call from the people responsible. If God hasn't burdened their hearts the same way, I would understand my desire to be from the flesh or the pit rather than from God.

A more subtle form of this is name dropping. Like the lovesick man who says to his date, 'I have prayed about it, and God has revealed to me that we should get married.' The man who asks for my daughter's hand had better come with the proposal, not a mandate. My wife calls this 'pulling spiritual rank.' Those who use God's name to get leverage for what they want can only expect disaster down the road. God says He's against the prophet who pulls spiritual rank by using His name to achieve personal objectives.

Finally God says, 'I am against those who have prophesied false dreams and related them, and led My people astray by their falsehoods and reckless boasting' (Jer 23:32).

I'm troubled by those who have to keep promising great things in order to keep the money coming in. 'God is going to do a great work, a mighty work,' or worse, 'a new thing,' they proclaim. None of these people is a candidate for the Nobel Peace Prize, but Mother Theresa received one. Reckless boasting is not of God.

Identifying New Testament false prophets and teachers

The gift of prophecy in the New Testament has the same purpose of turning people's hearts back to God as did the Old Testament prophets. According to 1 Corinthians 14:24,25:

> But if all prophesy, and an unbeliever or an ungifted man enters, he is convicted by all, he is called to account by all; the secrets of his heart are disclosed; and so he will fall on his face and worship God, declaring that God is certainly among you.

God's Word is like fire; it purifies the church: 'For it is time for judgement to begin with the household of God' (1 Pet 4:17). God is far more concerned about church purity than church growth. Because only the pure church can grow and bear fruit, Satan will use signs and wonders to lead people off the path of righteousness. He will deceive people to become obsessed with physical healings and external phenomena instead of heart purification. God's Word is like a hammer that breaks up the hard ground and softens the heart. If people were living in immorality in our churches and a word of prophecy came from the Lord, rest assured it would not be some generic source of comfort but an exhortation to purify ourselves.

The warnings against false prophets are numerous in the New Testament:

Beloved, do not believe every spirit, but test the spirits to see whether they are from God; because many false prophets have gone out into the world (1 Jn 4:1).

The warnings intensify as the Lord prepares to return. In the Olivet discourse, Jesus said:

And many false prophets will arise, and will mislead many... For false Christs and false prophets will arise and will show great signs and wonders, so as to mislead, if possible, even the elect (Mt 24:11,24).

Knowing that they will appear is one thing, but detecting who they are is another.

In determining the credibility of a prophet, the first thing I would look for is a *righteous life*. Jesus said, 'You will know them by their fruits' (Mt 7:20). The next three verses identify the counterfeits. They may say, 'Lord, Lord!' They may prophesy, cast out demons and even perform miracles in the name of the Lord. Yet they will not enter the kingdom of heaven because they are not doing the will of the Father in heaven. Satan is obviously able to pull off miracles and get his demons to cooperate by leaving those they afflict at the right time. Thus it would appear that the false teacher had cast out demons. Jesus is not into 'show time' and declares, 'He who does the will of God will enter heaven.'

It isn't what we do for God externally that gets us into heaven. It's what God has done for us internally. God's will for our life is our sanctification (1 Thess 4:3). God has changed our nature; we must change our behaviour. We are to be holy for He is holy (1 Pet 1:16). There will be those who will show great signs and wonders, but they will also hear from God, 'Depart from Me you who practised lawlessness' (Mt 7:23). The false teachers hide their sin, but eventually their deeds will find them out. Paul reveals in 2 Corinthians 11:13–15:

> For such men are false prophets, deceitful workers, disguising themselves as apostles of Christ. And no wonder, for even Satan disguises himself as an angel of light. Therefore it is not surprising if his servants also disguise themselves as servants of righteousness; whose end shall be according to their deeds.

Eventually, the immorality of their lifestyle will be revealed.

The above passage reveals a second characteristic of false prophets and teachers. *They work within the church.* These are not cult leaders. Cults can be identified by their doctrine, and they make no attempt to hide it. Not so with false prophets and teachers:

> But false prophets also arose among the people, just as there will also be false teachers among you, who will secretly introduce destructive heresies, even denying the Master who bought them, bringing swift destruction upon themselves. And many will follow their sensuality, and because of them the way of the truth will be maligned; and in their greed they will exploit you with false words; their judgement from long ago is not idle, and their destruction is not asleep (2 Pet 2:1–3).

False teachers work secretly and under disguise as ministers of righteousness. What we *see* will seldom threaten the church. External opposition has had a purging effect on the church that usually leaves the church stronger. But these false teachers are infiltrators. Many are hard-core Satanists trained to infiltrate the church. Their purpose is to secretly introduce destructive heresies. Heretics are people who cause schisms. Heresy seldom begins with blatant error. It usually begins with truth out of balance. They will set us up with enough truth to choke us on subtle deviations. They may lure people by their dynamic personalities, causing people to follow their sensuality. The result is that many people will be mesmerised and follow their destructive ways.

A third characteristic of false prophets and teachers is their *rebellious heart*. They despise authority (2 Pet 2:10). If they are not in a leadership position, they will seek to discredit legitimate Christian leaders. This may be the easiest way to spot them. They won't answer to anyone. They have an independent spirit and not a compatible spirit with those desiring to do God's will. True Christian leaders have a servant's heart. True leaders don't seek to lord it over others, but prove to be an example.

Cautions are in order

As you guard against false prophets, I caution you not to go on a witch hunt. Many heresy hunters are self-righteous and as bad as the heretics they find. They become experts on what's wrong as opposed to what's right. Remember that good people can be deceived. If you come across someone who is a victim of bad teaching, show him the light — not the exit. The best way to eliminate the darkness is to turn on the light. Be a proclaimer, not a denouncer. And commit yourself to the truth. Fellowship in a place where truth is proclaimed in a balanced way.

Care is also needed in the area of judging morality. Don't throw someone out because of one moral indiscretion. The issue is 'those who practice lawlessness.' Even then be careful, because there are many who have accepted God's standards and seem to desire to live a righteous life, but for some reason they cannot. They aren't false teachers because they aren't trying to teach anybody. Our hearts need to go out to such people because they are enslaved to sinful habits or are being blinded and held captive by Satan.

The gift of prophecy

I'm concerned about the growing misuse of the gifts of prophecy and words of knowledge. Perspective is the value of distance. Step back from the details of 1 Corinthians 12-14, the classic passage on spiritual gifts. What is Paul trying to say? There are a variety of spiritual gifts and manifestations of the Spirit. In the midst of this diversity, there is unity, because there is only one Spirit and one Lord. God gives the gifts as He wills. Gifts and manifestations come and go and come again for the purpose of accomplishing God's will. What remains is faith, hope and love. These are the lasting and continuous standards by which we evaluate our ministry and lives.

Paul says, 'I write so that you may know how one ought to conduct himself in the household of God, which is the church of the living God, the pillar and support of the truth' (1 Tim 3:15). Truth is the object of our faith. If we know the truth, it will set us free to grow in love with the hope of eternity before us. The church is gifted to accomplish that objective. Gifts are only a means to an end, never an end in themselves. When 'gifts' become an end in themselves they are counterfeit, or else they become the basis for spiritual pride. Godly character is our goal, and it must take precedence over the gifts.

In 1 Corinthians 14, Paul is specifying the proper use of the gifts of prophecy and tongues in public worship. Some have understood verse 1 to be teaching that we are to desire earnestly the gift of prophecy. I understand the passage to teach that we are to desire the gift of prophecy over the gift of tongues in public worship. The congregation can only be edified by that which they can comprehend with their minds, therefore the elevation of prophecy over tongues.

Tongues were not even to be used in public worship unless there was an interpretation.

The overwhelming thrust of the rest of Scripture encourages us to seek God and trust Him to gift us as He sees fit for the edification of the church. 'Seek not, forsake not' seems to be the balance we need. Our responsibility is to yield to the Holy Spirit. However He chooses to fill us is His responsibility.

The misuse of prophecy

The Bible says there is only one intermediary between God and man, and that is Jesus. When God does send a prophet like Nathan to someone like David, for example, it is for the purpose of bringing conviction in order to establish righteousness. In the church age, bringing conviction is a primary ministry of the Holy Spirit.

The proper use of the gift of prophecy would reveal unrighteousness in order to establish people in Christ. Once people are living righteously with the Lord, the Holy Spirit will lead them. False gifts will not consistently promote holiness but will specify decisions concerning direction in life. That function is the role of the Holy Spirit alone: 'For all those being led by the Spirit of God, these are the sons of God' (Rom 8:14).

Too many churches encourage their members, including the immature, to come into the fullness of the Spirit with manifestations. I ask, 'Why not the fullness of the truth?' It's the fullness of the truth the Holy Spirit has promised to lead us into. I'm deeply concerned for young converts in ministries that push for them to seek total manifestations of the Spirit. Many have not had the time to understand the foundation laid by the apostles and the prophets. The church at Corinth had similar problems. They were exhorted by Paul to get back to the basics of faith, hope and love, and govern very closely the use of tongues and prophecies in public worship because God does everything decently and in order (1 Cor 14:40).

A pastor friend of mine received a letter from a former staff member who was also pastoring a church in his community. The letter contained a prophecy for my friend's church. I asked, 'Why would God give a prophecy for your church through the pastor of another church?' I suggested that they shouldn't listen to it since it would function like a curse. From the time they heard it, everything that happened in the church was evaluated by the prophecy (either to substantiate it or invalidate it). They called the pastor of an exceptionally good charismatic church who advised them in the same way. If a person or church is earnestly seeking the Lord, God will work through the lines of authority that He has established in His Word.

Paul says, 'Examine everything carefully; hold fast to that which is good' (1 Thess 5:19–21).

Keeping your faith in balance

If you accept prophetic utterances as valid for today, I would encourage you to test them in the following ways.

First, is the person giving the prophetic utterance living a balanced and righteous lifestyle?

Second, is the person committed to building God's kingdom or his own; is Christ being lifted up or is he?

Third, does the prophetic utterance establish confidence in the Word of God and is it consistent with a balanced presentation of it? Are people going to have a greater dependency upon God's revelation or man's inspiration? Are prophetic utterances a substitute for the serious, personal study of God's Word?

Fourth, does the use of the spiritual gift bring unity to the church and build up one another? Be careful in this test, because those who hold to a form of godliness but deny its power are not in balance either. They will quench the Spirit through censorship and very little will be accomplished in the church. They can cause disunity as well.

Last, do the spiritual manifestations bypass the mind? God operates through our mind; Satan bypasses it. If a person takes on a medium-like trance, be assured it is occultic. God renews our mind and brings back to our mind all that He has taught us. We are to think so as to have sound judgement.

All of us receive input from a myriad of sources today. With Satan still using false prophets in his battle for our minds, will you join me in this prayer that we may discern the truth God wants us to know to set and keep us free?

Dear Heavenly Father, I desire above all else to know Your will. I long for Your presence to be known in my life and ministry. I seek to glorify You by bearing much fruit.

But dear Lord, I don't want to possess any counterfeit gifts or follow any false teachers or prophets. Every spiritual manifestation in my life I bring to You. If it isn't of You, I renounce it and ask Your forgiveness for not being more discerning. If what I experience in my life is from You, then I pray that You will enable me to use it for Your glory. I will have only one Lord in my life, and that is You, Heavenly Father.

I commit myself to maturing in love and to meeting the needs of those around me. I choose to develop my faith by the truth of Your Word. I wish not to be identified with a wicked and adulterous generation that seeks only after a sign. You have already proved Your love for me by sending Your Son to die in my place. I love You and ask again for You to fill me with Your Holy Spirit that I may be holy as You are Holy. Amen.

NOTE

1. For the serious student who would like to know the biblical place for prophecy and its use in the church today, I suggest *Showing the Spirit* by D.A. Carson (Grand Rapids, MI: Baker Book House, 1987).

5
Facing Fear

Fear either compels us to do what is irresponsible
or it impedes us from living responsibly

After speaking at a pastor's breakfast, I was swapping stories
with several former students. We are sharing our experiences of helping people find freedom. One pastor, who was
a stranger to the rest of us, was taking it all in. Seizing the
right opportunity, he commented, 'This is really interesting.
Tell me, what would you do with the lady I'm seeing this
afternoon? She's having terrible nightmares, she hears
voices in her head and she has a lot of fear. That's just neu-
rosis, isn't it?'

'What's she afraid of?' I responded. 'She appears to have
the classic symptoms of spiritual conflict. With cooperation, it usually takes less than two hours to free a person
from that kind of attack.'

I responded in that way because in helping people
resolve their spiritual conflicts, I have yet to see one who
wasn't struggling with fear. How can we walk with God if
fear is running our lives?

Fear is a powerful controller. It either compels us to do
what is irresponsible or it impedes us from living responsibly. Recently a denominational executive spoke in our
chapel and his opening statement was, 'As I travel among
our pastors, I'm overwhelmed by the realisation that the
number one motivation in their lives is fear of failure.'

After several years of teaching evangelism and oversee-
ing evangelistic outreaches, I can tell you with confidence
that the number one reason people don't share their faith is

fear. Agoraphobia, fear of being in public, is one of the fastest growing psychological disorders. Fear of failure, fear of the devil, fear of man, fear of everything is plaguing our society.

Did you know that the most frequent command of Jesus in the Gospels is, 'Fear not'? In anticipation of the entrance into the promised land, God tells His people four times, 'Be strong and courageous' (see Joshua 1). The writer of Proverbs says, 'The wicked flee when no one is pursuing, but the righteous are as bold as a lion' (Prov 28:1). It is characteristic of the Spirit-filled life to be bold:

> And when they had prayed, the place where they had gathered together was shaken, and they were all filled with the Holy Spirit, and began to speak the word of God with boldness (Acts 4:31).

The early church didn't pray for 'divine appointments'; they prayed for boldness. God's kingdom can only be established by faithful and courageous people.

The fact that God doesn't look favourably on cowards and unbelievers is made evident in Revelation 21:7,8:

> He who overcomes shall inherit these things, and I will be his God and he will be My son. But for the cowardly and unbelieving and abominable and murderers and immoral persons and sorcerers and idolaters and all liars, their part will be in the lake that burns with fire and brimstone, which is the second death.

Does it surprise you that cowardly, unbelieving people were listed in a rogue's gallery with murderers and liars?

Why we fear what we fear

Fear and anxiety are similar, but not exactly the same. People are anxious because they don't know what is going to happen and they concern themselves with the worst. Fear, on the other hand has an object. People fear *something*.

In order for a fear object to be legitimate, it must have two attributes. First, it has to be potent. Second, it has to be imminent. We fear that which threatens our well-being, but only when it's present.

For instance, I have a healthy fear of rattlesnakes. But as I'm writing this, I am not afraid. Why? Because there are no rattlesnakes present. If someone dropped by my office and threw one of them at my feet, you would see an immediate fear response. The snake is now both present and potent. But if you threw a dead snake in my office, I would again not be afraid once I made sure it was dead! The snake is present, but it's not potent. You can overcome fear by eliminating one (or both) of the attributes of the fear object.

Fear objects range from the inanimate and abstract (abandonment, heights, failure, fire) to the personal and real (parents, boss, God, Satan). Fears are learned. For example, a child learns a healthy fear of fire by getting burned. Unless the lesson is extreme or abusive, such development is good for self-preservation. But some early learning may not reflect reality. For instance, a little child may be warned not to go outside because the bogeyman is there. That child grows up into an adult who fears leaving the house at night. Learned fears are not always rational and may result in phobias.

Phobias are irrational fears that don't reflect present-day reality. In early childhood, my wife witnessed a major aeroplane crash. Years later she lost a loved one in another aeroplane disaster. Her processing of those tragedies left her with a fear of flying. While it's a fact that aeroplane travel is

far safer than motorcars, such reasoning may not resolve
my wife's problem. Her fear is triggered in the present, but
it was developed in the past.

Whether the original fear object was real or imagined
doesn't affect the present emotional response. To the person
experiencing fear, the fear is real.

There is a trilogy of fear objects which frighten almost
everyone. Yet Scripture tells us we don't have to fear them.
If we can conquer our fear of these three things, we will set
ourselves free from the crippling fear Satan uses to destroy
our walk with God. We'll take a look at these fear objects
and examine what God has to say about them.

People who intimidate

The first major fear object is *man*. Consider Psalm 118:5–9:

> From my distress I called upon the Lord; The Lord
> answered me and set me in a large place. The Lord is for me;
> I will not fear; What can man do to me? The Lord is for me
> among those who help me; Therefore I shall look with satis-
> faction on those who hate me. It is better to take refuge in
> the Lord than to trust in man. It is better to take refuge in
> the Lord than to trust in princes.

The timid man is quick to respond, 'What can man do to
me? I'll tell you what man can do to me. He can abuse me,
he can sack me from my job, he can even kill me.'

True, but Jesus tells us to lay those fears aside: 'And do
not fear those who kill the body, but are unable to kill the
soul; but rather fear Him who is able to destroy both soul
and body in hell' (Mt 10:28). If you fail to take God as your
refuge, the fear of man will control your life.

God appointed Saul to be the first king of Israel and
commanded him to utterly destroy Amalek along with all

of his family, followers and possessions. Unfortunately, Saul didn't listen:

> But Saul and the people spared Agag and the best of the sheep, the oxen, the fatlings, the lambs, and all that was good, and were not willing to destroy them utterly; but everything despised and worthless, that they utterly destroyed (1 Sam 15:9).

Then God said, 'I regret that I have made Saul king, for he has turned back from following Me, and has not carried out My commands' (1 Sam 15:11). Samuel confronted Saul, and after Saul's excuses ran out, he confessed, 'I have sinned; I have indeed transgressed the command of the Lord and your words, because I feared the people and listened to their voice' (1 Sam 15:24). Then the Lord rejected Saul as king of Israel. More than one king has gone down the tubes for fearing man more than God.

Suppose a secretary is intimidated by her boss. She works in fear of him from eight to five because he is both imminent and potent. What power does the boss have over the secretary? He could sack her! How could she overcome that power? She could quit or be willing to quit. By not allowing her boss to hold the job over her head, she would free herself from his intimidations.

I'm not suggesting that she rebel against her boss or become irresponsible. Servants are to obey their masters and we are to work heartily as for the Lord rather than men (Col 3:22,23). However, when the secretary makes God her sanctuary, she frees herself up to live a responsible life. If she loses her job in the process, she has the assurance that God will meet all her needs.

Disarming the fear of people

The means by which we overcome people's intimidations is to sanctify Christ as the Lord of our lives. When we make God our refuge, other fear objects pale in comparison. Look at 1 Peter 3:13–15:

> And who is there to harm you if you prove zealous for what is good? But even if you should suffer for the sake of righteousness, you are blessed. And do not fear their intimidations, and do not be troubled, but sanctify Christ as Lord in your hearts, always being ready to make a defence to every one who asks you to give an account for the hope that is in you, yet with gentleness and reverence.

It's important to note when standing up to intimidating people that we are not to become like them in their belligerence. Our response in Christ is to give evidence of the fruit of the Spirit. We are to speak in gentleness and reverence.

Peter continues, 'And keep a good conscience so that in the thing in which you are slandered, those who revile your good behaviour in Christ may be put to shame' (1 Pet 3:16). As long as we abide in Christ and respond in grace, be assured that the other person's character will reveal itself. Let your intimidator bear the shame if anyone must.

Learning how to respond to the intimidations of people is essential to overcoming the first fear in the fear trilogy — man.

The fear of dying

The second member of the fearful trilogy is *death*. Most phobias can be reduced to a fear of death. It looms over many as the ultimate fear object. The fact that death is imminent is clearly established in Scripture: 'It is appointed

for men to die once, and after this comes the judgement'
(Heb 9:27).

But Christians need not fear death. Jesus removed death
as a legitimate fear object by taking away its power when He
died for our sins: 'Death is swallowed up in victory. O death,
where is your victory? O death, where is your sting?' (1 Cor
15:54,55) Jesus Himself said, 'I am the resurrection and the
life. He who believes in Me shall live even if he dies. And
everyone who lives, and believes in Me shall never die' (Jn
11:25,26).

Every child of God is spiritually alive, and even physical
death cannot separate us from the love of God (Rom 8:38).
Paul says, 'For to me, to live is Christ, and to die is gain'
(Phil 1:21). Why? Because we have made God our sanctuary. When we physically die, we will receive a resurrected
body and be far better off than we are today. Try putting
something else into Paul's formula, for instance: 'For me to
live is success.' Then to die would be what? Loss! 'For me to
live is a good physical body.' Again, to die would be loss.

I often ask people, 'What is the worst thing that could
happen to you?' 'Well, I could die,' they answer. To which I
respond, 'Then you have nothing to fear, since the Bible
says that may be the best thing that could happen to you!'
The ultimate value is not physical life, but spiritual life. If
our life is hidden in Christ, then we won't suffer loss when
we physically die. We can only gain. The person who is free
from the fear of death is free to live again.

The fear of Satan

The third member of the phobia trilogy is *Satan*. Fear is one
of Satan's greatest strategies. We are cautioned in 1 Peter
5:8, 'Be of sober spirit, be on the alert. Your adversary, the
devil, prowls around like a roaring lion, seeking someone to
devour.' Lions roar in order to paralyse their prey in fear so
they can consume them. I'm often asked, 'Aren't you afraid

to deal with demonic issues?' I respond, 'I don't know of one verse in the Bible that instructs us to fear Satan.' Satan is a defeated foe, but through deception he paralyses the church in fear.

In *The Bondage Breaker* I give the following illustration. When I was a young boy on the farm, our neighbours had a yappy little dog that scared the socks off me. I recall one day when my brother, father and I drove over to their farm. As soon as we got out of the truck, that dog came roaring around the corner barking like crazy. Terrorised, I ran! Guess who the dog chased? I found sanctuary on the top of the truck. My brother and father stood right by the dog who was barking only at me. The dog didn't chase or bother them one bit. What power did that dog have to put me on top of that truck?

It had no inherent power at all. It was a puny little runt! The only power which it had was the power I gave it. I'll tell you how I ended up on the top of the truck. That dog used my mind, my will, my emotions and my muscles. My dad thought it was a little embarrassing. He wanted me to stand my ground. The next time we went to that farm, I worked up my courage and when the dog came after me I kicked a rock at it. To my great relief, it put its tail between its legs and took off.

James 4:7 offers this strategy: 'Submit therefore to God. Resist the devil and he will flee from you.' The order is critical. Make God your sanctuary first, then the devil can easily be resisted.

Another of Satan's tactics is the common psychological disorder, anxiety attacks. They're called anxiety rather than fear attacks because people don't know what they're afraid of. In my experience, when people can't identify the fear object, I can almost assure you it's Satan.

Because of the nature of my ministry, I've had several such attacks. I'm not by nature a timid person, but I have awakened at night terrorised. Knowing what it is, I know how to resolve it. Most people try to respond physically but can't. Anxiety attacks often feel like a pressure on the chest or something grabbing the throat. Since they can't respond physically, it seems as though the power is overwhelming. Responding in the flesh will not resolve it: 'For the weapons of our warfare are not of the flesh, but are divinely powerful for the destruction of fortresses' (2 Cor 10:4).

Saying no to Satan

How then can we resist these attacks? Since Satan cannot touch who we are as children of God, inwardly we can always turn to God. The moment we turn to our authority and acknowledge Christ as the Lord of our life, we will be free to respond verbally. All we have to say is, 'Jesus!' The need to say it cannot be overstated. Satan is under no obligation to obey our thoughts. We must take our stand verbally against that kind of attack. Notice the words in Matthew 10:25–27:

> It is enough for the disciple that he become as his teacher, and the slave as his master. If they have called the head of the house Beelzebub, how much more the members of his household! Therefore, do not fear them, for there is nothing covered that will not be revealed, and hidden that will not be known. What I tell you in the darkness, speak in the light; and what you hear whispered in your ear, proclaim upon the housetops.

Why verbally? Because all occult practices are dark, mysterious and hidden. As soon as we expose them by bringing them to the light, their power is broken. God requires us to verbally take our stand in the world: 'If you confess with your mouth Jesus as Lord, and believe in your heart that God raised him from the dead, you shall be saved' (Rom 10:9). People are intimidated by deceiving spirits. But as soon as the lie is exposed, the power of Satan is broken. I can illustrate this from my personal experience.

What would you do if a demonised person suddenly started to approach you? That's happened to me more than once in counselling. In one case, a rather large lady got out of her chair and started to come toward me. All I did was verbally say, 'I'm a child of God. The evil one cannot touch me' (1 Jn 5:18). She stopped dead in her tracks.

A man on the east coast heard that account in a series of tapes that I had done. Shortly after that he was confronted by three thugs at a train station demanding his money. 'It was as though I could see right through them,' he told me later. So he responded, 'I'm a child of God. The evil one can't touch me.' 'What?' they asked. He repeated, 'I'm a child of God. The evil one can't touch me.' 'Oh!' they responded and walked away.

Satan can't do anything about our position in Christ. But if he can get us to believe it's not true, then we will live as though it's not, even though it is true. Knowing who we are as children of God cannot be overstated in making a stand against Satan. Notice the complete text of 1 John 5:18–20:

> We know that no one who is born of God sins; but He who was born of God keeps him and the evil one does not touch him. We know that we are of God, and the whole world lies in the power of the evil one. And we know that the Son of God has come, and has given us understanding, in order that we might know Him who is true, and we are in Him who is true, in His Son Jesus Christ. This is the true God and eternal life.

Acting responsibly

Overcoming the fears of man, death and Satan is what frees us to live a responsible life. Irrational fears compel us to act irresponsibly, or they impede us from living a responsible life. In that sense fear and faith are mutually exclusive.

A severe storm was hitting the east coast, and the Coast Guard was summoned to respond to a ship in crisis. A young sailor, new on board, was terrorised by the prospect and proclaimed, 'We can't go out. We'll never come back!' The seasoned captain responded, 'We must go out. We don't have to come back.' Duty called and responsibility overcame the fear.

If we're going to walk by faith, there can be only one fear object in our life, and that's God. We are responsible to Him. He is the ultimate fear object because He is omnipotent and omnipresent. The fear of the Lord is healthy because it is the one fear that expels all other fears. Notice how this is true from Isaiah 8:11–14:

> For thus the Lord spoke to me with mighty power and instructed me not to walk in the way of this people...and you are not to fear what they fear or be in dread of it. It is the Lord of hosts whom you should regard as holy. And He shall be your fear, and He shall be your dread. Then He shall become a sanctuary.

All other fear objects pale in comparison to our holy God. We need to be like David who proclaimed before Goliath, 'For who is this uncircumcised Philistine that he should taunt the armies of the living God?' (1 Sam 17:26) The Hebrew army saw Goliath in relation to themselves and cowered in defeat. David saw Goliath in relation to God and conquered in His strength.

When the twelve spies checked out the promised land, ten of them came back and responded, 'We are not able to go up against the people, for they are too strong for us' (Num 13:31). They didn't see God in the land, they saw the giants. So they reasoned, 'We became like grasshoppers in our own sight, and so we were in their sight' (Num 13:33). (I saw myself as a grasshopper compared to that stupid dog I mentioned earlier, so I was a grasshopper in the dog's sight.) With that perspective, 'all the congregation lifted up their voices and cried, and the people wept that night' (Num 14:1). (I felt like crying on top of that truck!) Joshua and Caleb responded:

> Only do not rebel against the Lord; and do not fear the people of the land, for they shall be our prey. Their protection has been removed from them, and the Lord is with us; do not fear them (Num 14:9).

The people did rebel. They accepted the majority report instead of listening to Caleb and Joshua. By accepting the Canaanites' will over God's will, they elevated the power and eminence of the Canaanites over the omnipotence and omnipresence of God. To honour God as the ultimate fear object is to worship Him. To be controlled by any other fear object is to allow it to usurp God's place in our lives.

Pleasing God

Obeying the commandment to have no other gods before us is the first act of worship. The writer of Proverbs says, 'The fear of the Lord is the beginning of knowledge; fools despise wisdom and instruction' (Prov 1:7). To worship God is to acknowledge His divine attributes. He doesn't need us to tell Him who He is. We need to keep our minds renewed to the reality of His presence. The fear of God is the highest motivation to do good. Notice how this is brought out in 2 Corinthians 5:9–11:

Therefore also we have our ambition, whether at home or absent, to be pleasing to Him. For we must all appear before the judgement seat of Christ, that each one may be recompensed for his deeds in the body, according to what he has done, whether good or bad. Therefore, knowing the fear of the Lord, we persuade men, but we are made manifest to God; and I hope that we are made manifest also in your consciences.

Realising that God knows the thoughts and intentions of our hearts, we should be motivated to live our lives to please Him. Someday we're going to stand before Him and give an account. The judgement that Paul is talking about in this passage is not for punishment but for rewards. We don't fear God because of the possibility of punishment: 'There is no fear in love, but perfect love casts out fear because fear involves punishment, and the one who fears is not perfected in love' (1 Jn 4:18). We have already been judged as to where we will spend eternity. But how we spend eternity depends on how we respond to God in this lifetime.

I personally don't want to limp into heaven and have Him say, 'Well, okay, come on in.' I want to stand before God someday and hear Him say, 'Well done, good and faithful servant. Enter into the joy of your Lord.' That's the greatest motivation in my life. As a child I didn't fear the punishment of my father nearly as much as the fear of disappointing my parents.

Resolving your fears

At the end of the chapter you will find a 'Phobia Finder'. I use it to help people identify and hopefully eliminate any irrational fears in their lives. Let's go through it and apply it to possible fear situations in our lives.

First, *analyse your fear*. Identify all fear objects. What is it you're afraid of? A problem well-stated is half solved.

Most people aren't aware of what is controlling their lives. Remember, 'God has not given us a spirit of timidity, but of power, and love, and discipline' (2 Tim 1:7).

If you are struggling with anxiety attacks, determine when they first occurred. What experience preceded the first attack? People struggling with agoraphobia can usually identify one precipitating event. It is often associated with some tragedy or failure in their lives. Satan takes advantage of victimised people if they don't seek a scriptural solution to their crisis. For example, I have found that affairs and abortions often precede anxiety attacks. When I established the connection, I discovered that the person had not resolved the sin before God. The person rationalised it instead of confessing it. The psalmist says, 'For I confess my iniquity; I am full of anxiety because of my sin' (Ps 38:18).

Second, *determine where God's place in your life has been usurped.* In what way does any fear prevent you from responsible behaviour or compel you toward irresponsible behaviour? You may need to confess any situations where you've allowed your actions to be controlled by fear. Remember, 'The wicked flee when no one is pursuing, but the righteous are as bold as a lion' (Prov 28:1). We will always live less than a responsible life if we fear anything other than God. Sanctify Christ as the Lord of your life. Make God your sanctuary and commit yourself to live a responsible life according to His will.

Third, *work out a plan of responsible behaviour.* A university student shared with me that she was living in terror of her father. They hadn't spoken to each other in six months. Obviously there was irresponsible behaviour on both their parts. I asked her what she would be afraid of if she went home and assumed her role as her father's daughter. I suggested she take the initiative that evening and say, 'Hi, Dad!' We reasoned that there were three possible responses he could give. First, he could get mad. Second, he could respond with a greeting. Third, he could remain silent. It was the possibility of the third response that created the most fear.

We then discussed the fourth point in the Phobia Finder: *Determine in advance what your response will be to any fear object.* The young woman and I talked about what her response would be in each of those three cases we had mentioned. I then asked her if she would be willing to carry out our plan. She agreed to do it. I got a call that evening from a happy daughter who exclaimed, 'He said "Hi" back!'

Do the thing you fear the most, and the death of fear is certain. See what the Lord says in Psalm 91:1–5,9,10:

> He who dwells in the shelter of the Most High will abide in the shadow of the Almighty. I will say to the LORD, 'My refuge and my fortress, my God, in whom I trust!' For it is He who delivers you from the snare of the trapper, and from the deadly pestilence. He will cover you with His pinions, and under His wings you may seek refuge; His faithfulness is a shield and bulwark. You will not be afraid of the terror by night, or of the arrow that flies by day; for you have made the LORD, my refuge, even the Most High, your dwelling place. No evil will befall you, nor will any plague come near your tent.

All of us have had the experience of being afraid, but how often have we stopped to realise how much fear can control our lives? Its paralysis can prevent us from knowing the direction, freedom and ministry God wants us to have. Join me in prayer, affirming God's dominion in our lives so that the power of fear is broken.

Dear Heavenly Father, You are the fortress, shield and strength of my life. I refuse to be intimidated by any fear object. I choose to sanctify Christ as the Lord of my life. You

are the only omnipotent, omnipresent God. You have not given me a spirit of fear. By Your presence in my life I have power, love and a sound mind. Your presence enables me to live a responsible life. Your presence in my life has made me a partaker of Your divine nature so I can love others as You love them. You are my sanctuary, and I ask You to protect my family and ministry. Amen.

Phobia Finder

1. *Analyse your fear.*
   a. Identify all fear objects (What are you afraid of?)
   b. When did you first experience the fear (anxiety attack)?
   c. What events preceded the first occurrence?
2. *Determine where God's place in your life has been usurped.*
   a. In what way does any fear:
      Prevent you from responsible behaviour?
      Compel you towards irresponsible behaviour?
   b. Confess any active or passive participation on your part where you have allowed fear to control your life.
   c. Commit yourself to God with the understanding that you are willing to fulfil your responsibility in the matter.
3. *Work out a plan of responsible behaviour.*
4. *Determine in advance what your response will be to any fear object.*
5. *Commit yourself to carry out that plan.*

6
The Essential Prerequisite

Do you believe that the will of God is good,
acceptable and perfect for you?

Knowing the will of God is not just a twentieth-century
problem. People were struggling at the time of Christ. Some
people were saying of Him, 'He's a good man.' Others were
saying, 'He leads the multitudes astray' (see John 7:12).
How could these people know whether He was leading
them into truth?

Seizing the opportunity, Jesus set forth standards of
divine guidance. His first admonition was, 'My teaching is
not mine, but His who sent me. If any man is willing to do
His will, he shall know of His teaching, whether it is of
God, or whether I speak from myself' (Jn 7:17). The essential prerequisite to knowing the will of God, according to
Jesus, is a willingness to do it. Yet before we seek to understand why that is the case, let's ask an even more basic question: What is the will of God?

Understanding what God wants

Notice the opening words of the Lord's Prayer:

> Our Father Who art in heaven, hallowed be Thy name. Thy
> kingdom come. Thy will be done on earth as it is in heaven
> (Mt 6:9,10).

When praying this prayer, we are asking for God's will to be accomplished on earth as it presently is in heaven. Apparently God's will is being perfectly executed in heaven but not on earth. What has gone wrong on earth, and how is this to be understood in light of the coming of His kingdom? Let's step back to the beginning of time to understand the unfolding plan of God.

God created mankind in His own image. He breathed into them, and they became living beings. The first Adam was both spiritually and physically alive. He was physically alive in that his soul/spirit was in union with his body, and spiritually alive in that his soul/spirit was in union with God. Eve was created out of Adam and they were told to be fruitful and multiply. God charged them to rule over the birds of the sky, the beasts of the field and the fish of the sea. They were given dominion on earth over God's creation.

Then Satan approached Eve, tempting her in the same three ways we are tempted today: the lust of the flesh, the lust of the eyes and the boastful pride of life. Being deceived, she took the fruit and ate, and Adam followed likewise in sin. Because they acted independently of God through disobedience, they died spiritually and were separated from God. Satan became the rebel holder of authority — a position Jesus never questioned, calling him the 'ruler of this world' (Jn 14:30).

Separated from God, Adam and Eve lived their lives independently of Him. Attempts at establishing an ongoing relationship through the government and law in the Old Testament would prove futile.

Like all offspring of Adam, we come into this world physically alive but spiritually dead. During the formative years of our lives, we learn how to survive, cope, defend ourselves and hopefully succeed. We are conformed to this world because we had no other choice. We had neither the presence of God in our life nor the knowledge of His ways. Lacking a relationship with God, we sought to find our identity and purpose for living in the natural world. Paul expressed it this way:

> And you were dead in your trespasses and sins, in which you formerly walked according to the course of this world, according to the prince of the power of the air, of the spirit that is now working in the sons of disobedience. Among them we too all formerly lived in the lusts of our flesh, indulging the desires of the flesh and of the mind, and were by nature children of wrath even as the rest (Eph 2:1–3).

How Jesus fulfilled God's plan

What a hopeless mess! If Jesus came to undo all of that, He had His work cut out for Him. Mankind was dead in trespasses and sin, and Satan was the ruler of the world. Nothing short of Jesus' death on the cross could undo both, so that is why He came. 1 John 3:8 says, 'the Son of God appeared for this purpose, that He might destroy the works of the devil.' Jesus said He came that we might have life (Jn 10:10). Was He successful? Look at Colossians 2:13–15:

> And when you were dead in your transgressions and the uncircumcision of your flesh, He made you alive together with Him, having forgiven us all our transgressions, having cancelled out the certificate of debt consisting of decrees against us and which was hostile to us, and He has taken it out of the way, having nailed it to the cross. When he had disarmed the rulers and authorities, He made a public display of them, having triumphed over them through Him.

Jesus accomplished both tasks: He saved mankind and he disarmed Satan.

The complete gospel

First, let's take a look at what happened to mankind. If Jesus wanted to save a dead person He would have to do two things. He would first have to deal with what caused the dead man to die. In this case, 'the wages of sin is death' (Rom 6:23). So He went to the cross and died for our sins. But that's only half the gospel.

We understand the fact that we are sinful and need a Messiah to die for our sins. So if we believe and trust in Jesus, our sins will be forgiven and when we die we will go to heaven. The greatest issue is that we were dead in our trespasses and sins and desperately needed life. The second thing Jesus did for mankind was that He gave us eternal life as a present reality and not just something we get when we die:

> And the witness is this, that God has given us eternal life, and this life is in His Son. He who has the Son has the life; he who does not have the Son of God does not have the life (1 Jn 5:11,12).

Every child of God is spiritually alive right now. Before we experienced salvation, we were conformed to this world and our minds were programmed to live independently of God. This learned independence is what constitutes the flesh. And though we have received eternal life, nobody pushed the 'clear' button in our memory bank. We still have to deal with the flesh. That's why the apostle Paul writes in Romans 12:2:

> And do not be conformed to this world, but be transformed by the renewing of your mind, that you may prove what the will of God is, that which is good and acceptable and perfect.

God has given us eternal life but we must 'work out our salvation with fear and trembling for it is God who is at work in us, both to will and to work for His good pleasure' (Phil 2:12,13). Since our citizenship is in heaven, we need to prepare for that eternal state by living righteous lives. We are to become the children of God that our heavenly Father has called us to be.

The lion tamed

Jesus Christ has defeated Satan. Scripture assures us that Satan is a defeated foe, but according to 1 Peter 5:8 he roars around like a hungry lion seeking for someone to devour. He no longer has the teeth to do as he wishes, but he is hounding Christians to death! It is our responsibility to submit to God, resist the devil and he will flee from us (Jas 4:7). Jesus announced that 'all authority has been given to Me in heaven and on earth' (Mt 28:18). If we are going to go into the world and make disciples, we need to know that God has given us the authority to do His will. We should exercise authority over Satan when necessary.

Not only did Jesus complete that which He came to do (He said, 'It is finished'), but He left us an example to follow in His steps (1 Pet 2:21). And what was His example? 'My food is to do the will of Him who sent me, and to accomplish His work' (Jn 4:34). Was it easy? Oh no! It may bring comfort to some that, in His humanity, Jesus struggled with the will of God. Jesus agonised in His darkest hour: 'Father if Thou art willing, remove this cup from Me, yet not My will but Thine be done' (Lk 22:42). The Lord Jesus Christ modelled a life of total dependence upon God the Father.

Let me summarise God's will for our lives:

God's will for those who believe in him is to be alive in Christ for the purpose of establishing His kingdom by over-

coming the evil one and becoming fully the people He has called us to be.

The heart of God's will

In a personal sense, God's will for our lives is that we conform to the image of God, something the apostle Paul makes clear in 1 Thessalonians 4:3: 'For this is the will of God, your sanctification.' In his letter to Roman Christians, Paul writes, 'For whom He foreknew He predestined to become conformed to the image of His son' (Rom 8:29) and adds in 1 Timothy 1:5, 'The goal of our instruction is love from a pure heart, a good conscience, and a sincere faith.'

I can hear the protests, 'But that doesn't answer the questions you raised at the beginning of chapter 1.' You're right. But divine guidance will never come to those whose primary goal is not first and foremost conforming to the image of God.

There is no instruction in the Bible concerning career choice, where we live or who we should marry. There is, however, an abundance of instruction on how we're to relate to our employer and behave on the job we already have (Col 3:22–25). And there is much about how to relate with one another (Col 3:10–14) and live with our families (Col 3:18–21).

The Bible overwhelmingly instructs that to do God's will means living in harmony with God and man:

> You shall love the Lord your God with all your heart, and with all your soul, and with all your mind. This is the great and foremost commandment. The second is like it, you shall love your neighbour as yourself. On these two commandments depend the whole law and the prophets (Mt 22:37–40).

The whole purpose of the Bible is to teach us how to

have a relationship with God and live in harmony with one another. We do this by assuming our responsibilities for today and trusting God for tomorrow.

Most people want to know what God has in store for them tomorrow. That's why prophecy has always been a popular subject. But most prophecy buffs know that the critical issue concerning the Lord's second coming is, 'What sort of people ought you to be in holy conduct and godliness?' (2 Pet 3:11). Jesus said, 'But seek ye first His kingdom and His righteousness, and all these things shall be added to you, therefore do not be anxious for tomorrow' (Mt 6:33,34). Biblical prophecy is given to us as a hope (the present assurance for some future good) so we will have the courage to live righteously and confidently today.

Again I can hear the protests, Are you trying to tell us that we aren't to make any plans for the future or establish any goals for our ministry or work?' No, I'm trying to say that the primary focus of God's will is that we seek His kingdom by becoming the person He wants us to be *today*. I'm not really sure that God's will enters into the choice of whether we become an engineer, plumber or nurse. But I am convinced that God's will is concerned with what kind of engineer, plumber or nurse we are.

I teach leadership and church management, so I believe in setting goals and making plans. But a biblical vision for the future and godly goals for ministry or work have no value if they don't provide direction for our steps today. Goals for tomorrow that don't prioritise present activities are nothing more than wishful thinking. We make plans for tomorrow in order to establish meaningful activities for today. We need to ask the Lord each day if we are still on target, and give Him the right to order mid-course changes in direction.

Making the most of every opportunity

There are two important concepts about the will of God that my students hear at seminary. The first is, 'Bloom where you are planted.' Be the best you can be at your present assignment, and stay there until God calls you elsewhere.

Oftentimes my students will say, 'There are no openings to serve at my church!' My response, 'Oh, yes there are. They're probably begging for someone to teach eight-year-old boys.' The momentary silence reveals this thought: 'But anyone can teach eight-year-old boys. I had something higher in mind.' Like maybe an opening in the Trinity!

Take the opportunity before you and teach those eight-year-old boys. Decide to be the best teacher they've ever had. You may start with only three little boys, but at the end of that year you've got twelve boys excited about God, Sunday school and church. Next year, when the personnel committee needs to fill leadership positions, they say, 'We need some new life on the Christian education committee.' Somebody aware of the fruit you are bearing says, 'There's this guy doing a great job with our eight-year-olds. Let's ask him to be on the committee.'

Now that you are on the Christian education committee, decide to be the best committee member you can be. It won't be long before they recognise your initiative and say, 'We could use this person on the board.' Determine to become the best possible board member you can. Then an opening develops for an intern and guess who the people suggest! People hearing of your faithfulness and aware of the fruit you are bearing ask you to consider a full-time pastoral position. So you become the best youth pastor, small group pastor or college minister you can possibly be. Before long you'll be bearing so much fruit that other churches will be inquiring about your availability. God guides those who bloom where they are planted.

When D. L. Moody found his life in Christ, he looked for some opportunities to teach at a church, but no one wanted to use the uneducated man. He started his own Bible study in a shoe shop, and it wasn't long before children were coming out of the woodwork. People couldn't help but notice him because he was bearing fruit, and few have left such an imprint as his upon the world.

Paul said, 'I thank Christ Jesus our Lord, who has strengthened me, because He considered me faithful, putting me into service' (1 Tim 1:12). Show yourself faithful by exploiting the opportunities around you. The needs of people are everywhere, so what are you waiting for?

What an elementary concept, but many simply bide their time waiting for the 'big' opportunity. Sure, these people will humble themselves to teach eight-year-olds, but at the end of the year they have the same three boys they started with — boys who are now looking forward to being promoted out of their class. Jesus said to those who had bloomed where they were planted, 'Well done, good and faithful servant; you were faithful with a few things, I will put you in charge of many things, enter into the joy of your master' (Mt 25:21). If you aren't responsible in your present assignment and taking advantage of the opportunities that are there, don't expect God to call you elsewhere.

A man in my church often expressed his frustration with his job. For twenty years he'd been working as a construction worker, and he hated it! Frustrated with his career, he wondered why God wouldn't call him out of there.

I asked him if he had ever expressed dissatisfaction about his job with his fellow employees who weren't Christians. He said, 'Oh, sure. I complain right along with the rest of them.' I continued, 'What do you suppose that does to your witness?' He was a little startled by my question. I added, 'Do you realise that God has you exactly where He wants you? When you assume your responsibility to be the person God wants you to be as a construction worker, He may open a new door for you.'

The Holy Spirit must have brought conviction because this man became a missionary at work. He displayed concern for the needs of his co-workers and their families and soon had a series of witnessing experiences to share. Within six months an opportunity arose and he left construction work. And all because he started to bloom where he was planted.

Moving in obedience

The second important concept I teach about God's will is that God can only guide a moving ship. He is the rudder, but if the ship isn't under way it can't be directed. Willingness to obey His will gets the ship moving.

I was assigned to a destroyer when I was in the Navy. We had just passed through the Panama Canal on our way to San Diego when we had a flame-out in the middle of the night. The oil king (the man responsible for even distribution of the oil on board the ship) had allowed a compartment of oil to be pumped dry. In a short time the boilers went cold for lack of fuel, and we lost all our power. Within minutes the ship was doing 30- and 40-degree rolls. A ship without power is helpless in the sea. The helmsman could do nothing because the rudder only works if the ship is under way.

In Acts 15:36, Paul had decided to revisit the churches he helped establish on his first missionary trip. The churches were being strengthened and increasing in number (Acts 16:5). Luke reports:

> And they passed through the Phrygian and Galatian region, having been forbidden by the Holy Spirit to speak the word in Asia; and when they had come to Mysia, they were trying to go into Bithynia, and the Spirit of Jesus did not permit

them; and passing by Mysia, they came down to Troas. And a vision appeared to Paul in the night: a certain man of Macedonia was standing and appealing to him, and saying 'Come over to Macedonia and help us' (Acts 16:6–9).

Sometimes God's leading does not make sense. If God wanted Paul to go to Macedonia in the first place, why didn't He make it easier and faster by having Paul travel by land to Caesarea and sail to Macedonia? Because God starts us out on a life course to fulfil a certain purpose and then, only when we are ready, He gives us course corrections. Like a good river pilot, He steers us away from troubled waters, and like a good coach, he never puts us in the game until we are ready.

If God wanted me to be a seminary professor, why didn't he direct me to a good Bible college and then immediately to seminary? Instead He allowed/guided me through a variety of experiences — farm boy, sailor, wrestling coach, aerospace engineer, campus pastor, youth pastor, minister of adult education and senior pastor. All the time I was gaining experience and developing character. Every new assignment was a stretching experience; each had a greater responsibility.

I believe in divine guidance. We read in Isaiah 58:11, 'The Lord will continually guide you.' But the context reveals that there are prerequisites that have to be satisfied. The Israelites were seeking God's leading through fasting (v 2), but God revealed that their fasting was a farce which ended in strife (v 4). The fast that God desired was proof of their repentance. He desired for them to set the captives free and meet the needs of the poor around them (vs 6,7). 'Then your light will break out like the dawn' (v 8). Then guidance would come.

Instead the Israelites were like a person who seeks to be an athlete by simply suiting up for the race. That's not how the skills are gained. It's in the course of dedication, training and the contest itself that the one gains the skill of an athlete.

It's in the doing of God's work that His will becomes known.

Abandonment to God's will

Now I want to return to the essential prerequisite that I mentioned at the beginning of the chapter, that in order to know God's will there must be a willingness to do it.

Imagine, if you would, a door in the path ahead of us. God's will is on the other side of that door. We crave to know what it is. Will God show us what's on the other side of that door? No. Why not? Because we have to resolve an issue on this side of the door first. If He is Lord, He has the right to determine what's on the other side of the door. If we don't afford Him that right, then we are not acknowledging Him as Lord.

Why do we want to know what's on the other side of that door? Isn't it because we want to reserve the right to determine whether or not we will go through it? Some boldly walk halfway through, but keep their foot in the door just in case they don't like what they see and want to go back. It's going to be awfully hard to continue walking with God if your foot is stuck in the door. Jesus said, 'No one putting his hand to the plough and looking back is fit for the kingdom of God' (Lk 9:62).

One man probably spoke for many when he said, 'I'm so used to running my own life. I'm not sure I even can or want to trust someone else. Besides, God would probably haul me off to some mission field I can't stand.' What we need to realise is that if we did give our heart to the Lord, and God did call us to that mission field, by the time we got there we wouldn't want to be anywhere else.

Question: Do you believe that the will of God is good,

acceptable and perfect for you? That's the heart of the issue. In the Lord's Prayer we are taught to approach God with the intent that His will be accomplished on earth. It makes no sense to petition God if we are not predisposed to do His will.

In the last half of the nineteenth century, George Müller founded the Bristol Orphan Home which would become known all over the world as one of the most remarkable monuments of human faith and divine guidance in history. Year after year, without a single advertisement to the public or appeal to Christian friends, hundreds of children were fed, clothed and educated. The home was maintained simply through prayer and faith. George Müller epitomises the essential prerequisite to divine guidance in these thoughts:

> I seek in the beginning to get my heart in such a state that it has no will of its own in regard to a given matter. Nine-tenths of the trouble with people is just here. Nine-tenths of the difficulties are overcome when our hearts are ready to do the Lord's will. When one is truly in this state, it is usually but a little way to the knowledge of what His will is.

Knowing that 'what's on the other side of the door' is something planned by our loving, omnipotent heavenly Father, would you pray this prayer with me?

Dear Heavenly Father, I choose to acknowledge You as the Lord of my life. Your loving kindness extends to all generations. You are the only all-powerful, all-knowing and ever-present Lord. I will have no other gods before me.

Forgive me for the times I have acted as my own god and sought to determine my own destiny. Forgive me for ever questioning that Your will for my life is anything but good, acceptable and perfect. I no longer choose to be conformed to this world, but to be transformed by the renewing of my mind.

I, therefore, commit myself to be a workman who need not be ashamed, rightly dividing the word of truth. By Your grace I determine to be faithful with what You have already entrusted me.

For this day, I commit myself to be the person You want me to be. I ask You to fill me with Your Holy Spirit and grant me the wisdom and guidance as I seek to do Your will. May Your kingdom rule extend to me. You are the King of my life. I submit to You. Amen.

7
Glorifying God

How do we give glory to another when we are desperately looking for affirmation ourselves?

By now your mind may be swirling with a lot of questions: 'How do I know the will of God? What difference will it make if I discover the will of God, since I can't seem to run my life now? How can I ever please God with my rotten background?

Let's examine some additional issues about knowing God's will, then we'll see how it impacts on all of us, especially people who are hurting.

Heaven is where we say to God, 'Thy will be done.' Hell is where God says to us, 'Thy will be done.' As I said in the last chapter, the essential prerequisite to knowing the will of God is our disposition towards it. In dealing with the question of what is true and what isn't, who is right and who isn't, Jesus responds by saying, 'If any man is willing to do His will, he shall know of the teaching, whether it is of God, or whether I speak of Myself' (Jn 7:17).

If we are predisposed to question or reject the will of God, we will never know what it is. Disobedience affects discernment. Getting my own way excludes God's way. God, speaking through the prophet Isaiah, says:

> For My thoughts are not your thoughts, nor are your ways My ways, declares the Lord. As the heavens are higher than the earth, so are My ways higher than your ways, and My thoughts than your thoughts (Is 55:8,9).

If I wanted to determine the spiritual vitality of an individual using only one criteria, I would evaluate whether the person desires to live according to the will of God, or if he desires to do his own thing. The prayer of a vital, growing Christian is, 'Make me know Thy ways, oh Lord, teach me Thy paths' (Ps 25:4). Jesus taught us to pray, 'Thy kingdom come, Thy will be done, on earth as it is in heaven,' so we should be seeking to establish God's kingdom, not ours.

Beyond being willing

Once our will is bent in the right direction, Jesus raises the additional question of motive: 'He who speaks from himself, seeks his own glory, but he who is seeking the Glory of the one Who sent him, he is true and there is no unrighteousness in him' (Jn 7:18). The person who is true glorifies the one who sent him.

This is perfectly modelled in the Godhead. Notice first the example of Jesus: 'For I proceeded forth and have come from God, for I have not even come on My own initiative, but He sent Me' (Jn 8:42). In talking with His Father, Jesus said:

> I glorified Thee on the earth, having accomplished the work which Thou has given Me to do.... Now they have come to know that everything Thou hast given Me is from Thee; for the words which Thou gavest Me I have given to them; and they received them, and truly understood that I came forth from Thee, and they believed that Thou didst send Me (Jn 17:4,7,8).

The Holy Spirit acts in the same way. In John 14:16 Jesus said, 'I will ask the Father and He will give you another Helper that He may be with you for ever, that is the Spirit of Truth.' When the Holy Spirit comes, this is what He will do:

When He, the Spirit of Truth comes, He will guide you into all truth, for He will not speak on His own initiative; whatever He will speak, He will speak and disclose to you what is to come. And He shall glorify Me, for He shall take of Mine and shall disclose it to you (Jn 16:13,14).

I can take this one step further. Are you ready for this? Jesus said in John 20:21, 'As the Father has sent Me, I also send you.' Granted, that was said to the apostles, but we are all under the Great Commission. Do you want to be true? Then glorify the one who has sent you! Paul asked:

Do you not know your body is a temple of the Holy Spirit Who is in you, Whom you have from God, and that you are not your own? For you have been bought with a price, therefore glorify God in your body (1 Corinthians 6:19,20).

People who know they are God-sent and are committed to live like that, glorify God. Self-sent people seek their own glory.

I know this is a tremendous struggle for those of you who are hurting. You are saying to me, 'God gave me lousy parents. I have no money for a decent education. I've been mistreated by others my whole life. And God wants me to sit around and stroke His ego!'

How do we give glory to another when we are desperately looking for affirmation ourselves? Why should we be excited about glorifying God if we believe that it is God who dealt us a bad hand? Does the Bible teach a worm theology, where God is everything and we are nothing? How is God glorified if His children are required to grovel in some pitiful existence? No wonder the New Age teaching that 'You are God and all you have to do is realise it' is very attractive to those who have been beaten down by life.

The cry of the hurting

I have spent thousands of hours with hurting people who were longing to hear from God. To many of them, the thought of doing the will of God is a tiresome duty with no immediate results. Giving glory to God seems like bowing to a king who demands homage from the poor peasants forced to scramble for the crumbs that fall from his table. Give glory to God! For what?

Let me tell you about someone. If I were to pick the top ten prospects who graduated from our seminary in the last decade, this man would be one of them. He was an excellent student and an outstanding communicator with a winsome personality. Upon graduation he accepted the challenge of a small pastorate, but within two years he was out of the ministry. Two more years passed and God called him back into a pastorate, at which time he attended one of my conferences. Several months after the conference, he wrote me this letter:

I've always figured I was just a no-good, rotten, dirty, stinking sinner, saved by grace yet failing God miserably every day. And all I could look forward to was a lifetime of apologising every night for not being the man I know He wants me to be. 'I'll try harder tomorrow, Lord.'

As a firstborn son, I spent my life trying to earn the approval of highly expectant parents. I've related to God the same way. I felt He just couldn't love me as much as other, 'better' believers. Oh sure, I'm saved by grace through faith, but I'm just hanging on until He gets tired of putting up with me here and takes me home to finally stop the failure in progress. Whew, what a treadmill!

Neil, when you said that in our new identification in Christ we're not sinners but saints, you totally blew me away. Isn't that strange, that a guy could go through a good seminary and never latch on to the truth that he is a new creation in Christ?

This has been so helpful and liberating to me. I'm beginning to grow out of my old ways of thinking about myself and about God. I don't constantly picture Him as disappointed in me any more. If He can still love me, be active in me and find use for even me, after I've failed Him as badly as I have, then surely my worth to Him can't be based on my performance. He just plain loves me. Full stop.

What a new joyful walk I'm experiencing with Him. Praise God. I have been so deeply touched by the realisation of who I am in Christ that I am taking our people through a study in Ephesians to learn who we are in Christ and what we have as believers in Christ. My preaching is different, and our people are profiting greatly by being built up in strength and confidence. I can't tell you how gracious the Lord has been to me, allowing me to try again. Each day of service is a direct gift from God, and I bank each one carefully in heaven's vault for all eternity to the honour and glory of my Saviour.

Give glory to God because He can restore and renew the life of a hurting person.

It was my privilege to spend a Saturday morning with a sharp couple who had driven several hundred miles in hopes that I could resolve a conflict going on in their home. He was a successful man — a superintendent in a public school district. He attended church regularly and, by all external evidence, appeared to be normal. But he was struggling with compulsive thoughts, explosive anger and incredible nightmares that left him depleted every morning.

Within hours we were able to resolve his spiritual conflicts and found freedom in Christ.

Several months later, being assured that what had happened was lasting, he wrote me a letter. I'd like to share part of it with you:

> I never really understood the relationship God wanted to have with me. I saw God as an omnipotent but distant and stern father. You helped me to realise that God is like a real father in how He loves me, meaning that He wants me to enjoy His presence and live a fulfilling life on this earth. I used to see Him as an aloof disciplinarian, a benevolent disciplinarian, but nevertheless a disciplinarian. I knew that I was to have a personal relationship with Him, but I had no way of knowing what that meant.
>
> I equated my own earthly father's attitude toward a father/son relationship to the kind of kinship that would be appropriate between God and myself. I was dead wrong. God not only wants to see me obediently happy, but He also takes joy in my accomplishments. I have struggled with my purpose in life. What did it matter whether I achieved anything? If all my achievements were the result of God's will, and all the credit belonged to Him, it followed in my small mind that I was nothing but a non-efficacious vessel of the Almighty.
>
> Of course I was willing to accept that concept, as I believed it to be biblical. But I was wrong, and I was basing my belief system on a non-scriptural foundation. My downfall was inevitable. There was no way I could experience happiness with this belief. Humility was very important to me. It meant taking no personal satisfaction for a job well done. Without some sort of personal satisfaction for one's endeavours, much of life is missed, and God does not want this. He wants me to

do good things and take pleasure in doing them well. Just as an earthly father is pleased when his son does well, so too is God pleased when His children do His will.

This revelation instilled a great deal of meaning in my life. I now have a new concept of God's love and my place in His divine plan. I have meaning, and what I do has meaning. I can take pleasure in doing good without risking the sin of pride. Now I see the truth — that God is a loving and caring Father. He gave me a will that I am supposed to use to please Him, and that is exactly what I intend to do.

If God is a consuming fire, you're going to stay away. But if He's a loving Father, you're going to draw near. Your motive for serving Him is not to gain His approval; you're already approved. We don't perform for Him in order to be accepted; we are already accepted. Therefore, we joyfully serve Him. We don't labour in the vineyard so that someday He may notice us and hopefully love us. God has known us from the foundation of the world, and He already loves us. Christians will instinctively give glory to God when they know what God has freely bestowed upon them.

God's glory revealed

So what is the glory of God? And how do we glorify God in our body? To begin with, the answer is not joining a health club with the hope that we will acquire the affirmation of others. It's not running endless miles every day, or eating the perfect foods or dieting to the point where we look like an emaciated model. If we do that, who gets the glory?

Don't get me wrong. I believe we're to take care of the temple that houses the Holy Spirit, but not for the sake of drawing attention to ourselves. According to 1 Corinthians 9:27, we are to buffet our body and make it our slave so as not to be disqualified from preaching. In other words, don't lose your witness and ability to serve because you don't take care of yourself. Your body is to serve you, not the other way around.

The glory of God is the manifestation of His presence. In the Old Testament, Moses said, 'I pray Thee, show me Thy glory' (Ex 33:18). God did give Moses a sense of His glory. He said:

> You cannot see My face, for no man can see Me and live. …Behold there is a place by Me and you shall stand there on the rock. And it will come about that when My glory is passing by, that I will put you in the cleft of the rock and cover you with My hand, until I have passed by. Then I will take My hand away and you shall see My back, but My face will not be seen (Ex 33:20–23).

God also manifested His presence over the Ark of the Covenant in the Holy of Holies:

> And the Lord said to Moses, 'Tell your brother Aaron that he shall not enter at any time the holy place inside the veil, before the mercy seat which is on the Ark lest he die, for I will appear in the cloud over the mercy seat' (Lev 16:2).

The progressive departure of the glory of God is revealed in the book of Ezekiel. In Ezekiel 8:4–6, the glory is present in Jerusalem. In Ezekiel 9:3, the glory of God moves to the threshold of the temple, then returns to the sanctuary. In Ezekiel 10:4, the glory moves back to the threshold. In 10:18,19, the glory moves to the east gate. Then in Ezekiel 11:23 the glory of the Lord goes up from the midst of the city and stands over the mountain which is east of the city. Then, 'Ichabod' — the glory departs. Four hundred silent years for Israel begin.

The glory of God doesn't appear again until we read in John 1:14: 'And the Word became flesh and dwelt among us, and we beheld His glory, glory as of the only begotten from the Father, full of grace and truth.' Jesus was a manifestation of the presence of God. That's why He could say, 'He who has seen Me, has seen the Father' (Jn 14:9). Now we glorify God by manifesting His presence: 'By this is my Father glorified, that you bear much fruit, and so prove to be my disciples' (Jn 15:8).

Right behaviour for people of God

The world system in which we were raised says that we are nothing, so compete, scheme, achieve and get ahead. The biblical system teaches that we are something, so be submissive. Here's how Peter said it:

> And coming to Him as to a living stone, rejected by men but choice and precious in the sight of God.... But you are a chosen race, a royal priesthood, a holy nation, a people for God's own possession that you may proclaim the excellencies of Him Who has called you out of darkness into His marvellous light. For you once were not a people, but now you are the people of God. You had not received mercy, but now you have received mercy (1 Pet 2:4,9,10).

Only after that affirmation of us being the people of God does Peter say, 'Submit yourselves, for the Lord's sake, to every human institution' (v 13), and 'Servants be submissive to your masters' (v 18). He even relates it to the home: 'In the same way you wives be submissive to your own husbands' (1 Pet 3:1).

Do I believe in the depravity of man? I certainly do. I believe I was utterly dead in my trespasses and sins, separated from God, and there was nothing I could do about it. I had nothing to look forward to but a godless eternity.

God took the initiative and, praise Him, I'm not depraved any more! I'm a child of God, and so are all born-again believers.

One of my students wrote me this note:

> What really struck me was the concept that we are saints and not sinners. I remember how surprised I was when I took Greek and saw that a Christian is often called *hagios* ('holy one'). I was so steeped in the idea that I was a totally depraved sinner. The concept of who we are in Christ didn't break through until I read your book *Victory Over the Darkness*.
>
> I'm still adjusting to the lofty concept that my real self is holy instead of wretched. I have been saved more than twelve years, and I have never really appreciated what happened to me at my conversion. I always knew that my future destiny was secure, but I didn't understand that I was truly a brand new creation in Christ Jesus.

Why live below your privilege?

I love the illustration Bob George gives in his book *Classic Christianity*. Suppose you are a prostitute. One day you hear that the king has decreed that all prostitutes are forgiven. Since you're a prostitute, that's great news. But would it necessarily change your behaviour or your self-perception? Probably not. You may dance in the streets for a while, but chances are you would continue in the same vocation. You would see yourself as nothing more than a forgiven prostitute.

Now suppose the king not only forgave you, but he made you his bride as well. You're a queen. Would that change your behaviour? Of course. Why would you want to live as a prostitute if you were the queen?

The church is the bride of Christ. You are far more likely

to promote the kingdom if you are the queen rather than a forgiven prostitute. We are not redeemed caterpillars; we are butterflies. Why would you want to crawl in some false humility when you are called to mount up with wings as eagles?

'I would be filled with pride if I believed that,' says the sceptic. You are defeated if you don't believe it. Humility is not putting yourself down when God is trying to build you up. Self-abasement has the appearance of wisdom, but it has no value against fleshly indulgence according to Colossians 2:23. Humility is confidence properly placed. We need to be like Paul and 'put no confidence in the flesh' (Phil 3:3). Let's put our confidence in God: 'For it is God working in you both to will and to work for His good pleasure' (Phil 2:13).

A sharp student at Talbot shared that he struggled with a poor sense of self-worth. Finding out who he was in Christ became the primary motivation to seek God and to do His will. He took a couple of lists of Scriptures that I use and rearranged them so he could clearly understand that he was significant, accepted and secure in Christ. Whenever he felt low or questioned his worth, he would read through the list. Let me share his list with you:

IN CHRIST

I AM SIGNIFICANT:

Matthew 5:13	I am the salt of the earth.
Matthew 5:14	I am the light of the earth.
John 1:12	I am God's child (Rom 8:14–16; 1 Jn 3:1–3).
John 15:1,5	I am a branch of the true vine, a channel of His life.
John 15:16	I have been chosen and appointed to bear fruit.

Acts 1:8	I am a personal witness of Christ.
1 Corinthians 3:16	I am God's temple.
1 Corinthians 12:27	I am a member of Christ's body.
2 Corinthians 5:17,18	I am a minister of reconciliation for God.
2 Corinthians 6:1	I am God's co-worker (1 Cor 3:9).
Ephesians 1:1	I am a saint.
Ephesians 2:6	I have been raised up and I am seated with Christ.
Ephesians 2:10	I am God's workmanship.
Philippians 3:20	I am a citizen of heaven (Eph 2:6).

I AM ACCEPTED:

John 15:15	I am Christ's friend.
Romans 5:1	I have been justified.
1 Corinthians 6:17	I am joined to the Lord and I am one spirit with Him.
1 Corinthians 6:20	I have been bought with a price. I belong to God.
1 Corinthians 12:27	I am a member of Christ's body.
2 Corinthians 5:21	I have been made righteous.
Ephesians 1.5	I have been adopted as God's child.
Ephesians 2:18	I have direct access to God through the Holy Spirit.
Ephesians 2:19	I am of God's household.
Ephesians 2:19	I am a fellow citizen with the rest of the saints.
Ephesians 3:12	I may approach God with boldness and confidence.
Colossians 1:14	I have been redeemed and forgiven of all my sins.
Colossians 2:10	I am complete in Christ.

I AM SECURE:

John 1:12	I am a child of God (Gal 3:26–28).

Romans 8:28	I am assured that all things work together for good.
Romans 8:35	I cannot be separated from the love of God.
Romans 8:1	I am free forever from condemnation.
Romans 8:33	I am free from any condemning charges against me.
2 Corinthians 1:21	I have been established, anointed and sealed by God.
Ephesians 1:13,14	I have been given the Holy Spirit as a pledge, guaranteeing my inheritance to come.
Colossians 1:13	I have been delivered from the domain of darkness and transferred to the kingdom of Christ.
Colossians 3:3	I am hidden with Christ in God.
Philippians 1:6	I am confident that the good work that God has begun in me will be perfected.
Philippians 4:13	I can do all things through Him who strengthens me.
2 Timothy 1:7	I have not been given a spirit of fear, but of power, love and a sound mind.
Hebrews 4:16	I can find grace and mercy in time of need.
1 John 5:1	I am born of God and the evil one cannot touch me.

Those verses aren't true because of what you and I have done. They are true because of what Christ has done. Knowing who we are becomes a primary motivation of wanting to serve God. Listen to Paul's testimony in 1 Corinthians 15:10:

But by grace of God I am what I am, and His grace toward me did not prove vain, but I laboured even more than all of them, yet not I but the grace of God in me.

I'm convinced that we will 'labour even more' when we understand the tremendous position we have in Christ.

A pastor's wife attended my conference on 'Resolving Personal and Spiritual Conflicts.' She discovered who she was as a child of God and found her freedom in Christ. She wrote, 'I crave to share Jesus with people out of my own love for Him, whereas before it was largely an 'I should' activity.'

A seminary student stopped by my office and told me he was changing his major from missions to practical theology. He said, 'My motivation to go into missions was to gain God's approval. I suppose it was a carry-over from my childhood days because I'd never been able to live up to my father's expectations.' The following summer he participated in a short-term missions programme. When he got back he made another appointment to see me. He said, 'I'm changing my major back to missions. But now I'm going not because I have to, but because I want to.' Only a liberated child of Christ joyfully gives glory to God and seeks to establish His kingdom.

Let's stop trying to become something we already are. That can only lead to futility. If we refuse to accept who we are, then no amount of self-effort or works on our part can possibly result in freedom from our hurt. We labour for an unattainable goal and God truly becomes a stern taskmaster to us.

But once we see ourselves from God's perspective, and know who we are in Christ, we are then freed to serve our loving heavenly Father. We experience the guiding hand of Him who has sent us and are able to live freely to the glory of God.

Hurting people...the world is filled with hurting people. People who suffer injustices as well as the consequences of their own bad choices. People who, in their struggle for freedom from their hurt, focus on causes outside of themselves and others to blame, including God. But to those who hurt, God offers a total release. As we seek to glorify Him, He will manifest His glory in us. Would you pray with me for this reality in your life?

Loving Father, I would ask like Moses, 'Show me Your glory.' I desire for Your presence to be manifested in this world. I ask You to fill me with Your Spirit that I may glorify You in my body. Forgive me for the times that I have sought my own glory and acted independently from You.

Thank You for giving me life and calling me Your child. I declare my dependency upon You. I want nothing more than to reflect Your image as I grow in Christ-likeness.

I commit myself to seek no other glory but Yours. You are the only One deserving all honour, glory and praise. I lift up the name of Jesus and pray that You will draw all men to Him. I will work from this day forward by Your grace to establish Your Kingdom. You are the king of my life. Amen.

8
A Light To My Path

God's Word offers a timeless message for our
changing culture

I have fond childhood memories of playing the board game
Monopoly with my younger sister — probably because I
always won!

I'm sure we initially read the directions and attempted to
play by the rules. However, every time we played, the rules
changed according to our personal desires. Not only that,
but I must confess my deviousness in persuading my sister
to make trades of property. I would make her feel she was
getting a terrific deal when, in fact, I was the one who came
out ahead. Sibling rivalry and family tradition gradually set
aside the rules of the game while the motive of the players
grew increasingly suspect.

Such was the case of the Jewish community at the time
of Christ. But the game they were playing had eternal significance. Their traditions had set aside the commandments
of God and gone beyond being devious by imposing legalistic behaviour on their followers to keep them in bondage.
Jesus not only revealed their sick motives, but He also
established the Word of God as the only authoritative rule
that can guide us through the game of life.

Today we need to understand how we have distorted the
truth of God's Word and/or set it aside for the sake of
church or family traditions or personal comfort. Jesus confronted the issue when He was attacked by the Jews for
healing on the Sabbath and accused of having a demon:

'Did not Moses give you the law, and yet none of you carries out the law? Why do you seek to kill Me?' The multitude answered, 'You have a demon. Who seeks to kill You?' Jesus answered and said to them, 'I did one deed, and you all marvel. On this account Moses has given you circumcision (not because it is from Moses, but from the fathers), and on the Sabbath you circumcise a man. If a man receive circumcision on the Sabbath that the Law of Moses may not be broken, are you angry with Me because I made an entire man well on the Sabbath?' (Jn 7:19–23)

Regarding the Sabbath issue, Jesus argued that the Mosaic law required circumcision on the eighth day. If a child was born eight days before the Sabbath, then the law required that he be circumcised on the Sabbath. If it is lawful to circumcise a child on the Sabbath, why not bring healing to the whole person on that day? If Scripture is interpreted wrongly, it will be applied wrongly.

Jesus said, 'You nicely set aside the commandment of God in order to keep your tradition' (Mk 7:9). Jesus was never one to beat around the bush. In essence He was saying, 'Moses gave you the rule book, and none of you are following it! Not only that, but some of you are seeking to kill me.' The last charge was a fact recorded earlier in John 5:18: 'For this cause, therefore, the Jews were seeking all the more to kill Him, because He not only was breaking the Sabbath, but also was calling God His own Father, making Himself equal with God.'

The accusation that Jesus had a demon resulted from the Israelites' bewilderment that Jesus could discern the nature of their hearts. Blinded to the truth, they concluded that Jesus received His information from a demonic source. I think it is interesting to note that the early church also believed Satan was capable of putting thoughts into our minds. Let the modern church not be ignorant of the warning in 1 Timothy 4:1: 'But the Spirit explicitly says that in the latter times some will fall away from the faith, paying attention to deceitful spirits and doctrines [teachings] of demons.'

God's view of false guidance

Let me illustrate from the Bible God's attitude towards those who would turn to the occult for guidance instead of the living God and His Word.

When King Ahaziah of Israel fell through the lattice in his upper chamber, he sent messengers to inquire of Baal-zebub, the god of Ekron, whether he was going to recover from his sickness. But the angel of the Lord said to Elijah, 'Arise, go up to meet the messengers of the king of Samaria and say to them, "Is it because there is no god in Israel that you are going to inquire of Baal-zebub the god of Ekron?"' (2 Kings 1:3). The message he did receive from God was that he would surely die, and die he did.

Isaiah 8:19,20 records:

> And when they say to you, 'Consult the mediums and the spiritists who whisper and mutter,' should not a people consult their God? Should they consult the dead on behalf of the living? To the law and to the testimony! If they do not speak according to this word, it is because they have no dawn.

Even though the Hebrew nation had the law and the prophets, their history abounds with leaders seeking false gods, turning away from the commandments of Moses, not heeding the warnings of the prophets and severely distorting the true intent of the Word of God.

In the New Testament, Jesus affirmed the validity of the law and the prophets and warned against distorting that truth. He said in Matthew 5:17-19:

Do not think that I came to abolish the law or the prophets;
I did not come to abolish, but to fulfil. For truly I say to you,
until heaven and earth pass away, not the smallest letter or
stroke shall pass away from the law, until all is accomplished. Whoever then annuls one of the least of these commandments, and so teaches others, shall be called least in
the kingdom of heaven; but whoever keeps and teaches
them, he shall be called great in the kingdom of heaven.

We are warned in James 3:1, 'Let not many of you
become teachers, my brethren, knowing that as such we
shall incur a stricter judgement.' The Bible warns of severe
penalties for those who would distort its meaning since it is
the only infallible source for understanding the will of God.

Matthew 23 reveals that Jesus considered the religious
establishment of His day as the least in the kingdom of
God, calling its leaders (among many other things) 'blind
guides' (v 24). The Pharisees sat themselves in the seat of
Moses (v 2) and thus shut off the kingdom of heaven from
men (v 13).

Rightly using God's Word

It goes beyond the scope of this book to tackle the problem
of hermeneutics (principles of biblical interpretation). I do
want to identify several issues, however, that affect the way
we understand and apply the Bible to life. From that we'll
see how we stray into error — and fall prey to Satan's half
truths and lies.

First, if our interpretation of Scripture is going to be
right, it must be *systematic*. Individual parts need to be seen
in the context of the whole. There are two potential hindrances which keep our theology from being systematic.

1. *Many Christians don't see the whole picture.* They
come to church weekly and receive a piece of the puzzle.
Occasionally they miss a week, so most don't even have all

the pieces. Imagine how difficult it would be to put a puzzle together without the picture on the box. Individual pieces remain disassociated from the whole.

2. *We view the picture through the grid of our own limited perspectives.* In conferences, I'll have a volunteer come forward to illustrate this point. Holding up my hand with the palm facing up, I'll ask the volunteer to describe what he sees. Eventually, he'll get to the fingernails, and I'll protest, 'Wait a minute. There are no fingernails on this hand. How can you say there are fingernails when I don't see any? Are we looking at the same hand?' We are looking at the same hand, but from different perspectives.

Truth has many dimensions. In order to perceive the whole truth we need to accept the other person's perspective. That's why there are four Gospels. All four wrote about the life, death, burial and resurrection of Christ. All four are different. Which one is the correct perspective? All four! If you want a complete picture, you have to read all four.

When I first got married, I thought it was important (being the head of the home) that the right perspective would bear light on all issues. Of course that perspective was mine. Then I matured a little and tolerated my wife's perspective. Then I matured a little more and appreciated my wife's perspective. Then I matured a little more and began to seek it out.

Let me illustrate. If my son Karl fell down and scratched his knee when he was a baby, my wife's first response was, 'Oh, poor baby!' My response was, 'Get up. Be a man!' Twenty years later when Karl scratches his knee my wife says, 'Oh, poor baby, get up.' And I respond, 'Get up, poor baby.' We've been influenced by each other's perspective, and it has affected how we respond to life.

The tragedy of our time is that few intellectuals admit to their bias. Dispensationalists remain dispensational. Covenant theologians remain covenant in their understanding of Scripture. And Catholics remain Catholic. There's nothing wrong with having distinctions, if we are open to hearing other perspectives. One of my privileges is to teach at an interdenominational school in Southern California where cultural pluralism abounds. While this setting helps purge out traditions that no longer serve a purpose, there is a limit to what we can tolerate. It's one thing to disagree with another's interpretation; it's another to question whether the Bible is the only authoritative source for faith and practice.

Second, to have a biblical hermeneutic, we must adhere to a *grammatical, historical method of biblical interpretation.* How does this apply as we study the Bible? We must understand how the Bible was put together.

1. *God has revealed Himself in time and space.* I have travelled twice to Israel. There is a Jerusalem, a temple, a Jordan River and a Sea of Galilee. The basis for the Christian faith is rooted in geography and history. History in His story fleshed out in our three-dimensional world. This is not the case with many cults which base their faith in mystical time and space.

2. *The self-disclosure of God was an unfolding process.* It occurred over a time span of 1400 years. It wasn't complete until John received his vision on the island of Patmos, resulting in the book of Revelation. Historical Christianity has accepted the fact that the canon (the number of books that belong in the Bible) is closed. There is no new revelation of scriptural quality. Although God is certainly guiding His church through the presence of the indwelling Holy Spirit, no present guidance from God will be contrary to His will already revealed in Scripture.

The Holy Spirit is first and foremost the Spirit of truth (Jn 14:17). Jesus said, 'When He, the Spirit of Truth, comes, He will guide you into all truth' (Jn 16:13). When Jesus prayed, He said, 'I do not ask Thee to take them out of the world, but to keep them from the evil one' (Jn 17:15). Then He says, 'Sanctify them in the truth, Thy Word is truth' (v 17). The primary function of the Holy Spirit is to establish God's presence in our lives and enable us to understand the Word of God.

Most conservative biblical scholars do not believe the Bible was dictated by God in the sense that God told human sources what to write by some audible means. That would be like the occultic practice of automatic writing which requires the writer to function as a medium. An occultic medium or a New Age Channeller functions by assuming a passive state of the mind. Instead, God worked through the minds of the prophets and apostles and super-intended the choice of words. We have a reliable text inspired by God with the personalities of the writers coming through.

In a similar fashion, the guidance of God does not bypass our responsibility to think or to search the Scriptures. We need to be like the Bereans who were considered 'noble minded' because they examined the Scriptures daily to see if these things were so (Acts 17:11).

3. *The grammatical, historical method of interpretation requires that we understand what it meant to the hearers at that time,* in their language and their culture. A similar need exists today when missionaries struggle with the problem of contextualisation (translating the Bible and biblical truth in the context of the culture). Missionaries need to isolate the truth of God's Word from their own cultural bias and rightly apply it to the culture in which they are ministering. Truth is transcultural and, if understood correctly, is true for all people at all times.

4. *The fourth requirement of an historical, grammatical method of interpretation is to understand the literary context.* Nothing has meaning without context. Who was the book written to, and why was it written? What is the major point

of the passage under consideration? Never isolate a passage, text, sentence or work from its literary context. There is only one true interpretation. However, there may be many applications.

Why we misunderstand the Bible

While God has given us an infallible guide to life — His Word — the truth He wants us to follow for our freedom can be obscured by our bias and selfish indulgence. In the twentieth-century Western church, I see at least five major hindrances which affect our understanding and application of the Word of God.

First, *there is a tendency to make doctrine an end in itself.* A major problem in Christian education is having the wrong goal. Christian maturity is not understanding principles of the Bible; Christian maturity is character. According to 1 Timothy 1:5, 'The goal of our instruction is love from a pure heart, a good conscience, and a sincere faith.' If our doctrine is right, it will govern our relationship with God and man. If what we come to accept as truth doesn't affect our love for God and man, something is radically wrong. Knowledge 'makes arrogant, but love edifies' (1 Cor 8:1).

Second, *we can learn a lot about God from Scripture and not know Him at all.* Before his conversion, Paul knew the law, but he didn't recognise God in Christ when he saw Him. After Paul was struck down by the Lord on the Damascus Road, his life pursuit was, 'I count all things to be loss in view of the surpassing value of knowing Christ Jesus my Lord' (Phil 3:8). We're not asked to fall in love with doctrine. We're to fall in love with the Lord Jesus Christ.

Third, *we often encourage memorising Scripture instead of thinking scripturally.* Rote memory without integration is a Western world concept of learning. Our model should be, 'The Word became flesh and dwelt among us.' We are to incarnate the Word of God. We are to have our lives transformed by it, and our minds renewed by it. We need to integrate truth into the very fabric of our lives, not simply memorise it.

Fourth, *we often hear the Word and then don't do it.* The Western world concept of education is characterised by acquiring data. The Hebrew concept was determined by obedience. For instance, the Great Commission requires us to go into the world, making disciples and teaching them to observe all that Christ commanded. It's in the observation (obedience) that we learn and not in the hearing. The will of God is thwarted by educating people beyond their obedience. Jesus taught, 'If you know these things, blessed are you if you do them' (Jn 13:17). James expanded on this idea:

> But the one who looks intently at the perfect law, the law of liberty, and abides by it, not having become a forgetful hearer, but an effectual doer, this man shall be blessed in what he does (Jas 1:25).

Fifth, like the Pharisees, *we tend to 'neglect the commandment of God, and hold to the tradition of man'* (Mk 7:8). I believe this is one of the most serious problems affecting our churches today. Many of our graduates leave seminary with a desire to serve God and bear fruit for His glory. They labour in their last year to discern God's guidance. Many fear that there will be no 'call'. Most are young and filled with idealism. I fear the possibility that their first 'call' may come from an old wineskin (a church rooted in the traditions of men), and we send them out as new wine (zealous to serve God according to the truth of His Word).

A timeless message for a changing culture

The world at the end of the twentieth century is changing at an alarming rate. People are under tremendous stress to keep up with the rapid rate of change. The ecclesiastical challenge is to give anxious people the timeless message of Christ and present it in a contemporary way that relates to a changing culture.

Many of the older and mature saints who rightfully constitute the boards and committees in our traditional evangelical churches resist change. They are comfortable with the form of worship, style of music and methods of teaching that brought them to Christ and helped them mature. They get uncomfortable when a young pastor comes in with new ideas and a desire to change their Christian practices. I, myself, am deeply committed to the authority of Scripture and desire to see both the old and the new wine preserved, so I offer these comments as God seeks to guide us into the twenty-first century.

Jesus not only came to fulfil the law, but He also came to usher in a new age. The Jewish community was locked into tradition. Most of the opposition to Jesus didn't come when He presented the truth, but when He confronted their traditions. When one doesn't conform to the customs and practices of the status quo, the establishment will be offended. The new wine often comes under the scrutiny, and sometimes the wrath, of the old wineskins.

Jesus was taking bold steps in the process of change and such steps are by far the most perilous. Machiavelli wrote in *The Prince*, 'There is nothing more difficult to take in hand, more perilous to conduct, or more uncertain in its success, than to take the lead in the introduction of a new order of things.'

In my first pastorate, I had the privilege of leading our church from rented facilities to the acquisition of new property and buildings. That was only one of many changes that as a young pastor I attempted to bring about. Others included a revision in the constitution that changed the form of our church government. And while the preceding pastor was formal and conservative in style, I advocated more freedom of expression and contemporary worship.

The board members I worked with were at least twenty years my senior, and most were charter members. Many of them would agree that the new property and government were better than what we had before, but when I left the church I had 'bullet holes' all over my body!

I can give you a different, more refreshing experience. More recently I had the privilege of helping an established church through an organisational change. The pastor had been there for thirty years and had led the church from its beginning to more than 1,000 attenders. The organisation had evolved with little planning or purpose, so we reorganised twenty-six committees into seven. Although the organisational change was significant, it took place without any dissention. The major key in this case was the cooperation and credibility of the pastor.

If God is leading us into the twenty-first century, we must learn how to adapt our ministry to a changing culture. But while we do, there are some biblical criteria that Jesus taught and modelled that must shape our thinking as we consider revising established practices. Let's look at the example of Christ and see how He responded to Pharisaic traditions that conflicted with the Scriptures.

When not to conform to Pharisaic practices

One of the beautiful things about Jesus is His universal appeal. If you are an ultraconservative, it will thrill your heart to know that He changes not: 'Jesus Christ is the same yesterday and today, yes and for ever' (Heb 13:8). If you are a flaming liberal, you will love the way He refused to participate in Pharisaic practices, particularly the customary traditions of fasting, ritual washings and observing the Sabbath.

The Gospels reveal the conflict that arises when truth, purpose and meaning are at odds with tradition. The fact that Jesus was willing to suffer the rejection of the establishment clearly shows that there is something greater at stake than simply getting one's own way. There are three criteria by which we should determine when a stand for truth should be made against church traditions:

1. Don't conform if the traditions place people under an unnecessary burden (Lk 11:37–41)

The law of Moses called for cleansing after touching an unclean animal or contact with a corpse and ceremonial cleansings for religious practices. To those laws the Rabbis added many petty little rules to guard against every possible defilement. Hygiene was no longer the issue — purification was. They reasoned, 'If we have contact with anything impure, we are impure, and therefore we must be cleansed by washing.' The water must also be pure and if the water must be pure then the vessel carrying the water must be pure, and so forth.

The *Talmud*, a collection of ancient Rabbinic writings, relates the story of Rabbi Akiba who was imprisoned. Rabbi Joshua brought him some water but the guard spilled half of the container. There was too little water to both wash and drink and Rabbi Akiba faced the possibility of death for lack of water if he chose to wash. He reasoned, 'He who eats with unwashed hands perpetuates a crime that ought to be punished by death. Better for me to die of thirst than to transgress the traditions of my ancestors!'

Any preoccupation with trifles as matters of conscience will make one either a moral imbecile or an intolerable hypocrite. Jesus responded harshly to such reasoning: 'You blind guides who strain out a gnat and swallow a camel!'

(Mt 23:24) The Lord cautions that the weightier matters of the law (such as justice and mercy) are overlooked when attention focuses on strict observance of religious practices. This leads to a corresponding negligence of the eternal laws of God. Jesus told the people to pay more attention to cleansing their hearts and not be like their leaders who cleanse only their hands.

The laws of God are liberating and protective. They are restrictive only when they protect us from the evil one. The rules of any institution should ensure the freedom of each individual to reach their God-given potential. They should serve as a guide so we don't stray from our purpose, and they should protect us from those who abuse the system.

The principle that Jesus modelled could be stated as follows: If people are commanded to follow a traditional practice that makes life more difficult and no longer contributes to the purpose of the organisation, then we must not participate as a matter of religious conscience. Jesus simply didn't observe such traditions, and He defended His disciples for not observing them as well.

2. Don't conform if the traditions distort the law they are intended to serve (Lk 6:1–11)

In His ministry, Jesus often violated the traditional instructions surrounding the observance of the Sabbath because they were a clear distortion of God's commandment. A common practice, born out of a desire to protect a known law or principle, is to establish additional rules to keep us from breaking the laws or violating the principles. We establish fences around the laws, but within a short time the fences become laws.

For instance, we are not to be unequally yoked (2 Cor 6:14,15). To ensure that this doesn't happen, we sometimes build a fence around the law by establishing additional rules such as, 'You can't associate with or date a non-Christian.'

That may be advisable in some cases, but don't make it a law. Some have gone to the extreme by requiring that their children never associate with non-Christians. This makes the Great Commission a formidable task!

Here's another example. A common practice in many churches, left over from the Prohibition era, is to require total abstinence from alcohol. Again, that may be wise in many cases, but the Bible instructs against strong drink and drunkenness and teaches us to do all things in moderation. The major biblical concern is not the alcohol, but whether we're being a stumbling block to a weaker brother. Total abstinence may actually keep some from the medicine they need or it may be detrimental when relating to a weaker brother.

I was confronted by this last point when a neighbour whom I had led to Christ found out I was at home with a terrible cold. She came by that evening with a 'hot toddy' to cure me. Being a Baptist pastor, did I accept this act of love? I'll leave you with the tension of not knowing what I did, but I will admit to this — I slept like a baby that night!

The point is, we can easily distort the true Word of God by adding our own traditional practices and making them equal with the original intent of God. We may need to stand against Pharisaic practices as the Lord did — before we find ourselves in bondage to man-made traditions.

3. Don't conform if the traditions are contrary to the will of God (Mk 7:6–9)

Time devoted solely to the traditions of man is often morally corrupt time. Out of necessity there is a corresponding decrease in the commitment to the commandments of God for every commitment to the traditions of man. Remember, 'You nicely set aside the commandment of God in order to keep your tradition' (Mk 7:9). It is easy to see this in others, yet very difficult to see it in ourselves.

Santa Claus at Christmas and the Easter Bunny at Easter are obvious, but what isn't obvious are the little traditions that churches and Christians keep observing year after year, although their purpose is no longer evident.

We cannot ignore the clear example of Jesus. If the Word of God is being abused or distorted in any way, if traditional practices no longer serve their purpose or add to the burdens of people, we must take an active stand.

Changing Christian practices for effective ministry

I really don't mind taking a stand on biblical grounds and living with the conflict that comes from those who oppose the gospel. I think that is part of our calling. What grieves God is when our ministry and work is stopped because well-intentioned people resist the inevitable and needlessly fight change.

I tell my students that the greatest asset they will have in their early years of ministry is older mature saints in the church. The greatest liability they will have is old saints who stopped growing years ago. All these saints want to do is censor. They reflect no more love or kindness than they did twenty years ago. They don't worship — they critique the worship service. They no longer sit under the judgement of Scripture — they sit in judgement of the pastor. They no longer bear fruit — they actually prevent it. They insist that they are right when what they need to be is holy.

Another problem arises when Christian leaders act impulsively as change agents without giving thought to what the consequences will be to the fellowship. Any movement forward that costs the price of fellowship is too high. We must be diligent to preserve the unity of the Spirit. Such change agents seem to be unaware that patience is a fruit of the Spirit. The modern generation wants it now. They seem to have forgotten the fact that God does everything decently and in order. He is not the author of confusion.

To both groups I offer the following suggestions.

The law had required an annual fast on the Day of Atonement. By the time of Zechariah, there were four days of fasting per year. In Jesus' time, strict Jews were fasting twice a week (Lk 18:12). John's disciples were fasting, but the Lord's disciples weren't. The Pharisees wanted to know why. Jesus used this occasion to share four principles that are timeless and critical for our day. I will be using Luke 5:33–39 to show the process of change:

> And they said to Him, 'The disciples of John often fast and offer prayers; the disciples of the Pharisees also do the same; but Yours eat and drink.' And Jesus said to them, 'You cannot make the attendants of the bridegroom fast while the bridegroom is with them, can you? But the days will come; and when the bridegroom is taken away from them, then they will fast in those days.' And He was also telling them a parable: 'No one tears a piece from a new garment and puts it on an old garment; otherwise he will both tear the new, and the piece from the new will not match the old. And no one puts new wine into old wineskins; otherwise the new wine will burst the skins, and it will be spilled out, and the skins will be ruined. But new wine must be put into fresh wineskins. And no one, after drinking old wine wishes for new; for he says, "The old is good enough."'

1. Jesus taught that Christian practices should be appropriate for the situation

Jesus doesn't condemn or condone John's disciples. It was all right for John's disciples to fast, and it was all right if Jesus' disciples didn't. The point that Jesus makes is that it isn't necessary for His disciples to fast while He is with them. The day will come when He won't be with them, and then they will fast. It's not a question of ritual, but of purpose.

Determining the purpose, and whether it is appropriate requires an answer to the question, WHY? 'We have always done it this way before' is unacceptable. Christian practices continue for years, often outliving their purpose, until someone asks, 'Why do we do that?' Then watch the defences come up!

For instance, having three church services a week is generally practiced by evangelical Christians, but few know why. Originally, Sunday morning was for instruction and worship. Sunday evening was for evangelism, and the Wednesday service was for prayer. Today few churches have three services for those same purposes. In many churches, evangelism has switched to Sunday morning (if there is an evangelistic service). Sunday evenings range from body life gatherings to an informal repeat of the morning service. (I think the major reason for the decline in Sunday evening attendance is the lack of purpose.) Wednesday stopped being a prayer meeting years ago.

Few people can say why they have an adult fellowship group and, consequently, most never fulfil the greatest purpose for which they exist. Without a clear purpose, planning dribbles down to who is going to be the teacher and what is the next monthly social! The purpose of fellowship groups is to provide a base for incorporating new people into the church, going after those who stray, and meeting the needs of one another. Routine activities that lack purpose produce mindless participation. How is God going to guide such a group?

The greatest avenue for productive change is to clarify the purpose of any existing ministry or group. I sat with the leaders of an adult group and helped them hammer out a purpose statement. Some major changes took place in their class. Within two years they had doubled. Asking 'Why?' forced them to evaluate their purpose and ministry, and necessary changes came.

2. Jesus taught that Christian practices should be consistent with the inward condition of the heart

Holding to external practices which no longer correlate with the heart is repugnant to God. Jesus railed against praying in vain repetitions and putting on a gloomy face while fasting. Consistency cries for an affirmative answer to the question, 'Is it real?' The Christian community searches for truth while the world searches for reality. These are large overlapping circles, but I'm convinced that we must be real in order to be right. Change is most needed when Christians sit stoically week after week reciting endless creeds in utter hypocrisy.

Tragically, those who are coming to a church simply to fulfil a religious obligation are the most resistant to change. They have resisted the need to change under the instruction of the Word and are in a state of carnality. They are not coming to the changeless Christ and saying, 'Change me so I may be like You.'

Paradoxically, the ones who have a real Christian experience are the ones who are free to change their Christian practices. They are committed to the substance of their faith, not the form. Form always follows function, but people have a tendency to fixate on the form. The way to avoid that is to focus on the heart as Jesus did.

Organisational renewal will not bring spiritual renewal. When the spiritual tide is out, every little tadpole wants his own little tide pool to swim in. When the spiritual tide is in, the fish swim in one big ocean where someone is synchronising every move. When the Holy Spirit is leading, almost any organisation will work. But when He isn't, it doesn't matter how good the programme and organisation is, it won't work.

3. Jesus taught that the forms of our Christian practice must change

Here the Lord carefully chooses His metaphors. The garment and the wineskins are the external dress and the container, not the substance of our faith. They represent the religious customs, practices and traditions which the substance of our faith is packaged in. Jesus is stating a fact — the garment needs mending and the old wineskin is old! What worked before isn't working any more. Times change, cultures change and what worked twenty years ago may not work today. But what doesn't change is the object of our faith.

'Time-honoured faith' and 'long-established practice' blend together and become indistinguishable to the status quo. When someone advocates another form of practice, it becomes painfully apparent that the security of the old wineskins rests in the long-established practice instead of the time-honoured faith.

The reasoning behind the resistance is logical: 'I came to Christ singing that song,' or 'It worked for me. I don't see why it won't work for my children.' I have sat in worship services all choked up listening to a piece of music or a favourite passage and then noticed that it didn't mean a thing to my children. We have to ask, 'Is it relevant? Does it relate?' The older generation is the stable force in our churches. They are faithful and mature, and they represent the financial stability that every church needs. They also make up the boards and committees that determine the style of ministry, and they have a natural tendency to perpetuate the long-established practices because they find them meaningful.

This problem is not spiritual; it's sociological. Why is it that a good Bible-believing church which faithfully carries out its ministry struggles to hold onto its young people, when down the street a contemporary ministry rents a store building and has four times more young people in a matter of months? Because the contemporary ministry relates to the young and their style of music. It caters to their desire for expression and participation. The forty-and-under crowd was raised in a different culture than the forty-and-above. And this brings up the fourth principle.

4. Jesus taught that Christian practices should preserve the old and the new wine

The old wine is vastly superior to the new. The old wine eulogises the venerable past and loves to contrast it with the present. Make no mistake: They are wise, gentle, reverent and good. Because of the quality of their vintage, they create a strong prejudice against any proposed change. Even Jesus conceded to loving the old wine of Jewish piety: 'And no one, after drinking the old wine wishes for the new; for he says, "The old wine is good enough."' But its supply will run out!

New wine can be bitter and harsh in the natural order of things. But can we object to its existence? Can we deny the need for new forms of worship and styles of music, art and even instruction? We may not straightway desire it because it is strange and novel, but wisdom says not to spurn, spill or spoil it.

This last principle asks the question, 'Does it unify?' The unity of the Spirit is already present. The task is to instruct believers that it is the responsibility of all to practise unity by tolerating the preferences of others and accepting the diversity of the body as a good thing. The task is difficult, but not impossible.

If we are to accomplish our purpose, we must ask ourselves four questions:

- Why are we doing what we are doing?
- Is it real?

- Does it relate?
- Does it unify?

I believe that God will lead us into the twenty-first century if we are diligent to separate the substance of our faith from its various forms.

If you join me in wanting to be free from person prejudices and follow the essentials of the faith in a changing world, then would you pray with me?

Dear Heavenly Father, I thank you for Your Word. I ask You to rid me of my biases. I want to know the truth and to see life from Your perspective, not from my limited viewpoint. I want to know You and be conformed to Your image.

Keep me from just being a hearer of the Word and not a doer. I ask You to sort out the Christian practices in my life that are setting aside Your commandments. I don't want to go to church just to go to church. I want to meet together with You and Your children in a real, living fellowship. Show me what I need to do in order for that to happen. I don't want to criticise others and the worship service. I want to love others and to worship You. I don't want to sit in judgement of the message, but let it sit in judgement of me.

Lead me, Lord, through Your Word. Transform my mind so I can prove that Your will is good, acceptable and perfect. Amen.

9
A Peace In My Heart

What a priceless commodity is the peace that results
from judging rightly the influences that invade our lives

We live in a world where the flip of a switch instantly light-
ens or darkens a room. The lamps in biblical times, on the
other hand, burned brightly but required proper tending. If
not cared for, they would become a dwindling flame. God's
Word uses the metaphor of a lamp to teach us about guidance for our lives. And it proves the opportunity for some
graphic applications of this teaching.

The psalmist wrote, 'Thy word is a lamp to my feet, and
a light to my path' (Ps 119:105). Earnestly seeking the clear
teaching of God's Word allows the lamp to burn brightly
and us to stay on a straight path. When we fail to acknowledge our theological bias and limited perspective, the light
lessens and our path becomes twisted. The lamp flickers
when form replaces function and traditions push aside the
commandments of God. The light dims when we stay away
from God's Word and the fellowship of believers. It goes
out when we serve another master.

Sometimes we overlook the obvious: God's will is
expressed by His Word. As a child, I didn't struggle with
knowing my earthly father's will. He clearly expressed it to
me. I learned early on that we lived together peacefully if I
was quick to obey. Being a farm boy, it made sense to help
my father establish his kingdom (the family farm). Farmers
know from nature that we reap what we sow. Not only that,
I stood to inherit the family farm along with my brothers
and sisters as my father had with his sisters. Yet I wonder

how many Christians realise that what they are presently sowing in the kingdom of God is what they will reap for all eternity.

The need to know truth

I have learned from successes and failures that I live peacefully with my heavenly Father when I am quick to obey Him. Jesus said, 'If anyone loves Me, he will keep My Word; and My Father will love him, and We will come to him, and make Our abode with Him' (Jn 14:23). It only makes sense to pray, 'Thy kingdom come,' because as children of God we are destined to inherit it: 'Come, you who are blessed of My Father, inherit the kingdom prepared for you from the foundation of the world' (Mt 25:34).

But 'do you not know that the unrighteous shall not inherit the kingdom of God?' (1 Cor 6:9) If righteousness determines our destiny, it is little wonder that Jesus made this further point: 'Do not judge according to appearance, but judge with righteous judgement' (Jn 7:24).

Using God's Word rightly

I want to assert again the pre-eminence of God's Word. It is our guide for judging others with righteous judgement. Is the person proclaiming the Word of God? Is it biblically true? Accepting the fact that God's Word is both foundational and central, however, is not the only criterion. Satan will quote Scripture. He even had the audacity to quote it to Jesus. Any organisation can make up a doctrinal statement. We have even encountered hard-core Satanists who have infiltrated the church and occupied leadership positions in evangelical ministries.

Paul warned:

> For such men are false apostles, deceitful workers, disguising themselves as apostles of Christ. And no wonder, for even

Satan disguises himself as an angel of light. Therefore it is
not surprising if his servants also disguise themselves as servants of righteousness; whose end shall be according to their
deeds (2 Cor 11:13–15).

There is a false teacher in the Southern California area
who teaches the Bible. In fact, he teaches the Bible very well
but his moral life is decadent. Two of our seminary students
were mesmerised by his intellectual brilliance. I personally
wouldn't care to do intellectual battle with him, but I
wouldn't want to battle Satan either. this man indulges the
flesh in its corrupt desires and despises authority, which are
traits identified in 2 Peter 2:10 as those of a false prophet.

I'm always amazed at how gullible some people are and
how easily deceived. 'He's such a wonderful speaker!' 'What
a charismatic person!' 'I could feel the electricity in the air!'
They're not judging righteously; they're judging by appearance (or worse, by how they feel). John wrote, 'Little children, let no one deceive you; the one who practises
righteousness is righteous, just as He is righteous; the one
who practises sin is of the devil' (1 Jn 3:7,8).

Our guide to truth

If we know the truth, the lie is obvious. Our focus is not dis-
pelling the darkness, but turning on the light. Our major
concern is the righteous leading of the Holy Spirit who will
lead us into all truth. The presence of the Holy Spirit in our
lives serves as the only foundation for the development of
godly character. Notice how truth, righteousness and peace
come together in the following three verses:

Surely His salvation is near to those who fear Him, that
glory may dwell in our land. Lovingkindness and truth have
met together; righteousness and peace have kissed each
other (Ps 85:9,10).

The work of righteousness will be peace, and the service of righteousness, quietness and confidence forever (Is 32:17).

Blessed are those who hunger and thirst for righteousness, for they shall be satisfied (Mt 5:6).

Christians have frequently relied upon a sense of peace as evidence of the Holy Spirit's leading. It is common to hear people say, 'I just don't have a peace about it.' I think that is legitimate. I would be concerned about the person who proceeds when his spirit is disturbed. God doesn't lead through anxiety. We are to cast our anxiety upon Jesus, because He cares for us (1 Pet 5:7).

Still, a lot of money is spent on the temporary 'cure' of anxiety. People consume alcohol, take illegal drugs, turn to the refrigerator, have sex, mindlessly repeat mantras and escape to cabins, boats and motor homes — all to reduce their anxiety. One lady said, 'Whenever I feel anxious, I go on a shopping spree!' Prescription drugs are regularly dispensed for the ails brought on by anxiety.

The bartender, drug pusher, occult practitioner and other peddlers of escapism all have one thing in common: They really don't care about the consumer. They are out to make a profit. Even worse, when the temporary 'cure' wears off, we have to return to the same world with the added problem of hangovers and other negative consequences of fake healers.

This 'cure' is not new. Nearly 2,500 years ago the prophet Jeremiah proclaimed:

For from the least of them to the greatest of them, everyone is greedy for gain, and from the prophet even to the priest everyone deals falsely. And they have healed the brokenness of My people superficially saying, 'Peace, peace,' but there is no peace. Were they ashamed because of the abomination they have done? They were not even ashamed at all; They did not even know how to blush (Jer 6:13–15).

With truth comes peace

Eternally, we have peace with God: 'Therefore having been justified by faith, we have peace with God through our Lord Jesus Christ' (Rom 5:1).

Externally, we want peace on earth, but we may not always have that: 'If possible, so far as it depends upon you, be at peace with all men' (Rom 12:18). Some things are beyond our right or ability to control. Insecure people often seek peace by ordering their external world. Their peace depends on controlling people and circumstances. There is no person more insecure than a controller.

Let's face it: External peace doesn't always depend upon us. We should always seek to be peacemakers (see Matthew 5:9), but our sense of self-worth cannot be based on an external world that we may or may not be able to control. The fruit of the Spirit is 'self-control,' not spouse-control or child-control or circumstance-control.

Internally, we desperately need the peace of God:

> Be anxious for nothing, but in everything by prayer and sup-
> plication with thanksgiving let your requests be made
> known to God. And the peace of God, which surpasses all
> comprehension, shall guard your hearts and your minds in
> Christ Jesus (Phil 4:6,7).

The awareness of a troubled spirit should drive us to find the peace of God by turning to Him and assuming our responsibility to use our minds:

> Finally, brethren, whatever is true, whatever is right, what-
> ever is pure, whatever is lovely, whatever is of good repute, if

there is any excellence and if anything worthy of praise, let your mind dwell on these things (Phil 4:8).

We seek the peace of God by ordering our internal world. Consider it like this:

Eternal:	Peace *with* God	What we have
Internal:	Peace *of* God	What we need
External:	Peace *on* earth	What we want

Resolving barriers to peace

To be anxious is to be double-minded, and a double-minded man is unstable in all his ways (Jas 1:8). I believe there are two tensions in our minds that rob us of God's peace and thus inhibit His guidance in our lives. Both are addressed by Jesus in the Sermon on the Mount (Mt 6:19–34).

Tension 1: Where our treasure is

The first tension is double-mindedness over treasure or possessions. We're basically in love with what we believe to be our highest good. There are material goods which Jesus identifies as 'treasures upon earth.' And there are immaterial goods which Jesus calls 'treasures in heaven.' 'Treasures upon earth' have two characteristics. First, all things decay physically. If rust doesn't destroy what we have, then moths or termites will. I had a friend who owned what most Americans only dream of: a cabin in the hills and a boat in the marina. What impressed me was the tremendous amount of energy he expended to keep both in repair. He probably would have experienced a lot more peace if he'd rented a cabin or a boat and let somebody else take care of repairs.

Second, because of the value of earthly treasures, there is always a concern for security. It is hard to be anxiety-free if we are worried about our possessions. The more we possess, the more we cause others to covet. Hence, the reason for 'thieves to break in and steal.'

On the other hand, 'treasures in heaven' are beyond the reach of thieves and secure from the ravages of moths and rust. Paul puts it this way:

> On the other hand discipline yourself for the purpose of Godliness. For bodily discipline is only of little profit, but Godliness is profitable for all things, for it holds promise for the present life and for the life to come (1 Tim 4:7,8).

People seem to want the best of both worlds. But if we concentrate on treasures in this one, we will miss out on treasures in the next. If we store our treasures in the next life, God may throw in an extra blessing in this one. Jesus states it plainly:

> Do not lay up for yourselves treasures upon earth, but lay up for yourselves treasures in heaven. For where your treasure is, there will your heart be also (Mt 6:19).

Question! What do you treasure in your heart? What would you exchange for love, joy, peace, patience, kindness, goodness, faithfulness, gentleness and self-control? Would you exchange those for a new car, a cabin in the hills, a boat in the marina, exceptional status at the top of the corporate ladder? Jesus reminded the crowd, 'Beware, and be on guard against every form of greed; for not even when one has an abundance does his life consist of his possessions' (Lk 12:15).

A man's life consists of who he serves. There is a moral healthiness and simple, unaffected goodness present in the single-minded person that is absent from the one serving many masters. Jesus said:

> No one can serve two masters. For either he will hate the one
> and love the other, or he will hold to one and despise the
> other. You cannot serve God and mammon. For this reason
> I say to you, do not be anxious (Mt 6:24,25).

There will be no peace serving two masters. To which-
ever master we yield, by that master we shall be controlled.

Tension 2: Double-mindedness over tomorrow

The second tension is double-mindedness over tomorrow.
The first tension dealt with possessions. This one deals with
provision. The materialist struggles with the first tension;
the doubter struggles with the second.

The question is, can we trust God? Jesus answered by
saying:

> Look at the birds of the air, they do not sow, neither do they
> reap, nor gather into barns, and yet your heavenly Father
> feeds them. Are you not worth much more than they? (Mt
> 6:26)

Trusting God for tomorrow is a question of our worth.
Birds are not created in the image of God. We are! Birds will
not inherit the kingdom of God, but we shall. Birds are
mortal; mankind is immortal. If God takes care of the
birds, so much more will He take care of us. That's why the
apostle Paul could write, 'My God shall supply all your
needs according to His riches in glory in Christ Jesus' (Phil
4:19).

Observe the lilies of the field:

> If God so arrays the grass of the field, which is alive today
> and tomorrow is thrown into the furnace, will He not do
> much more for you O men of little faith? Do not be anxious
> then! (Mt 6:30,31)

God lays His own reputation on the line. If we trust and obey, He will provide. This is a question of God's integrity.

> For God knows we have need of all these things.... Therefore do not be anxious for tomorrow; for tomorrow will care for itself. Each day has enough trouble of its own (Mt 6:32,34).

The essential will of God is that we live responsibly today and trust Him for tomorrow. Are we people of little faith, or do we really believe that the fruit of the Spirit will satisfy us more than earthly possessions? Do we really believe that if we hunger and thirst after righteousness, we shall be satisfied? Do we really believe that if we seek to establish God's kingdom, God will supply all our needs according to His riches in glory? If we do, then we will 'seek first His kingdom and His righteousness, and all these things shall be added to you' (Mt 6:33).

Limiting anxious feelings

Let's assume your first priority is the kingdom of God, and you deeply believe that God and His righteousness will satisfy. You have sought God's will for a certain direction, and you believe that He has led you to make specific plans. The problem is, you are still worried about whether your plans will come about as you had hoped. That's okay. I believe a little anxiety is needed to motivate us to responsible behaviour. When I'm facing such situations, I try to follow the six steps described below to limit my anxious feelings. They have been summarised in an 'Anxiety Worksheet' at the end of the chapter.

First, *state the problem*. A problem well-stated is half-solved. In anxious states of mind, people can't see the forest for the trees. Put the problem in perspective. Will it matter for eternity? Generally speaking, the process of worrying

takes a greater toll on a person than the negative consequences of what they are worrying about. I've had a lot of
anxious people come into my office who only need their
problem clarified.

The danger at this juncture is to seek ungodly counsel.
The world is glutted with magicians and sorcerers who will
promise incredible results. Their appearance may be striking. Their credentials may be impressive. Their personality
may be charming. But their character is bankrupt. 'Judge
righteously not according to appearance,' Jesus said (Jn
7:24). 'How blessed is the man who does not walk in the
counsel of the wicked, nor stand in the path of sinners, nor
sit in the seat of scoffers' (Ps 1:1).

Second, *divide the facts from the assumptions*. People
may be fearful of facts, but not anxious. We're anxious
because we don't know what's going to happen tomorrow.
Since we don't know, we make assumptions. A peculiar trait
of the mind is its tendency to assume the worst. If the
assumption is accepted as truth, it will drive the mind to its
anxiety limits. If you act upon the assumption, you will be
counted among the fools! Therefore, as best as possible, separate the assumptions from the facts.

Third, *determine what you have the right or ability to control*. You are responsible for that which you can control,
and you are not responsible for that which you can't. Your
self-worth is tied only to that for which you are responsible.
If you aren't living a responsible life, you should feel anxious! Don't try to cast your responsibility onto Christ; He
will throw it back. But do cast your anxiety onto Him. His
integrity is at stake in meeting your needs if you are living a
responsible life.

Fourth, *list everything you can do which is related to the
situation that is under your responsibility*. When people don't
assume their responsibility, they turn to temporary cures
for their anxiety. Remember, 'The work of righteousness

will be peace' (Is 32:17). Turning to an unrighteous solution will only increase anxiety in the future.

Fifth, *once you are sure you have fulfilled your responsibility, see if there is any way you can help others.* Turning your attention away from your self-absorption and onto helping people around you is not only the loving thing to do, but it also brings a special inner peace that comes from knowing you have helped someone in need.

Sixth, *the rest is God's responsibility,* except for your prayer, according to Philippians 4:6–8. Any residual anxiety is probably due to assuming responsibilities that God never intended you to have.

A friend of mine called after several months of sleepless nights and anxious days. She had served the Lord through a missions organisation for many years. A philosophical difference resulted in a parting of the ways. Declining health resulted in much physical pain. Her list of doctors was endless. Now she was asking me if seeing a secular counsellor who specialises in hypnosis for pain reduction was advisable. I expressed my reservations and asked if we could get together. I suspected a little spiritual pride kept her from seeking the help of Christian friends for counsel.

After a couple of hours resolving spiritual conflicts, she found her peace with God. Her entire countenance changed and she said on her way out, 'I feel like I have been set free!'

'You have,' I responded. The peace of God that passes all understanding was now guarding her mind.

What a priceless commodity is the peace that results from judging rightly the influences that invade our lives. And to think that God gives us His Word and His Spirit so that we can know the truth and receive His calm. Would you join me in this prayer to receive His peace?

Dear Heavenly Father, I desire Your peace. I therefore commit myself to live a righteous life. Forgive me for seeking trea-

sures on earth instead of treasures in heaven. I thank You for the possessions You have entrusted to me in this life, but I choose to believe that my life does not consist of my possessions. My life is in Christ, and I want the fruit of the Spirit to be evident in me so that I may glorify You.

I bring my anxious thoughts before You concerning Your provision for tomorrow. I choose to trust You by seeking first Your kingdom and Your righteousness. I know that all other things will be added to me, and I trust You to meet my needs. I commit myself to order my internal world around You. Forgive me for the times I have tried to control people and circumstances that I had no right or ability to control. I cast my anxiety upon You and commit myself to be responsible for what You have entrusted with me. Amen.

Anxiety Worksheet

1. State the problem.
2. Divide the facts from the assumptions.
    a. Identify the facts relating to the situation.
    b. Identify the assumptions relating to the situation.
    c. Verify the assumptions.
3. Determine what you have the right or ability to control.
    a. What you can control as a matter of personal responsibility.
    b. What you cannot or should not control.
4. List everything related to the situation that is your responsibility.
5. If you have fulfilled your responsibility, how can you help others?
6. The rest is God's responsibility, except for prayer, according to Philippians 4:6.

10
Sanctified Common Sense

How does God work through human responsibility to bring about His will?

Have you heard about the devout Christian who heard an urgent news report on his radio that a flash flood was within minutes of entering the peaceful valley where he lived? Immediately he went to his knees and committed his life to the Lord and prayed for safety. The words were still on his lips when He became aware that water was gushing under his door. He retreated to the first floor and finally onto the roof of his house.

While he sat on the roof, a helicopter flew by and the pilot asked over the loudspeaker if they could lift him off. 'It's not necessary since I have the Lord's protection,' he replied.

Moments later the house began to break up and he found himself clinging to a tree. A police boat, braving the waters, approached him for rescue, but he assured them that the Lord would save him. Finally, the tree gave way and the man went to his death.

Standing before the Lord, he asked, 'Lord, I'm glad to be here, but why didn't you answer my prayer for safety?' The Lord responded, 'Son, I told you over the radio to get out of there. Then I sent you a helicopter and a motor boat!'

Nowhere in the Bible are we given the idea that God works only in the extraordinary. Much of the time He supernaturally works through His created order. Many people think God is present only when there is a miracle and that He leads only through signs and wonders.

This kind of mindset is seen in John 7:25–27. The Jewish people were commenting about Jesus: 'Is this not the man who they are seeking to kill? Look, He is speaking in public. The rulers do not really know that this is the Christ, do they? However, we know where this man is from; but whenever the Christ may come, no one knows where He is from.'

They were looking for a mystery man, seeking a sign when the real signs of Jesus' divine character and fulfilment of Scripture were there all the time.

Looking for signs is understandable. There is always some anxiety concerning the decision we have made or are about to make. Naturally, we want to make the right decision and be in God's will, so there is the temptation to ask for some sign of confirmation from God.

Then there are those people who *always* look for a sign. They walk by sight, not by faith. To them, God is present only in the miraculous. God was 'really' at the church service if something unusual happened. Many desire and look for 'visitations' from God.

But how does that square with God's omnipresence and the fact that He will never leave nor forsake us? Isn't God at every church service? Since God created the fixed order of the universe, would you expect Him to work primarily within that fixed order or outside of it? If God gave us an instruction manual, shouldn't we expect Him to operate within the confinements of it? If God gave us a watch, would we be honouring Him more by asking what time it is, or by simply consulting the watch?

God's way

I believe in miracles, and I accept as fact every one recorded in the Bible. I believe that our entire Christian experience is a miracle. It simply cannot be explained by natural means. And God's power is seen in other miraculous ways today, but must He always prove Himself by stepping outside His created order? If God doesn't primarily guide us through His Word (which never changes) and take into account the fixed order of the universe, how can we ever have any stability? How can we make any plans if God doesn't reveal His ways and then stay consistent with them?

I challenge you to take an exhaustive concordance and look up every reference for 'way' and 'ways'. You will find that God is not capricious in His dealings with man. He has clearly established ways and He is faithful to them. Let me illustrate with just a few references:

> I pray Thee, if I have found favour in Thy sight, let me know Thy ways, that I may know Thee (Ex 33:13).
> Therefore, you shall keep the commandments of the Lord your God, to walk in His ways and to fear Him (Deut 8:6).

Moving to the New Testament, we see John the Baptist storming on the scene announcing, 'Make ready the way of the Lord' (Mk 1:3). And Jesus said, 'I am the way' (Jn 14:6).

I believe God has revealed His ways, and we are to walk in them. The question is, how does God work through human responsibility and the natural order of the universe to bring about His will? Somehow He works through a less-than-perfect church, orchestrating human affairs in such a way as to guarantee the outcome of the ages. What really impresses me is His timing, not His miraculous interventions.

Notice how Jesus responded to those who insisted on a sign:

> Then some of the scribes and Pharisees answered Him saying, 'Teacher, we want a sign from You.' But He answered and said to them, 'An evil and adulterous generation craves

for a sign; and yet no sign shall be given to it but the sign of Jonah the prophet' (Mt 12:38,39).

Satan wanted a sign too. He said, 'If You are the Son of God, throw Yourself down' (Mt 4:6). To this Jesus responded, 'You shall not put the Lord your God to the test' (Mt 4:7). Jesus was saying that the sign we need is the Word of God, and we are to use the Word to guard against Satan's temptations to force the Lord to prove Himself.

What about signs and wonders?

Signs and wonders validated the ministry of Jesus and the apostles. After quoting from the prophet Joel and demonstrating that the outpouring of the Spirit at Pentecost was biblical, Peter preached:

> Men of Israel, listen to these words: Jesus the Nazarene, a man attested to you by God with miracles and wonders and signs which God performed through Him in your midst, just as you yourselves know (Acts 2:22).

Of the apostles, Paul said, 'The signs of a true apostle were performed among you with all perseverance, but signs and wonders and miracles' (2 Cor 12:12).

However, signs and wonders would also accompany false teachers and false prophets (Mt 7:21–23; 2 Pet 2:1–22). In fact, biblical references to signs and wonders in the last days are nearly all credited to false teachers, false prophets and false Christs (Mt 24:11,24). The false prophet in the tribulation will perform great signs, 'and he deceives those who dwell on the earth because of the signs which it was given to him to perform' (Rev 13:14).

Jesus is no longer with us in the flesh, and there are no more apostles. Jesus identified the sign of a disciple as markedly different: 'By this all men will know that you are My disciples, if you have love for one another' (Jn 13:35).

Does this mean that signs and wonders have ceased? I certainly don't want to be identified with an evil generation that seeks a sign, but I also don't want to be associated with the powerless anti-supernaturalism evidenced in Western rationalism. Both the power of God and the wisdom of God are expressed in Christ. Paul said,

> For indeed Jews ask for a sign, and Greeks search for wisdom; but we preach Christ crucified, to Jews a stumbling block, and to Gentiles foolishness, but to those who are the called, both Jews and Greeks, Christ the power of God and the wisdom of God (1 Cor 1:22–24).

The wisdom of God

Wisdom was certainly the way of the Old Testament as the book of Proverbs and other wisdom literature attest. However, in the Old Testament, wisdom was not understood as our ability to reason independently of God. Rather, it was an acceptance and knowledge of divine revelation. Biblical wisdom is seeing life from God's perspective. In contrast, Western world rationalism is interpreting life from man's perspective. When wisdom degenerates to rationalism, our walk with God is reduced to an intellectual pursuit rather than a living relationship. Proverbs 3:5–7 pictures the relationship God desires with us:

> Trust in the Lord with all your heart, and do not lean on your own understanding. In all your ways acknowledge Him, and He will make your paths straight. Do not be wise in your own eyes; Fear the Lord and turn away from evil.

Turning away from evil signifies that there are moral boundaries. Some believe that the will of God is to live inside those boundaries. They think that if we are morally right with God, He has no fixed plan for our lives. We are free to live as we please as long as we stay morally pure and exercise biblical wisdom. Since all unbelievers are outside the moral boundaries of God, they can expect judgement. Christians living outside the moral boundaries can expect discipline. The writer of Hebrews would attest to the latter: 'But if you are without discipline, of which all have become partakers, then you are illegitimate children and not sons' (Heb 12:8).

It's true that God does give us freedom to make choices on non-moral issues, but He expects us to know His Word and make wise decisions. He has made His will known primarily in His Word, and He delights when we humbly submit to it and obey. But we are not Old Testament saints. We are New Testament Christians. Christ has reconciled Jew and Gentile, and we possess both power and wisdom. What marks the church age is that we now have the presence of the Holy Spirit who will guide us into all truth.

For the rest of this chapter, we'll look at seven ways in which we commonly seek God's guidance and conclude with ten factors that will help lead you toward a wise decision. Much of this book deals with God's presence, both counterfeit and true. His presence brings conviction when I'm out of His will and a peace when I'm in it. The Holy Spirit enables us to discern when we're being influenced by a counterfeit spirit.

Seven common methods of seeking God's guidance

1. Conscience
Folklore advises, 'Let your conscience be your guide.' This has serious limitations since our conscience is a function of our mind. Having been conformed to this world, it can be

programmed wrongly. A conscience is always true to its own standard. Until we come to Christ, the standard is the world system we were raised in. Many people are falsely guided by a guilty conscience — not a true guilt, but a psychological guilt usually developed in early childhood. Satan works through this stronghold to accuse the brethren day and night (Rev 12:10).

People like this are usually perfectionists who labour under condemnation, even though the Bible says, 'There is no condemnation for those who are in Christ Jesus' (Rom 8:1). They aren't led; they are driven. They constantly look for affirmation. They have a tendency to be man-pleasers. Paul said, 'If I were still striving to please men, I would not be a bond-servant of Christ' (Gal 1:10). If you are striving to please men, who are you a bond-servant of?

Since our minds were conformed to this world we need to renew them in such a way that what we believe is in accordance to truth. Chapter 14 of Romans is dealing with how we should walk in regard to non-moral issues. Paul says,

> The faith which you have, have as your own conviction before God. Happy is he who does not condemn himself in what he approves. But he who doubts is condemned (Rom 14:22,23).

In other words, be very cautious about going against your own conscience once you are committed to Christ. The Holy Spirit does work through our conscience as He seeks to renew our minds. However, we are to restrict our freedom if it causes a weaker brother to stumble. We never have the right to violate another person's conscience. Paul says, 'I also do my best to maintain always a blameless conscience both before God and before men' (Acts 24:16).

2. *Fleeces*

'If the sun is shining in the morning, I'll do it.'

'If he's there when I open the door, I'll know he's the one.'

'If I pass the class on world missions, I'll be a missionary. If not, I'll be a local pastor.'

We all know better than this, but it's amazing how often scenarios just like those pop into our heads. We refer to such propositions as laying a 'fleece' before the Lord. The term *fleece* comes from the account of Gideon.

In Judges 6, Gideon is called by God to deliver Israel from the Mideonites. Gideon questions whether God is even for Israel (6:13), and he doubts his own ability (6:15). So he asks God for a sign (6:17). God gives him one, then tells him to take the family ox and tear down the altar of Baal. Gideon is afraid to go during the day, so he goes at night. Then he questions again whether God will deliver Israel. This time he puts a lamb's fleece on the ground. If God will deliver, the lamb's fleece will be wet in the morning and the ground around it will be dry. The next morning it is so. That ought to satisfy him, right?

Wrong! Wanting to be sure, and hoping God won't get too mad, Gideon asks Him to do it again, but this time with the opposite results (ie, the fleece dry and the ground wet). Not exactly the stuff heroes are made of. But God answers Gideon's request and then He reduces Gideon's army down to 300 men!

The whole point of the passage is that God, not man, is the deliverer. God chose a man desperately seeking assurance and reduced an army down to nothing so that the victory would clearly be His. The fleece wasn't a means of demonstrating faith; it was just the opposite. And it certainly wasn't used to determine God's will. God had already told Gideon what to do. Gideon was questioning the integrity of God, just as we do if we ask for a fleece when God has already shown us His will.

3. Circumstances

Some of us tend to assume that it is God's will if the circumstances are favourable and it isn't God's will if the circumstances are unfavourable. Next to the Bible, I would guess that more Christians are 'guided' by this means than any other. Yet of all the possible means of guidance, this is the least authoritative and trustworthy.

As I mentioned before, I had the privilege of pastoring a church that purchased a new property and went through a building programme. Through most of the process the circumstances didn't seem favourable. Twice I sat with the mayor, who was also a local property dealer, and asked him if he thought our plans were feasible. He advised us not to make the land trade, and he didn't think the city would allow us to build. He knew the real estate and the political climate better than anyone in the city.

But even the advice of experts didn't prove reliable. The land swap increased our assets by millions and the city planning commission voted 7–0 in favour of our building plans. You may have to set sail by the tide, but you'd better be guided by the stars or you're going to end up on the wrong shore. Circumstances may have their effect on your plans, but you have a far greater accountability to God. Make sure you follow Him, not the tide of circumstance.

I heard a motivational speaker say, 'I don't like to recruit Christians because when the going gets tough they quit, concluding that it must not be God's will.' Generally speaking, I believe that Christians should live above life's circumstances and not be guided by them. Establishing God's kingdom on earth is going to be an uphill fight. But Paul says, 'I have learned to be content in whatever circumstance I am' (Phil 4:11).

Also, be careful about applying too much significance to unusual circumstances or coincidences. 'It must be God's will. Why else would that book be lying there?' It could be God's will, but I would never take that kind of sign on its own merit. If, for example, you keep coming across another person's path, maybe you should check it out. If it is more than a coincidence, you will quickly find out when you talk with the person.

I have counselled too many people in occultic bondage who have made bizarre associations or attached far too much significance to irrelevant events.

4. Godly counsel
Proverbs 11:14 says, 'Where there is no guidance, the people fall, but in abundance of counsellors there is victory.' The reason for this is obvious. No one person has complete knowledge, and everyone has a limited perspective on the truth. God has structured the church in such a way that we need each other. I have made some dumb decisions that would never have been made if I had consulted someone. However, some people will only consult those who agree with them. That's a sign of immaturity.

At the same time, the counsel of others does have to be weighed. There is a fascinating account in Acts 21 where the Holy Spirit seemed to be warning Paul not to go to Jerusalem. Disciples in Tyre 'kept telling Paul through the Spirit not to set foot in Jerusalem' (21:4). Then a prophet named Agabus gave a visual demonstration by binding himself and saying, 'This is what the Holy Spirit says: "In this way the Jews at Jerusalem will bind the man who owns this belt [Paul] and deliver him into the hands of the Gentiles"' (21:11). Everyone began begging him not to go. Paul responded:

'What are you doing, weeping and breaking my heart? For I am ready not only to be bound, but even die at Jerusalem for the name of the Lord Jesus.' And since he would not be persuaded, we fell silent, remarking, 'The will of the Lord be done!' (Acts 21:13,14)

Was the Holy Spirit guiding the disciples and Agabus? The information was mostly true, but the conclusion of the disciples wasn't. The Holy Spirit wasn't trying to prevent Paul from going; He was preparing Paul for coming persecution. Paul was right in not wanting to take the easy way out.

The missionary Hudson Taylor went against advice, and circumstances nearly destroyed him. But he, more than anyone, opened up China to the gospel. Sometimes people can tell you the truth, but they draw selfish conclusions. Sometimes we need to ascertain our own motives as well as those of the people we seek counsel from, for our motives can be in error as well. The value of counsel is to get an unbiased opinion from a spiritually sensitive person which you can add to the recipe of ingredients God is giving to guide you.

5. Gifts and abilities

After I taught a class on spiritual gifts, a young man came to me and asked, 'Is my gift prophecy or exhortation?' Knowing him very well, I was careful as I responded. 'I don't think either one is your gift,' I began. 'But if I have ever known someone who has the gift of helps, you're it. You're sensitive to the needs of other people and always ready to help.'

A look of disappointment came over his face. 'I knew it!' he responded. Struggling with a low self-esteem, he was pursuing what he wrongly perceived to be a greater gift.

God hasn't distributed gifts and talents equally, and for

that reason alone we can be assured that our sense of self-worth isn't to be based on what we do. Our self-acceptance comes from our identity in Christ and our growth in character. Show me someone who understands who he is as a child of God and whose character exemplifies the fruit of the Spirit, and I will show you someone with a healthy self-image.

Every child of God has the same identity and opportunity to grow. Only when our identity is firmly established and we have matured to the point where the fruit of the Spirit is evident will we use the gifts and talents to edify others.

God has known us from the foundation of the world. He has entrusted us with certain life endowments. He will certainly lead us in a way that makes use of our gifts and talents. It is our responsibility to take advantage of every opportunity as it arrives. Tragically, many people go to the grave with their music still in them, never contributing to the symphony of God's work. They never realise their potential nor take the risks that faith requires. They hang onto the security of the tree trunk, but the fruit is always on the end of the limb.

6. Duty

Do you know how much of our Christian calling is simply a matter of duty? Most of it. You don't need God to tell you to live a responsible life. He already has. You don't need some subjective confirmation for every decision.

I confess that I don't 'feel led' to do a lot of things. There are mornings I don't feel like getting out of bed. And I have never felt led to visit a convalescent hospital. The smell inside the front door has never confirmed my 'leading' to be there. I have left feeling blessed, however, experiencing the truth of what Jesus said: 'If you know these things, you are blessed if you do them' (Jn 13:17).

7. Desires

The psalmist wrote, 'Delight yourself in the Lord; and He will give you the desires of your heart' (Ps 37:4). The key is to delight yourself in the Lord. If you do, your desires will change. I believe this process unfolds as we seek to do God's will.

I had very little desire to read until I came to Christ. Now I read volumes. After I received Christ, I wanted to serve Him full time. I had completed engineering school and was prepared to do anything God wanted, except go back to school. Within a year I could hardly wait to get to seminary. It was the best educational experience of my life, and the only one I enjoyed up to that point. Since then I have finished four more degrees. I never had a desire to write a book until three years ago, and this is my third one. If we delight ourselves in the Lord, He does change our desires!

We struggle between the desires of the flesh and the desires of righteousness. Jesus told us, 'Blessed are those who hunger and thirst for righteousness, for they shall be satisfied' (Mt 5:6). Do you believe that? I guarantee that if you try to satisfy the desires of the flesh, you will never satisfy them. The more you feed them, the greater the hunger.

When we first come to Christ, nothing contests our will more than the lusts of the flesh: 'For the flesh sets its desires against the Spirit, and the Spirit against the flesh; for these are in opposition to one another' (Gal 5:17). Our will is like a toggle switch, but it's initially spring-loaded to the flesh. In a mature Christian, it's spring-loaded to the Spirit. In determining God's will for your life, do you intend to satisfy the flesh or the Spirit?

Ten factors leading to a wise decision

At the end of the chapter you will find a checklist titled, 'Ten Deciding Factors'. These are ten questions you'll want to ask yourself and pray about when you're faced with a decision. The first five are generic. They represent moral issues and godly wisdom that are normative for all times. The next five are questions that you need to ask when facing a change in direction. Let's take a look at what each question entails.

First, *have you prayed about it?* The Lord's Prayer begins with a petition for His will. Prayer was never intended to be a fourth-down punting situation in which we ask God to bail us out of our hasty decisions. It was intended to be a first-down huddle. We aren't supposed to ask God to bless our plans; we are supposed to ask God for His plans.

God could just give us what we need, but He taught us to pray, 'Give us this day our daily bread.' Nothing established dependency more than prayer. Dependency puts us in a right position with God since the flesh operates independently of God. The tendency is to try everything but God first and then when that fails say, 'Well I guess there is nothing else to do now but to pray.' But we are to 'seek first His kingdom and His righteousness.'

Second, *is it consistent with the Word of God?* In our culture, ignorance is no excuse since resources abound. I believe that every home should have at least a concordance, Bible dictionary, topical Bible, a good commentary and a study Bible with notes. Most communities in America have a pastor within driving distance or one who is reachable by phone. Most pastors would love to share what God has to say about a given matter. If they wouldn't, you have called the wrong pastor!

We also have an abundance of radio programmes with great messages, and some even invite people to phone in with questions. Christian literature discusses every imaginable problem. You can receive valuable input to help you make a decision if you will make a habit of consulting the Bible and godly resources.

Third, *can I do it and be a positive Christian witness?* Asking that question years ago prompted me to give up bridge and golf. Now that I have matured a little, I can play them again!

A seminary student stopped by my office and told me about a job he had been offered. It would take care of his financial needs, but he had some reservations concerning the sales pitch he was required to use. I asked him if he could use the sales technique and be a positive witness for Christ. He didn't take the job.

This simple question will govern a lot of behaviour. Several spin-off questions are helpful: Would I do that if Jesus were here? Would I go to that movie if Jesus were my escort? Can I tell that joke from the pulpit?

Fourth, *will the Lord be glorified?* Can I do this and give glory to God? In doing it, would I be glorifying God in my body? Am I seeking the glory of man or glory of God? Am I doing this to be noticed by man or am I seeking to please the Lord? Driven people will do it just to get the approval of others. Those sent by God seek His glory.

Fifth, *am I acting responsibly?* God doesn't bail us out of our irresponsibility. He will let us suffer the consequences of our sins and irresponsible choices. But when we are faithful in little things, he will put us in charge of greater things. Don't get ahead of God's timing or you will be over your head in responsibilities. Seek to develop your life and message, and God will expand your ministry.

Sixth, *is it reasonable?* God expects us to think. His guidance may transcend human reasoning, but it never excludes it. God doesn't bypass our mind; He operates through it: 'Brethren, do not be children in your thinking; yet in evil be babes, but in your thinking be mature' (1 Cor 14:20). We are warned in Scripture not to put our mind in neutral. We are to think and practise what we know to be true (Phil 4:8,9).

Seventh, *does a realistic opportunity exist?* Closed doors

are not meant to be knocked down. If you have a hopeless scheme, let it go. If it isn't God's timing, wait. If a realistic opportunity exists, and all the other factors are in agreement, then take the plunge. God may open a window of opportunity, but it will close if not taken advantage of. The faithless man asks, 'What do I stand to lose if I do?' The faithful man asks, 'What do I risk losing if I don't?'

Eighth, *are unbiased, spiritually sensitive associates in agreement?* Be careful not to consult only those who will agree with you. Give your advisors permission to ask hard questions. Don't be afraid of no answers. If it isn't God's will, don't you want to know before you make the mistake of acting impulsively?

Ninth, *do I have a sanctified desire?* Don't think that being in the will of God must always be an unpleasant task. The joy of the Lord should be our strength. I find my greatest joy in serving God and being in His will. But don't get the idea that if everything is wonderful you must be in the will of God. Is this a desire to satisfy a lust of the flesh, or a Spirit-filled desire to see God's kingdom established and people healed?

Tenth, *do I have a peace about it?* This is an inner peace. In the world you will have tribulation, but in Christ we have the assurance of overcoming the world. Is the peace of God guarding your heart and your mind?

If you have been able to answer yes to all ten of these deciding factors, what are you waiting for?

I'm not sure who the author is, but Kyle Rote, Jr., shared the following article at a Fellowship of Christian Athletes gathering:

> I am part of the 'Fellowship of the Unashamed.' I have Holy Spirit Power. The dye has been cast. I've stepped over the line. The decision has been made. I am a disciple of His. I won't look back, let up, slow down, back

away or be still. My past is redeemed, my present makes sense and my future is secure. I am finished and done with low living, sight walking, small planning, smooth knees, colourless dreams, tame visions, mundane talking, chincy giving and dwarfed goals!

I no longer need pre-eminence, prosperity, position, promotions, plaudits or popularity. I don't have to be right, first, tops, recognised, praised, regarded or rewarded. I now live by presence, lean by faith, love by patience, lift by prayer and labour by love.

My face is set, my gait is fast, my goal is heaven, my road is narrow, my way is rough, my companions few, my guide reliable, my mission clear. I cannot be bought, compromised, detoured, lured away, turned back, diluted or delayed. I will not flinch in the face of sacrifice, hesitate in the presence of adversity, negotiate at the table of the enemy, ponder at the pool of popularity or meander in the maze of mediocrity.

I won't give up, shut up, let up or burn up till I've preached up, prayed up, paid up, stored up and stayed up for the cause of Christ.

I am a disciple of Jesus. I must go till He comes, give till I drop, preach till all know and work till He stops.

And when He comes to get His own, He'll have no problems recognising me. My colours will be clear.

We have seen that God's ways are established. He has spoken through His Word and He already is working in our lives. The question is whether we see and seek His direction or are influenced by false guides. If you would like to tell God of your desire to find and follow His will for your life in ways that honour Him, then would you pray with me?

Dear Lord, I thank You that I do not have to drift through life in uncertainty, never really being sure that my steps are being

guided by You. I thank You that I can have the privilege of walking according to Your way.

Lord, keep me from looking for signs when You have already spoken so clearly in Your Word. And don't let me be bound by circumstances, but help me to seek the wisdom that is from above through Your Word and the godly counsel of others.

I again commit myself to desiring Your will, Your glory and the fruit that will result in my life and others as I walk with You. Thank You, Lord. I know the way will not always be easy, but it will be the path of joy and peace. Amen.

Ten Deciding Factors

For all decisions	Yes	No
1. Have I prayed about it?	❏	❏
2. Is it consistent with the Word of God?	❏	❏
3. Can I have a positive Christian witness?	❏	❏
4. Will the Lord be glorified?	❏	❏
5. Am I acting responsibly?	❏	❏

Direction-changing decisions

	Yes	No
6. Is it reasonable?	❏	❏
What makes sense?		
What doesn't make sense?		
7. Does a realistic opportunity exist?	❏	❏
Factors for:		
Factors against:		
8. Are unbiased, spiritually sensitive people in agreement?	❏	❏
Those for:		
Those against:		
9. Do I have a sanctified desire?	❏	❏
Why?		
Why not?		
10. Do I have a peace about it?	❏	❏
Why?		
Why not?		

11
The Life of Faith

Faith is not a means of getting man's will done in heaven;
it is the means of getting God's will done on earth

After Sunday school one morning, a mother asked her little
girl what she had learned. The daughter responded, 'I
learned how Moses built this pontoon bridge across the
Red Sea, and how all these people were transported across
with tanks and half-tracks. As soon as they were across, the
bridge was blown up just as the Egyptians were coming
across and they were all drowned in the Red Sea.'

The mother was astonished and asked if that's what the
teacher had told her. 'Oh no,' the little girl replied, 'but you
would never have believed what she really said.'

That little girl is like a lot of people. They think that faith
is believing what isn't true. And for others, faith is little
more than just wishful thinking.

After Jesus claimed to be sent by God, some were seeking to seize Him, having come to the conclusion that He
was not a good man. But others did believe Him, 'and they
were saying, 'When the Christ shall come, He will not perform more signs than those which this man has, will He?'
(Jn 7:31) All the evidence was there. Some chose to believe;
others chose not to. People do the same today. Yet to live
within the will of God, you have to believe in the Lord Jesus
Christ.

Faith is the operating principle of life. It is the means by
which we relate to God and carry out His kingdom activity.
Just think of the many ways faith must be operative in our
lives.

> For by grace you have been saved through faith; and that not
> of yourselves, it is the gift of God; not as a result of works,
> that no one should boast (Eph 2:8,9).

We're not only saved by faith, but we also 'walk by faith,
and not by sight' (2 Cor 5:7).

Being found faithful is a prerequisite for ministry: 'I
thank Christ Jesus our Lord, who has strengthened me,
because He considered me faithful, putting me into service'
(1 Tim 1:12). Paul then adds: 'And the things which you
have heard from me in the presence of many witnesses, these
entrust to faithful men, who will be able to teach others
also' (2 Tim 2:2). This is more than being reliable, since a
person could be counted on to follow through on an assignment and not be a believer. The added ingredient in faithful
people is that they know the truth and can be counted on to
be reliable.

Really, the quality of any relationship is determined by
faith or trust: 'Many a man proclaims his own loyalty, but
who can find a trustworthy man?' (Prov 20:6) The words
faith, *trust* and *believe* are all the same word (*pistis*) in the
original language. The man who has faith believes in something. The one who believes also trusts, or he doesn't truly
believe. There is no concept that looms larger in life than
faith because what we believe determines how we live.

Let's look at three standards of faith which will keep us
on the right path if understood and practised.

1. Faith is dependent upon its object

The question is not whether we walk by faith, but what or
whom we believe. Everybody walks by faith; it is the operating principle of life. For instance, we drive our cars by
faith. When we observe a green traffic light, we don't slow
down or stop — we drive right through the intersection. We
believe drivers coming from the other direction will see a

red light and stop. We never see the red light, but we believe they do. Suppose you didn't believe that. How would you approach the intersection?

When I was a little boy, I popped a coin in a soft drink machine and out came a bottle of pop. (Remember those days?) Without looking, I quickly took a drink of the soda, but immediately spat it out. Then I noticed that the bottom of the bottle was completely filled with junk. I never drank that brand again. Now we drink sodas out of cans by faith! We can't even see what's in the can, but we believe the manufacturer put in the can what the label says.

We already have some beliefs about the world we live in. Whatever we think will make us happy, satisfied or successful is what constitutes our belief system. We are walking by faith according to what we already believe. Be assured that the world system we were raised in didn't establish a biblical belief system in our minds. Because we came into this world separated from God, we learned to live our lives independently from Him. We were conformed to this world. Unless we were raised in a perfect Christian home, much of what we learned to believe didn't reflect biblical truth.

If you believe that you will only be satisfied by owning things, then you will probably never be satisfied. If you believe you are successful because of the amount of toys you accumulate, you will certainly be at odds with Scripture. And if the world system hasn't distorted our faith enough, the New Age movement has given it several new twists. The New Ager operates under the principle that if you believe hard enough, anything will become true. But believing doesn't make it true, and not believing doesn't make it not true. Not believing in hell, for example, doesn't drop the temperature down there one degree!

We don't create reality in our minds. We are incapable of creating anything. We can creatively shove around and rearrange what God has already created, but we are not gods.

To think that we will get what we want if we believe with all our hearts is a faith based on selfish desires. It originates within ourselves and depends on our own ability to believe. It's a form of religious self-hypnosis. It's like the Christian who says, 'I don't know the Bible, but I have faith.' For that person, faith is a substitute for knowledge and a compensation for ignorance.

The visible versus the invisible

Hope is not wishful thinking: 'Now faith is the assurance of things hoped for, the conviction of things not seen' (Heb 11:1). Hope is the present assurance of some future good. Biblical faith is not a preference for what we would like to see, but a conviction that what is unseen is real. Biblical faith enables us to see the reality of the spiritual world we presently live in, and we have the assurance of heaven. Only with that kind of faith can we say with Paul, 'For I consider the sufferings of this present time are not worthy to be compared with the glory that is to be revealed to us' (Rom 8:18).

According to Scripture, the invisible world is more real than the visible world: 'By faith we understand that the worlds were prepared by the word of God, so that what is seen was not made out of the things which are visible' (Heb 11:3). The ultimate reality is spiritual, not physical. God is a spirit. Every physical thing we see is only temporal and passing away:

> While we look not at the things which are seen, but at the things which are not seen; for the things which are seen are temporal, but the things which are not seen are eternal (2 Cor 4:18).

When Jesus appeared to the frightened band of disciples

after His resurrection, He showed them both His hands and His side. Later the disciples informed Thomas of what they had seen, but he responded, 'Unless I shall see in His hands the imprint of the nails, and put my finger into the place of the nails, and put my hand into His side, I will not believe' (Jn 20:25). Thomas was determined to walk by sight, not by faith. The only thing that was real to Thomas was what he could see. Eight days later Jesus appeared again, and said to Thomas:

> 'Reach here your finger, and see My hands; and reach here your hand, and put it into My side; and be not unbelieving but believing.' Thomas answered and said to Him, 'My Lord and my God!' Jesus said to him, 'Because you have seen Me, you have believed. Blessed are they who did not see, and yet believed' (Jn 20:27–29).

The object worthy of genuine faith

Scripture asserts that Jesus is the author and perfecter of our faith (Heb 12:2). He is the ultimate faith object because he never changes; He is immutable:

> Remember those who led you, who spoke the word of God to you; and considering the result of their conduct, imitate their faith. Jesus Christ is the same yesterday and today, yes and forever (Heb 13:7,8).

The sun is perhaps the most credible object of faith for the world. It appears to be immutable. It has always been there, 24 hours of every day, 365 days a year. Without the sun, people couldn't live. If the sun didn't rise tomorrow morning, what would happen to the world's faith? All of humanity would be thrown into confusion.

If we have such great faith in the sun, why don't we have

even greater faith in the Son who made the sun and all the rest of the fixed order of the universe?

Our faith is in God. Genuine faith is born out of a knowledge of the will of God and exists only to fulfil that will. Faith is not a means of getting man's will done in heaven; it is the means of getting God's will done on earth.

After hearing me speak on spiritual conflict, a young man came by to talk about his personal life. He said he'd had several experiences of not being able to speak the name of Jesus aloud. I asked him about his faith. He thought he had made a decision for Christ years earlier in an evangelistic meeting. He tried living with some American Indians to continue his spiritual journey, but that proved to be disastrous. He finally ended up living in a pastor's home where he was helped with the assurance of his salvation. This pastor believed in a 'second work of grace,' so he encouraged the young man to go into the woods and fight his lonely battle until he received it. Believing that he had, the young man reported this to the pastor. The pastor then encouraged him to just go live by faith.

The young man said to me, 'I've been trying to live by faith for three years, and it has been one trial after another.'

'Faith in what?' I asked.

He didn't know how to respond. This young man was trying to live by faith in faith. But faith itself is not a valid object. The only valid object for faith is God and the revelation we have of Him in His Word.

2. Faith is dependent upon knowing its object

How much faith we have is determined by how well we know the object of our faith. When my son, Karl, was a year old, I stood him on the table, backed away and told him to jump into my arms. He hesitated only momentarily, then with childlike faith he leaned forward and fell into my arms. As we repeated this activity, he became bolder and bolder. It wasn't long before he was jumping several feet into my arms.

At the age of two he was ready for the major leagues, so we moved from a table to the lower limb of a tree. It was a greater leap of faith to jump down into my arms from a tree, but he obediently did it. His faith in me continued to grow, provided I continued to catch him.

Suppose one day he jumped, but I didn't catch him. Would he climb up the tree and do it again? Probably not. Once faith is lost, it's hard to regain. One act of unfaithfulness in marriage will affect the relationship for years. The hurt spouse can forgive and decide to continue the relationship, but it will take a long time to re-establish the trust that was lost. Faith increases through repeated and ever larger steps of faith, provided the object of faith remains faithful.

Lets put my son back on the tree limb again. Instead of me catching him, I ask his older sister to catch him. Will he jump into her arms? Probably not, because I've changed the object of his faith. What happens if Karl climbs to the top of the tree. Will I continue to be a valid object for his faith? No! If he climbs high enough, there will be a point at which I will no longer be able to catch him.

There was a time when Karl thought I could answer any question or beat anybody (a confidence doomed to be shaken, since I'm neither omniscient nor omnipotent). There is only one who can catch him as he scales the higher limbs of life. It becomes my goal as a parent to remove myself as the ultimate object of his faith and introduce him to his heavenly Father. His identity must change from a child of Neil Anderson to a child of God. Then no matter how high God calls him, he will always be safe.

Big God, big faith

God doesn't change according to how we see Him. But there is a sense in which some today have a little God, while others have a big God. What makes the difference?

Paul writes, 'So faith comes from hearing, and hearing by the word of Christ' (Rom 10:17). If we have little knowledge of God's Word we will have little faith. If we have a lot of knowledge of God's Word, we can have a lot of faith. The heroes of Hebrews 11 had great faith because they had a great God. Big God, big faith. Little God, little faith. If we know and put our trust in seven promises from Scripture, we have a seven-promise faith. If we know and believe seven thousand promises of Scripture, we have a seven-thousand-promise faith.

I'm not talking about being super intelligent as though only smart people can have faith. There are a lot of things in the Bible I don't understand, but I believe them. I don't fully understand the virgin birth, but I believe it.

You see, belief is a choice. We choose to believe what we have been convinced is true. Believing doesn't make it true, but it is true. Therefore, we believe.

Let me quickly add, however, that nobody (including myself) is presently living up to their faith potential. That's why we are to encourage one another in our faith. We are to encourage people to step out in faith according to what they already know to be true. Understanding increases with obedience. I may not know why God would have me do something, but as I commit myself to doing it, I often understand sometime later.

If God wants it done, it can be done

Question! If God wants it done, can it be done? Yes! 'All things are possible to him who believes' (Mk 9:23). If God wants me to do it, can I do it? Of course! 'I can do all things through Him who strengthens me' (Phil 4:13).

What are the 'all things' mentioned in those verses? Is this 'miracle-a-moment' living? Can we just name it and claim it? No. 'All things' pertains to God's will. What God makes possible is the doing of His will; what he empowers us to do is what He desires done. Every miracle outside the will of God is made possible by the god of this world. Satan can work miracles, but he cannot please God. Notice the sobering warning of Jesus in Matthew 7:20–23:

> So then, you will know them by their fruits. Not every one who says to Me, 'Lord, Lord,' will enter the kingdom of heaven; but he who does the will of My Father who is in heaven. Many will say to Me on that day, 'Lord, Lord, did we not prophesy in Your name, and in Your name cast out demons, and in Your name perform many miracles?' And then I will declare to them, 'I never knew you; depart from me, you who practise lawlessness.'

Jesus shocked His disciples when He cursed a fig tree which bore no fruit for Him. The next day Peter noticed the tree was withered from the roots up. When Peter pointed it out to Him, Jesus answered:

> Have faith in God. Truly I say to you, whoever says to this mountain, 'Be taken up and cast into the sea,' and does not doubt in his heart, but believes that what he says is going to happen, it shall be granted him. Therefore I say to you, all things for which you pray and ask, believe that you have received them, and they shall be granted you (Mk 11:22–24).

Can such a miraculous thing happen by prayer and faith? Yes, if we understand what a God-wrought miracle is. A miracle from God is a supernatural intervention in the fixed order of the universe for the sole purpose of establishing His kingdom. A true miracle can only be accomplished by God and only to help fulfil His redemptive purpose.

Moving a mountain into the sea fulfils no redemptive purpose. Besides, given enough time and earth-moving equipment, we could accomplish that without God. The point that Jesus is making is, 'If God wants it done, it can be done.' Nothing can keep us from doing the will of God, if we believe. Nobody can stop us from being the person God wants us to be. 'Mountains' are often obstacles standing in the way of accomplishing God's will. Faith removes such barriers.

I'm sometimes impressed by how much the world can accomplish when they believe in themselves. When I worked on the Apollo space programme in the 1960s, we bid on a contract for the space shuttle. The technology to build the type of rocket it would take to boost that size payload into space had not yet been developed, but NASA believed that given enough time and resources, it could be done. Ten years later it was. Some who believe only in science exhibit greater faith than Christians. How much more should we be able to accomplish if the object of our faith is God?

Every commandment of God is a promise: 'For as many as may be the promises of God, in Him they are yes' (2 Cor 1:20). God will never command us to do something that He will not also empower us to do. The will of God never leads us where the grace of God cannot enable us. It is never a question of whether God can, but if He wills. If He wills, then we can if we believe. Those predisposed to do His will understand what it is (Jn 7:17), and by the grace of God will do it.

It is critical to realise that God is under no obligation to man. God is only under obligation to Himself and to the covenants He has made with us. He will faithfully respond according to His Word which becomes operative in our lives when we choose to believe and act upon it. We don't need

God jumping around in heaven catering to our every whim! There will never be a day when we say something and God has to do it because we said it. We cannot box God in.

There was a woman in my pastorate who wouldn't let me pray for her dying husband if I concluded my prayer with, 'Be it done according to Thy will.' I will never apologise for bowing to a higher authority. We are told to pray, 'Thy will be done.' Any other way would put us in the position of Lord. The misuse of God's Word and divine attributes is precisely how Satan tempted Jesus. Jesus withstood the temptation to act independently of God the Father and declared that His food was to do the will of His father who sent Him. That is our food as well.

3. Faith results in action

Faith is an action word. We cannot passively respond to God.

You may have heard the story of the circus performer who strung a wire over a river and proceeded to ride across it on a unicycle. When he returned, everyone applauded. Then he asked, 'Who believes I can do that with a man on my shoulders?' Everyone responded in affirmation. He said, 'All right, who will hop on?' The person who hops on is the person who really believes. Faith is not just giving credence to something or someone. Faith is demonstrated reliance upon something or someone.

Faith has the same operating dynamic as *agape* love. When we refer to love as a noun, we're talking about character: 'Love is patient, love is kind' (1 Cor 13:4). When we say that God is love, we are describing His character. Paul says the goal of our instruction is love (1 Tim 1:5); therefore, the goal of our Christian education is character transformation.

When love is used as a verb, it is expressed by action: 'For God so loved the world that He gave' (Jn 3:16). If we say we love someone and do nothing on their behalf, it's only sentimental and not *agape* love. True love is expressed by meeting the needs of others:

> We know love by this, that He laid down His life for us; and we ought to lay down our lives for the brethren. But whoever has this world's goods, and beholds his brother in need and closes his heart against him, how does the love of God abide in him? Little children, let us not love with word or with tongue, but in deed and truth (1 Jn 3:16–18).

Faith has a similar dynamic. When using faith as a noun, we're talking about what we believe. But if we're talking about faith as a verb, then it is expressed in the way we live. James says it like this:

> Even so faith, if it has no works, is dead, being by itself. But someone may well say, 'You have faith, and I have works; show me your faith without the works, and I will show you my faith by my works.' You believe that God is one. You do well; the demons also believe and shudder (Jas 2:17–19).

The devil believes in the existence of Jesus and knows that God's Word is true. But he doesn't seek to glorify Jesus or to obey Him. He seeks his own glory, being a rebel at heart: 'For they exchanged the truth of God for a lie, and worshipped and served the creature rather than the Creator' (Rom 1:25).

Let's go back to when I placed my son on the table and encouraged him to jump into my arms. What if Karl had never left that table, but kept insisting, 'My daddy can catch me!' Does he really believe it? The answer is obvious. We demonstrate what we believe by how we live our lives. If we believe it, we will do it. If we don't, then what we believe is just wishful thinking.

Faith that talks

One primary means by which we express our belief is confession — verbally expressing what we believe. In fact, God requires us to take our stand in this world. Jesus says:

> For whoever is ashamed of Me and My words in this adulterous and sinful generation, the Son of Man will also be ashamed of him when He comes in the glory of His Father with the holy angels (Mk 8:38).

The power of words is evident throughout the Bible: The worlds 'were prepared by the word of God' (Heb 11:3); 'By the word of the Lord, the heavens were made' (Ps 33:6); 'For He spoke and it was done; He commanded, and it stood fast' (Ps 33:9); Jesus 'upholds all things by the word of His power (Heb 1:3).

Paul writes:

> If you confess with your mouth Jesus as Lord, and believe in your heart that God raised Him from the dead, you shall be saved; for with the heart man believes, resulting in righteousness, and with the mouth he confesses, resulting in salvation (Rom 10:9,10).

In rebuking the Pharisees, Jesus said, 'For by your words you shall be justified, and by your words you shall be condemned' (Mt 12:37). Look again at Mark 11:23:

> Truly I say to you, whoever says to this mountain, 'Be taken up and cast into the sea,' and does not doubt in his heart, but believes that what he says is going to happen, it shall be granted him.

Notice that Jesus does not say we shall have whatever we believe, but we shall have whatever we believe and say.

Confession gives expression to what is believed. It is the confession of the mouth that releases the belief of the heart.

When the disciples couldn't deliver a demon-possessed boy, Jesus said, 'If you have faith as a mustard seed, you shall say to this mountain, 'Move from here to there,' and it shall move; and nothing shall be impossible for you' (Mt 17:20). In Luke 17:6, Jesus said, 'If you had faith like a mustard seed, you would say to this mulberry tree, "Be uprooted and be planted in the sea," and it would obey you.' Jesus is revealing the power of faith when expressed in words.

I believe the primary purpose for speaking what we believe is to overcome the god of this world. Satan is under no obligation to obey our thoughts. He doesn't perfectly know them. Only God perfectly knows the thoughts and intentions of our heart (Heb 4:12). Satan can only observe our conduct, and having observed humanity for thousands of years, it's no great trick for him to figure out in a general way what we are thinking. We usually live out our thought life since every behaviour is first preceded by a thought.

To defeat Satan, we must speak forth the Word of God, which is the sword of the Spirit (Eph 6:17). In our English translations, two different words are used for the 'Word of God.' The most common is *logos* and it indicates the whole revealed Word of God. For instance, Jesus is the *logos* in John 1:1. the other word is *rhema*. *Rhema* is the communication of *logos*. It is the same Word of God, but the emphasis of *rhema* is in its expression. We are to hide the whole Word (*logos*) in our hearts, and when Satan attacks, we stand against him by confessing God's Word (*rhema*).

Confessing what we believe gives proof of our faith. Confession doesn't create faith; faith makes possible true confession. Confession is agreeing with God. When we confess our sins, we are responding to the convictions of God and agreeing with Him about our moral condition.

Forgiveness and cleansing come when we are in agreement with Him.

Satan will distort the truth of God and make confession a self-induced profession. The New Age movement teaches that something can become true if we believe it. In a similar fashion, the positive confession movement asserts that whatever we profess will become true. The emphasis has shifted from 'Thy word is truth' to 'My word is truth.' 'I said it, it must be true!' 'I confessed it, so it must happen!' When this theology is questioned, the positive confessioners say that *logos* is the written Word of God, and *rhema* is the present revelation of God to their mind. When these modern-day 'prophets' speak, they expect people to obey. When their authority is questioned, they respond, 'Touch not God's anointed.' When their inaccuracies are revealed, they say, 'I'm only learning.' If they had tried to pull that off in the Old Testament, they would have been stoned to death.

Satan will do all within his power to discredit God and undermine our confidence in His Word. But if there is a counterfeit, there must be a truth. If there are deceiving spirits, there must be a Holy Spirit who will lead us into all truth. Notice how we are to respond to the counterfeit and choose the truth:

> Beloved, do not believe every spirit, but test the spirits to see whether they are from God; because many false prophets have gone out into the world. You are from God, little children, and have overcome them; because greater is He who is in you than he who is in the world.... For whatever is born of God overcomes the world; and this is the victory that has overcome the world — our faith. And who is the one who overcomes the world, but he who believes that Jesus is the Son of God? (1 Jn 4:1,4; 5:4,5)

Faith worth the risk

The story is told of a prospector in the last century who had to make a four-day journey across a burning desert. He couldn't carry enough water to make the journey without dying of thirst, but he was assured there was a well halfway across the desert. So he set out, and sure enough there was a well right where the map indicated. But when he pumped the handle, the well only burped up sand. Then he saw this sign: 'Buried two feet over and two feet down is a jug of water. Dig it up and use the water to prime the pump. Drink all the water you want, but when you are done, fill the jug again for the next person.'

Sure enough, two feet over and two feet down was enough water for the prospector to prime the pump or to finish his two-day journey. Should he pour the water down the well or should he drink it?

To tell you the truth, I'd drink the water that was buried! I don't know who wrote the sign on that rusty old pump. It could be a cruel joke. I'd pour that water down a worthless well, only to watch my life drain away for lack of water.

I don't have to worry about things like that when it comes to trusting God. I know who wrote the sign. When I pour myself into a life of faith, I know that out of my inner being shall flow rivers of living water. God said so, history verifies it and I, for one, can testify that it is true. In the final analysis, God is not only true, He's right.

Is faith a risk? Of course. But failing to step out in faith is to risk missing life.

Risk

To laugh is to risk appearing the fool.

To weep is to risk appearing sentimental.

To reach out for another is to risk involvement.

To expose feelings is to risk exposing who we really are.

To place our ideas, our dreams before the crowd, is to
   risk their loss.
To love is to risk not being loved in return.
To live is to risk dying.
To hope is to risk despair.
To try is to risk failure.
Risks must be taken because the greatest hazard in life
is to risk nothing. The person who risks nothing does
nothing, has nothing, is nothing. He may avoid suffering and sorrow, but he simply cannot learn, feel,
change, grow, love...live. Chained by his certitudes, he
is a slave; he has forfeited freedom.

                                — *Author Unknown*

What a privilege for us to be able to walk by faith when the
object of our faith is God Himself and all of the promises
of His Word. Let's express our gratitude and ask for His
continuing guidance in prayer:

**Dear Heavenly Father, You are the object of my faith. It is
You I believe. You are the way, the truth and the life. By the
counsel of Your will, all things hold together.**

**Forgive me for the times I acted presumptuously, thinking
I was acting in faith. Forgive me for times when I didn't take
Your Word seriously and failed to act when I know I should
have.**

**I want to know You and know Your ways so I can walk by
faith. I ask You to fill me with Your Spirit and guide me in the
way of truth. I ask that You not lead me into temptation but
deliver me from evil. I pray that You would never allow me to
lead another person astray by my words or my example. As
You direct my steps, may I glorify You in all that I do and say.
Amen.**

12
Spiritual Discernment

Discernment is our first line of defence when our ability to reason is insufficient

I had dear friends who were being used by the Lord in full-time ministry. Some difficulty developed in their marriage so they consulted a pastor/counsellor. The wife's response after the initial meeting was negative, but they continued with this particular counsellor because other people they respected said he was a good man.

Over the next year the ministry my friends were in as well as our relationship deteriorated. A short time later their pastor/counsellor was exposed for having sex with a number of counsellees. The damage he did to several women was incredible. He justified his behaviour by explaining, 'What we do in the flesh doesn't matter. Only what we do in the spirit counts!'

My friends were confronted with an ultimatum by their ministry group: 'Choose your ministry or choose him.' They chose to stay with him!

Why won't people judge righteously? 'Little children, let no one deceive you; the one who practises righteousness is righteous, just as He is righteous; the one who practises sin is of the devil' (1 Jn 3:7,8). The authoritative, arrogant spirit of this man had some kind of demonic hold on many, since half his church stayed with him. The initial discernment of my friends was correct, but they ignored the warnings of the Holy Spirit.

I believe discernment is a critical part of our walk with God. This divine enablement is our first line of defence when our ability to reason is insufficient. Jesus demonstrated spiritual discernment throughout His earthly ministry. We need to examine His example and learn how to develop our ability to discern good from evil, truth from lies.

The discernment of Jesus

While many Jews were questioning whether Jesus was a good man, they couldn't help but marvel at His teaching: 'How has this man become learned, having never been educated?' (Jn 7:15) Jesus responded, 'My teaching is not Mine, but His who sent Me' (Jn 7:16). (Would that we who teach the Bible could say that!)

After the Sermon on the Mount, the multitudes were amazed at His teaching, 'for He was teaching them as one having authority, and not as their scribes' (Mt 7:29). Jesus never had a formal education nor any secular position of authority, and still the sceptics recognised a teaching and authority not of this world.

Jesus also had the ability to discern beyond the normal means of external observation: 'But Jesus, on His part, was not entrusting Himself to them, for He knew all men, and because He did not need anyone to bear witness concerning man for He Himself knew what was in man' (Jn 2:24,25).

It's not hard to know the truth if you are the truth, and speaking with authority would come quite natural if you're God! Discernment is also easier if you know, as Jesus does, what's in the hearts of men. Though we don't possess those attributes, we do have the Holy Spirit. If we are going to continue the work of Jesus, we must yield to the Holy Spirit and allow Him to possess us. Then we can know the truth, speak with authority and discern good and evil. Let's briefly analyse these three functions.

Our guidance from the Spirit

First, *we have within us the Spirit of truth.* When Jesus
promised to send the Holy Spirit, He said:

> When He, the Spirit of truth, comes, He will guide you into
> all truth; for He will not speak on His own initiative, but
> whatever He hears, He will speak; and He will disclose to
> you what is to come. He shall glorify Me; for He shall take
> of Mine, and shall disclose it to you. All things that the
> Father has are Mine; therefore I said, that He takes of Mine,
> and will disclose it to you (Jn 16:13–15).

This promise has primary reference to the apostles, but
its application extends to all Spirit-filled believers (1 Jn
2:20–27). The Holy Spirit is first and foremost a Spirit of
truth, and He will lead us into all truth.

When Jesus prayed, He requested, 'I do not ask Thee to
take them out of the world, but to keep them from the evil
one... Sanctify them in the truth; Thy word is truth' (Jn
17:15,17). Truth is what keeps us from the evil one. Truth is
God's will made known through His Word. The Holy
Spirit's role is to enable us to understand the Word of God
from God's perspective. Because of His presence in our life,
we incarnate the Word of God as we abide in Christ.

Second, *we can speak with authority.* The ability to do so
stems from the same source as was true of Jesus Himself.
The authority Jesus possessed was not based in any earthly
position, but in the quality, conduct and character of His
life.

The true shepherd exercises spiritual leadership with the
heart of a servant. Spiritual leadership cannot be based in a
position of authority since there is no position lower than a
servant. We can speak with authority only when our character is Christ-like. As servants, we are subject to the needs
of those we are called to lead. That's why He said we will

know His disciples by their love. The requirements to be a spiritual leader in 1 Timothy 3 and Titus 1 are all character requirements. All of this is made possible by the indwelling presence of God the Holy Spirit. Peter writes:

> Shepherd the flock of God among you, not under compulsion, but voluntarily, according to the will of God; and not for sordid gain, but with eagerness; nor yet as lording it over those allotted to your charge, but proving to be examples to the flock (1 Pet 5:2,3).

You never hear Jesus say, 'You do this because I'm God.' What happens to a marriage relationship when a husband authoritatively demands obedience because he is the head of the home? Nothing good, let me assure you. The spiritual head of a home assumes his responsibility by meeting the needs of his family. Being the head of a home is an awesome responsibility, not a right to be demanded. A wise husband listens carefully to the counsel of his wife and depends upon the Holy Spirit. With the Holy Spirit's enablement, he can live a righteous life out of which he can lead with loving authority.

Third, *the Holy Spirit enables us to discern.* According to John 16:8, He 'will convict the world concerning sin, and righteousness and judgement.' The Holy Spirit doesn't take up residence in our lives and then sit passively by while we participate in sin. Since we are in Christ, we have become partakers of the divine nature (2 Pet 1:4), and we sense conviction when we choose to behave in a way that isn't consistent with the Spirit's presence in our lives. The Holy Spirit is not compatible with the world, the flesh or an evil spirit. The Holy Spirit enables us to discern good from evil.

How discernment comes

I don't know any legitimate Christian who questions the role of the Holy Spirit in leading us to truth or living a righteous life or helping us discern good from evil. The debate is not if He does, but how He does it. I would like to make some observations from 1 Corinthians 2:9–16:

> But just as it is written, 'Things which eye has not seen and ear has not heard, and which have not entered the heart of man, all that God has prepared to those who love Him.' for to us God revealed them through the Spirit; for the Spirit searches all things, even the depths of God. For who among men knows the thoughts of a man except the spirit of the man, which is in him? Even so the thoughts of God no one knows except the Spirit of God. Now we have received, not the spirit of the world, but the Spirit who is from God, that we might know the things freely given to us by God, which things we also speak, not in words taught by human wisdom, but in those taught by the Spirit, combining spiritual thoughts with spiritual words. But a natural man does not accept things of the Spirit of God; for they are foolishness to him, and he cannot understand them, because they are spiritually appraised. But he who is spiritual appraises all things, yet he himself is appraised by no man. For who has known the mind of the Lord, that he should instruct Him: But we have the mind of Christ.

Though this is a difficult passage to understand, I believe it's safe to draw the following conclusions. One, a natural man cannot discern what is spiritually true; he can only know his own thoughts. Two, the Holy Spirit knows all things and is capable of revealing the nature of God and His will. The Spirit of God knows the thoughts of God. Three, we have not received the spirit of the world but the Spirit who is from God. The Spirit makes known to us the things freely given by God. Four, we have the mind of Christ.

Five, the Holy Spirit takes words *(logos)*, which are not taught by human wisdom but by the Spirit and combines (brings together, compares or explains) them. What is actually being combined or compared is fuzzy, though, because the original language literally says, 'spirituals with spirituals.' The NASB translates that as 'combining spiritual thoughts with spiritual words.' The NIV translates it as 'words taught by the Spirit, expressing spiritual truths in spiritual words.'

The natural man looks like this:

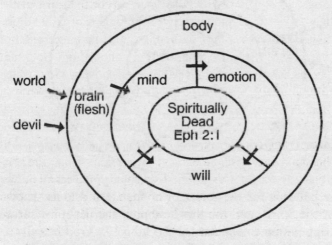

The natural man is spiritually dead, separated from God. He has neither the presence of God in his life nor the knowledge of God's ways. He has learned to live his life independently of God. Essentially, this is what constitutes the 'flesh'. His mind has been conformed to this world. The brain, which is physical and part of the body, functions like a computer. This mind is the programmer. The body picks up data from the world through its five senses. The mind chooses and interprets the data, and the brain stores it. The emotions are essentially a product of how the mind chooses to think and interpret life's events.

When we are born again, the Holy Spirit takes up residence in our life. Because we are now spiritually alive and united with Christ, we have the mind of Christ. We have become a partaker of the divine nature. However, nobody pushed the clear button in the computer. The brain is still programmed to live independently of God. The Christian now looks like this:

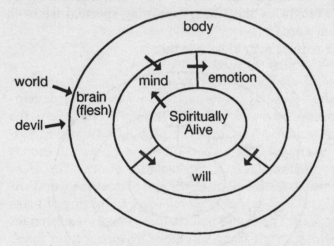

The battle is for the mind: 'For the flesh sets its desire against the Spirit, and the Spirit against the flesh; for these are in opposition to one another' (Gal 5:17). God has given us the responsibility to choose. The carnal Christian chooses to walk according to the flesh. What governs his behaviour are the old habit patterns and thoughts that were programmed over time. The spiritually defeated Christian fails to put on the armour of God, and ends up paying attention to deceiving spirits. The spiritual man has crucified the flesh and put on the armour of God; he chooses to think upon that which is true.

We are to be renewed in the spirit of our minds (Eph

4:23). The Holy Spirit discloses the mind of Christ. We must no longer choose to be conformed to this world. We are to be diligent to present ourselves approved to God as a workman who does not need to be ashamed, handling accurately the word of truth (2 Tim 2:15). When we do, we are transformed by the renewing of our minds. We choose to think the truth, and the Holy Spirit enables our thoughts and renewed our minds with the *logos*. Then the peace of God guards our hearts and minds. We let the peace of Christ rule in our hearts by letting the word of Christ richly dwell in us (Col 3:15,16). We are now equipped to discern.

Distinguishing right and wrong

In a world saturated with deceiving spirits, false prophets and false teachers, the importance of exercising discernment cannot be overemphasised. In the Old Testament, the Hebrew word *bin* is used 247 times and is translated as 'discern', 'distinguish' and sometimes 'understand'. It means 'to make a distinction, or separate from.' The New Testament counterpart, *diakrino*, also means 'to separate or divide.' It is used primarily in reference to judging or making decisions. The Holy Spirit enables us to distinguish right from wrong, truth from lies, God's thoughts from man's thoughts.

An incident in Solomon's life is helpful in understanding discernment. David had died and Solomon had taken his place as king of Israel. Solomon admitted he felt too young and inexperienced to be the king: 'And now, O Lord my God, Thou has made Thy servant king in place of my father David, yet I am but a little child; I do not know how to go out or come in' (1 Kings 3:7). In Gibeon the Lord appeared to Solomon in a dream at night, and God said, 'Ask what you wish Me to give you.' Solomon asked and the Lord responded:

'Thy servant is in the midst of Thy people which Thou has chosen, a great people who cannot be numbered or counted for multitude. So give Thy servant an understanding heart to judge Thy people to discern between good and evil. For who is able to judge this great people of Thine?' And it was pleasing in the sight of the Lord that Solomon had asked this thing. And God said to him, 'Because you have asked this thing and have not asked for yourself long life, nor have asked riches for yourself, nor have you asked for the life of your enemies, but have asked for yourself discernment to understand justice, behold, I have done according to your words. Behold, I have given you a wise and discerning heart, so that there has been no one like you before you, nor shall one like you arise after you' (1 Kings 3:8–12).

This passage reveals several key concepts about discernment. First, *God gave Solomon the ability to discern because of the purity of his motives.* Solomon wasn't asking for personal gain or advantage over his enemies. He was asking for the ability to discern good and evil, and God gave it to him. The ability to discern is completely dependent upon God who is able to look at the heart. This is true for the proper use of any spiritual gift. Wrong motives open the door for Satan's counterfeits.

A few years ago, an undergraduate girl was following me around to various speaking engagements. After an evening service at a local church, she was shaking visibly. I saw her plight and asked if I could help. Learning she was a student, I asked her to stop by my office the next day. When we got together, she told me she was seeing one of our Christian counsellors. I asked her how that was going, and she replied it was like a game. She could tell everything the counsellor was going to do next. When I realised she enjoyed playing mind games with her counsellor, I challenged her, 'You like doing that, don't you? You like the advantage it gives you over other people.' As soon as I exposed the deception, an evil spirit manifested itself.

She believed God had given her a spiritual gift that enabled her to point out people's sins. She could walk on campus and say, 'That person is struggling with sex, that person with alcohol,' etc. As near as I could tell, she was right. Yet when she found her freedom in Christ, the ability disappeared. That wasn't the Holy Spirit enabling her to discern. It was an evil spirit compatible with the evil spirits that were causing the moral problems in the other people. Her goal had been to go into counselling and use this 'gift' to 'help' people. Instead, she went to the mission field. Now she is helping people, but this time by the Spirit of God.

Second, this passage clearly establishes that *true biblical discernment is always on the plane of good and evil.* The distinguishing of spirits the Bible teaches is the Holy Spirit enabling us to distinguish between a good spirit and an evil spirit (1 Cor 12:10). I was working with a young lady who was plagued with compulsive thoughts that contributed to an eating disorder. As she was going through the process of forgiving others, I sensed that it wasn't the girl talking any more. 'That's not her,' I said. There were several other people in the room observing the counselling process, but nobody else sensed it. They wondered how I knew. I don't know how I knew, but I knew. The fact that I was right was evident immediately. The expression on her face changed, and a voice said, 'She will never forgive that person.'

While spiritual discernment is primarily a function of the Spirit and not the mind, it doesn't bypass the mind, nor does it replace the need to know the truth from the Word of God. Rather, it builds upon the truth already understood in our hearts. There are numerous occasions when our minds want to know what's wrong. We may not receive the answer right away, but the Holy Spirit is alerting us that something is wrong — like a built-in alarm system.

Let me illustrate. Suppose my son comes home and I sense something is wrong. So I ask him, 'What's wrong Karl?' He says, 'Nothing!' Again I ask him what's wrong, and again he claims nothing is wrong. My 'buzzer' is going off because I am discerning that something is wrong. At this point we typically blow the discernment. We try to be objective, so we guess what it is. (Isn't that being objective?) 'Karl, have you been doing such and such again?' If I guess wrong (and I probably will), I blow the discernment. Karl will stalk away into his room, mad at me for falsely charging him.

So what should I have done? Just share the discernment. 'Karl, something is wrong.' 'No Dad, nothing's wrong!' 'Karl I know something is wrong.' He shrugs his shoulders and goes to his room. Is that it? No, that's not it! Remember, the Holy Spirit is going to convict the world of sin. The Holy Spirit made me aware that something is wrong and after I express that, God has a direct shot at Karl in his bedroom. Guess what happens in his room? Conviction! I can almost imagine what he is thinking — *Dad knows!* I really don't know what's wrong, but my discernment knows something is wrong.

When I was pastoring, I would sometimes enter a family's home and sense something was wrong. There was nothing visible. The people were smiling, they had a pot of coffee on and they had even dusted off the Bible. But I could cut the air with a knife. I knew something wasn't right, but I never knew what to do about it. We tend to ignore that kind of discernment and conduct business as usual. If we discern something is wrong, we should stop and pray. God can give us wisdom in knowing what to do. If we ignore the discernment, we will just continue ignoring the warning of the Holy Spirit.

Discernment, a spiritual weapon

Discernment is like an early warning system, the first line of defence in a spiritual world. There's nothing mystical about this. It makes sense that the Holy Spirit is not going to bear witness when an evil spirit is present: 'You cannot drink the cup of the Lord and the cup of demons; you cannot partake of the table of the Lord and the table of demons' (1 Cor 10:21).

I can't imagine the Holy Spirit remaining passive in the face of adversity. But don't confuse this with human intuition. This is the Holy Spirit bearing witness with my spirit and counteracting the influence of the world, the flesh and the devil. When they are incompatible, the buzzer goes off. Perhaps you've had the positive experience of sensing a compatible spirit in a stranger whom you just 'knew' was a Christian, even though nothing has been said.

Hebrews 5:12 – 6:2 offers further insight:

> For though by this time you ought to be teachers, you have need again for someone to teach you the elementary princi ples of the oracles of God, and you have come to need milk and not solid food. For every one who partakes only of milk is not accustomed to the word of righteousness, for he is a babe. But solid food is for the mature, who because of practice have their senses trained to discern good and evil. Therefore leaving the elementary teaching about Christ, let us press on to maturity, not laying again a foundation of repentance from dead works and of faith toward God, of instruction about washings, and laying on of hands, and the resurrection of the dead, and eternal judgement.

What the writer of Hebrews identifies as elementary teaching is heaving theology for most people. A good systematic theology is the foundation upon which we build our lives. It is to our walk with God what our skeleton is to our body. It holds us together and keeps us in the right form. But right doctrine is never an end in itself. True doctrine governs our relationship with God and man. Many Christians have a relationship with God that is only theological, not personal. Those accustomed to the word of righteousness are sensitive to the personal leading of the Holy Spirit.

Solomon started with a love for God. He 'became greater than all the kings of the earth in riches and in wisdom. And all the earth was seeking the presence of Solomon, to hear his wisdom which God had put in his heart (1 Kings 10:23,24). He had the ability to discern, but moral demise led to his downfall. His wives turned his heart away, and he was no longer accustomed to the words of righteousness. His heart was not wholly devoted to the Lord, and the kingdom of God was torn in two.

Many Christians come faithfully to church on Sunday and the words sink into their ears, but not into their hearts. Their eyes aren't opened because their senses haven't been trained to discern good and evil.

I'm not sure my senses would have been trained if God hadn't called me into the ministry of setting captives free. If we are going to minister in a world of deception, we had better learn to rely upon God and not lean on our own understanding.

Discerning specific issues

The Holy Spirit is resident in our lives for more than warning. Sometimes He gives us impressions of what the problem really is. While ministering, it isn't uncommon to have thoughts come to my mind. For instance, a person could be sharing their story, and I'm sensing they are struggling with homosexuality. I never treat such impressions as authoritative; I test every one as I believe Scripture requires us to do. I do this by waiting for the right opportunity and ask something like this, 'Have you ever struggled with homosexual feelings or tendencies?' If it triggers no response, I know the impression isn't valid or the person doesn't want to disclose it at this time. In either case, I continue to develop trust and understanding.

As I have matured in the Lord, I find that these impressions are generally true, and they get to the heart of the issue. But I never ascribe scriptural quality to them, nor do I believe they are a substitute for knowing the Bible. Our ability to discern grows in proportion to our spiritual maturity and knowledge of God and His ways. God brings to our minds the Scripture we have already put into our hearts through studying His Word. There are no shortcuts to maturity. The Holy Spirit doesn't bypass the parts of Scripture that require us to show compassion, develop trusting relationships and exercise patience. The spiritual leading of the Holy Spirit works through the whole counsel of God.

Deceiving spirits encourage shortcuts, bypass the mind and seek to create a dependency upon esoteric knowledge (knowledge that can only be understood by a few elite people). Spirit guides can give you the knowledge you seek by bypassing your mind. You won't even have to think. Just go by what you hear in your head. Sounds good, doesn't it? That's how a medium works. New Age channellers are making big money with their esoteric knowledge. Some will even profess to be Christians. Satan gives them enough truth to hook a gullible public.

John writes, 'Beloved, do not believe every spirit, but test the spirits to see whether they are from God; because many false prophets have gone out into the world' (1 Jn 4:1). This is not optional. We are required by God to test the spirits. There is only one infallible source of faith and practice, and that's the Word of God. It's the *logos* hidden in our hearts that the Holy Spirit bears witness to.

Our power to perceive the light of God is, of all our powers, the one which we need most to cultivate and develop. As exercise strengthens the body and education enlarges the mind, so the spiritual faculty within us grows as we use it in seeing and doing God's will.   — *Friends Book of Discipline*

Let's not waste such a precious resource that God has made available to us — our minds quickened by the Holy Spirit to be able to discern good and evil, right and wrong. If you desire to see your discernment strengthened, I invite you to pray with me:

Dear Heavenly Father, I desire to know You and Your ways. I don't want to take any shortcuts and be deceived by evil spirits. I want to know the truth and You are the truth. Teach me to think so as to have sound judgement. I want to base my leadership in character, not position, so I commit myself to be like You.

I want people to know me for my love. May that be the proof that I am Your disciple. Deliver me from a knowledge that would make me arrogant. I confess to You my pride. I humble myself before You and ask that You will fill me with Your Spirit.

I ask You to lead me into all truth, so that I can discern good and evil. I ask for the courage to take my stand in the world, with the authority that comes from truth and righteousness. I ask this in the name of Jesus. Amen.

13
Walking By The Spirit

If we find ourselves huffing and puffing our way through life, maybe we're not walking with God

A young pilot had just passed the point of no return when the weather changed for the worse. Visibility dropped to a matter of feet as fog descended to the earth. Putting total trust in the cockpit instruments was a new experience to him, for the ink was still wet on the certificate verifying that he was qualified for instrument flying.

The landing worried him the most. His destination was a crowded metropolitan airport that he wasn't familiar with. In a few minutes he would be in radio contact with the tower. Until then, he was alone with his thoughts. Flying with no visibility, he became aware of how easy it would be to panic. Twice he reached for the radio to broadcast, 'Mayday!' but he forced himself to go over and over the words of his instructor instead. His instructor had practically forced him to memorise the rule book. He didn't care for it at the time, but now he was thankful.

Finally he heard the voice of the air traffic controller. Trying not to sound apprehensive, the young pilot asked for landing instructions. 'I'm going to put you on a holding pattern,' the controller responded. *Great!* thought the pilot. However, he knew that his safe landing was in the hands of this person. He had to draw upon his previous instruction and training and trust the voice of an air traffic controller he couldn't see. The words of an old hymn, 'Trust and obey for there's no other way,' took on new meaning. Aware that this was no time for pride, he informed the controller, 'This is not a seasoned pro up here. I would appreciate any help you could give me.' 'You've got it!' he heard back.

For the next forty-five minutes, the controller gently guided the pilot through the blinding fog. As course and altitude corrections came periodically, the young pilot realised the controller was guiding him around obstacles and away from potential collisions. With the words of the rule book firmly placed in his mind, and with the gentle voice of the controller, he landed safely at last.

The Holy Spirit guides us through the maze of life much like that air traffic controller. The controller assumed that the young pilot understood the instructions of the flight manual. His guidance was based on that. Such is the case with the Holy Spirit: He can only guide us if we have the knowledge of God's Word and His will established in our minds.

The urgent need

Early in church history, the Jerusalem council convened to discuss two critical issues that were threatening the body of believers (see Acts 15). One issue was circumcision and the other was socialising with the use of food. They were debating the boundaries of legalism and licence. That tension still exists today.

It is important to note how the early Christians finally came to an agreement. First, they searched the Scriptures: 'And with this the words of the prophets agree, just as it is written' (Acts 15:5). After consulting the Scriptures, they drafted a letter that was sent with Paul, part of which says, 'They had become of one mind.... For it seemed good to the Holy Spirit and to us' (Acts 15:25,28). Their search for guidance through their crisis was balanced: They consulted the Scriptures and came to the mind of Christ by the aid of the Holy Spirit.

We desperately need God's guidance through the moral demise of our country today. But I'm puzzled at the evangelical response. We see divorce, so we preach against divorce. We see drunkenness, so we preach against the excessive use of alcohol. We see drugs, so we preach against drugs. How's it working? Preaching morality never has worked and it never will! If we are only moralists, we aren't proclaiming the gospel. And jumping to the other extreme of whitewashing sin is equally devastating. The only balanced hope we have is stated in Galatians 5:16–18:

> But I say, walk by the Spirit, and you will not carry out the desires of the flesh. For the flesh sets its desire against the Spirit, and the Spirit against the flesh. For these are in opposition to one another, so that you may not do the things that you please. But if you are led by the Spirit, you are not under the law.

The flight instruction manual is the authoritative means by which we fly. But who would deny that the plane is empowered by something other than the pilot or question the need for an air traffic controller? In the same way, we sense our need for someone to guide us. The real difficulty lies not in the need, but in the 'how to' of walking by the Spirit. If I answered the question with three steps and a formula, I'd be putting you back under the law. To walk by the Spirit is not a legal issue — it's a personal issue. The air traffic controller is a living personality, not a recorded message from a computer. The Holy Spirit is not an 'it'; the Holy Spirit is a He.

It is easier to explain what walking by the Spirit is not, rather than what it is, so let's start with what it isn't.

Not undisciplined freedom

First, from the above passage in Galatians, we can clearly see that *walking by the Spirit is not licence. Licence* is defined as an excessive or undisciplined freedom constituting the abuse of a privilege. It gave way to the Old King James term, *licentious*, meaning lacking moral discipline with no regard for accepted rules and regulations. Paul says walking by the Spirit ensures that we don't carry out the desires of the flesh, and His presence guards against doing whatever we please.

When I was born, I was completely dependent upon my mother and father for human survival. If they hadn't fed me, changed me and taken care of me, I would have died. My goal as any little child was to be independent. Like most children, my striving for independence began with the 'terrible twos'. So my parents set parameters. They knew that for my safety, they simply could not let me do what I pleased.

Since I came into this world physically alive but spiritually dead, I learned to live my life independent of God. Essentially, this is what constitutes the flesh. I had neither the presence of God in my life nor the knowledge of God's ways, so I learned to cope and defend myself as I was being conformed to this world. This learned independence is what makes the flesh hostile toward God. That is why the flesh and the Spirit are in opposition to one another.

Being children of God, the presence of the Holy Spirit restrains us so we will not do the things that we please. If there were no moral restraints and no boundaries to govern our behaviour, we would drive ourselves into moral decadence. Imagine the air traffic controller saying to the pilot, 'You have my permission to land any time and any place you want.' That pilot would most likely crash and burn!

Paul writes, 'You were called to freedom, brethren, only do not turn your freedom into an opportunity for the flesh, but through love serve one another' (Gal 5:13). God wants us free, but freedom is not licence. I believe we are free by the grace of God to live a responsible life. In the early part of the twentieth century, a rigid fundamentalism had left our churches frozen in legalism. In the '50s it began to thaw, and the Jesus People movement of the '60s and '70s melted it into licence for many. The pendulum had swung from the justice of God to the mercy of God. 'God loves me,' believers reasoned, 'so I can do whatever I want. There's no way He would send me to hell.' A libertine spirit led to free sex and free drugs. The result is a society on the brink of disaster.

There's always a price to pay for licence. True freedom doesn't lie in the exercise of choices, but in the consequences of the choices made. You may reserve the right to tell a lie, but you'll be in bondage to it because you'll have to remember the nature of the lie and to whom it was told. You may choose to rob a bank, but you will always be looking over your shoulder, fearing you may be caught. That's bondage.

If we choose to walk by the flesh, we are responsible for the consequences of the choices we make. If we walk by the Spirit, God says He assumes responsibility for the consequences.

Not chained by the law

Second, *walking by the Spirit is not legalism*: 'But if you are led by the Spirit, you are not under the law' (Gal 5:16).

If we choose to relate to God on the basis of the law, then we need to be aware of three biblical truths. First, the law will function as a curse. Look at Galatians 3:10–14:

All who rely on observing the law are under a curse, for it is written: 'Cursed is everyone who does not continue to do everything written in the Book of the Law.' Clearly no one is justified before God by the law, because, 'The righteous will live by faith.' The law is not based on faith; on the contrary, 'The man who does these things will live by them.' Christ redeemed us from the curse of the law by becoming a curse for us, for it is written: 'Cursed is everyone who is hung on a tree.' He redeemed us in order that the blessing given to Abraham might come to the Gentiles through Christ Jesus, so that by faith we might receive the promise of the Spirit (NIV).

If we want to base our relationship with God on how well we keep the law, we should first consider James 2:10, 'For whoever keeps the whole law and yet stumbles on one point, he has become guilty of all.' Thankfully, our relationship with God is based on who we are in Christ, not on our ability to keep the law. We are not saved by how we perform, but by how we believe: 'For the law has become our tutor to lead us to Christ that we may be justified by faith' (Gal 3:24). The blessings of Abraham have come to the Gentiles because we are alive, right now, in Christ Jesus. Look again at Galatians 3:14: 'He redeemed us in order that the blessing given to Abraham might come to the Gentiles through Christ Jesus, so that by faith we might receive the promise of the Spirit' (NIV). We are recipients of the Holy Spirit through faith and He is operative in our life through faith.

Many Christians labour under the moral fog of legalism. To them the gospel isn't good news, it's bad news. They don't go to church to celebrate what Christ has already done; they go to receive another dose of guilt. Legalistic pastors know no other way to keep their people within the moral boundaries of Scripture other than holding them over the fires of hell and threatening, 'Turn or burn.' These types of pastors are moralists. They focus on the external, not the internal. They quote, 'As a man thinks in his heart, so is he,' but all they see is the 'so is he.' Their entire focus is to change behaviour.

What they fail to understand is that the real battle is for the mind. People's thoughts determine what they do. We need to find out what's happening on the inside, then we will know why people are behaving the way they are. The moralist looks only on the outside of man, but Jesus looks upon the heart.

The second limitation of the law is that it is powerless to give life. Telling people that what they are doing is wrong does not give them the power to stop. In and of itself, the law is impotent:

> Is the law then contrary to the promises of God? May it never be! For if a law had been given which was able to impart life, then righteousness would indeed have been based on law (Gal 3:21).

We were dead in our trespasses and sins, but now we are alive in Christ: 'We are servants of a new covenant, not of the letter, but of the Spirit. For the letter kills, but the Spirit gives life' (2 Cor 3:6). This life establishes our true identity as to whom we are as children of God. Jesus said, 'I came that you might have life and have it more abundantly' (Jn 10:10).

Not slaves to sin

No person can consistently behave in a way that is inconsistent with how he perceives himself: 'And every one who has this hope fixed on Him purifies himself, just as He is pure' (1 Jn 3:3). The gospel says that we are not just forgiven but that we have become new creations in Christ. God changed our nature, but it is our responsibility to change our behaviour. I'm not whitewashing sin; I'm trying to establish how God intends us to be free from it: 'Knowing this, that our old self was [past tense] crucified with Him, in order that our body of sin might be done away with that we should no longer be slaves to sin' (Rom 6:6).

In order to live a life free from sin, we have to understand an important fact. A grim determination of our will to overcome sin won't work if we keep insisting that Christians are still sinners. Because what do sinners do? They sin! The Bible doesn't call a child of God a sinner; it calls the child of God a saint who sins.

The third startling fact about the law is that it can stimulate the desire to do that which it tries to prohibit. Try telling a child he can go one place but not another, and where does he want to go immediately? When I was young, I had some friends who were Catholic. Their church posted a list of movies they couldn't see which quickly became a list of movies to see. My friends actually tore the list off the wall of the church and shared it with the entire school campus.

According to Romans 7:5, some sinful passions are actually aroused by the law: 'For while we were in the flesh, the sinful passions, which were aroused by the law, were at work in the members of our body to bear fruit for death.' Paul argues in Romans 7 that the law isn't sinful, even though it stimulates the desire to sin:

> What shall we say then? Is the law sin? May it never be! But sin, taking the opportunity through the commandment produced in me coveting of every kind; for apart from the law sin is dead (Rom 7:7,8).

I'm not trying to tell you we shouldn't have a moral standard! Of course we need a moral standard. But the means by which we relate to God is by faith, and the presence of the Holy Spirit will enable us to walk between the two extremes of legalism and licence.

The Christian life is like a journey down a road. The

Holy Spirit proves sanctuary for those who walk the narrow path. To the right of the path is a sharp drop. It's a tempting option. You could sail off that cliff and enjoy an exhilarating 'flight'. But that kind of freedom has serious consequences, especially when you hit the bottom! Wanting to have my own way and demanding my 'right' for freedom of choice without considering the consequences is licence. It's a deadly step in the wrong direction.

To the left of that road is a roaring fire of legalism. The 'accuser of the brethren' has a field day with those who choose to deviate from the narrow path by going back under the law. Many are burned by legalism. If you are led by the Spirit, you are not under the law: 'There is now no condemnation for those who are in Christ Jesus' (Rom 8:1).

So if walking by the Spirit is not licence, and it's not legalism, then what is it? Is it liberty: 'Now the Lord is a Spirit, and where the Spirit of the Lord is there is liberty' (2 Cor 3:17). So how do we experience this liberty? It's in the walking.

Moving with God

Walking by the Spirit implies two things that it's not. First, walking by the Spirit is not sitting passively expecting God to do everything. And second, it is not running around in endless, exhaustive activities as though everything depended on our efforts. Do you know how much would get accomplished for the kingdom of God if we expected God to do everything? Nothing! Do you know how much gets accomplished for the kingdom of God if we try to do it all by ourselves? Nothing! You and I have the privilege to water and plant, but God causes the increase. Yet if there is not watering or planting, there is no increase.

There was a pastor whose favourite hobby was gardening. One day a neighbour walked by and said, 'The Lord sure gave you a beautiful garden.' The pastor responded,

'This garden is the Lord's and mine. You should have seen the plot of ground when the Lord had it all by Himself.'

In counteracting Pharisaic slavery, Jesus said, 'Come to Me all who are weary and heavy-laden, and I will give you rest. Take My yoke upon you and learn from Me, for I am gentle and humble in heart, and you shall find rest for your souls. For my yoke is easy and my load is light' (Mt 11:28–30).

Jesus is alluding to the yoke that harnessed two oxen together. When a young ox was being broken in, it was paired with a lead ox. After much training, the lead ox knew the best way to accomplish a day's work was to neither run nor sit. He knew they would accomplish more if they walked down the narrow row, looking neither to the left nor to the right. And if the team was going to accomplish anything, they had to pull together.

Young oxen get impatient with the slow pace and want to run ahead. Do you know what they get? A sore neck! Other young oxen feel like doing nothing and just sit. Guess what they get? A sore neck! That lead ox is going to keep right on walking no matter what the young ox does. Life has a way of continuing on whether we like it or not. Count on Jesus, our lead ox, to continue a steady pace down the centre of that narrow path.

We had a perfect family dog that grew up with our children. When little Missy died, it was traumatic for us. I hurried to a pet store the same day and bought a replacement dog. Much like marrying on the rebound, it was a disaster. Buster grew up to be a DAWG! He is the most neurotic mess I've ever seen. My son signed up for twelve lessons of dog-obedience, but after two weeks it was my son who was thoroughly trained by Buster!

I tried putting a choke-chain around that dog and taking it for a walk. I had one conviction firmly planted in my mind: I was the master, and I was going to set the direction and pace of our walk. That dumb dog, however, wanted to run. He would strain at the end of the leash and choke all the way through our walk. Occasionally, Buster would stop and do his own thing. I kept on walking, however, and Buster would be choked into reality. Sometimes he would stray off the path and end up winding his leash around a tree. The result was like a wild ride at an amusement park as I kept on walking. Did the dumb dog ever learn to walk obediently by my side? No, he never did. I've known a few Christians like that.

Jesus said, *Come to Me. I'm the lead ox. Is your Christian life weary and heavy-laden? I'll give you rest. Take My yoke.* The flesh quickly responds, 'That's all I need is another yoke!' But you can't put on the yoke of Christ without throwing off the yoke of legalism and licence. *Learn from Me*, Jesus says. If we walked with Jesus, what do you think we would learn? To start with, we would learn to take one day at a time. We would learn the priority of relationships. We would learn that our walk is one of faith and not sight...one of grace, not legalism.

My yoke is easy, and My load is light, Jesus says. If we find ourselves huffing and puffing our way through life, maybe we're not walking with God. Maybe we're running in the flesh. I ask myself that very often. This is the only passage in the New Testament where Jesus describes himself. And He says He's gentle and humble in heart. We need to share the yoke with the gentle Jesus and pull together with Him: 'As you therefore have received Christ Jesus, so walk in Him' (Col 2:6).

Following our guide

We not only walk by the Spirit, but we are led by the Spirit as well. Being led by the Spirit implies two things that it's not. First, we are neither being pushed nor pulled. And second, we are neither driven (legalism), nor are we lured away (licence).

There are a lot of driven Christians who know little of resting in the Spirit. Motivated by guilt, they can't say no. They expend a lot of energy, but they bear very little fruit. They measure success in ministry by the number of activities. They measure spirituality by the expenditure of human energy.

I've had people push me for an answer — now! I find it very easy to respond, 'No'. 'Why not?' they ask. 'Because God doesn't lead that way,' I answer. The devil leads that way. He always demands an answer right now and withdraws the offer if time for consideration is requested. The guidance of God may come suddenly, but it never comes to the unprepared. Pentecost was sudden, but the disciples had spent days in prayerful preparation.

Many believers are lured away by various impulses. The lure of knowledge and power has trapped some. As undisciplined and lazy people, though, they don't want to study to show themselves approved. They accept the esoteric knowledge of the occult. They want the air traffic controller to explain the instruction manual to them while they are in the air. Why study when you can receive your knowledge from God directly? Others are pulled off the path by the lure of incredible power. They don't seem to understand the fact that they already have the power. It is the truth they need. Satanists pursue power; Christians pursue truth.

Growing up on a farm, I had the privilege of raising championship sheep. I can tell you from experience that sheep are not the smartest animals on the farm. They're right down there with chickens. For instance, you can self-feed cattle and pigs, but you can't sheep. If you turn sheep loose in a green pasture, they will literally eat themselves to death. One thing's for certain: Sheep without a shepherd will soon perish.

In the Western world, we drive our sheep from the rear, using sheep dogs. However, that is not the case in Israel. In my trips to the Holy Land, I observed that the herds of sheep were generally small, and the shepherd would sit patiently by while the flocks grazed. The shepherd seemed to have personal knowledge of every sheep. When an area was sufficiently grazed, the shepherd would say something and walk off. To my amazement, the sheep looked up and followed him. What a beautiful illustration of what the Lord said in John 10:27: 'My sheep hear My voice, and I know them, and they follow Me.'

Walking by the Spirit is neither legalism nor licence. It's not sitting passively, waiting for God to do something, nor is it running around in endless, exhausting circles trying to do everything by ourselves. If we walk by the Spirit, we are neither driven nor lured off the path of faith.

Walking by the Spirit is walking with God: 'For all who are being led by the Spirit of God, these are the sons of God' (Rom 8:14). It's not a legal issue; it's a personal issue.

Would you pray with me for the peace and fulfilment of a life that simply keeps pace with God?

Dear Heavenly Father. You are the strength of my life. Forgive me for trying to fly alone. I not only need Your strength, but I also need Your guidance. I accept the times You put me in a holding pattern. I now realise that it was for my own good.

I desire to walk the narrow path, so I gladly accept Your invitation to come to Jesus. I take His yoke upon me, and I throw off the yokes of legalism and licence.

I commit myself to know Your Word so I can be guided by You. I no longer expect You to guide me without Your Word richly dwelling within me. And I no longer lean on my own understanding.

Lead me not into temptation, but deliver me from evil.

Help me to know You so well that I can discern Your voice from the voice of the evil one.

I desire the liberty that comes only as I submit to You. I acknowledge my dependency upon You. I ask You to fill me with Your Holy Spirit that I may be led by You.

You are my God and I am a sheep in Your pasture. I love the security that comes from knowing You are my Shepherd. Amen.

14
Walking In The Light

If prayer is so important, why is it so difficult?

Even as a young Christian, I realised that prayer was a vital link for God's guidance. But prayer was also the most frustrating part of my early Christian experience.

At seminary I remember reading about great saints who would spend two, three or four hours in prayer — sometimes even all night. I was struggling to spend five minutes! I would labour through my prayer list for two or three minutes then glance at my watch. I would wonder what I was going to say for the next two minutes. Prayer was supposed to be a dialogue with God, but for me it seemed like I was talking to the wall.

My greatest struggle was trying to stay focused. I knew what I wanted to pray about and I had my list, but distracting thoughts were a fierce competition. Every activity of the day was parading through my mind or pesky thoughts were reminding me of my many temptations. I would spend a lot of time rebuking Satan, assuming he was trying to distract me from my devotional life.

If prayer is so important, why is it so difficult?

In church we arranged our chairs in little circles. If the second person to pray happened to be seated by the first person who prayed, a pattern had been established: Each person would have to pray in turn as we went around the circle. But what if a person didn't pray when it was his turn and you were expected to follow that person? My thoughts were, 'Why isn't that guy praying? In the awkward silence I would wonder how long I should wait before I skipped him.

And did the next person to pray ever listen to the prayer of the previous person? Probably not. They were too concerned with what they were going to say when it was their turn. And then there was always the one who droned on and on and on, who everyone wished would stop praying! They never heard that long prayers are for the closet and short prayers are for public, and the devil will orchestrate the opposite.

When the opportunity came for me to pray the pastoral prayer in the morning service, it wasn't long before I realised, *I'm not talking to God, I'm talking to the people.* Initially, I was more conscious of the congregation's presence than I was of the presence of God. I found myself summarising the sermon or giving the week's announcements in the prayer: 'Dear Lord, bless our church picnic next Saturday at 9 am at the city park on the corner of Fifth and Central, and help us to remember that last names beginning with A through G are to bring salads.' That was no prayer; that was an announcement. One pastoral staff member would pray in King James English for so long that people were timing him: 'Would you believe eleven minutes this morning!'

I don't want to make fun of prayer, but where is the reality? When we pray publicly, what are we modelling?

Realising that prayer was important for our marriage my wife and I would spend time discussing what we needed to pray about: 'Let's pray about this, and we need to pray about this.' After a lengthy discussion, we would pray by going through the same list again, only this time we would include God. I began to wonder where God was the first time we went through the list!

I know that God accepts and appreciates even our feeble efforts, but I sometimes wonder what He thinks. He's probably saying, 'Why don't you just include Me from the begin-

ning?' or 'There they go around the prayer circle again.
Come on, people, get real!'

Pray with thanksgiving

I reached a turning point in my first ministry when I was
doing a series of lessons on prayer. The first five lessons
were theological, so I had little problem preparing for them,
and I had determined well in advance that the last lesson
would be, 'How to Pray in the Spirit.' But the night before
I was to give that talk, I became acutely aware that I didn't
have the foggiest idea how to pray in the Spirit. I was hours
away from giving a message I personally couldn't relate to.
I sat bankrupt before God. Those are special moments if
you never have been there!

Sometime before midnight the Lord began to direct my
thoughts through the Bible in one of the most important
evenings of my life. I reasoned, *If I'm going to pray in the
Spirit, I must be filled with the Spirit.* So I went to Ephesians
5:18–20:

> Do not get drunk with wine, for that is dissipation, but be
> filled with the Spirit, speaking to one another in psalms, and
> hymns and spiritual songs, singing and making melody in
> your heart to the Lord, always giving thanks for all things in
> the name of our Lord Jesus Christ, even the Father.

I leafed over to the parallel passage in Colossians
3:15–17:

> Let the peace of Christ rule in your hearts, to which indeed
> you were called in one body and be thankful, and let the
> Word of Christ richly dwell within you, with all wisdom,
> teaching and admonishing one another with psalms, and
> hymns, and spiritual songs, singing with thankfulness in
> your hearts to the Lord, and whatever you do in word or

deed, do all in the name of our Lord Jesus Christ giving thanks to Him and to God the Father.

I noticed that being filled with the Spirit and letting the Word of Christ richly dwell within us was closely associated with the concept of giving thanks. I looked ahead to Colossians 4:2: 'Devote yourselves to prayer keeping alert in it with an attitude of thanksgiving.' Then Philippians 4:6: 'Be anxious for nothing, but by prayer and supplication, with thanksgiving....' I turned to 1 Thessalonians 5:17,18: 'Prayer at all times without ceasing and in everything giving thanks for this is God's will for you in Christ Jesus.' Prayer and thanksgiving seemed to be bound together. That evening I walked through the Epistles and this is what I found:

I do not cease giving thanks for you while making mention of you in my prayers (Eph 1:16).

I thank my God in all my remembrance of you always offering prayer (Phil 1:3,4).

We give thanks to God the father of our Lord Jesus Christ, praying always for you (Col 1:3).

We give thanks to God always for all of you making mention of you in our prayers (1 Thess 1:2).

First of all then I urge that entreaties and prayers and petitions and thanksgivings be made on behalf of all men (1 Tim 2:1).

I thank God, whom I serve with a clear conscience, the way my forefathers did, as I constantly remember you in my prayers day and night (2 Tim 1:3).

I thank my God always making mention of you in my prayer (Philem 1:4).

I turned to one of my favourite Old Testament passages, Psalm 95:

Oh come let us sing for joy to the Lord, let us shout joyfully
to the Rock of our salvation, let us come before His presence
with thanksgiving. Let us shout joyfully to Him with psalms
for the Lord is a great God, and a great king above all Gods,
in whose hands are the depths of the earth, the peaks of the
mountains are His also, the sea is His for it was He who
made it and His hands formed the dry land. Come, let us
worship and bow down, let us kneel before the Lord our
maker, for He is our God and we are the people of His pasture and the sheep of His hand. Today if you would hear His
voice...

The last three words grabbed me: 'Hear His voice.' I
thought, *Today I'd love to hear Your voice!* Maybe I wasn't
hearing His voice because I wasn't coming before Him with
an attitude of thanksgiving.

In Psalm 95:7, the word *hear* is the Hebrew word *shema*,
which means to 'hear as to obey.' Verse 8 quickly follows,
'And do not harden your hearts.' I turned to Hebrews 4:7
which quotes Psalm 95: 'Today if you hear His voice, do not
harden your hearts.' I then read of the 'Sabbath rest that
remains' in Hebrews 4. It is an exhortation to cease trusting
in our own works and begin to trust in God's. Resting in the
finished work of Christ didn't typify my prayer time. I
became painfully aware that my prayer time was a work of
the flesh. It was not saturated with an attitude of thanksgiving and praise for all that He had, was and would do in
my life.

Praying what God wants prayed

That same night I turned to Romans 8:26,27:

In the same way the Spirit also helps our weakness, for we
do not know how to pray as we should, but the Spirit
Himself intercedes for us with groanings too deep for utter-

ance. And He who searches the heart knows what the mind
of the Spirit is, because He intercedes for the saints according to the will of God.

We really don't know how to pray or what to pray for,
but the Holy Spirit does and He will help us in our weakness. *Help* is a fascinating word in Greek (*sunantilambano*),
two prepositions placed in front of the word *take*. The Holy
Spirit comes along side, bears us up and takes us to the
other side. The Holy Spirit connects us with God. He intercedes for us on our behalf. The prayer that the Holy Spirit
prompts us to pray is the prayer that God the Father will
always answer.

How does the Holy Spirit help us in our weakness? I
didn't know, but I tried something that evening. I said,
'Okay, Lord, I'm setting aside my list, and I'm going to
assume that whatever comes to my mind during this time of
prayer is from You or allowed by You. I'm going to let You
set the agenda.' Whatever came to my mind that evening
was what I prayed about. If it was a tempting thought, I
talked to God about the area of weakness. If the busyness
of the day clamoured for attention, I discussed my plans
with God. I dealt with whatever came to my mind.

I wasn't passively letting thoughts control me, though. I
was actively taking every thought captive to the obedience
of Christ (2 Cor 10:5). Let me warn you that if you passively
listen to your thoughts, you may end up paying attention to
a deceiving spirit (1 Tim 4:1).

If my mind entertained a lying thought or an evil
thought I didn't ignore it. I brought it before the Lord. It
doesn't make any difference whether our thoughts come
from an external source or from our preprogrammed past
or from a deceiving spirit, we are still responsible to take
every thought captive to the obedience of Christ. If an evil
thought was coming from Satan, God was allowing it. In

my experience, it typically identified an area of weakness that I had not previously been honest with God about. God will allow us to get banged around by Satan until we bring our struggles before the only one who can resolve them.

In my personal prayer, I was trying to shove evil thoughts away without much success. When I brought them to the light, it was amazing how much freedom I had. All the issues I was trying to ignore during prayer were issues God wanted me to deal with. He wanted to make me aware of matters that were affecting our personal relationship. Now when there is a tempting thought, I go naked before God and don't try to hide my human frailty.

Warning: If you try this, you will find out how personal God really is. Now you know why the phrase, 'Today if you would hear His voice,' is followed by, 'Do not harden your heart.' If God determined and prioritised our prayer list, He would begin with personal issues that affect our relationship with Him. 'Come on,' God says. 'You keep telling others you have a personal relationship with Me. Let's get personal!'

I have challenged hundreds of seminary students to take a walk with God for forty-five minutes during class. They start their walk by thanking God for all He has done for them. I encourage them to take their Bible and a pad of paper to write down what comes to mind. I then instruct them to deal with those issues by bringing them before the Lord. If nothing comes to mind, they are to reflect upon God's goodness and thank Him for all He has done for them. I've had students return and tell me they have accomplished more in that forty-five minutes than they ever had in their prayer life before. Some have dealt with personal issues never before discussed with God. Almost all have found it a refreshing encounter.

God seeks intimacy with us

Fellowship with God is not an abstract theological concept, but a living relationship. Living in continuous agreement with God is to walk in the light: 'If we walk in the light as He Himself is in the light, we have fellowship with one another, and the blood of Jesus His Son cleanses us from all our sin' (1 Jn 1:7). Satan can't accuse me if I live in the light, but walking in the light is not moral perfection: 'If we say that we have no sin, we are deceiving ourselves' (1 Jn 1:8). The confession mentioned in 1 John 1:9 is agreeing with God about our present moral condition before Him.

What makes it possible to be this open with God about our condition is the fact that we are already His children. Our eternal state is not at stake, only our daily victory. We don't have to pretend with God in hopes that He will accept us. As children we're already accepted, so we are free to be honest with Him. We have no relationship to lose, only fellowship to gain. Knowing that we're secure in Christ, we can express ourselves honestly to Him. He already knows the thoughts and intentions of our hearts (Heb 4:12).

Have you ever wondered why it's so difficult to sit in the presence of God? God is our Father, and like any parent He doesn't appreciate grumbling, complaining children, especially since this Father sacrificed His only begotten Son for us. He will not be very interested in our list of demands if we haven't been obedient to Him. I also don't think He is going to be very interested in helping us develop our own kingdoms when we are to work at establishing the only one that will last — His!

To sit in the presence of my Father who loves me, who has made an incredible sacrifice so I can be there, doesn't have to be a dismal, failing experience. Listen to the heart of our heavenly Father:

For we do not have a high priest who cannot sympathise with our weaknesses, but one who has been tempted in all things as we are, yet without sin. Let us therefore draw near with confidence to the throne of grace that we may receive mercy and may find grace to help in the time of need (Heb 4:15,16).

Let us draw near with a sincere heart in full assurance of faith, having our hearts sprinkled clean from an evil conscience (Heb 10:22).

Rest assured that a personal God is first concerned about the condition of our hearts. He encourages us to pray, 'Our Father Who art in heaven.'

The natural progression of prayer

In my eighteen years of ministry, I have observed three approaches to prayer which progress from level to level. The first level is *petition*. We are encouraged to let our requests be made known to God (Phil 4:6,7), though some never get beyond personal petitions. Often our petitions reflect the burdens that God has placed on our hearts. If it helps us to keep a list of daily prayer reminders, we should do so. However, most people weary of this, and their devotional life disappears over time. Often they don't see immediate results from their prayers, so they conclude that more can be accomplished if they just get busy for the Lord.

Of the ones who persist, many are motivated by guilt because they know that prayer is a Christian duty. I'm convinced that God is pleased with their efforts, although they are not as effective as they could be. He certainly is more pleased with them than with those who quit.

We've progressed to the second level when prayer becomes *personal*. We have discovered a new dimension when we are comfortable in His presence and don't feel obliged to talk. It's much like a marriage relationship. A mature couple can ride together in the car for hours, enjoying each other's company without having to say a thing. But have you noticed how different it is when you're alone with a stranger? Silence is awkward.

It's okay to remain silent in God's presence. Realising that I need not feel obliged to keep the conversation going when I'm with God changed my prayer life dramatically. I can walk with God for as long as I walk in the light. I can commune with Him as I drive to work. This kind of prayer makes my relationship with God a 24-hour-a-day experience. Setting aside special times is still important, but when I leave my quiet times, God doesn't stay there and He doesn't go with me — rather I go with Him!

I call the third dimension of prayer *true intercession*. True intercessors hear from God. They know how to pray and what to pray for. In my observation there are very few intercessory prayer warriors. The ones I know are usually older than fifty, and most are ladies. They pray privately in their homes and often at night. God wakes them up, and they know who and what to pray for. These warriors often invite others for prayer in their home, and they'll pray through problems for as long as it takes. If you are a pastor, find out who the prayer warriors are in your congregation. Every church has at least one or two of them. Share your schedule and family needs with them. When these people pray, things happen.

Praise and thanksgiving are part of every level of prayer. They are continuous as we walk in the light. To come before God with thanksgiving is no different than coming before our earthly parents with an attitude of gratitude. Nothing disturbs a parent more than a child who is always demanding, forever complaining and never satisfied. How would you feel if you've given as much as you can as a parent and your child still wants more, more, more? On the other hand, how would you feel towards the child who snuggles up and says, 'Thanks for being who you are. I just love you and I know you're doing the best you can for me.' What a great parent-child relationship.

Praising God is simply describing His attributes. I try to be aware when I pray that God is the ever-present, all-powerful, all-knowing, loving heavenly Father. I don't praise Him because He needs me to tell Him who He is. He knows who He is. I am the one who needs to keep His divine attributes constantly in my mind. And the knowledge of God's presence is foremost in my thoughts. No matter where I go, He is with me.

I'm always disturbed when I hear people asking God to 'be there.' What a blatant denial of His omnipresence. The same goes for asking God to be with our missionaries. We have the assurance of Scripture that He will be with them unto the ends of the earth. We can confidently acknowledge that He will neither leave us nor forsake us. We ought to thank God for His presence and ask Him to bring to our minds anything that may be keeping us from having perfect fellowship with Him.

Choosing truth, dispelling darkness
When prayer becomes personal, the Christian life corresponds with the level of growth depicted in 1 John 2:14:

> I write to you, young men, because you are strong, and the word of God lives in you, and you have overcome the evil one (NIV).

Until you have overcome the evil one, you may not have a lot of mental peace. If you are attempting to deal with deceiving thoughts by trying to rebuke them, you'll be like the person treading water in the middle of the ocean whose whole life purpose is to keep twelve corks which are bobbing close by submerged with a little hammer!

Acknowledge the presence of the corks, but ignore them and swim to shore! Don't pay attention to deceiving spirits.

The whole thrust of Scripture is to choose truth. We dispel the darkness by turning on the light. If you are plagued by tempting thoughts, bring the issue before God and seek to resolve that which is keeping you from having perfect fellowship with Him. The devil isn't the primary issue — he is only taking advantage of the fact that your fellowship with God has been broken. James 4:7 has the right priorities: 'Submit therefore to God. Resist the devil and he will flee from you.' The primary issue is to submit to God.

Satan knows that if he can keep our minds distracted, we won't have much of a prayer life with God. Prayer is the vital link for God's guidance. If we are going to walk with God through the darkness, we must have the peace of God which surpasses all comprehension and guards our hearts and minds in Christ Jesus (Phil 4:7). It is beyond the scope of this book to describe how that can be achieved, but I have sought to do that in my two previous books, *Victory Over the Darkness* and *The Bondage Breaker*.

Take a look at 1 John 2:12–14. 'Little children' of the faith have not learned how to overcome the evil one. They are at the petition level of prayer. 'Fathers' are those who have a deep experiential knowledge of God. They have known Him from the beginning (1 Jn 2:13). To them everything begins with God and nothing that lasts starts without Him. They walk with a personal God and they pray without ceasing. They have reached the intercession level of prayer.

We need to understand where we are in our relationship with God in order to know how to ward off the devil's schemes. An undergraduate student stopped by my office to ask some questions about Satanism. I answered some of her questions and then said, 'I don't think you should be researching this.' She asked, 'Why not?' I answered,

'Because you're not free.' Surprised by my straightforward-ness, she said, 'What do you mean by that?' I responded, 'I'm sure you struggle with your devotional life, and your prayer life is probably zero. You probably have difficulty paying attention in your Bible classes, and I'm pretty sure your self-esteem is down in the mud. You may even enter-tain suicide thoughts.' Surprised, she asked, 'How do you know that?' She told her friend later, 'That guy read my mind.'

I didn't read her mind, but I've counselled lots of people who have not overcome the evil one. Most have not under-stood the battle going on for their minds and they've got in over their heads. I encouraged this student to take my class on spiritual conflicts and biblical counselling. After the class, she wrote me this letter:

> I guess I was expecting an emotionally moving experi-ence. But what I've discovered this last week is a feel-ing of control, like my mind is my own. I haven't had my usual strung-out periods of thought and contemplation. My mind simply feels quieted
>
> It really is a strange feeling. My emotions have been stable. I haven't felt depressed once this week. My will is mine. I feel like I have been able to choose to live my life abiding in Christ.
>
> Scripture seems different. I have a totally new perspective. I actually understand what it is saying. I feel left alone, but not in a bad way. I'm not lonely, just a single person. For the first time, I believe I actually understand what it means to be a Christian, who Christ is and who I am in Him. I feel capable of helping people and capable of handling myself.
>
> I've been a co-dependent for years, but this last week I haven't had the slightest feeling or need for someone. I guess I'm describing what it is like to be at

peace. I feel this quiet, soft joy in my heart. I have been more friendly and comfortable with strangers. It hasn't been a struggle to get through the day. And I have been participating actively in life and not merely passively, critically watching it. Thank you for lending me your hope. I believe I have my own now in Christ.

Having overcome the evil one, she is a 'young woman' in her relationship with God (1 Jn 2:14). Because of her mental peace, she is experiencing the guidance of God in her daily life. Finding freedom in Christ is what allows people to relate personally to God in prayer.

If you hear His voice, don't harden your heart. Deal with issues He brings to your mind, and take every thought captive to the obedience of Christ.

If it's your desire to actively pursue God and find out just how personal He really is, would you pray with me?

Dear Heavenly Father, I want my heart sprinkled clean so I can come boldly before Your throne of grace. Forgive me for ever shutting You out of my life. Search me, O God, try me and see if there is any hurtful way in me. Lead me in an everlasting way. I want to walk in the light as You are in the light. I bring my life before You as an open book, realising that You already know the thoughts and intentions of my heart. I trust my entire life to You. Amen.

15
Walking Through
The Darkness

Why does God lead us down faith-testing paths?

The life led by the Spirit of God is marvellous. Sensing His presence, living victoriously and knowing the truth are characteristics of a free person. But what if you couldn't sense His presence? What if God, for some reason, suspended His blessing? What would you do if you were faithfully following God and suddenly all external circumstances turned sour?

Job was enjoying the benefits of living righteously when, unexpectedly, it was all taken away. Health, wealth, family — all gone! If we found ourselves in Job's shoes, our minds would spin with questions:

'What did I do to deserve this?'

'Did I miss a turn in the road?'

'Is this what I get for living a righteous life?'

'Where is God?'

'God, why are You doing this to me?'

And like Job, we may even feel like cursing the day we were born.

My family and I have been through two extremely dark periods in our lives. There were days I wasn't sure if we were going to make it. If it weren't for the message of Isaiah 50:10,11, I'm not sure we would have spiritually survived:

> Who is among you that fears the Lord, that obeys the voice
> of His servant, that walks in darkness and has no light? Let

him trust in the name of the Lord, and rely on his God. Behold all you who kindle a fire, who encircle yourselves with firebrands, walk in the light of your fire, and among the brands you have set ablaze, this you will have from My hand, and you will lie down in torment.

Isaiah is asking if there is a believer, somebody who fears the Lord, who walks in darkness. But he is not referring to the darkness of sin, or even the darkness of this world. He is talking about the darkness of uncertainty — that blanket of heaviness that settles in as though a black cloud has drifted over our very being. The assurance of yesterday has been replaced by the uncertainties of tomorrow. God has suspended His conscious blessings. Church has become a dismal experience. Friends seem more like a bother than a blessing.

What is a person to do during these times? What's the purpose? Why would this happen to a true believer? Using Isaiah 50:10,11 as our guide, we'll look at what a Christian should and should not do when he finds himself walking through the darkness of uncertainty. And we'll discuss how God leads (and why He would lead) us down such a faith-testing path.

Never stop

One of the most important things Isaiah tells us is that, no matter how dark it gets, we are to keep on walking.

In the light we can see the next step. The path ahead is clear. We know a friend from an enemy, and we can see where the obstacles are. But when darkness settles in, every natural instinct says to drop out, sit down, stop! We begin to doubt the truth of the Word that had been a lamp unto our feet. We become fearful of the next step.

Isaiah encourages us that, no matter how dark it gets, we are to keep on walking.

I wrote earlier about an exciting church building programme where God had obviously guided us to a new property and enabled the construction of new facilities. Few are
the times when God so dramatically leads as He did in that
situation. Usually it's more subtle and sometimes it doesn't
seem like He's guiding us at all — as the months following
that miracle showed me.

After the building programme was finished, God
released me from that pastorate. I was nearing the end of
my doctoral studies and facing the major task of a dissertation. I also knew that my seminary education was not quite
complete. I resigned in the summer and began one of the
most difficult educational years of my life. In one year I
completed forty-three semester units, seventeen of them foreign language (Greek and Hebrew). In the middle of the
year I took my comprehensive exams and by the end of the
year I had finished my doctoral dissertation. I also taught
part-time at Talbot School of Theology. A back-breaking
year to say the least.

Joanne and I started that year with the assurance that
$20,000 would be made available for our use interest free.
Our plan was to pay off the loan when we sold our home
after I graduated and found a ministry. Upon completion of
my education, I was confident God would have a place for
us in His kingdom plan. So I proceeded with a great deal of
anticipation of finishing my doctorate and a second master's degree. For the next six months our life unfolded as
planned.

Then God turned out the light.

News came that the second half of the $20,000 wasn't
going to come in. I had no job and my educational goals
were only half-completed at best. I always considered
myself a dependable, faithful man, but now I was on the
brink of not being able to provide for the basic needs of my
family. Having no other source of income, our cupboards

became bare. I had been so certain of God's calling six months earlier, but now my confidence was shaken.

Everything came to a head two weeks before my comprehensive exams. Only ten per cent of the doctoral candidates had passed the previous testing, so there was a lot of pressure. If I didn't pass the exams, I couldn't start my dissertation, and I had already invested three years and $15,000 in the programme. And at this point I didn't even know where my next meal would come from. I had equity in my home, but interest rates at the time were so high that houses simply weren't selling. I looked into a couple of ministry opportunities, but they weren't for me and I knew I couldn't accept them. The problem wasn't an unwillingness to work — I would have sold sausages to provide for my family.

I wanted God's will!

I began to wonder if I had made the wrong decision. His leading was so clear the past summer, so why all the doubts now? Why this darkness? It was as though God had dropped me into a funnel and the farther I fell, the darker it became. When I thought it couldn't get any darker, I hit the narrow part. Then at the absolute darkest hour, God dropped me out of the bottom of that funnel and everything became clear.

About 2 am on a Thursday morning the dawn broke. Nothing changed circumstantially, but everything changed internally. I remember waking up and jumping up and down on the bed. My startled wife woke up and wondered what was going on, but she, too, could sense something had taken place. There was a conscious awareness of God in a remarkable way. Without audible voices or visions, God, in His quiet and gentle way, renewed my mind: *Neil, do you walk by faith or do you walk by sight? Can you walk by faith now? You believed Me last summer. Do you believe Me now? Neil, do you love Me or do you love My blessings? Do you*

worship Me for who I am or do you worship Me for the bless-
ings I bring? What if I suspended My conscious presence in
your life? Would you still believe in Me?

I knew I would. In my spirit I responded, 'Lord, You
know I love You, and I walk by faith, not by sight. Lord, I
worship You because of who You are, and I know that You
will never leave me nor forsake me. Forgive me, Lord, that I
ever doubted Your place in my life or questioned Your ability to provide for all our needs.'

Precious moments like these can't be planned or predicted. They're never repeatable. What we have previously
learned from the Bible becomes incarnate during these
times. Our worship is purified and our love clarified. Faith
moves from a textbook definition to a living reality. Trust is
deepened when God puts us in a position where we have no
other choice but to trust. We truly learn to live by faith
when circumstances are not working favourably for us.

Do I need to share what happened the next day? The
dean of Talbot School of Theology phoned to ask if I had
taken another position. He asked me not to accept anything
until we had the opportunity to talk. That Friday afternoon
he offered me the position I've held for the past eight years.

Friday evening a man from my previous ministry
stopped by at 10 pm. When I asked him what he was doing
at our home at that hour of the night, he said he wasn't sure.
I invited him in with the assurance, 'We'll figure out something.' I half jokingly asked him if he'd like to buy my house
and he responded, 'Maybe I would.' The next Tuesday he
and his parents made an offer on our house which we
accepted. Now we could sell our house because we knew
where we were heading.

Nothing had changed externally before that morning,
but everything had changed internally. In a moment, God
can change what circumstances can never change.

My wife and I had previously made a commitment

together that helped sustain us during the hard times: We will never make a major decision when we are down. That alone has kept me from resigning after difficult board meetings or not-so-perfect messages. The point is, never doubt in darkness what God has clearly shown in the light. We are to keep on walking in the light of previous revelation. If it was true six months ago, it's still true. If we're serious about our walk with God, He will test us to determine whether we love Him or His blessings. He may cloud the future so we can learn to walk by faith and not by sight or feelings.

Understand that God has not left us; He has only suspended His conscious presence so that our faith will not rest on feelings or be established by unique experiences or blessings. Suppose when we were children our parents found themselves in difficult financial circumstances and we didn't get any Christmas presents. Would we stop loving them? Would we stop looking to them for direction and support? Of course not.

If God's ministry of darkness should envelop you, listen to Isaiah's advice: Keep on walking.

The consequences of doing it your way

Isaiah's next piece of advice is a warning of what not to do when the way gets dark: Don't light your own fire. The natural tendency when we don't see it God's way is to do it our way. Resist the urge to create your own light.

Notice the text again: 'Behold all you who kindle a fire, who encircle yourselves with firebrands, walk in the light of your fire.' God is not talking about the fire of judgement; He's talking about fire that creates light. Notice what happens when people create their own light: 'And among the brands you have set ablaze, this you will have from My hand, you will lie down in torment.' Go ahead, do it your own way. God will allow it, but misery will follow.

Let me illustrate from the Bible. God called Abraham

out of Ur into the promised land. In Genesis 12, a covenant was made in which God promised Abraham that his descendants would be more numerous than the sands of the sea or the stars in the sky. Abraham lived his life in the light of that promise, then God turned out the light.

So many years passed that his wife Sarah could no longer bear a child by natural means. God's guidance had been so clear before, but now it looked like Abraham would have to assist God in its fulfilment. Who could blame Abraham for creating his own light? Sarah supplied the match by offering her handmaiden to Abraham. Out of that union came the Arab nation which has been in conflict with the Jewish nation ever since.

Moses tried to create his own light. God superintended his birth and provided for his preservation. Raised in the home of Pharaoh, Moses was given the second most prominent position in Egypt. But God had put a burden on his heart to set his people free. Impulsively Moses pulled out his sword and God turned out the light. Abandoned to the back side of the desert, Moses spent forty years tending his father-in-law's sheep. Then one day, Moses turned to see a burning bush that wasn't consumed. God had turned the light back on.

I'm not suggesting that we will have to wait forty years, but our darkness may last for weeks, months and possibly, for some exceptional people, even years. God is in control and He knows exactly how big a knothole He can pull us through. When we are stretched to our limit, He pulls us out the other side.

After the night, the day

Our second period of darkness occurred a number of years ago when my wife developed cataracts in both eyes and slowly lost her sight. She had two operations within four months, but because she couldn't have lens implants, she had to be fitted with cataract glasses and finally contacts. Five years later, technological advances allowed her to have implant surgery.

The surgery was successful, but Joanne didn't recover physically or emotionally. She became fearful, paranoid and depressed. For months she went from doctor to doctor. Because she was forty-five years old, most of the doctors wanted to declare her a head case or a hormone case. She was neither. All they could figure out to do was to fill her full of tranquillisers and sleeping pills. She was hospitalised five times.

Needless to say, this whole process became exceedingly expensive. Our insurance ran out and we had to sell our house to pay the medical bills. I struggled with what my role should be in relation to my wife. Should I be her pastor, counsellor or husband? I decided there was only one role I could fulfil in her life, and that was to be her husband. If someone was going to fix my wife, it would have to be someone other than myself. My role was to hold her every day and say, 'Joanne, someday this will pass.' I was thinking it would be a matter of a few weeks or months, but it turned into a long, fifteen month ordeal.

During this dark time, Isaiah 21:11,12 was very meaningful to me:

> One keeps calling to me from Seir, 'Watchman, how far gone is the night? Watchman, how far gone is the night?' The watchman says, 'Morning comes but also night.'

I base my life on the hope that morning comes. No matter how dark the night, morning comes. And it's always darkest before the dawn. At our darkest moments, I wasn't even sure Joanne was going to make it.

We had a day of prayer at Biola University. I had nothing to do with the programme other than to set aside spe-

cial time for prayer in my classes. In the evening the undergraduate students had a communion service. I hadn't
planned on going, but since work had detained me on campus I decided to participate. I sat on the gym floor with the
undergrad students and took communion.

I'm sure nobody in the student body was aware that it
was one of the loneliest times of my life. I was deeply committed to doing God's will, and I was walking as best I
could in the light of previous revelation, but I felt abandoned. God had stripped my family of everything we
owned. All we had left was each other and our relationship
to God.

But when there was nowhere else to turn, morning came!

If God has ever spoken to my heart, He did in that communion service. It didn't come through the pastor's message
or the testimonies of the students, but it did come in the
context of taking communion. I suppose the essence was
this: *Neil, there's a price to pay for freedom. It cost My Son
His life. Are you willing to pay the price?*

'Dear God,' I prayed, 'if that's the reason, I'm willing.
But if it's some stupid thing I'm doing, then I don't want to
be a part of It any more.' I left with the inner assurance that
it was over. The circumstances hadn't changed, but in my
heart I knew that morning had come.

Later that week Joanne woke up one morning and said,
'Neil, I slept last night.' Sixteen days before, she had visited
a family practice doctor who specialised in the treatment of
clinical depression. He got her off the medication that had
been prescribed by other doctors and treated her chemical
imbalance with proper medication. On that morning she
knew she was finally on the road to recovery. She never
looked back and continued on to full and complete health.

Learning true resources

You may be asking, 'What's the point of the dark times? What's God trying to do? What's He trying to teach us?'

In God's ministry of darkness, we learn a lot about ourselves. Whatever was left of my old nature that gave simplistic advice such as, 'Read your Bible' or 'Just work harder' or 'Pray more,' was mercifully stripped away. Most people going through dark times would love to do the right thing, but many can't and don't know why.

In God's ministry of darkness we learn compassion. We learn to wait patiently with people. We learn to respond to the emotional needs of people who have lost hope. We weep with those who weep. We don't try to teach or instruct or advise. We had some 'friends' advise us in our time of darkness, and I can tell you it hurts.

Job had friends like that. In his hour of darkness Job needed a few good friends to just sit with him. His friends did that for one week and then their patience ran out. The meaningful help Joanne and I received was from people who just stood by us and prayed.

If God took away every external blessing and reduced our assets to nothing more than meaningful relationships, would that be enough to sustain us? Yes, I believe it would.

In our case, within two years God replaced everything we lost. And this time it was far better in terms of home, family and ministry. Be encouraged: God makes everything right in the end.

Perhaps God brings us to the end of our resources so we can discover the vastness of His. We don't hear many sermons about brokenness in our churches these days, yet in all four Gospels Jesus taught us to deny ourselves, pick up our cross daily and follow Him. When it was time for the Son of Man to be glorified, He said: 'Truly, truly I say to you, unless a grain of wheat falls into the ground and dies, it remains by itself alone; but if it dies it bears much fruit' (Jn

12:24). I don't know any painless way to die to ourselves, but I do know that it's necessary and that it's the best possible thing that could ever happen to us: 'For we who live are constantly being delivered over to death for Jesus' sake, that the life of Jesus also may be manifested in our mortal flesh' (2 Cor 4:11).

If we are relying on degrees, diplomas, status and self-confidence, God is going to strip that confidence away. Paul had to learn that power is perfected in weakness:

> Beloved, do not be surprised at the fiery ordeal among you which comes upon you for your testing as though some strange thing were happening to you. But to the degree that you share the sufferings of Christ, keep on rejoicing, so that also at the revelation of His glory you may rejoice with exaltation (1 Pet 4:12).

We need the attitude of the early church, who rejoiced because they were considered worthy to suffer shame for His name (Acts 5:41). Are we afraid of the truth in 2 Timothy 3:12: 'And indeed all who desire to live godly in Christ Jesus will suffer'?

'No pain, no gain,' says the body builder. Isn't that true in the spiritual realm as well? 'All discipline for the moment seems not to be joyful, but sorrowful; yet to those who have been trained by it, afterwards it yields the peaceful fruit of righteousness' (Heb 12:11). Proven character comes from persevering through the tribulations of life (Rom 5:3–5).

Maybe the ultimate purpose of walking in darkness is to learn to trust in the Lord, Isaiah says, 'Let him trust in the name of the Lord and rely on His name' (Is 50:10). Every great period of growth in my life and ministry has been preceded by a major time of testing.

Learning to wait

Possibly the greatest sign of spiritual maturity is the ability to postpone rewards. The ultimate test would be to receive nothing in this lifetime, but to look forward to receiving our reward in the life to come. The writer of Hebrews expresses it this way:

> All these died in faith without receiving the promises, but having seen them and having welcomed them from a distance and having confessed that they were strangers and exiles on this earth, for those who say such things, make it clear that they are seeking a country of their own.... And all these having gained approval through their faith did not receive what was promised because God had provided something better for us, so that apart from us they should not be made perfect (Heb 11:13,39).

If I had known beforehand what my family would have to go through to get where we are today, I probably wouldn't have come. But looking back, we all say, 'We're glad we came.' Remember, God makes everything right in the end, though it may not even be in this lifetime. I believe with all my heart that when life is done and we're looking back, we will be able to say that the will of God is good, acceptable and perfect.

It is not the critic who counts, nor the man who points how the strong man stumbled, or where the doer of deeds could have done better. The credit belongs to the man who is actually in the arena, whose face is marred by the dust and sweat and blood; who strives valiantly; who errs and comes short again and again; who knows the great enthusiasms, the great devotions, and spends himself in a worthy cause; who at best, knows in the end the triumph of high achievement; and who, at the worst, if he fails, at least fails while daring greatly, so that his place shall never be with those cold and timid souls who know neither victory or defeat.

— Theodore Roosevelt

We may be in the arena, but we don't have to fear the outcome of the battle. I can say that with confidence. The battle is not ours; it is the Lord's. We have His truth and He has made every provision for us. Satan has no place in our lives. The Holy Spirit will guide us in the continuing experience of God's will for our lives.

I will not close this chapter as I have done before with a suggested prayer. Instead, it is just my prayer that your heart will be filled with words that you would now want to express to your Lord — words of praise, words of pain, words of commitment, words about knowing God's truth and His will in the New Age.

Would you now pray?

Book 2
**LIVING FREE
IN CHRIST**

Acknowledgements

I'm indebted to Ron and Carole Wormser, my tireless partners in ministry. They did the serious editing and offered valuable feedback. I deeply appreciate Dr Robert Saucy for reading the manuscript and caring enough to ask the tough theological questions.

Roger McNichols, our manager at Freedom in Christ Ministries, coordinated the project. His mother, Laura McNichols, typed much of the manuscript from audiotapes I recorded as I travelled to and from conferences.

I can't thank Bill Greig Jr. and his staff enough for supporting my ministry. He and the entire family at Gospel Light have been an inspiration to me. You're all great and easy to work with.

My dear wife, Joanne, endured yet another one of my projects. She is my companion for life and makes my ministry possible, real and relevant. She is always there to verify, validate and vindicate what this book has to say.

To my daughter, Heidi, and new son-in-law, Keith Anderson, I dedicate this book. You are starting a new journey in life together with the joyful blessing of both sets of your parents. May the message of this book be what keeps you together in Christ.

Introduction

I am thankful for my heritage. I was born and raised on a farm in Minnesota, where I walked a mile to a country school for my first six years of education. My social life revolved totally around my family, school, and church. Church was a regular experience for me, but somehow during those formative years of my life, I was never confronted with the need to make a decision about my relationship to Christ. I never really understood what the gospel was all about. I was twenty-five-years-old before I finally realised who God is and why Jesus came. It would be another fifteen years before I finally realised who I am as a child of God.

Tragically, most Christians *never* come to appreciate who they are in Christ. From the time of birth we are programmed by our environment and the people in our lives. We interpret the meaning of life's experiences through the grid of our personal orientation and react accordingly. For the many who have experienced rejection, abandonment or abuse from earliest childhood, entrenched in their belief system is an attitude that says, 'I am of no value,' 'I don't measure up,' 'I am unlovable.' Even those of us whose childhood seemed wholesome have been victimised in some way by the enemy's subtle deceptions.

Without exception, all the people I have counselled have had some unscriptural belief the enemy has used to keep them in bondage. It is important to recognise faulty beliefs from the past, to renounce them as lies, and to reprogramme and renew our minds with truth.

Physically alive, spiritually dead

Genesis 2:7 says, 'The Lord God formed the man from the dust of the ground and breathed into his nostrils the breath of life, and the man became a living being.' Adam was alive in two ways: First, he was alive physically — his soul, or soul-spirit, was in union with his physical body. Second, he was alive spiritually — his soul, or soul-spirit, was in union with God.

In Genesis 2:16,17 we read, 'The Lord God commanded the man, "You are free to eat from any tree in the garden; but you must not eat from the tree of the knowledge of good and evil, for when you eat of it you will surely die."' Well, Adam disobeyed God, and he ate of that tree. Did he die physically? Not initially, although the physical process of dying did begin, but he died spiritually, and it was dramatically realised by his separation from God.

From that time on, everyone born into this world is physically alive but spiritually dead, separated from God. Before coming to Christ, we had neither the presence of God in our lives nor the knowledge of His ways, so we learned to live independently of Him. Ephesians 2:1 says, 'As for you, you were dead in your transgressions and sins.' What does it mean that we were dead? Were we dead physically? Of course not, but we were dead spiritually, we were separated from God.

Jesus came to remove that separation. He said in John 10:10, 'I have come that they might have life, and have it to the full.' In the early years of my Christian experience, I thought eternal life was something I got when I died, but 1 John 5:11,12 says, 'And this is the testimony: God has given us eternal life, and this life is in his Son. He who has the Son has life; he who does not have the Son of God does not have life.' Every Christian is alive in Christ *right now*. To be alive means that your soul is in union with God. Throughout the New Testament you will repeatedly see the truth that you

are in Christ or that Christ is in you. It is this life that gives
us our essential identity.

Our new identity

Colossians 3:10,11 says we 'have put on the new self, which
is being renewed in knowledge in the image of its Creator.
Here there is no Greek or Jew, circumcised or uncircumcised, barbarian, Scythian, slave or free, but Christ is all,
and is in all.'

In other words, how we formerly identified ourselves no
longer applies. When asked to describe themselves, people
usually mention race, religion, cultural background or
social distinctions. But Paul said none of those apply anymore, because our identity is no longer determined by our
physical heritage, social standing or racial distinctions. Our
identity lies in the fact that we are all children of God and
we are *in Christ*.

Although I am thankful for my physical heritage, I am
far more grateful for my spiritual heritage. The practical
significance of this essential truth cannot be overstated. A
Christian gains forgiveness, receives the Holy Spirit, puts on
a new nature and gets to go to heaven. A Christian, in terms
of his or her deepest identity, is also a saint, a child born of
God, a divine masterpiece, a child of light, a citizen of
heaven.

'But you are a chosen people, a royal priesthood, a holy
nation, a people belonging to God, that you may declare
the praises of him who called you out of darkness into his
wonderful light. Once you were not a people, but now you
are the people of God, once you had not received mercy, but
now you have received mercy' (1 Pet 2:9,10).

At a conference I conducted several years ago, a missionary attended who was required to come back from the
field because of deep emotional problems. She had a very
difficult childhood, having been raised in a dysfunctional

family. At the conference, she realised for the first time who she was in Christ and resolved her spiritual conflicts. It was as though she was born again.

When she went home to her family some time later, she heard even more devastating news about her upbringing. She made an appointment with me and told me about the family problems she was having. I commented to her, 'Aren't you glad that you learned this new information after you found out who you are as a child of God?'

She responded, 'Oh, if I had heard this about my family two months ago, it would have been the final blow.'

I said, 'Now that you know this about your family, what does that do to your heritage?'

She started to answer. Then a smile broke across her face and she said, 'Nothing!'

She realised she is a child of God and had appropriated the truth of 2 Corinthians 5:17: 'Therefore, if anyone is in Christ, he is a new creation, the old has gone, the new has come!'

Learning our new identity

We are no longer products of our past. We are primarily products of Christ's work on the cross. But remember, when we were dead in our trespasses and sins, we had learned to live our life independently of God. Our identity and perception of ourselves were formed and programmed into our minds through the natural orders of this world. That's why Paul says in Romans 12:2, 'Do not conform any longer to the pattern of this world, but be transformed by the renewing of your mind. Then you will be able to test and approve what God's will is — his good, pleasing and perfect will.'

Renewing our minds does not come naturally; there is no automatic 'delete button' that erases past programming. We have to know the Word of God consciously so that we can understand who we are from God's perspective. And who are we? As 1 John 3:1–3 says, 'How great is the love the Father has lavished on us, that we should be called children of God! And that is what we are! The reason the world does not know us is that it did not know him. Dear friends, now we are children of God, and what we will be has not yet been made known. But we know that when he appears, we shall be like him, for we shall see him as he is. Everyone who has this hope in him purifies himself, just as he is pure.'

Who we are determines what we do

The most important belief we possess is a true knowledge of who God is. The second most important belief is who we are as children of God, because we cannot consistently behave in a way that is inconsistent with how we perceive ourselves. And if we do not see ourselves as God sees us, then to that degree we suffer from a wrong identity and a poor image of who we really are.

It is not what we do that determines who we are. It is who we are that determines what we do, as illustrated by a letter I received from a missionary:

> I am writing in response to reading *Victory over the Darkness*. I am sure you have received many letters, at least I hope you have, because that means people like me have had their eyes opened to God's truth.
>
> I am a missionary, and even though I have been a Christian for twenty-one years, I never understood God's forgiveness and my spiritual inheritance. I have been bulimic since 1977. I was in Bible college at the time I began this horrible practice. I never thought this living hell would end. I have wanted to die, and I would have killed myself had I not thought that was a sin. I felt God had turned His back on me and I was doomed to hell because I couldn't overcome this sin. I hated myself. I felt like a failure.

But the Lord led me to purchase your book and bring it with me. I began reading it last week. I feel like a new Christian, like I have just been born again. My eyes are now open to God's love. I realise I am a saint who sins, not a sinner. I can finally say I am free, free of Satan's bondage and aware now of the lies he has been filling me with. Before, I would confess to God and beg His forgiveness when I binged and purged. Yet the next time, I fell deeper into Satan's grasp because I couldn't forgive myself, and I couldn't accept God's forgiveness. I also thought the answer lay in drawing closer to God, yet I went to Him in fear and confusion, acting as a sinner who couldn't be loved. No more!

Through the Scriptures and the way you presented them, I am no longer a defeated Christian. I don't consider myself a bulimic; I consider myself a saint, salt of the earth, Christ's friend, a slave of righteousness. Food has no power over me. Satan has lost his grip on me.

This missionary's testimony is typical of the hundreds of people I have had the privilege of counselling. As these troubled people shared their stories with me, one common thread was woven throughout: None of them knew who they were as children of God. They had no personal, internal sense of their identity in Christ.

We are not 'sinners in the hands of an angry God'! It is my prayer that you will see clearly what the Bible teaches — that every child of God is a saint held securely in the hands of a loving God.

Satan doesn't want you to know

This section is broken into three parts; each part contains a number of verses related to the section topics: Our Acceptance, Our Security and Our Significance in Christ.

Each of the verses in these three parts will broaden your concept of what it means to be a child of God.

Probably the most common question I receive from people who have read and been blessed by *Victory over the Darkness* and *The Bondage Breaker* is: 'Now I understand the power of my identity in Christ. As well, the Lord has broken the bondage in my life. But how do I remind myself of my position in Christ? It's so easy to forget!'

It *is* easy to forget our position in Christ. Why? Because Satan doesn't want you to be free. How do you live each day consciously aware and active as a child of God? First and foremost, through Bible reading, prayer and fellowship. As well, this book can help you remember — on a daily basis — your wonderful position in Christ.

I am burdened for those who have never discovered their identity in Christ nor the freedom He brings. 'My God will meet all your needs according to His glorious riches in Christ Jesus' (Phil 4:19). Our tendency is to think only of our physical needs, but the critical needs are the 'being' needs, and they are the ones most wonderfully met *in* Christ.

The secular world has identified these needs but is pitifully inadequate to meet them. Trying to pick ourselves up by our own bootstraps or stroking one another's ego is not going to get it done. What a privilege we have to tell the world how Christ has come to meet our most critical and foundational needs: identity, acceptance, security and significance.

It is my prayer that at the conclusion of this book you will have entered into the experience assured us in Galatians 4:6,7, 'Because you are sons, God sent the Spirit of his Son into our hearts, the Spirit who calls out, "*Abba*, Father." So you are no longer a slave, but a son; and since you are a son, God has made you also an heir.' In other words, I'm praying that you will experience a bonding relationship with your heavenly Father. This may be the primary role of the Holy Spirit. 'The Spirit himself testifies with our spirit that we are God's children' (Rom 8:16).

As you read, study and meditate upon the meaning of these passages, be aware that Satan does not want you to know this. You may actually struggle in your thought life with opposing arguments about what God has to say about who you are. Let me encourage you to stand against that. If a lie is formed in your mind that is contrary to what the Bible says, then renounce that lie and accept God's truth. If possible, say aloud the prayers at the end of each chapter.

As well, at the back of the book I have included a list of Scripture truths regarding who we are in Christ. This is a composite list to help you remember your position as a child of God. You may want to tear out this page and keep it in your Bible, or place it on your refrigerator or bathroom mirror. Don't let the enemy blind you to the truth of your precious identity!

One person suggested, 'I would be prideful if I believed all these verses about myself.' The answer is, 'No, you would be defeated if you didn't.' You are not who you are in Christ because of the things you have done, you are in Christ because of what He has done. He died and rose again so that you and I could live in the freedom of His love.

16
I Am Accepted

*'Accept one another, then, just as Christ accepted
you, in order to bring praise to God.'*   ROMANS 15:7

Rejection is one of the most painful experiences known to
humanity. Years ago, I was having a devotional time with
my children when I raised the question, 'What is rejection?'
My daughter, Heidi, gave a nice answer, but my son, Karl,
followed by nailing the issue right on the heart. He said, 'I
know, rejection is when Johnny won't play with me any
more and I have to play with Heidi.' Unconditional love and
acceptance is one of the most basic needs of all humanity.

Striving for acceptance
Notice the children around you. From earliest childhood,
you can see them striving for acceptance and the approval
of 'significant others' in their lives. 'Do you like my picture,
Mummy?' 'Did I play well, Daddy?' The social system in
which most of us were raised gave us the impression that if
we appeared good, performed well or had a certain amount
of social status, we would finally be somebody. But try as we
might to gain approval, we always come up short. Whatever
pinnacle of self-identity we are able to achieve eventually
crumbles under the pressure of rejection or the criticism of
self-condemnation.

   We cannot do anything to qualify for unconditional and
voluntary love. We labour under the false assumption that

if we live perfectly everybody will accept us, while there was One who lived His life perfectly, and everybody rejected Him.

I regularly meet mature adults who still struggle for the approval of their parents or others. Ultimately, they compromise their spiritual integrity to avoid the rejection of man, as the following letter illustrates:

I came from a Christian family, and though there was a lot of bickering and hostility between my parents, I think I had an average childhood.

Everyone always said I looked like my dad, but unfortunately, my mother was often angry at my dad and resented his family. Many times, when I displeased my mother, she would say I was just like my father's sister, the one she often criticised.

My parents provided for our needs well and intellectually I knew I was loved, but the feeling and assurance of being totally accepted and okay always seemed to escape me. Even after thirty-five years of marriage and several grandchildren of my own, I was still subconsciously trying to earn my mother's approval and prove my love to her, resulting in many arguments between my husband and myself.

I first realised unconditional love at the age of fourteen when I understood Christ's invitation in Revelation 3:20 and began a personal walk with Him. I was overwhelmed by His love, devoured Scripture and witnessed to all of my friends. I have never consciously chosen to leave that precious relationship, but as I look back on my life I see how Satan has attacked me in my most vulnerable area, the need to know total love and acceptance.

During our years of marriage and a lifetime of ministry, I have been on some rabbit trails because I did not realise who I am in Christ. I have listened to negative thoughts against myself, thinking they were my own. I did not realise that Satan can use our past experiences and put thoughts in our minds to condemn and defeat us.

Neil, what blessed news to hear your teaching on our identity in Christ. I am no longer a product of my past, I am a product of the work of Christ on the cross. I know who I am now. I'm a child of God, and the basis for my acceptance is in Him, not in man. I got the chills when we sang the words of the theme song of your conference, 'Resolving Personal and Spiritual Conflicts':

'In the Beloved' accepted am I,
Risen, ascended, and seated on high;
Saved from all sin thro' His infinite grace,
With the redeemed ones accorded a place.

'In the Beloved,' God's marvellous grace
Calls me to dwell in this wonderful place;
God sees my Saviour and then He sees me
'In the Beloved' accepted and free.[1]

Relating to others

Understanding and receiving God's unconditional love is foundational for all future growth. We don't have to do things so God will some day accept us. We are accepted by God completely as we are. Our actions and works should be in response to God's love for us, not an attempt to earn His favour.

Finding our acceptance in Christ serves as a basis for our relationship with other people as well. Paul writes in Romans 15:7, 'Accept one another, then, just as Christ accepted you, in order to bring praise to God.'

Our need for acceptance and belonging are legitimate needs, they are God-given. But if we attempt to meet them independently of God, we are doomed to reap the dissatisfaction the self-life brings.

Peter admonishes us to lay aside the relentless pursuit of the approval of man. 'Therefore, rid yourselves of all malice and all deceit, hypocrisy, envy, and slander of every kind. Like newborn babies, crave pure spiritual milk, so that by it you may grow up in your salvation, now that you have tasted that the Lord is good. As you come to him, the living Stone — rejected by men but chosen by God and precious to him — you also, like living stones, are being built into a spiritual house to be a holy priesthood' (1 Pet 2:15). Malice is wicked behaviour that is often born out of our own sense of inadequacy when we look to others who have something we desperately need in order to be fulfilled.

Peer pressure is so powerful and the pursuit of man's approval so prevalent that people will compromise even their most basic moral principles to gain the acceptance of others. Lacking this, they begin to scheme and manipulate people or present a false image to gain approval. When this fails, they envy those who seem to have what they don't have, and then the natural consequence is to slander them to bring them down to their own level. So strong and devious is man's inner craving for significance apart from Christ!

No need to compete

But when you know who you are in Christ, you no longer need to be threatened by people or compete with them, because you are already secure and loved.

The Christian is to be like a newborn baby who knows nothing about guile, hypocrisy and envy. In reality we are like babies; we are newborn in Christ, and we are to long for the pure milk of the Word, because it is there we discover our true identity. Sure, we will sometimes experience the rejection of man, but we will never be cast away by our heavenly Father. He has promised never to leave us nor forsake us.

Let me encourage you as a newborn babe in Christ to long for the pure milk of the Word, that by it you may grow in respect to salvation, tasting the kindness, love and acceptance of the Lord. Take a moment to express your gratefulness to the Lord in prayer:

Dear heavenly Father, I pray that You will open my eyes so I may know and personally receive Your unconditional love and acceptance. I renounce the lies of Satan that question Your love and insist I must earn Your love and approval. I choose to believe that I am accepted in Christ. I ask for Your grace to sustain me as I face the rejection of mankind, and may You enable me to stand against the peer pressure that tempts me to compromise. In Jesus' precious name I pray. Amen.

NOTE

1. Lyrics by Cevilla D. Martin 'In the Beloved' (Carol Stream, IL: Hope Publishing Co., © 1930, renewal 1958). Used by permission.

17
I Am God's Child

*'Yet to all who received him, to those who believed
in his name, he gave the right to become children of
God — children born not of natural descent, nor of
human decision or a husband's will, but born of
God.'*   JOHN 1:12,13

The most important belief about ourselves is that we are
children of God and that being His child is a right given to
us by God Himself.

Let me use my family heritage as an illustration of some
important truths about our spiritual heritage. If my father
had never been born, would I have been born? If my grand-
father had never existed, would my father have existed?
Obviously, the answer is no. That my father and grandfather did exist is the basis for my being here. If you continue
with this logic, you can see that we are all related, or 'in
Adam.' Between descendants, there exists a blood relationship, born of the flesh and the will of mankind.

Would I still be a son?
Once I was born, was there anything I could have done to
undo my relationship with my dad? What if he kicked me
out of the home? Would I still be his son? If he attempted to
disown me, would I still be his child? Yes, I would, because
we are blood related.

But was there something I could have done that would
cause me no longer to live in harmony with my father? Sure,
and I probably discovered almost every way by the time I
was five. But that had nothing to do with the blood rela-

tionship. Living in harmony with my father hinged on one issue: my obedience. If I obeyed my father, we got along fine; if I didn't, we had problems. My father was a taskmaster, and I learned from my earliest days that if he told me to run and get a wrench, he meant 'run'. I suppose that I, like Christ, learned obedience from the things I suffered (see Hebrews 5:8). Today, I am eternally grateful God gave me a father who taught me to obey.

My relationship with my dad was born out of natural descent, based on the human decision of my parents. Years later, I was privileged to enter a new relationship, to be born of God. The decision to enter into that relationship was not of my mother, nor of my father. The only one who had a volitional choice was me. I alone could choose to believe and receive Christ. Now that I am God's child, is there anything I could do that would cause me to lose that relatedness? Personally, I don't think so. Why? Because I am blood related. 'For you know that it was not with perishable things such as silver or gold that you were redeemed from the empty way of life handed down to you from your forefathers, but with the precious blood of Christ, a lamb without blemish or defect' (1 Pet 1:18,19).

Will God leave me?

The issue isn't really whether or not I choose to, or am able to, hang on to this relationship with God. The issue is whether or not God will ever leave me or forsake me, which He promised He would never do. By choice, I could disobey and no longer live in harmony with my heavenly Father, but that would not affect the blood relationship, and as long as I obey God, I will live in harmony with Him.

Making these distinctions is critical. If I thought it was my obedience that determined whether or not I would stay related to God, I would be subjecting myself again to legalism. And if I did, I would logically conclude that I was related to God by my obedience, so if I disobeyed I would lose my relationship with Him. But that's not true; we are saved by grace, through faith, not by works.

On the other hand, there are those who glibly say, 'I know God will never leave me,' but they fail to live a happy, victorious life because they don't obey Him. But Jesus says, 'If anyone loves me, he will obey my teaching' (Jn 14:23). And that is not only for His sake but for ours. I like the simple truth of the classic old song:

> Trust and obey,
> For there's no other way
> To be happy in Jesus,
> But to trust and obey.[1]

We are not saved by how we *behave*, we are saved by how we believe. When we enter into a relationship with God by faith, we can exclaim with John, 'How great is the love the Father has lavished on us, that we should be called children of God! And that is what we are!…Dear friends, now we are children of God, and what we will be has not yet been made known. But we know that when he appears, we shall be like him, for we shall see him as he is. Everyone who has this hope in him purifies himself, just as he is pure' (1 Jn 3:1–3).

This important passage drives home again how critical it is to know who we are as children of God, because that serves as the basis for how we live our lives. No person can consistently behave in a way that is inconsistent with how he perceives himself.

The child of a heavenly Father

When Jesus instructed the disciples to pray, how did He start? He started with 'Our Father.' Through the Freedom in Christ seminars and ministry, we lead people through seven 'Steps to Freedom', which are a central part of the bondage-breaking process. (See the Appendix for a complete listing of the seven Steps to Freedom.)

The prayers in the Steps to Freedom begin with 'Dear heavenly Father.' One lady was unable to pray those words during the first two prayers, but at the third step, the step on forgiveness, she chose to forgive her father for sexually abusing her as a small child. Then she renounced the lie Satan had been telling her — that God, her heavenly Father, is like her earthly father. At the next prayer, a joyous smile broke out on her face as she prayed, 'Dear heavenly Father.'

That is the most important inward, personal thing we can say as we address God. And if He is our Father, then we must be His children. Do you have this assurance? If not, why not settle it right now? The devil may come along and say, 'What right do you have to call yourself God's child?' Renounce that as a lie, because the truth is, God has given to you that right. It's not a right you have earned; John 1:12 says He *gave* it to you.

If you have never made certain of your relationship with God, let me encourage you to pray this way:

Dear heavenly Father, thank You for dying on the cross, taking my place and taking my sin upon Yourself. I realise that I could not have any relationship with You on the basis of my works. But I thank You that in Christ I am forgiven, and right now, if I have never done so before, I receive You into my life. I believe that Jesus died for my sin, was raised on the third day, and I confess now with my mouth that Jesus is Lord.

I come to You as Your child. I thank You for giving me eternal life. I renounce any lie of Satan that I have no right to be called Your child, and I thank You that You have given me that right. I no longer put any confidence in myself; my confidence is in You and the fact that I am saved, not by what I have done, but by what You have done through Christ on the cross. I now accept myself as a child of God because of the

free gift You have given to me. I gladly receive it and accept it for all of eternity. In Jesus' name I pray. Amen.

NOTE

1. 'Trust and Obey'. Text by John H. Sammis (1846–1919). Public domain.

18
I Am Christ's Friend

*'My command is this: Love each other as I have
loved you. Greater love has no one than this, that
he lay down his life for his friends. You are my
friends if you do what I command. I no longer call
you servants, because a servant does not know his
master's business. Instead, I have called you
friends, for everything that I learned from my
Father I have made known to you. You did not
choose me, but I chose you and appointed you to go
and bear fruit — fruit that will last. Then the
Father will give you whatever you ask in my name.
This is my command: Love each other.'*

JOHN 15:12–17

Several years ago a young man entered my college ministry
like a storm. It was the most incredible song-and-dance
routine I had ever seen in my life. If you looked in the dictionary under 'extrovert', it would probably say, 'see
Danny'. For about a month, he showed off his sharp wit
and fun-loving nature. Then one day he came to my office
deeply depressed and asked me, 'Why don't I have any
friends?'

I looked at him and said, 'I think it's because we don't
know who you really are. You come across as this funny
guy, but deep down you are really hurting, aren't you?' I
told him I thought I could be his friend if I got to know
him.

What is a friend?
A friend is someone who takes you into his confidence. It's a reciprocal relationship. At my conferences, I always ask the question, 'In the short time we are together, if I really got to know you, I mean *really* got to know you, would I like you?' Then I always respond, 'I think I would; in fact, I'm sure I would.' Without exception, this is true of the people I have come to know intimately. Even if they have trouble relating socially or are afraid of getting close to others. After hearing the difficulties from their pasts, I find that as a result of knowing them, I come to enjoy them and love them.

A friend is always someone who loves you, who has your best interests at heart, who stands by you in your lowest moments and sacrifices himself to meet your need. Have you ever had someone you thought was a friend desert you when the chips were down? Maybe you have seen friends scatter during times of adversity. But I hope you've also had a friend stick by you through a tough time, demonstrating commitment and love. Proverbs 17:17 says, 'A friend loves at all times, and a brother is born for adversity.' One counsellee wept openly when one of our staff members offered to spend several hours helping her through the Steps to Freedom. 'No one has ever spent that much time with me before,' she said.

Jesus, the ultimate friend
In Christ, you have the best friend you could ever have. Many may desert you during times of trouble, but Jesus invites you to draw near to Him. In John 15:12–17, He says that you are no longer a servant doing only what is commanded, without understanding the purpose. Jesus takes His friends into His confidence. In John 15:15, He says, 'Everything that I learned from my Father I have made known to you.' He also said, 'But when he, the Spirit of truth, comes, he will guide you into all truth.... All that belongs to the

Father is mine. That is why I said the Spirit will take from what is mine and make it known to you' (Jn 16:13,15). Jesus discloses Himself to us...we know Him...He invites us to draw near...He is the friend who sticks closer than a brother, the One who stays with us through all adversity.

Another proof that Jesus is the ultimate friend is that He purposely gave Himself for us. He sacrificed Himself to meet our greatest need. 'This is how we know what love is: Jesus Christ laid down his life for us' (1 Jn 3:16). I have heard many people express the sentiment, 'Oh, I wish Jesus was my friend.' That wish has already been granted. He is your friend because He chose to be your friend; He chose you.

Have you ever wished that a certain person in your life would be your friend? Perhaps you thought, *I am going to do whatever I can to make him my friend,* only to be disappointed because he had his own agenda and didn't share your desire for friendship. But consider what you already have. We are talking about the God of the universe — the most significant other that you could possibly have in your life. And He chose you!

How can I be a friend to Christ?

The critical question then is, 'How can I reciprocate our relationship? How can I be His friend?' First of all, let's go back to what makes a friend. The most important thing you can do is disclose yourself to God, be totally honest with Him, walk in the light, and unburden yourself before Him, knowing that He loves you and has your best interests at heart.

Another dimension of friendship is to love a person sacrificially, to meet his or her needs. But you say, 'God doesn't have any needs.' In essence, that's true. But what does He deeply desire and require? Not only to love Him above all else, but also to love those around you. 'And he has given us this command: Whoever loves God must also love his brother' (1 Jn 4:21).

To dwell above with those we love,
To me that will be glory.
But to dwell below, with those we know,
Well that's another story.[1]

Yet, Christ has commanded us to love one another.

What it takes to love a brother as a friend
First, we have to be real. Someone shared with me this lovely little story Margery Williams wrote called *The Velveteen Rabbit*, in which stuffed animals in a playroom talk to each other:

> 'What is real?' asked the Rabbit one day. 'Does it mean having things that buzz inside and a stick-out handle?'
> 'Real isn't how you are made,' said the Skin Horse. 'It's a thing that happens to you when a child loves you for a long, long time, not just to play with, but really loves you, then you become real.'
> 'Does it hurt?' asked the Rabbit.
> 'Sometimes,' said the Skin Horse, for he was always truthful. 'When you are real you don't mind being hurt.'
> 'Does it happen all at once like being wound up?' he asked, 'or bit by bit?'
> 'It doesn't happen all at once. You become. It takes a long time. That's why it doesn't often happen to people who break easily, or have sharp edges, or have to be carefully kept. Generally by the time you are real, most of your hair has been loved off, your eyes drop out, and you get loose in the joints, and very shabby. But these things don't matter at all, because once you are real you can't be ugly, except to people who don't understand.'[2]

Second, as we don't live with perfect people, being real

will require us to forgive one another. In no way has God shown His friendship to us more than by laying down His life so we can be forgiven. When we lose our hair and become shabby rubbing up against one another, we are learning to live with the consequences of another's sin.

We are to forgive as Christ has forgiven us (see Ephesians 4:32). When He forgave us, He agreed to accept upon Himself the consequences of our sin. He will not use our past offences against us. What a friend we have in Jesus! 'He who covers an offence promotes love, but whoever repeats the matter separates close friends' (Prov 17:9).

In helping people find their freedom in Christ, I've come to see that unforgiveness is the number one basis for Satan having access to the Church. Satan revels when Christians fight or harbour grudges and separate one another.

Forgiving yourself

Many Christians have not realised that they must also forgive themselves. Without that, it is very difficult to forgive and love others. When you forgive yourself, you are simply agreeing with God and receiving His forgiveness. When one counsellor suggested a woman forgive herself for having an abortion, she suddenly went catatonic. She had already asked God's forgiveness, but forgiving herself was obviously where Satan wanted to keep her in bondage. After she forgave herself, the harassment she had lived with for so long ceased. The day after her appointment, she approached the counsellor again and said, 'My mind has never been so quiet and peaceful.'

Another lady wrote:

> I had spent so much time fasting and undergoing deliverance of my hatred of my father, but to no avail. Going through the Steps to Freedom was so much easier, and it worked. I have experienced immediate transforma-

tion. I know who I am in Christ. Now that I'm free of unforgiveness of my father, I see my husband with new eyes, and I appreciate him and love him so much more than ever before. The mind torment and voices have stopped. I am sleeping through the night for the first time in my life. The self-hatred is gone.

Christ commanded us to love our Christian brothers, and He also prayed for us to be one in His love so the world would know He was sent from God (see John 17:20–23). Because I am Christ's friend, I choose to love Him back by obeying Him, and by God's grace, He will enable me to bear fruit and to love others.

Why not settle it once and for all. You are Christ's friend because He appointed and chose you personally. You can respond to Him right now with this prayer:

Dear heavenly Father, what a privilege to call You Father, and how thankful I am that You have chosen me to be Your friend. I renounce the lie that I am not worthy to be Your friend, because You have made me worthy. I renounce the lie that everybody is Your friend except me. And I announce the truth that I, too, am Your friend, because You have chosen me. From this day forward, I want to express my love towards You by being open and honest about myself to You and by loving and being real with the brethren. Thank You for the privilege, thank You for the calling, thank You for choosing me. In Jesus' precious name I pray. Amen.

NOTES

1. Author and source unknown.

2. Margery Williams, *The Velveteen Rabbit*. Public domain.

19
I Have Been Justified

'Therefore, since we have been justified through faith, we have peace with God through our Lord Jesus Christ.'   ROMANS 5:1

The school district in the small farming community where I was raised used to release students from school early every Tuesday afternoon for religious day instruction. Those who didn't want to go to the church of their choice went to the school's study hall instead. The rest of us went to our churches for an hour of Bible study. One Tuesday afternoon, a friend and I decided that we would skip this time. We went and played in the gravel pit.

The next day the principal called me in and confronted me with the fact that I had skipped school. He concluded his remarks by saying he had arranged for me to be home from school on Thursday and Friday of that week. I was shocked. I thought, *I can't believe it! I've been suspended from school for two days for skipping religious day instruction.*

As I rode the school bus back home that afternoon, I was terrified. I walked slowly up the long lane that led to our house, fearing my parents' wrath. I thought about faking an illness for two days or getting dressed for school as usual but hiding in the woods all day. No, I couldn't do that to my parents. Lying wasn't the answer.

There was great unrest in my heart as I trudged up that lane. Because I was suspended from school, there was no way I could hide from my parents what I had done. When I finally told my parents, my mother was at first surprised, and then she started to smile. Unknown to me, she had phoned the principal earlier that week and asked permission for me to be released from school for two days to help with the autumn harvest. I had already been justified for not going to school those two days!

There's nothing left for you to do

Many Christians fear the prospect of facing an angry God, knowing that He is holy and we are sinful. They haven't grasped the fact that we have already been justified. The Greek language makes the concept of our justification very clear. Because of the precision of the verbs, the language is explicit in describing when something has already been done (past tense), is being done (present tense), will be done (future tense), or is a continuous action. In Romans 5:1, it clearly says we *have already* been justified before a Holy Father, Jesus *has already* paid the penalty for our sins, establishing our peace with God the Father.

When something has already been done, there is nothing left for you to do. Many Christians try desperately to become something they already are while the Bible declares that you cannot do for yourself what has already been done for you by Christ. The enemy's lie is that you must atone for your sin by works of some kind and thereby prove your love for God. The occult and non-Christian religions teach that.

So often, people will be aware of past sins, will have confessed them (perhaps many times), and will have forsaken them. Yet, they still have nagging thoughts of remorse and condemnation. One lady said, 'I studied the Bible and prayed as many as eight to ten hours a day, but I still could not get free from my past until I went through the *Steps to Freedom* and accepted what Christ has done for me.' Satan, who accuses us day and night (see Revelation 12:10), had kept her in bondage with his lies.

What can wash away my sin?

It's also true that much Christian service is done out of drivenness or guilt. Let me hasten to say, 'Don't quit serving the Lord, but do check your motivation.'

Other people punish themselves by cutting themselves, purging or hurting their bodies in various other ways. They do not realise that such deeds and thoughts are directly from the deceiver who does not want us wholly dependent on Christ. The enemy wants to keep us in bondage, having us attempt to pay for our own sins. I asked one lady who binged and purged several times a day, 'Why do you do it?' She said she felt cleansed afterward. I asked her if she would be willing to renounce her purging and trust only in the cleansing work of Christ; she did and joyfully exclaimed, 'That's it! My cleansing is in the shed blood of Christ on the cross!' As the old hymn says, 'Nothing in my hand I bring, simply to Thy cross I cling.'[1]

Justified in, through and by Christ alone

Faith is the only means by which you and I can enter into a relationship with God. Galatians 2:16 says, 'Know that a man is not justified by observing the law, but by faith in Jesus Christ. So we, too, have put our faith in Christ Jesus that we may be justified by faith in Christ and not by observing the law, because by observing the law no one will be justified.' I cannot do for myself what only Christ alone could and has done for me.

The little preposition 'in' plays a critical role in the New Testament. The fact that you are *in Christ*, that you are *in union* with Him, means that you are spiritually alive right now — you have *already been justified* before God.

What does that mean exactly? Look at Romans 5:9–11: 'Since we have now been justified by his blood, how much more shall we be saved from God's wrath through him! For if, when we were God's enemies, we were reconciled to him through the death of his Son, how much more, having been reconciled, shall we be saved through his life! Not only is this so, but we also rejoice in God through our Lord Jesus Christ, through whom we have now received reconciliation.'

Much, much more

Here are four results of our justification, as revealed in Romans 5:9–11:

First, we are saved from God's wrath; our future is secure because God's wrath has been satisfied. You say, 'Great, I have escaped eternal damnation.'

True, but there is *much more*. We have peace with God. Before we were His enemies; now we are friends with God. Facing God would be an unpleasant prospect if we had not been justified. I mean, would you pursue God if He were a consuming fire? When I skipped school that one day, I was not looking forward to facing the judgement, rejection or punishment of my parents. Knowing I was already justified and forgiven would have caused me to want to run to their loving arms rather than feeling dread and fear. We have peace with God. We don't have to pursue that peace; by the grace of God we have it now.

But that's not all! There's still *much more*. We have been saved through His life. My present life is already alive in Christ; I have spiritual life now. Eternal life is not something we get when we die; we possess it right now.

Well, is that it? No, *much more*. We also rejoice. John's stated purpose for his first epistle is, 'We proclaim to you what we have seen and heard, so that you also may have fellowship with us. And our fellowship is with the Father and with his son, Jesus Christ. We write this to make our joy complete' (1 Jn 1:3,4). Many Christians are trying to appease an angry God to avoid punishment, when they should be pursuing a loving God whose justice has been satisfied by the sacrifice of His only Son. We have been justified, therefore we have, *right now*, the joy of peace with God. Why don't you thank Him as follows:

Dear heavenly Father, I thank You for sending Your only begotten Son to pay the price in order that I may be justified. I now accept by faith that I have peace with You through my Lord Jesus Christ. I renounce the lie that we are enemies and claim the truth that we are friends, reconciled by the death of Your Son. I rejoice in the life that I now have in Christ and I look forward to the day when I shall see You face-to-face. In Jesus' precious name I pray. Amen.

NOTE

1.   'Rock of Ages'. Text by Augustus M. Toplady (1740–1778). Public domain.

20
I Am United with the Lord and One with Him in Spirit

'But he who unites himself with the Lord is one with him in spirit.'   1 CORINTHIANS 6:17

When I first became a Christian, the most exciting truth I encountered was that the Holy Spirit had somehow taken up residence within me. I was united with the Lord and one spirit with Him — a concept totally foreign to my previous spiritual understanding. When I first worked through the discipleship material that explained this, I wondered if it was heresy, but as I began to look at the Word of God I realised it is true. Prior to receiving Christ, my identity was found in the things I did. I was a farmer, a sailor, a wrestling coach, and finally, an engineer. My purpose and meaning in life were found in the natural world. In a real sense, I suppose, I was one with the world because that was all I knew.

New Age distortions
The New Age movement now sweeping the world focuses upon a tired old philosophy. It focuses on a cosmic unity, that you are one with the world. It is a distortion of the Christian doctrine of atonement (that my sins have been atoned for). New Agers take the concept and make it 'at-one-ment' or 'at one with the world.' It is incredibly attractive because it promises spiritual 'wholeness' without having to face the problem of sin.

If we are all one, then we are all god. So they reason, 'All you really need to know is that you are god; you don't need a Saviour to die for your sin, you just need to be enlightened.' New Age doctrine has come full circle and bought the lie of the Garden of Eden, 'You shall be as God.' It is the ultimate lie.

The truth is, you are not God, but you are, by His grace, a *child of God*.

Your bodies are members of Christ

You may be questioning the truth of what the Word of God says because you don't *feel* united to the Lord. So you may ask, 'Is this only a spiritual unity that does not include my body?' Actually, the Bible teaches that it is far more than that. Romans 8:11 says, 'And if the Spirit of him who raised Jesus from the dead is living in you, he who raised Christ from the dead will also give life to your mortal bodies through his Spirit, who lives in you.'

In 1 Corinthians 6:15 we read, 'Do you not know that your bodies are members of Christ himself?' Then verses 15 and 16 go on to warn us about no longer being united with a prostitute, which would include any use of your body that would cause you to lose the sense of unity with God. Some close friends of mine and several Christian workers got caught up with a false teacher who taught that what they did in the flesh, with their physical bodies, didn't matter — the only thing that mattered was the spiritual reality that they were united with God. He used this false teaching to involve himself sexually with many of these people, leaving them in terrible bondage.

What to do with your body

The Bible is very clear about what we are supposed to do with our physical bodies: 'In the same way, count yourselves dead to sin but alive to God in Christ Jesus. Therefore do not let sin reign in your mortal body so that you obey its evil desires. Do not offer the parts of your body to sin, as instruments of wickedness, but rather offer yourselves to God, as those who have been brought from death to life; and offer the parts of your body to him as instruments of righteousness' (Rom 6:11–13). We don't have to work at becoming dead to sin; we simply accept it as being so. In Christ Jesus we are alive to God, so we are already dead to sin.

However, we do have the responsibility to safeguard our mortal bodies from sin and keep them from being instruments of unrighteousness. Failing to do so would be to violate the unity we have with the Lord and our spiritual oneness with Him. If we use our bodies as instruments of wickedness, we will allow sin to reign, actually rule, in our mortal bodies, and we will end up obeying its evil desires even though we don't have to.

Your body is meant for the Lord

Let's look at one of the biggest problems in the Church, which is sexual sin. According to 1 Corinthians 6:13, 'The body is not meant for sexual immorality, but for the Lord, and the Lord for the body.' Verse 18 says, 'Flee from sexual immorality All other sins a man commits are outside his body, but he who sins sexually sins against his own body.' And, I would remind you, sinning against your own body involves sinning against the One with whom you are united.

Scripture seems to set sexual sins in a class all by themselves. For one reason, it is impossible to commit a sexual sin and not use your body as an instrument of unrighteousness. The moment you do, you allow sin to reign in your mortal body.

Unholy bonding

A young mother confessed her adultery to me during a break at a conference. I agreed to meet with her the next day. Her opening comment was, 'I just can't imagine ever giving up this man' (her adulterous lover). She never had a real father, and childhood sexual abuse had obviously contributed to a distorted image of herself and God. She had no sense of an intimate relationship with God or her husband.

She agreed to walk through the *Steps to Freedom* with me. During that time, several sexual encounters surfaced and she renounced them all. Forgiving and forgiveness followed. 'I feel like a tremendous weight has been lifted from me,' she said.

Because she had never known her father, and I was old enough to be her parent, I asked if I could talk to her as though she were my daughter. She agreed, and I said, 'I would want for you to live a happy and satisfied life. I would also want for you to be able to talk with God and read your Bible without a guilty conscience. I would want for you to live comfortably with yourself and to get up in the morning, look at yourself in the mirror, and like what you see.' Tears began to form in her eyes.

I continued, 'I would want you to do what is right for my grandchildren and not have to apologise some day for being unfaithful ever again. I am going to pray that you will give your husband another chance.' Now we were both in tears. Something special happened. Maybe I was touched, because my daughter, Heidi, had just been married to a wonderful Christian man. But the reason she was touched was because she bonded — not to me, but to her heavenly Father.

God warns us not to be joined sexually with harlots, because we will become one body with them (see 1 Corinthians 6:16). We would be using our body as an instrument of unrighteousness, and thus allowing sin to reign in our mortal bodies. The result is spiritual bondage. In hundreds of cases, I have seen 'unholy' sex lead to unholy bonding, making God-ordained sex with a spouse undesirable and bonding with God seem impossible. Secular studies have also shown that excessive sexual expressions before marriage lead to inhibited marital sex. Many people have confessed to me, 'I enjoyed sex with others, but now that I am married, I can hardly stand to be touched.'

Satan's perversion of sex

The enemy distorts sex, which God created to be beautiful, wholesome and intended only for the marriage relationship. In our present culture, sex is synonymous with love, and it has become a 'god' to be worshipped. And many Christians believe that lie.

It is common for us to have a Christian young woman name thirty or more people with whom she has had intercourse, perhaps including several long-term affairs. Some will say, 'I was looking for a relationship where I felt loved.'

I spend the majority of my counselling time with Christian leaders, many of whom have fallen prey to the enemy in the area of forbidden sex. All of us in the Body of Christ have grieved as we've seen whole ministries severely damaged because a leader did not run from sexual immorality.

One Christian man who has a beautiful wife and child came to one of our staff members, desperate for help. He had been living a double life — a churchgoing family man, seemingly committed and faithful, all the while secretly visiting prostitutes and obsessed with pornography and sexual perversion. As he went through the *Steps to Freedom*, he was prompted to renounce any covenants he had made with Satan. He broke down, wept uncontrollably and said, 'I have given Satan control of parts of my life.' He remembered a time when he stood before a mirror, and Satan promised him all the beautiful women he wanted if only he would say he loved Satan.

This may seem like an extreme case, but I want to remind you that if Satan came into the room with a red suit and long tail, you would recognise him. So that isn't the way he works. He is very subtle at first. He'll approach you in your area of greatest need or vulnerability, and it will all begin in your mind. The battle is won or lost right there. That is why it is crucial to take every thought captive to the obedience of Christ (see 2 Corinthians 10:5).

Renounce wrong uses of your body

In helping people find their freedom in Christ, I have found it necessary to have them pray and ask the Lord to reveal every sexual use of their bodies as an instrument of unrighteousness. As God brings these sins to their minds, I suggest they say, 'I renounce that sexual use of my body as an instrument of unrighteousness.' We have found this to be important, whether something was done to them or something they participated in voluntarily. In every case I wrote about in my book *Released From Bondage*, the people walked through that process. Some people might think, *That would take me a long time.* So what if it took you all day? Wouldn't that be better than living in bondage for the rest of your life?

Even in physical illnesses that come upon me at times, I have found it important to pray and commit my body to God as a living sacrifice, and to command Satan to leave my presence. If I have knowingly used my body in a wrongful way, then I need to confess that.

In most cases, the reason we don't feel united with the Lord is because we have used our body as instruments of unrighteousness. No wonder Paul says in Romans 12:1, 'Therefore, I urge you, brothers, in view of God's mercy, to offer your bodies as living sacrifices, holy and pleasing to God — this is your spiritual act of worship.' Wouldn't you like to have that sense of unity with God and be one with Him in spirit? If you would, then I, as Paul, urge you to submit your body to God as a living sacrifice.

Dear heavenly Father, I come to You as Your child. I renounce the lie that I am separated from You just because I don't feel Your presence. I choose to believe that I am united spiritually with You. I now ask You to reveal to my mind every use of my body that was an instrument of unrighteousness. *(Note: As the Lord reveals them to you, specifically renounce each use of your body, especially every sexual use, as an instrument of unrighteousness.)*

I now submit my body to You as an instrument of righteousness, and I command Satan to leave my presence. I reserve the sexual use of my body for my spouse only *(if you are married)*. I now ask You to fill me with Your Holy Spirit. In Jesus' precious name I pray. Amen.

21

I Have Been bought with a Price; I Belong to God

'Do you not know that your body is a temple of the Holy Spirit, who is in you, whom you have received from God? You are not your own; you were bought at a price. Therefore honour God with your body.'
1 CORINTHIANS 6:19,20

Our souls were never designed by God to function as master, nor can we claim two masters at the same time. 'No one can serve two masters. Either he will hate the one and love the other, or he will be devoted to the one and despise the other. You cannot serve both God and Money' (Mt 6:24).

The humanist claims, 'I am the master of my fate; I am the captain of my soul.' Oh no, you're not! Self-seeking, self-serving, self-justifying, self-glorifying, self-centred and self-confident living are in actuality serving the world, the flesh and the devil. The world's definition of freedom is to do your own thing, to exercise your independence by being a 'free agent' morally. God's definition of true freedom is for us voluntarily to do His thing, which requires us to be dependent upon Him, the One who bought us with a price, the One to whom we belong.

What many call freedom is actually bondage

Several years ago, I was asked to speak at a secular university on the subject of Christian morality in the context of marriage and sex. The classroom was predominantly filled with young ladies. There was one young man, however, who pulled his chair off into a corner and made a show of being unconcerned about anything I had to say. Occasionally, he would interrupt with a little arrogant statement. One young lady in the back of the room asked me what Christians thought about masturbation. Before I could say anything he piped up, 'Well I masturbate every day.'

I paused for a second, then I said, 'Well, congratulations, but can you stop?'

I didn't hear another remark from him again until the end of the class when everybody left. He came up and said, 'So why would I want to stop?'

I said, 'That's not what I asked; I asked if you *could* stop. What you think is freedom, really isn't freedom at all — it's bondage.'

Anybody who acts as his own God is in bondage to his sinful nature. We were sold into the slave market of sin. Jesus purchased us from the kingdom of darkness and saved us from ourselves. We are not our own; we were bought at a very high price, the precious blood of Christ. We are no longer slaves to sin but servants to Christ. For the apostles, this truth was foundational to all that they had to say.

Notice how the apostles began their letters, 'Paul and Timothy, servants of Christ Jesus, to all the saints in Christ Jesus at Philippi' (Phil 1:1). 'James, a servant of God, and of the Lord Jesus Christ' (Jas 1:1). 'Simon Peter, a servant and apostle of Jesus Christ' (2 Pet 1:1). 'Jude, a servant of Jesus Christ' (Jude 1).

Being a servant brings freedom

The sceptic may say, 'So what? A servant is still a slave.' But that's not necessarily true. Don't be confused by the terminology. The most practical, present benefit of being a child of God is freedom. Being a servant of sin is bondage; being a servant of God is freedom.

As one who belongs to God, we have freedom in three

ways: First, we are free from the law. The law says 'don't do this' in order to be righteous, but Galatians 5:1 says, 'It is for freedom that Christ has set us free. Stand firm, then, and do not let yourselves be burdened again by a yoke of slavery.' The person who is driven by the legalism of the law will feel as though he is being cursed and condemned all of his life, but living by the Spirit gives life and liberty.

Second, we are free from the past. 'Because you are sons, God sent the Spirit of his Son into our hearts, the Spirit who calls out, '*Abba*, Father.' So you are no longer a slave, but a son; and since you are a son, God has made you also an heir. Formerly, when you did not know God, you were slaves to those who by nature are not gods' (Gal 4:6–8). What a privilege it is to watch as God sets people free from their past. As children of God, we are no longer products of our past; we have a new heritage — we are heirs of God.

Third, we can be free from sin. The only means by which we are capable of doing this is to realise that we have been bought with a price and that the Holy Spirit now lives in us, enabling us to live our lives for Him, free from sin's bondage. He sensitises us to Satan's attacks and gives us the power not to sin and to live in obedience to our heavenly Father. But the choice is still ours. Let me illustrate our freedom in Christ with the following parable:

Freeing the slaves

Slavery in the United States was abolished by the Thirteenth Amendment on 18 December 1865. How many slaves were there on 19 December? In reality, there should have been none. But many still lived like slaves, because they never learned the truth. Others knew and even believed they were free but chose to live as they always had.

Now suppose several plantation owners were devastated by the Emancipation Proclamation. 'We're ruined! Slavery has been abolished. We've lost the battle to keep our slaves.'

But their chief spokesman slyly responded, 'Not necessarily, as long as these people think they're still slaves, the Emancipation Proclamation will have no practical effect. We don't have a legal right over them any more, but many of them don't know it. Keep your slaves from learning the truth, and your control over them will not even be challenged.'

One cotton farmer asked, 'But what if the news spreads?'

'Don't panic. We have another barrel in our gun. We may not be able to keep them from hearing the news, but we can still keep them from understanding it. They don't call me the 'father of lies' for nothing. We still have the potential to deceive the whole world. Just tell them that they misunderstood the Thirteenth Amendment. Tell them that they are *going to be free*, not that they are free already. The truth they heard is just positional truth, not actual truth. Some day they may receive the benefits, but not now.'

'But they'll expect me to say that. They won't believe me.'

'Then pick out a few persuasive ones who are convinced that they're still slaves and let them do the talking for you. Remember, most of these free people were born as slaves and have been slaves their whole lives. All we have to do is deceive them so that they still *think* like slaves. As long as they continue to do what slaves do, it will not be hard to convince them that they must still be slaves. They will maintain their slave identity because of the things they do. The moment they try to profess that they are no longer slaves, just whisper in their ear, 'How can you even think you are no longer a slave when you are still doing things that slaves do?' After all, we have the capacity to accuse the brethren day and night.'

Years later, many had still not heard the wonderful news that they had been freed, so naturally they continued to live the way they had always lived. Some heard the good news

276 Part One: Our Acceptance in Christ

but told themselves, 'I'm still living like a slave, doing the same things I have always done. My experience tells me that I must not be free. Everything is the same as before the Proclamation, so it must not be true. I must still be a slave.' So they continued as if they had not received freedom!

Then one day, a former slave heard the good news and received it with great joy. He checked out the validity of the Proclamation and discovered that the highest of all authorities had originated the decree. Not only that, but it personally cost the authority a tremendous price so that slaves could be free. The slave's life was transformed. He reasoned that it would be hypocritical to continue living as a slave, even though his feelings told him he still was. Determined to live by what he knew to be true, his experiences began to change dramatically. He realised that his old master had no authority over him and did not need to be obeyed. He gladly served the one who set him free.[1]

Being a servant is belonging

Another practical benefit of being a servant of Christ is that we have a sense of belonging. Belonging meets one of the most basic needs we all have. If we don't understand that as a legitimate need, we will never understand peer pressure. The pressure to conform and avoid rejection is so powerful that Christians will also compromise in order to gain some sense of acceptance. But if I know I belong to God — my heavenly Father who will never leave me nor forsake me — then I have the power to stand and not compromise to gain acceptance, even if it means standing alone.

If you belong to any group, you carry the responsibility of living according to their established rules. If you break their rules, you will probably lose your membership. But when you belong to God, He promises never to leave you nor forsake you. And He gives you His Holy Spirit to bear witness that you are His child. Though you may break His rules, you will never lose your membership.

I remember a time when I was young, I came out of obscurity and pitched a rather phenomenal game of softball. People in the stands wondered who I was, and I heard one man say, 'Who is that guy? Who does he belong to?' I remember how good it felt to say I belonged to Marvin Anderson. It was a positive experience, but it can also be embarrassing if somebody misbehaves and people ask, 'Who does that troublemaker belong to?'

Now that I belong to God I carry a sense of responsibility. When people say, 'Well, who does he belong to?' the answer is, 'I belong to God.' The Scripture clearly says we belong to God; therefore, we are to honour Him with our bodies. It is not a negative thing to be a servant of God. It is a joyful thing to say that I have been bought with a price, and I belong to God.

Dear heavenly Father, I thank You that You have purchased me from the slave market of sin and brought me into Your own kingdom of light. I joyfully announce the fact that I belong to You. I renounce the lie that I am unworthy to be Your child and that You don't love me. I accept and proclaim the truth that You loved me and died for me while I was still a sinner. I am now alive in Christ, I have been bought with a price, and I belong to You for all eternity. I commit myself and my body to You as a living sacrifice, that I may glorify You. In Jesus' precious name I pray. Amen.

NOTE

1. The basis of this illustration was adapted from an article entitled 'Enslaved to My Self-Image' by Jamie Lash of Victory Seminar Ministries, Dallas, Texas. Used by permission.

22
I Am a Member of Christ's Body

'Now you are the body of Christ, and each one of
you is a part of it.'   1 CORINTHIANS 12:27

Anybody who regularly relates to people on a deep level knows that they don't inherently feel good about themselves. We are not born with an innate sense of worth or value. The natural man has no identity in Christ, so from the time we are born into this world, we are constantly pursuing some sense of identity, purpose or meaning in life.

The self-esteem movement has been profoundly affecting every aspect of life. More and more, people are searching for some sense of significance, and the philosophy of attempting to find it within yourself has even found its way into the Church.

I have heard Christians say a man finds his identity in a job and a woman finds her identity in her children or family. Some say this teaching comes out of Genesis 3, where it states that a man shall work by the sweat of his brow and a woman shall bear her child in pain. But that is the curse of the Fall, the result of man's choosing to live independently of God. If a man finds his identity in his job, what happens when he loses his job? If a woman finds her identity in her family or children, what happens if she never gets married?

Who we essentially are is not determined by what we do or the roles we live out in society. It is who we are that determines what we do, and then what we do brings a sense of satisfaction and fulfilment.

The search for self-worth

So the question is, 'Where *does* a person find a legitimate sense of identity or worth?' Is it in talents? No, it can't possibly be. God has given some one talent, some two talents, and others five talents (see Matthew 25:14–28). You may say, 'Well, God, how could You do that? Don't You know that the only person who can have any legitimate sense of worth or identity is the five-talented person?' But that is not true. I know a lot of five-talented people who are struggling for a sense of worth, just like the one-talented person.

Well, then, does our worth lie in intelligence? No, according to 1 Corinthians 1:27, 'God chose the foolish things of the world to shame the wise.' Okay, how about appearance? If we only appeared good, certainly we would have the acceptance and affirmation of others. But according to Isaiah 53:2, Jesus had 'no beauty or majesty to attract us to him.'

One time I asked my son, 'Karl, suppose there is a young girl at your school who has a potato body, stringy hair, bad complexion, a stuttering problem and no coordination — is there any hope for happiness for her?'

He paused for a moment and said, 'Hmmm. Probably not.' In the world's system, probably not, but could she have a legitimate sense of worth in God's system? Absolutely.

Is our worth found in spiritual gifts? No, I am sure it is not. God has not equally distributed gifts, talents or intelligence, but He has equally distributed Himself. Our identity comes from knowing who we are as children of God, and our sense of worth grows out of our commitment to become like Him.

Legitimate sense of worth in Christ

Show me people today who know who they are as children of God and have committed themselves to Him, and I will show you those who have a profound sense of self and of worth. Show me somebody who is continually growing in the fruit of the Spirit, whose life is characterised by love, joy, peace, patience, goodness, faithfulness, gentleness and self-control. Will that person have a good sense of identity and value? Yes, I am sure of it. And the beautiful part of that truth is that everyone has exactly the same opportunity.

Some people appear to play such a large observable role as a member of Christ's Body, others may feel they are not needed. But Paul writes in 1 Corinthians 12:21,22, 'The eye cannot say to the hand, "I don't need you!" And the head cannot say to the feet, "I don't need you!" On the contrary, those parts of the body that seem to be weaker are indispensable, and the parts that we think are less honourable we treat with special honour.' I'm glad God gives special honours, because we have a tendency to ignore those who are less gifted or talented.

When I accept speaking invitations, I am keenly aware that the outcome will be determined as much by the work of the sound man as by my own presentation. The attention afforded me is also directly related to the person who controls the thermostat. All 'players' have a part, and as with any team effort, all are dependent upon the others to fulfil their roles and use their unique gifts and talents.

Those who have the more noticeable gifts, unfortunately, get most of the attention. So what does God do? In 1 Corinthians 12:24,25, it says, 'Our presentable parts need no special treatment. But God has combined the members of the body and has given greater honour to the parts that lacked it, so that there should be no division in the body, but that its parts should have equal concern for each other.'

Pursue the giver, not the gifts

Our pursuit in life must be to fully utilise the gifts we have. One young man came to me several years ago all excited about his newly discovered perception of himself in relationship to gifts. He asked me if I thought his gift was prophecy or exhortation. I looked at him and knowing him quite well, I responded, 'Jimmy, I don't think either one is your gift. I think you have the gift of service. If ever I have met a person who has the gift of helps, you have it. You know instinctively what to do when you see another person in need, and you move quickly to act. When I see God operate through you in that way, it is exciting to see what happens.'

His head fell, and he said in a low voice, 'I knew it.'

I said, 'Well, Jimmy, there is no way you are going to be fulfilled trying to be something you are not. The only way you are going to live a productive life, feel good about yourself and carry out your calling in life is to discover who you really are. Find out what God has built into you, the talents He has given you. Use those gifts for the glory of God to edify the Body of Christ, and you will be fulfilled. Trying to be something you are not will only lead to failure and frustration.'

This young man took my advice and he pursued a life of service. Twenty-five years later, I still get Christmas cards affirming the joy he has discovered in serving in public school education and being involved in his church as a helper.

Know who you are — a child of God!

When I first entered ministry and before I understood these truths myself, a young girl came to our church college department. She was the epitome of the girl I asked my son about — not very attractive and seemingly untalented. She had nothing going for her physically. Her heritage was horrible: Her father was a drunk who left his family several years earlier; her older brother ran drugs in and out of the house, causing nothing but problems; her mother eked out a living working at two mediocre jobs. This young lady knew she could not compete with the world's system, but what she could and did do was to find out who she was as a child of God. I have never seen a girl who had a healthier sense of identity and worth. She became the friend of everybody, and she ended up with the nicest guy in our youth department.

In those days I used to wonder, *What is this girl's secret? What does she have?* Well, she understood at that time, more than I did, what it meant to be a child of God and to commit herself to being all He wanted her to be. She took on that identity, followed it faithfully and enjoyed her Christianity much more than most people do.

Would you join me in prayer right now, committing yourself to the enjoyment of knowing that you, too, are a member of Christ's Body and that your self-worth is grounded on that basic truth?

Dear heavenly Father, I thank You for making me a member of Your Body. I renounce the lie that I have no part to play or no significant contribution to make in the Body of Christ. I accept what You have created in me and the special spiritual gifts that come from You. I commit myself to grow in Your likeness so that my gifts and abilities can be used to edify Your Church.

I renounce the lie that my identity and sense of worth is found in my ability to perform. I accept the truth that my identity and worth is found in Christ and will be realised increasingly as I grow in Christ's likeness. I thank You for being a part of Your family and that I can realise I not only have You as my Father, but I have brothers and sisters in Christ with whom I can share my life. In the wonderful name of Jesus I pray. Amen.

23
I Am a Saint

'To the saints in Ephesus, the faithful in Christ Jesus.'
EPHESIANS 1:1

If I walked into any church in America and asked how many perceive themselves as a sinner saved by grace, almost everyone would raise their hands. But then if I asked how many perceive themselves as saints, few, if any, would raise their hands. My response would be: Which is the most biblically accurate statement of who you are as a Christian? Does the Bible refer to the believer as a sinner or as a saint? Did Paul address his letters to the sinners at Ephesus or to the saints?

Look at the truth in 1 Corinthians 1:2, 'To the church of God which is at Corinth, to those who have been sanctified in Christ Jesus, saints by calling, with all who in every place call upon the name of our Lord Jesus Christ, their Lord and ours' (NASB). Tragically, many Christians live their lives as though the passage reads, 'To others in the church who are struggling to be sanctified, sinners by calling (or saints by hard work), with some who call upon the name of the Lord, my Lord, but I'm not sure about theirs.'

Every child of God is a saint

The overwhelming and consistent message of the New Testament is that we are all saints by the grace of God, sanctified because we are *in* Christ Jesus. Every child of God is a saint because he is in Christ Jesus. The most overwhelming concept in the early parts of Ephesians is the tremendous inheritance we have in Christ. 'Praise be to the

God and Father of our Lord Jesus Christ, who has blessed us in the heavenly realms with every spiritual blessing *in Christ*. For he chose us *in him* before the creation of the world' (Eph 1:3,4, emphasis added).

Forty times in the one book of Ephesians, references are made to either you being in Christ or Christ in you. And for every verse throughout the Bible that talks about Christ being in you, ten verses can be found that talk about you being in Him. Go through the rest of Ephesians 1 and see how many times you can find this truth. In verse 7, you will find, '*In him* we have redemption.' In verse 11, it says, '*In him* we were also chosen.' Verse 12 will tell you that your hope lies *in Christ*. Verse 13 says you were included *in Christ* when you heard the word of truth.

The problem is not that the Bible does not clearly identify believers as saints — it does! The primary problem is, we just do not see it! So Paul says in Ephesians 1:18, 'I pray also that the eyes of your heart may be enlightened in order that you may know the hope to which he has called you, the riches of his glorious inheritance *in the saints*' (emphasis added).

Our identity in Christ

Being a saint represents the incredible work of Christ's redemption in the life of the believer. Man's old self is replaced by something that did not exist in him before. He is declared to be a new creation (see 2 Corinthians 5:17; Galatians 6:15). This newness of life is the very life of Jesus Christ within the believer himself (see Galatians 2:20; Colossians 3:4). He has become one spirit with the Lord (see 1 Corinthians 6:17). In the practice of daily living, the Christian is exhorted to 'put on the new self' (Eph 4:24). By faith, we are to function in the light of our true identity — who we really are in Christ Jesus.

Paul identifies the believer with Christ:

In His death	Romans 6:3,6;
	Galatians 2:20;
	Colossians 3:1–3
In His burial	Romans 6:4
In His resurrection	Romans 6:5,8,11
In His life	Romans 5:10,11
In His power	Ephesians 1:19,20
In His inheritance	Romans 8:16,17;
	Ephesians 1:11,12

The apostle Paul, through whom all the above identifications are expressed, describes himself in 1 Timothy 1:15 as the foremost of sinners. However, this statement is made in a context (vs 12–16), which clearly shows this as a reference to his unsaved condition. He makes a similar statement of self-depreciation in 1 Corinthians 15:9 but follows it in the next breath with, 'But by the grace of God I am what I am, and his grace to me was not without effect' (v 10).

This new man is the result of Jesus Christ's life implanted in the believer and manifested in practical ways as the Christian makes moral choices in the power of the Holy Spirit. We are not partly new and partly old, nor are we partly in light and partly in darkness; we are completely new creatures in Him.

Sin's power is broken

Does this mean we are sinless? By no means. Sin can continue to dwell in our bodies and make its appeal. But by virtue of our redemption, sin's power is broken (see Romans 6:7,14). We are under no obligation to serve, obey or respond to sin. By the grace of God, we can live as a child of light. If we choose to believe the lie that identity and purpose in life can be found in a course of action contrary to God, we will come under conviction, which is the result of choosing to act differently from who we really are in Christ.

Finding our identity in Christ is a concept taught repeatedly throughout the New Testament, because the way we live our lives is determined by our perceived identity. Our attitudes, responses and reactions to the circumstances of life hinge on our conscious or subconscious self-perceptions. As I said earlier, no one can consistently behave in a way that is inconsistent with how he perceives himself. If Christians are no different inwardly from non-Christians, or if they perceive themselves to be no different, then they will not live as new creatures.

A wrong identity

When people ask me to help them forgive those who have hurt them, I suggest they name the offence they are forgiving. And often I ask, 'How did that offence make you feel?' They answer with words such as, 'dirty', 'worthless', 'inadequate' or 'rejected'. When they forgive their offenders for those things, they are getting down to their hurt and pain, and they are also revealing how they have probably perceived themselves. That information was most likely believed and then programmed into their 'computer' (memory), becoming part of their perception. If in your belief system you see yourself as inadequate or no good, you will likely live that out. We are all living according to what we believe. If we have a wrong belief about ourselves, it will affect the way we live.

Repeated defeats in the life of Christians are capitalised on by Satan. He pours on guilt, and coupled with the negative influence of legalistic teachers, Christians often question their salvation or accept as normal an up-and-down spiritual existence. They confess their wretchedness and proneness to sin and strive to do better, but inwardly they consider themselves only as sinners saved by grace, hanging on until the rapture.

Why does this happen to so many Christians? Because of

ignorance of our true identity in Christ. Praise God, we are no longer just a product of our past. 'Therefore, if anyone is in Christ, he is a new creation; the old has gone, the new has come!' (2 Cor 5:17). When you see yourself as God sees you, as His child and a saint, it becomes a joy to cooperate with Him in His transforming work in your life.

God's great accomplishment

The work of atonement in changing sinners to saints was Jesus' greatest accomplishment on earth, an interchange that occurs at the moment of salvation. Its effect continues in the daily walk of the believer throughout life — this is the work of sanctification. But the progressive work of sanctification only has its full and powerful effect in our lives when that radical inner transformation, our newness in Christ, is realised and appropriated by faith.

All that is needed for godly living is ours by divine power, which is inherent in the Christ-life within. The believer's identity and purpose is in Christ. He becomes a doer of the Word because of who he already is. He does not need to perform to gain approval; rather, he is an obedient doer of the Word as a result of already being one with Christ (see James 1:22–25).

In the Bible, believers are called brothers, children, sons of God, sons of light, light in the Lord and saints. Nowhere are believers referred to as sinners, not even as sinners saved by grace. If a true Christian accepts himself as a sinner, then his core identity is sin. This is a direct contradiction to Scripture, because believers are justified by faith. But the implications of seeing oneself as a sinner are serious, for what do sinners do? They sin. What else would you expect of a sinner?

But again I would raise the question, 'Do believers never sin?' Yes, they do. We are not sinners saved by grace; we are saints who sin. And that designation given to believers in

the Bible corresponds to their new identity in Christ —
those who have died to sin and are now alive in Jesus Christ.
And by faith, a believer can choose to be what, in reality, he
already is in Christ. With our identity established and
understanding that the power of sin is broken, our will is
now able to choose truth by the power of the Holy Spirit
and the truth sets us free. Ephesians 5:8 says, 'For you were
once darkness, but now you are light in the Lord. Live as
children of light.' The problem is not that we are not saints;
it is that we do not live like saints.

**Dear heavenly Father, I renounce the lie that I am just a sin-
ner. I acknowledge that I am a saint not due to any effort on
my part but because of my redemption in Christ. I receive and
appropriate my new identity in Christ as a saint and I choose
to do so by faith. I ask You to fill me with Your Holy Spirit
and enable me to live out my true identity as a saint so I may
not sin. I choose to walk in the light that I may glorify You. I
pray this in the wonderful name of my Lord and Saviour,
Jesus Christ. Amen.**

24
I Have Been Adopted as God's Child

'In love he predestined us to be adopted as his sons through Jesus Christ, in accordance with his pleasure and will.'   EPHESIANS 1:5

In the middle of the last century, out on the plains of Nebraska, a circuit preacher made his rounds from church to church and from community to community. In one community, he found a little Greek orphan boy, an immigrant named Peter Popavich. Peter's family had been killed in one of the range wars that had taken its toll on many people. Peter was an incorrigible boy, causing others to shun him and run away.

Because nobody would take him into their homes, the preacher assumed Peter as his responsibility. He took the little boy wherever he went but soon realised this could not continue. Then he heard of a Christian couple named Mr and Mrs Smith who had a boy named Sammy, about the same age as Peter. The circuit preacher rode out to their farm and asked the Smiths if they would consider raising Peter. They prayed about it and agreed together as a family that this was God's will for their lives, so they took on the responsibility.

The chemistry of relationships is an interesting thing. Sammy was a loving, supportive little boy, while Peter remained his old incorrigible self. Regardless, the two boys became the best of friends. One day they were playing outside near a slough that had been quarantined because of contamination. A sign clearly announced the danger. Peter said, 'Let's go swimming.' But Sammy refused. Peter said, 'Well, I'm going to go anyway.' And in he went. He must have cut his foot on the surrounding barbed wire fence, because it became infected. Soon he grew gravely ill, and his temperature rose to 105 degrees. The antibiotics we have today probably would have cured him, but they were not available then. Daily, Peter's life hung in the balance.

One afternoon the mother and father had to go into town to get supplies. Concerned about spreading the illness, they told Sammy he could talk to Peter from the doorway but not to go into the room. While they were gone, the desire of the two boys to be together again was overwhelming, and when the parents came home they found them fast asleep in each other's arms. Nobody fully understands the providential nature of God, but in this case Peter got well, but Sammy got sick. Within days, Sammy died.

Several years passed. The circuit preacher again happened to be making his rounds in that same community. He remembered Peter, whom he had dropped off years earlier, so he decided to stop to see how he was. As he rode up to the farm, he recognised Mr Smith, but he didn't recognise the big, strong, strapping boy standing right beside him. The preacher asked, 'What happened to the boy I dropped by here several years ago?'

Mr Smith reached up, put his arm around the boy, and said, 'This is Peter Smith.' He said, 'We have adopted him as part of our family.'

Now you are the people of God
Before he was adopted, Peter was without a family. The Smiths didn't *need* Peter, but they *wanted* him. Peter could let go of the rejection he felt in the past and accept the love of his father who chose to adopt him. Our heavenly Father didn't *need* us, but He *wanted* us. This unconditional love

and acceptance of God is the essential foundation for our holy living.

'But you are a chosen people, a royal priesthood, a holy nation, a people belonging to God, that you may declare the praises of him who called you out of darkness into his wonderful light. Once you were not a people, but now you are the people of God; once you had not received mercy, but now you have received mercy' (1 Pet 2:9,10). There are no illegitimate children of God; none of us were unwanted or unexpected accidents. 'For he chose us in him, before the creation of the world to be holy and blameless in his sight' (Eph 1:4).

We are not castoffs in an orphanage acting on our best behaviour so someone might finally adopt us. Titus 3:4,5 tells us, 'But when the kindness and love of God our Saviour appeared, he saved us, not because of righteous things we had done, but because of his mercy.' Where once we had not received mercy, now we have. 'Consequently, you are no longer foreigners and aliens, but fellow citizens with God's people and members of God's household' (Eph 2:19).

Connecting with God

After speaking to a men's group about forgiving others, I was approached by two brothers. One had brought the other who had not gone to church for many years. His opening line was, 'Neil, my problem is canonicity. I've read seven books on the subject, and I just can't accept it.'

At first I wasn't sure what he meant. All I could picture in my mind was an old rusty cannon! I finally realised he was talking about the determination of which books could accurately and authoritatively be included in the Bible. 'Oh, you mean the closing of the canon!'

Do you really believe that was his problem? I couldn't believe his faith had been thwarted because he didn't agree with the rationale behind the collection of the books of the Bible. I pressed him further and discovered what was really the issue.

Both brothers related their story, which centred around their stepfather who never accepted them. He wasn't a bad person, but they never connected with him. There was never a bonding relationship, not even with their mother. Consequently, their relationship with God was only theological, as their relationship with their parents was only functional.

When I started to explain the nature of a bonding relationship, one of them looked at his watch and said, 'It's getting late.'

'See,' I responded, 'any time someone gets too close personally, you change the subject.' That night the backslidden brother forgave his stepfather, and the following month he asked to sing a song of testimony for the gathering of men. There wasn't a dry eye in the house.

Many people are like these brothers. When you get too close, they look for a way out. We will never connect with God until we confront the personal issues in our lives. Some people hide behind their theology. It is not uncommon at a conference to have someone, usually a man, approach me with his Bible and want to argue with me. If the situation warrants it, I will say, 'That's a legitimate question, but can I ask what you are personally struggling with? Is it your marriage or family? Is it your sense of purpose in life?' Some are touched that I care enough to ask, while others continue arguing, creating a smoke screen to keep me from getting too close.

We are all children of God
One of Satan's most common lies is that somehow you and I are different from other people. We may think, *God accepts these other people but not me.* I have researched

more than 1,725 professing Christian college students. Seventy-four per cent believed Christianity works for others, but it doesn't work for them. Is that true? Of course not. But if they believe that, will it affect the way they live their lives? Yes, it will. In privacy, I have actually had reasonably functioning adults tell me they think they may be aliens. This may sound bizarre, but Satan has done such a number on their thoughts, many have literally believed they are totally different from other people. But it's not true. All Christians are children of God, fellow citizens with God's people.

Dear heavenly Father, thank you for loving and choosing me. I reject the lies of Satan that You don't want me or care for me. I choose to believe that I am no longer a stranger to You. I am a fellow citizen with God's people and a member of God's household. With great joy I accept the fact that I have been adopted into Your family because of Your great love. Because of Your mercy, I have been saved. I thank You for this in the wonderful name of my Lord and Saviour, Jesus Christ. Amen.

25
I Have Direct Access to God Through the Holy Spirit

'He came and preached peace to you who were far away and peace to those who were near. For through him we both have access to the Father by one Spirit.'   EPHESIANS 2:17,18

When I was completing my basic training for the U.S. Navy, I was assigned to an evening watch with the officer of the day, a young lieutenant who was very personable. We had a lot in common and we enjoyed a pleasant evening chatting together. But he represented the ultimate authority on the base, and I was there to do his bidding.

Throughout my four-hour watch, several recruits came to his office for disciplinary reasons or with various requests. Regardless, everyone who approached him had to 'sound off' in a very specific way according to navy protocol. If they did it wrong, they had to do it again. In obvious fear, some had to do it again and again until they got it right. They were intimidated by him and they hoped for mercy.

Approaching the ultimate authority

When I reported for duty, I also approached this authority figure with some fear. However, I quickly realised I had a right to be there and that it was the safest place on the base as long as I had a good relationship with the lieutenant. My sense of security was dependent upon my obedience to and respect for this authority figure. It was a position I was not going to abuse by becoming disrespectful or disobedient. I also realised that every other recruit could have the same sense of safety and security if they were willing to humble themselves and approach him on the right basis.

There is only one way to approach God — through Jesus Christ, who said, 'I am the way and the truth and the life. No one comes to the Father except through me' (Jn 14:6). Jesus is the door; He is the access through whom we have the right to come to the throne of grace. Our only right to be there is because of the shed blood of the Lord Jesus Christ and His grace.

The writer of Hebrews says, 'Let us then approach the throne of grace with confidence, so that we may receive mercy and find grace to help us in our time of need' (Heb 4:16). 'In him and through faith in him we may approach God with freedom and confidence' (Eph 3:12). We have the *right* to come before God, we are *in Christ*, and Christ is seated with the heavenly Father.

You don't have to fear

Abuse of power and position has left many people fearful of authority figures. Many times, children are afraid to approach their parents, employees are intimidated by their bosses, and some church members fear confrontation with legalistic leaders. People often project the reaction of human authority onto God. If they can't approach their 'under-shepherds', how can they approach God? But God is not like that, He is love, and the punishment we deserved was placed upon His only Son. This is what John says in his first epistle: 'God is love. Whoever lives in love lives in God, and God in him. In this way, love is made complete among us so that we will have confidence on the day of judgement, because in this world we are like him. There is no fear in love. But perfect love drives out fear, because fear has to do with punishment. The one who fears is not made perfect in love' (1 Jn 4:16–18).

Confidence to enter

Being afraid of God is not a new problem. In the Old Testament, access to God was forbidden, and people feared His judgement. Only on the Day of Atonement could the high priest alone enter into the holy of holies, and that was an awesome experience. He first went through elaborate ceremonial cleansing in order to be qualified to enter. A rope was tied around his leg and bells were hemmed to the bottom of his garment so those outside could listen for the bells, indicating that he was still alive in the presence of God. If they no longer heard the bells, they used the rope to pull him out.

Under the former covenant, the way into the sanctuary of God's presence was closed to people, because the blood of animal sacrifices could never completely atone for their sins. Now, however, believers can come to the throne of grace because the perfect priest has offered the perfect sacrifice, atoning for sin once and for all. When Jesus died, the curtain separating the holy place from the Most Holy Place 'was torn in two from top to bottom' (Mk 15:38). The curtain symbolises the body of Christ in terms of His suffering. His body was torn to open the way into the divine presence.

The writer of Hebrews beautifully depicts this entrance into God's presence prepared for us by the Lord Jesus Christ: 'Therefore, brothers, since we have confidence to enter the Most Holy Place by the blood of Jesus, by a new and living way opened for us through the curtain, that is, his body, and since we have a great priest over the house of God, let us draw near to God with a sincere heart in full assurance of faith, having our hearts sprinkled to cleanse us from a guilty conscience and having our bodies washed with pure water. Let us hold unswervingly to the hope we profess, for he who promised is faithful. And let us consider how we may spur one another on toward love and good deeds' (Heb 10:19–24).

No bypass to God

I would not want to approach God on any other basis than through the blood of the Lord Jesus Christ. Arrogant people who show no respect for God's authority, or who seek by their own efforts to approach God, can only expect a terrifying judgement. The writer of Hebrews continues on, 'If we deliberately keep on sinning after we have received the knowledge of the truth, no sacrifice for sins is left, but only a fearful expectation of judgement and of raging fire that will consume the enemies of God. Anyone who rejected the law of Moses died without mercy on the testimony of two or three witnesses. How much more severely do you think a man deserves to be punished who has trampled the Son of God under foot, who has treated as an unholy thing the blood of the covenant that sanctified him, and who has insulted the Spirit of grace? For we know him who said, "It is mine to avenge; I will repay," and again, "The Lord will judge his people." It is a dreadful thing to fall into the hands of the living God' (Heb 10:26–31).

This passage is not threatening Christians with the loss of salvation, because true believers have not rejected the sacrifice of Christ. To reject Christ's sacrifice for sins is to reject the only sacrifice; there is no other. Hebrews 10:18 says, 'And where these have been forgiven, there is no longer any sacrifice for sin.' But Christ has died once and for all, and our sins are forgiven. If you are a child of God, you have not rejected the sacrifice of Christ, you have received it as the basis for your salvation. No Christian can commit the unpardonable sin, because the only unpardonable sin is unbelief, which will keep people forever from the grace of God. But now that you have received grace, your sins are forgiven.

These passages, however, do serve as a sober warning to Christians to take seriously the offensive nature of sin and the damage it does to ourselves, our testimony and the person of Christ.

Victory in Jesus

After years of helping people find their freedom in Christ, I can tell you that Satan uses fallacious teaching or personal misunderstanding of Hebrews 6 and 10 (the concept of the unpardonable sin) more than any other passages in Scripture. Consider this powerful testimony:

I had to write to you after reading *The Bondage Breaker* and listening to you on radio. God has delivered me from a Satanic bondage that held me for nine years. I lived in such a state of fear that I was hardly able to function normally.

I was going to a church that did not teach our security in Christ. The pastor told stories of people who had committed the unpardonable sin, and then tried to get forgiveness and couldn't. I wanted to brush it off, but soon afterward while cleaning house, I heard the first voice in my mind. It was blasphemous against God. It was as though I had been hit in the stomach. I doubled over, and a fear swept over me.

After that, the voices got worse and more frequent against God, Jesus, and finally, the Holy Spirit. Following the blasphemous thoughts came the accusations: 'Now you've done it — you're doomed for hell. God can't love you.' Over and over, I heard those voices in my mind until I thought I was going insane. I told no one, and I couldn't sleep. Nightmares caused me to fear the night. Once, I was awakened by a horrible voice calling my name. I saw a grotesque figure sitting on my dresser. The evil presence was so strong, I thought I was on the edge of hell.

When I tried to pray, the voices only got worse. I couldn't tell anyone, because I was afraid no one would understand. Fear totally dominated my life. I called the church, and the elders laid their hands on me, but no amount of prayer worked. I was losing my health, my family and my sanity. I even attempted suicide.

I started attending a different church that really taught the Word of God. I studied and memorised Scripture, and I started to grow again spiritually. One day, I came across Luke 10:19, and the presence of God came over me. Somehow I knew that His power had kept me through those tormenting nine years. Nothing could hurt me or separate me from God, just as it says in Romans 8:38,39.

His protection had been there all the time — all I had to do was to exercise the authority I had in Christ. But the fear had kept me from doing that. For the first time, I realised I had nothing to fear. God would never leave me. I felt His love so strong. He showed me I was His child; if I wasn't, I would never have survived Satan's attacks. I knew then I was totally free. I no longer struggle with fear. Just as you said in your book, Satan is a toothless lion. He only has a roar. I claim my victory in Christ.

I let years go by when all I had to do was take authority in Jesus Christ and resist the devil. But when you think you have committed the unpardonable sin and have lost your salvation, you feel you have no authority. This was the vicious trick of the devil; playing on my worst fears, and keeping me in bondage for years.

I thank God daily for my wonderful salvation, the deliverance He gave to me, and the security I have in Him. Now when Satan comes with his scare tactics, usually late at night, I just take my authority over him and he's gone. I wish every Christian knew who they were in Christ and the authority we have over Satan. What a great and awesome God we serve. As children of God, we should know that our past is forgiven, our present is secure, and our future looks bright!

By His grace alone

By what right do we approach the throne of God? Through the shed blood of our Lord Jesus Christ and by His grace alone. Because of Jesus, our Great High Priest, we have confidence to enter the most holy place. We stand there in His righteousness. The writer of Hebrews says, 'Let us draw near to God with a sincere heart in full assurance of faith.... Let us hold unswervingly to the hope we profess, for he who promises is faithful' (Heb 10:22,23). On the basis of Christ's finished work on the cross for us, we can pray:

Dear heavenly Father, You are the holy and sovereign Lord of the universe, and I acknowledge Your authority. I come before Your presence by way of the shed blood of the Lord Jesus Christ. I acknowledge that I have no other right to be in Your presence. I honour You as the Lord of my life, place my trust in You and commit myself to obey You. Because of Your love, I no longer fear punishment. Instead, I seek Your presence as the only place of safety and security. I renounce the lies of Satan that You do not love me or that I don't have any right to be in Your presence. So I come to You in freedom and in confidence with a sincere heart in full assurance of faith. In Jesus' precious name I pray. Amen.

26
I Have Been Redeemed and Forgiven of All My Sins

'For he has rescued us from the dominion of darkness and brought us into the kingdom of the Son he loves, in whom we have redemption, the forgiveness of sins.' COLOSSIANS 1:13,14

In my early years of ministry, I had no idea how evil and utterly black is the domain of darkness. Because I was blessed with good parents and a rich country heritage, I was not subjected to the incredible evil I now confront almost daily. As I listen to the horror stories from the victims of unspeakable atrocities, I cannot help but wonder how the secular world can listen to such abominations without ever seeing any resolution. I would be haunted by the stories I hear if I had not learned how to help people find their freedom in Christ. A caring person can't help being concerned, but without resolution, one would have to either pull away or become emotionally hardened to protect one's self.

Prisoners set free

Consider the letter I received from a chaplain in a prison ministry who attended one of our conferences:

> I attended your conference this past spring, and I wanted you to know that it has made a tremendous impact on my ministry. As a chaplain, most of the people I deal with are in bondage of some sort. I have had several opportunities to take inmates through the *Steps*

to Freedom. Each time, the individual has found freedom from bondage in his life. Your ministry is going to revolutionise my ministry. It hits right at the core of all the warfare issues.

One man who went through the *Steps to Freedom* was named Frederick. He was originally from South America and had experienced every evil thing you could imagine. His parents were involved with witch doctors, and so was he. For many years, he was a hit man for organised crime and had shot or stabbed many people. His body was full of evil tattoos: dragons, snakes and 666. He had been involved in every sexual perversion possible with both men and women, including being a male prostitute. He got involved in Satan worship.

Although Frederick received Christ three and a half years ago at a Christian halfway house, he was still oppressed, constantly hearing voices telling him to hurt people. Many times while in bed, he felt someone trying to strangle him. He often saw spirits appear beside him. Several weeks ago, I took him through the *Steps to Freedom*. He received immediate freedom and has never heard voices or seen spirits since that time. Praise the Lord.

Satan's bonds broken

At the other extreme, an attractive young university student from a good family walked into my office desperately seeking help for her life. We talked and prayed together, and several months later I received this note:

When we met together, the Lord released me totally from the grip Satan had on me. I can't quite explain it, and sometimes it's embarrassing to try, but my head feels totally free! There are no more voices or feelings of heaviness on my brain, only a physical release over my whole being.

Many times, Satan has tried to come back and clobber me with old, negative thoughts about God and my relationship with Him, but Satan's hold on my life has been unable to return. So much has happened since we prayed that it would take pages and pages to write it all down. I had honestly felt like there was no one to turn to and no one who could understand what I was feeling inside.

P.S. It has been wonderful and exciting to face and deal with problems with a clear head.

When Christ set us free, we are free indeed!

The price has been paid

Sometimes after I walk people through the Steps of Freedom, they will ask, 'How much do I owe you?' What a joy it is to say, 'You don't owe me anything. The price has already been paid.' What I have, and you can have as well, is the privilege to see suffering people find freedom in Christ. What remains in my memory after these sessions is not the abuse and the atrocities but the freedom.

The historical and orthodox teaching of the Church is that God paid a ransom price, the precious blood of the Lord Jesus Christ at the cross, to buy sinners from the slave market of sin (see 1 Peter 1:18,19). What is being spoken of here is the fact that we have been redeemed, which is to be given liberty upon receipt of a ransom. Titus writes, 'Our great God and Saviour, Jesus Christ, who gave himself for us to redeem us from all wickedness and to purify for himself a people that are his very own, eager to do what is good' (Titus 2:13,14).

Freedom changes behaviour

When spiritually imprisoned people are set free, they become zealous for good works. Suppose you were a prostitute, and the king had declared that all prostitutes were forgiven. You saw the decree and the seal on it. That would be great news wouldn't it? You probably would rejoice, but would that news alone change your perspective of yourself? You would probably still perceive yourself as a prostitute. Would it change your behaviour? Possibly not. You would just not have to sneak around and practise your trade in secret anymore. But what if the king's decree said that you were not only forgiven, but that the king had made you his bride? If you had become the queen, would that change your perspective of yourself? Would it change your behaviour? Of course it would! Why in the world would you live like a prostitute if you were the queen?

In Revelation 17:5, we are told that Satan's kingdom is:

MYSTERY
BABYLON THE GREAT
THE MOTHER OF PROSTITUTES
AND OF THE ABOMINATIONS OF
THE EARTH.

But in Revelation 21:9, we are told that the Church is the bride of Christ, 'the wife of the Lamb.' All of God's people are as special as a dearly loved bride from God's perspective, and if they only knew and believed that, they would do good works out of hearts full of love. That is why 1 John 3:3 says, 'Everyone who has this hope in him purifies himself.'

God's people are special people

I was asked a year in advance if I would speak to the staff and chaplains at a rescue mission. This was not the normal service when churches come in and share with those who are homeless and needy. This was a meeting of those off the streets who had trusted in Christ and made their first step. As I walked in, and even before I was introduced, everyone stood up and applauded. I was flabbergasted, knowing I had never met these men.

Then I found out they had been going through our video series *Resolving Personal and Spiritual Conflicts*. They weren't really applauding me. They were applauding the message they had received that they were not just a bunch of drunks, derelicts, and down-and-outs — they were children of God, special people who had been transferred out of the kingdom of darkness into the kingdom of light. And they had received redemption, the forgiveness of sins. Paul says in Ephesians 5:8, 'For you were once darkness, but now you are light in the Lord. Live as children of light.'

Dear heavenly Father, thank You for rescuing me from the domain of darkness. Because of Your great grace, I announce that I am no longer a child of darkness but a child of light, and I choose to walk in the light and ask that You will enable me to do so. I renounce the lie that I am just a product of my past, and I announce the truth that I am a product of Christ's work on the cross. I ask You to reveal to me anything in my life that would keep me in bondage to my past or to the lies of Satan. I ask for the grace to renounce all former activities of darkness and the lies of Satan. I now commit myself to You for all eternity. In Jesus' precious name and through His shed blood I pray. Amen.

27
I Am Complete

'For in Him dwells all the fullness of the Godhead bodily; and you are complete in Him, who is the head of all principality and power.'
COLOSSIANS 2:9,10 (NKJV)

Suppose a brand new car rolled off the assembly line, advertised as the most luxurious and powerful automobile ever made. It had a spark of life in it because of the battery, but it had yet to be filled with petrol. A tribesman from a remote part of the Amazon was flown in to inspect this beautiful car. Having no previous knowledge of cars, he wondered about the purpose of this object.

Observing the beautiful lines — the symmetry, the chrome, the paint job — he thought it might be for the sake of beauty, like a statue. As he sat in the bucket seats and tilted them forward and up and down, he wondered if it might be for comfort, like a small dwelling. He turned on the quadraphonic sound and thought the car might have been created for the enjoyment of music. When he turned on the headlights and the dome lights, he thought the car was for light. Tooting the horn, he thought the car was to give a warning. Then someone filled the car with petrol, put it in gear and the vehicle began to move forward. Finally, the tribesman understood the real purpose for which the car was created.

The purpose of an automobile is to provide transportation, but it can never fulfil its purpose without petrol. The body and accessories may be luxurious, but they won't move on their own. Nor does the engine itself have any power of its own; its only purpose is to convert the gasoline into a usable energy force. Then, and only then, can the automobile fulfil its purpose.

Fulfilling our purpose

We were never designed by God to function independently of Him. God created Adam and Eve spiritually alive; their souls were in union with Him. Only in this way could they fulfil the purpose for which they were created. But man, because of his rebellion, has chosen to live his life independently of God. Through sin, he has separated himself from God. However, God's plan is to present us again complete in Christ, for without Him we are incomplete.

The following testimony from a young woman illustrates this:

> The word 'handicapped' described my family. My mother had muscular dystrophy, my father polio, and my brother cerebral palsy. Though I had no physical problem myself, I saw the stares and glances of people, always feeling like somehow our family was weird.
>
> My father was very abusive, beating us regularly. One time in a fit of anger, he grabbed my mother's head as she sat in her wheelchair, and pounded it against the kitchen counter. He was enslaved to pornography and often called me horrible names, such as 'slut' and 'whore'. He tore the dress I made in sewing class off me, saying only a whore would wear a dress like that.
>
> Often I heard my mother weeping and crying out to the Lord for strength. I was slowly losing hope. By the seventh grade I was escaping through alcohol and then through sex, which resulted in an abortion. When I was seventeen, my mum died, and at eighteen, I was out of the house and supporting myself.

I thought I could finally find some peace, but instead I felt empty and full of guilt. I didn't know what to do with my life, but I knew I needed help. I stumbled into a church one day and heard about God's forgiveness and love. I sobbed as I responded and asked Jesus into my life. A huge weight lifted from my heavy heart, and I experienced indescribable joy. I was on a spiritual high for months as I went to Bible studies and met other Christians. But my non-Christian boyfriend kept saying I was getting weird. I was intimidated by him and didn't know much Scripture yet. Besides, I was living with him and felt I needed him, though I was really supporting him. We got married and everything became worse. He gambled, and I resumed drinking. I hoped our first child would somehow bring the fulfilment I craved, but that didn't happen. By the time our second baby was six months old, my husband had gambled away all of our money, and I left him.

I went through months of depression and darkness. Then one night I decided to 'start living again' and began partying and seeking attention from men. It didn't matter to me whether they were married or not; I just wanted someone to tell me I was okay. But after another devastating relationship, I heard the Lord saying to me, 'You don't need men to make you happy; you only need Me.' But I didn't listen to God's gentle call back to Himself.

Then I met a wonderful man and married. I was sure life would be great now. But the first years of our marriage brought out all that was ugly in both of us. Eventually, I realised my drinking was not helping my alcoholic husband, and I turned to the Lord for strength to quit. I sensed that His love had preserved me in spite of all my wrong choices and rebellion. I felt He was telling me that if I would just start concentrating on Him, abiding in Him as my All Sufficient One, that He would be responsible for my husband.

I found a little church with a wonderful pastor, and my husband was willing to attend with me once in a while. The pastor's wife became my friend and discipler. One day, I realised that my husband had changed; he was kinder and more at peace. I asked him about it, and he told me he'd received Christ a few weeks before at our church. But it was another year and a half before I heard him praying one night for God to deliver him from alcoholism. The Lord graciously did just that.

About that time, I attended a Freedom in Christ conference and later prayed through the *Steps to Freedom* with a friend. What an eye-opening, heart-revealing, truth encounter! Forgiving my father from my heart opened a new revelation of what my true Heavenly Father is like. I realised I no longer need to be bound by my past, that my identity is now in Christ, and I am made complete and fulfilled in Him. I was chosen in Christ before the foundation of the world to be holy and without blame. The armour of God is put on daily in this 'temple', and I praise God that by His grace I am what I am.

Perhaps like this dear lady, you have gone from experience to experience seeking fulfilment and completeness. I hope you see that no other person or material things can fill the vacuum you feel. You were created to relate to God in soul-union, and you can only find rest and purpose in your life when you put your total dependence upon Him.

Paul says in Ephesians 5:18,19, 'Do not get drunk on wine, which leads to debauchery. Instead, be filled with the Spirit. Speak to one another with psalms, hymns and spiritual songs. Sing and make music in your heart to the Lord.' We can go joyfully down the road of life, fulfilling our purpose, if we will only be filled with the Spirit of God. Wherever I am in my process of maturity, if I am not operating by the power of the Holy Spirit, I can accomplish nothing. I am complete only in Christ.

When you first became a Christian, you were like a small engine for a lawn mower. You could accomplish a needed task and fulfil a worthwhile purpose. However, your goal is to mature into a giant tractor, and accomplish even greater things. Even as you mature, never forget that neither the small engine nor the giant tractor can accomplish anything without the petrol. The only time we can fulfil our purpose for being here is when we are filled with the Holy Spirit.

Living complete in Christ

My entire concept of discipleship is that we work towards the goal of presenting everybody complete or established in Christ (see Colossians 1:28). According to Colossians 2:10, we are already complete in Christ. The idea is that we are incomplete without Him. The Greek word for 'complete' is different in Colossians 1:28. Here the idea is to bring everybody to a maturity in Christ. Discipleship is being firmly grounded and rooted in Him, and then going on to be built up in Him and continuing to live in Him.

God's gracious provision and offer to all Christians is that they might have a full assurance that they are, *right now*, complete in Christ. Paul says in Colossians 1:27–29, 'To them God has chosen to make known among the Gentiles the glorious riches of this mystery, which is Christ in you, the hope of glory. We proclaim him, admonishing and teaching everyone with all wisdom, so that we may present everyone perfect in Christ. To this end I labour, struggling with all his energy, which so powerfully works in me.'

Dear heavenly Father, I thank You for Your love and for making me aware that I was incomplete without You. I thank You

that I am now complete in Christ. I choose to no longer seek my purpose in life in any way independent of You. I put no confidence in the flesh. I now declare my dependence upon You and seek to fulfil my purpose by asking You to fill me with Your Holy Spirit. I renounce every occasion when I have sought power or fulfilment from any source other than You. I choose to be strong in You, Lord, and in the strength of Your might. In Jesus' precious name I pray. Amen.

28
I Am Secure

*'By wisdom the Lord laid the earth's foundations,
by understanding he set the heavens in place; by his
knowledge the deeps were divided, and the clouds
let drop the dew. My son, preserve sound
judgement and discernment, do not let them out of
your sight; they will be life for you, an ornament to
grace your neck. Then you will go on your way in
safety, and your foot will not stumble; when you lie
down, you will not be afraid; when you lie down,
your sleep will be sweet. Have no fear of sudden
disaster or of the ruin that overtakes the wicked,
for the Lord will be your confidence.'*

PROVERBS 3:19–26

The key to understanding security is learning to relate to
the eternal, not the temporal. Insecurity is caused by
depending upon temporal things we have no right or ability
to control. Lacking an eternal relationship and an eternal
perspective, man oftentimes is driven to find some sense of
safety or security.

Where not to look for security

Some people look for security in physical places. When I
was conducting a conference tour overseas, I called my wife
from the Philippines, and she asked how things were going.
At the time, Mount Pinatubo was about to erupt a second
time, the area was rattled by earthquakes and a raging

typhoon. What's more, I had just left my home in Southern California, where we had just experienced the worst earthquake in forty years, but that was still not the 'big one' everybody has predicted will come. A lot of places in the world are not safe, but in Christ we are always safe and secure.

Not in financial gain
Other people look for their sense of security in their financial holdings, but Jesus said:

'Watch out! Be on your guard against all kinds of greed; a man's life does not consist in the abundance of his possessions.'

And he told them this parable: 'The ground of a certain rich man produced a good crop. He thought to himself, "What shall I do? I have no place to store my crops."

'Then he said, "This is what I'll do. I will tear down my barns and build bigger ones, and there I will store all my grain and my goods. And I'll say to myself, 'You have plenty of good things laid up for many years. Take life easy; eat, drink and be merry.'"

'But God said to him, "You fool! This very night your life will be demanded from you. Then who will get what you have prepared for yourself?"

'This is how it will be for anyone who stores up things for himself but is not rich toward God' (Lk 12:15–21).

I believe that the financial structures of this world are being shaken to their very core. Who can predict with confidence where the money markets of this world will be in the next few years. Paul writes in 1 Timothy 6:6–10: 'But godliness with contentment is great gain. For we brought nothing into the world, and we can take nothing out of it. But if we have food and clothing, we will be content with that.

People who want to get rich fall into temptation and a trap and into many foolish and harmful desires that plunge men into ruin and destruction. For the love of money is a root of all kinds of evil. Some people, eager for money, have wandered from the faith and pierced themselves with many griefs.' Our major financial problem is not the lack of money; it is the lack of contentment with adequate food and clothing.

Not in temporal relationships

Many people look for a sense of security in temporal relationships: Spouses become insecure at the prospect that a mate may leave them, roommates live with the apprehension that the other may move out, employers fear the prospect of their help leaving, and employees are tense about the possibility of being made redundant. Any time people look for their ultimate security in temporal relationships, they set themselves up for a tremendous sense of insecurity and loss. I thank God for all my wonderful relatives and friends, but I also realise they are all temporal.

If we put too much stock in our earthly relationships, they may subtly replace God as the significant other in our lives. Paul warns us about trying to find our approval from men rather than from God: 'Am I now trying to win the approval of men, or of God? Or am I trying to please men? If I were still trying to please men, I would not be a servant of Christ' (Gal 1:10). If you were a man-pleaser, for whom would you be a servant? The consequence is to fear men more than God. Proverbs 29:25 says, 'Fear of man will prove to be a snare, but whoever trusts in the Lord is kept safe.'

Some people will try to find their sense of security by trusting only in themselves, but Proverbs 28:26 says: 'He who trusts in himself is a fool, but he who walks in wisdom is kept safe.' There is only One whom we can completely trust, and He controls the future.

Shaky foundations but sure promises

Standing on these shaky foundations of physical places, finances and temporal relationships, we face the reality of the second coming of Christ. We don't need to be afraid, but we do need to be aware of a sober warning in 1 Thessalonians 5:2–5, 'For you know very well that the day of the Lord will come like a thief in the night. While people are saying, "Peace and safety," destruction will come on them suddenly, as labour pains on a pregnant woman, and they will not escape. But you, brothers, are not in darkness so that this day should surprise you like a thief. You are all sons of the light and sons of the day. We do not belong to the night or to the darkness.' Destruction will come upon them, but not upon us, for we are all sons of light.

Security — our possession in Christ

I have often asked people what is the worst thing that could happen to them. Some respond, 'Well, I could die.' I am quick to say to them, 'That may be the *best* thing that could happen to you.' Philippians 1:21 says, 'For to me, to live is Christ and to die is gain.' Put anything else in that formula and see how it works. If you're living for your career, then to die would be loss. What if you're living solely for your family? Again, to die would be loss. If you're living for your palatial house and fancy cars, then again, to die would be loss.

There truly is only one way the formula will work: 'For to me, to live is Christ and to die is gain' (Phil 1:21). If we have an eternal perspective, even a loss of life can be seen as a profitable thing. 'I will lie down and sleep in peace, for you alone, O Lord, make me dwell in safety' (Ps 4:8).

The following eleven chapters all deal with our sense of

safety and security because of our possession in Christ. Pray that the Lord will open your eyes to the security you have in Him:

Dear heavenly Father, I thank You for my life in Christ. I know that my relationship with You is eternal. Teach me to see life from Your perspective. Open my eyes to the Scriptures in the coming chapters so I may see that I am safe and secure in Your arms. Protect my heart and my mind from the evil one. I place my trust in You for all eternity, and I put no confidence in the flesh. In Jesus' precious name I pray. Amen.

29
I Am Free Forever from Condemnation

'Therefore, there is now no condemnation for those who are in Christ Jesus, because through Christ Jesus the law of the Spirit of life set me free from the law of sin and death.' ROMANS 8:1,2

When I was in the navy, one of my favourite pastimes was photography. At one time, I had taken more than 800 slides while discovering the country of Japan. I turned them all in for development when we hit the next port. Because of an assigned duty, I had to trust another person to pick them up for me the day before we sailed. I was anxious to see them, so at the crack of dawn I was searching for my trusted friend. He was nowhere to be found.

Finally, I was informed that he was waiting for me on the second deck. Bounding up the ladder to the 02 level, I discovered my friend waiting for me with his fists raised. 'All right, let's get it over with,' he said.

'What in the world are you talking about,' I asked.

It turned out he had got drunk and lost all my pictures! I was furious. I have never beaten up anybody, though I confess I have thought about it a few times, and this was one of those times. If we had got into a fight, it wouldn't have gone well for my friend, as I was fifty pounds heavier and far more athletic.

'Put your fists down,' I said, 'I'm not going to do anything to you. Just tell me what happened and let's see what we can do about it.' He told me his story and there wasn't anything we could do about it! The pictures were gone. I had a choice: I could seek revenge or forgive him. I chose the latter and bore the consequence of his sin, which was the loss of something very valuable to me.

Ironically, I had rescued this same fellow from drowning several months earlier while he was swimming intoxicated off Midway Island. I felt as though I had some type of father relationship and responsibility for him.

When we have the life of Christ within us, we unwittingly bear the image of our heavenly Father more than we realise. The point is, Jesus saved us by bearing our sins upon Himself, therefore there is no condemnation, because we are forgiven.

It has been said that seventy-five per cent of all mentally disturbed people would be pronounced well if they could only be convinced that they are forgiven. Many seemingly healthy Christians find it difficult to believe that they are really free from condemnation. Some may say, 'I know that Jesus died for my sins and that I am forgiven for the sins I have already committed, but what if I should choose to sin tomorrow?'

Let me direct your thoughts to Romans 6:10: 'The death he died, he died to sin once for all; but the life he lives, he lives to God.' Christ died once for our sins, and He need not die again and again. Insecurity about forgiveness was common in the Old Testament because the blood of animal sacrifices was insufficient to atone for sins. 'He did not enter by means of the blood of goats and calves; but he entered the Most Holy Place *once for all* by his own blood, having obtained eternal redemption' (Heb 9:12, emphasis added). When Christ died once for all of our sins, how many of our sins were then future? They all were! There is no condemnation for the sins of the past or for the sins of the future because we are *in Christ*.

'God made him who had no sin to be sin for us, so that *in him* we might become the righteousness of God' (2 Cor

5:21, emphasis added). When Jesus went to the cross, all the sins of the world — past, present, and future — were placed upon Him. God the Father turned His back on His only Son, and He bore the condemnation for every sin ever committed. When Jesus ascended from the grave to sit at the right hand of the Father, there was no sin upon Him. There are no sins upon us that God would condemn us for either, because we as believers are *in Him*. We are alive *in Christ*.

Does this mean we never sin? Of course not, but we don't *have* to sin, and when we do, we are not condemned. 'My dear children, I write this to you so that you will not sin. But if anybody does sin, we have one who speaks to the Father in our defence — Jesus Christ, the Righteous One' (1 Jn 2:1).

Overcoming the law of sin and death

The basis for no condemnation in Romans 8:1 is explained in the next verse, 'Through Christ Jesus the law of the Spirit of life set me free from the law of sin and of death' (Rom 8:2). For the sake of illustration, let's consider the *law of sin* as similar to the law of gravity, and the *law of death* to be the consequence of the law of gravity. We know that the 'wages of sin is death' (see Romans 6:23), and sin, like gravity, will continue to pull us down. Unlike good ideas that may not last, laws are laws because they are continuously in effect.

We can fly in an aeroplane only because it has a power greater than the pull of gravity. If you don't believe that the law of gravity is still in effect, try cutting the engine and see how long it takes before you crash and burn. Can you imagine trying to 'fly' (live the Christian life) in the flesh. We would all end up walking like turkeys, when we are called to fly like eagles! If you were living in the flesh, you would be subject to the law of sin and death. The only way you can overcome any law is by another law that is greater.

But we are not trying to 'fly' in the flesh, for we are no

longer in the flesh but *in* Christ. Romans 8:9 says, 'You, however, are controlled not by the sinful nature [flesh] but by the Spirit, if the Spirit of God lives in you. And if anyone does not have the Spirit of Christ, he does not belong to Christ.' If you are *in* the flesh, you are not a Christian, because every child of God is *in* Christ. But even though we are in Christ, the flesh still remains with us, and we can choose to walk according to the flesh (old nature), or we can walk according to the Spirit.

Discerning your walk

One may ask, 'How do you know whether you are walking according to the flesh or the Spirit?' It's obvious according to Galatians 5:19: 'The acts of the sinful nature are obvious: sexual immorality, impurity and debauchery; idolatry and witchcraft; hatred, discord, jealousy, fits of rage, selfish ambition, dissensions, factions and envy; drunkenness, orgies, and the like.' Galatians 5:22 gives the flip side: 'But the fruit of the Spirit is love, joy, peace, patience, kindness, goodness, faithfulness, gentleness and self-control.'

To determine if you are walking according to the flesh or the Spirit, examine what's radiating out of your life. Though we are in Christ Jesus, we can still choose to operate according to the flesh. So if you have a fit of rage, what is the problem? Is somebody making you angry? Is it a deed of the other person's flesh or yours?

We must assume responsibility for our own attitudes and actions. When you sense you are walking according to the flesh, confess it, and ask the Lord to take control of your life again. If we are filled with the Spirit, we will sing and make melody in our hearts to the Lord (see Ephesians 5:18–20). The law of the Spirit of Life is always there, and we must learn to operate according to it. 'Walk by the Spirit, and you will not carry out the desire of the flesh' (Gal 5:16, NASB).

Don't allow sin to reign

Paul says, 'In the same way, count yourselves dead to sin but alive to God in Christ Jesus' (Rom 6:11). It is important to realise that we do not make ourselves dead to sin by considering it so; we consider it so because *it is so*. Has sin died? Of course not. The power of the law of sin is strong and alluring, but when it makes its appeal, you don't have to respond. You do not have to sin. But you must assume your responsibility to not allow sin to reign in your mortal body or choose to walk according to the flesh. If you do, you will not lose your salvation, but you will suffer the consequences of choosing to live independently of God. The deeds of the flesh will be evident.

The church in Corinth had become quite carnal. Paul encouraged them to stay in communion with God and to judge themselves accordingly. Because they hadn't assumed their responsibility, Paul writes in 1 Corinthians 11:30–32, 'That is why many among you are weak and sick, and a number of you have fallen asleep. But if we judged ourselves, we would not come under judgement. When we are judged by the Lord, we are being disciplined so that we will not be condemned with the world.'

God does not punish us out of condemnation. He disciplines us so we may share in His holiness. As Hebrews 12:10,11 says, 'Our fathers disciplined us for a little while as they thought best; but God disciplines us for our good, that we may share in his holiness. No discipline seems pleasant at the time, but painful. Later on, however, it produces a harvest of righteousness and peace for those who have been trained by it.'

Servants of a new covenant

In Romans 6:14, we read, 'You are not under law, but under grace.' Since you are no longer under the law, Satan has no basis to accuse you. Established law is the only basis for any accusation. Suppose you were pulled over by a policeman who wrote you a ticket for speeding. But you discovered that by some oversight of the lawmakers, there were no laws regulating the speed on that particular street. Could a judge find you guilty? Of course not.

The critic may scoff, 'Great, there are no laws, so everyone can sin all they want.' Wrong! Paul objects to that reasoning: 'Shall we go on sinning so that grace may increase? By no means! We died to sin; how can we live in it any longer?' (Rom 6:1,2). We shouldn't avoid sin because we fear eternal damnation. We should do so because we no longer want to live in bondage and bring shame upon our Lord and His Church. We are 'ministers of a new covenant — not of the letter [the law] but of the Spirit, for the letter kills, but the Spirit gives life' (2 Cor 3:6).

The only way a person can be condemned is to be found without Christ on the Judgement Day. We have already been judged and found innocent, because we are in Christ Jesus, who took the punishment for our sins upon Himself. 'Now the Lord is the Spirit, and where the Spirit of the Lord is, there is freedom' (2 Cor 3:17). Hallelujah, what a Saviour! Let's thank Him for freeing us from condemnation:

Dear heavenly Father, I thank You for sending Your Son to take my place on the Cross. I choose to believe the truth that there is no condemnation for those who are in Christ Jesus. I thank You for disciplining me as Your child so I may bear the fruit of righteousness. I believe the truth, 'There is no fear in love. But perfect love drives out fear, because fear has to do with punishment' (1 Jn 4:18). I know that You are not punishing me when You discipline me, because You love me. I renounce the lies of Satan that I am still subject to the laws of sin and death. I accept my responsibility to walk in the light, and I ask You to show me the times I have walked according to the flesh. I confess these times to You, and I thank You for

Your forgiveness and cleansing. I now ask You to fill me with Your Holy Spirit that I may walk according to Your Spirit. In Jesus' precious name I pray. Amen.

30
I Am Assured that All Things Work Together for Good

'And we know that in all things God works for the good of those who love him, who have been called according to his purpose. For those God foreknew he also predestined to be conformed to the likeness of his Son, that he might be the firstborn among many brothers. And those he predestined, he also called; those he called, he also justified; those he justified, he also glorified.'   ROMANS 8:28–30

Several years ago, while I was still working as an engineer, a co-worker shared with me the exciting news that his church was the beneficiary of an estate worth more than $700,000. That was an incredible sum of money for a small church to receive in the 1960s. For days, we speculated over the various possibilities of how the church would use that money.

Six months later, I remembered the incident and asked my friend, 'By the way, what became of that $700,000 your church received?'

'Don't ask,' he responded. 'Our church became divisive over what to do with the money and split right down the middle.'

What at one time was a happy little fellowship, trusting God for its daily provision, was torn apart over what seemed to be a good thing.

What is a good thing?
An old Chinese proverb tells of a young man who was raised in a peasant home with meagre material possessions.

One day, a stranger rode by his home leading several horses. He called out, 'If there is a young man in the household, I would like to give him a horse.' So the young man received the most incredible gift someone of his economic status could possibly receive. What a great thing to have his own horse!

The next day as he was riding, he fell off the horse and broke his leg. Well, maybe owning a horse was not a good thing after all, maybe it was a bad thing. However, the following day some warlords came out of the hills and insisted the young man ride with them into war. The boy could not go, because he had a broken leg. Suddenly having a broken leg was a good thing!

The proverb continues on and on, alternating between what appeared to be a good thing one day, turning out to be a bad thing the next day. The problem is, we really don't know what is good for us. God can work through anything. What is good is what God wills. This book is not large enough to contain all the stories I could tell of how God has used adversity to bring people to Himself.

Proven character from the good and the bad
God does not promise to make a bad thing good, nor has He assured us that He will keep us from bad things. He has promised us that in all things — even those that are terrible — good can come out of it for all those who love Him. In Romans 8:26–28, Paul is completing the thought he originally began in Romans 5:3–5, 'And not only this, but we also exult in our tribulations, knowing that tribulation brings about perseverance; and perseverance, proven character; and proven character, hope; and hope does not disappoint, because the love of God has been poured out within our hearts through the Holy Spirit who was given to us' (NASB).

In verse 3, 'exult' means heightened joy; 'tribulation'

means to be under pressure; 'perseverance' means to remain under pressure. As you consider this, it may seem that God is subjecting us to some kind of Christian masochism. But that is a wrong assumption. God is simply trying to show us that in the midst of trials and tribulations, He intends to produce the result of proven character, and that is where our hope lies.

Many people today believe their marriage is hopeless. Their solution? Change spouses! If their job is miserable, they change jobs! And if their church has problems, they switch churches! Running away from difficult situations is not where our hope lies. God's plan is that we 'hang in there' and grow up. Our hope lies in proven character, not in favourable circumstances. Hope based in favourable circumstances will always disappoint, but when based on the love of God and our proven character, we will never be disappointed.

Even so, we should be aware of false hopes. God never promised that everything would turn out exactly as we would like. Our hope is not in believing that life should be smooth sailing, and if things are rough right now, they'll be better in the morning. Our hope lies in the fact that God will make us better people and conform us to His image *through* our difficult circumstances.

Suppose you came to my office in great anguish and told me your spouse just left you. You would be crying out for hope, and I would want to give you some. But if I said, 'Oh, we'll win your spouse back,' I would be giving you a false hope. I cannot assure that. But I could say, 'Listen, if you have not committed yourself in the past to be the best possible spouse that God wants you to be, would you commit yourself to that now?' But even if your spouse didn't return, which we cannot guarantee, you could come through this tribulation with proven character. You can become a better person than you were before the crisis, and that's where your hope lies.

God's plan for us is based on His foreknowledge of us

God knew us from the foundations of the world and predestined us to be conformed to the likeness of His Son. In what way did He know us? Some teachers strongly believe in divine election, which means God chose us to be His children from the beginning of time. They would appeal to passages such as Ephesians 1:4,5: 'For he chose us in him before the creation of the world to be holy and blameless in his sight. In love, he predestined us to be adopted as his sons through Jesus Christ, in accordance with his pleasure and will.' Others believe salvation is primarily entered into by personal choice, citing verses such as Romans 10:13, 'Everyone who calls on the name of the Lord will be saved.'

I would caution against going to either extreme on this issue. One extreme sees divine election as being equivalent to fatalism — that there is no involvement of the human will. Others go to the other extreme that it is solely a matter of human choice. Divine sovereignty and human responsibility are both taught in the Word of God.

Someone suggested that if we looked upon the gateway to eternal life from the outside, we would see the sign: Whoever calls upon the name of the Lord shall be saved. But after we have called upon the name of the Lord and walked through that gate, looking back we would see the inscription: For you were known from the foundations of the world. Some things are simply beyond human comprehension, and we cannot advocate one portion of Scripture at the expense of another. Sovereignty and free will are like parallel railroad tracks that seem finally to converge as we look off into eternity.

What the 'all things' are for

The important thing is to realise that we have been known and predestined from the foundation of the world. Even if this refers only to the fact that in eternity past God knew those who would by faith become His people. Nevertheless, we *were* foreknown and predestined to be conformed to the image of God. That is what the 'all things' of Romans 8:28 are working together to accomplish in our lives — that we may take on the very character of Christ.

To this we add the present hope that we also shall be glorified. 'For in this hope we were saved. But hope that is seen is no hope at all. Who hopes for what he already has? But if we hope for what we do not yet have, we wait for it patiently' (Rom 8:24,25). Here lies our hope: In the present context of human suffering, trials and tribulations, we can, by the grace of God, emerge with proven character. Hope is not wishful thinking; biblical hope is the present assurance of God's plan and promises being fully realised in the future.

Dear heavenly Father, I am in awe that You have known me from the beginning of time. I confess that I don't fully understand what that really means. You alone are God. I accept Your purpose for my life to be conformed to Your image during times of trouble. Thank You for the hope this gives me and the assurance that in all things You work for good. I renounce the lies of Satan that I must not be a Christian or not walking in the Spirit if bad things happen. I renounce the lie that You have forsaken me during difficult times or that there is no hope. I assume my responsibility to allow You to fulfil Your purpose in my life — to conform me to Your image. I ask for Your grace to enable me to be like Christ. I now profess that my hope lies in the knowledge that You are working through all of the trials in my life to develop proven character. In Jesus' precious name I pray. Amen.

31
I Am Free from Any Condemning Charges Against Me

'If God is for us who can be against us? He who did not spare his own Son, but gave him up for us all — how will he not also, along with him, graciously give us all things? Who will bring any charge against those whom God has chosen? It is God who justifies. Who is he that condemns? Christ Jesus, who died — more than that, who was raised to life — is at the right hand of God and is also interceding for us.'   ROMANS 8:31–34

This tremendous passage is really dealing with the fact that if God is for us then no other opposition is of any account. If God isn't out to get us, then who is? The answer is Satan. Revelation 12:10 says that he accuses the brethren day and night. This relentless enemy of our souls blinds the unbelieving so they cannot see the light of the gospel of the glory of Christ (see 2 Corinthians 4:4). An emissary of Satan is assigned to keep us under the penalty of sin. Twenty-five years ago, he lost that battle in my life, thanks be to Jesus, but he didn't pull in his fangs and curl up his tail. Now he is committed to keep me, and you, under the power of sin; his chief means of doing this is through deception.

This father of lies (see John 8:44) is raising up thoughts against the knowledge of God (see 2 Corinthians 10:5), seeking to distort the nature of our relationship with Him and accusing us day and night. Paul warns us not to be ignorant of Satan's schemes (see 2 Corinthians 2:11), but Christians often operate like blindfolded warriors. Not knowing who our enemy is, we strike out at ourselves and each other.

The battle for the mind

Satan can't do anything about our position in Christ. However, if he can get us to *believe* our position isn't true, we will live as though it is not. For instance, evangelist Steve Russo and I surveyed 1,725 professing Christian young people, and we found that three out of four believed they are different from other young people, that Christianity works for others, but not for them. Is that true? Of course not, but if they believe they are different will it affect the way they live their lives? Of course, and it is affecting their lives. Of the same group, seven out of ten said they were hearing voices like a subconscious self talking to them.

Now do I believe that seven out of ten Christian young people are psychotic or paranoid schizophrenic? No, I do not believe that! What I believe is 1 Timothy 4:1: 'The Spirit clearly says that in later times some will abandon the faith and follow deceiving spirits and things taught by demons.' That's happening all over the world. No matter where I go, that battle is existing in the minds of people.

The primary nature of that battle is to destroy our concept of God, distort the relationship we have with Him, or discredit the truth of who I really am as a child of God. Satan's lies are aimed at causing me to think, *I'm stupid, I'm no good, I'm ugly, God doesn't love me, I can't be forgiven, Christianity doesn't work for me.*

This is often apparent as I lead people through the *Steps to Freedom.* For example, when I learn that a woman has had illicit sex and an abortion, I encourage her to assume responsibility and resolve the issue with the following prayer:

Lord, I confess that I have used my body as an instrument of unrighteousness and conceived a child. I did not assume stewardship of that life, and I ask Your forgiveness. I give that child to You for Your care in eternity. Amen.

In one incident, I asked the counsellee to also pray: 'And accept Your forgiveness, Lord, by choosing to forgive myself.' She immediately began experiencing interference, revealing how Satan was holding her in bondage. She believed she could not be forgiven for such a terrible act. Is that true? No, it's a lie. Those charging, condemning thoughts cannot be from God because He is the one who justifies, 'God demonstrates his own love for us in this: While we were still sinners, Christ died for us' (Rom 5:8).

Who does God rebuke?

Zechariah 3:1,2 says, 'Then he showed me Joshua the high priest standing before the angel of the Lord, and Satan standing at his right side to accuse him. The Lord said to Satan, 'The Lord rebuke you, Satan! The Lord, who has chosen Jerusalem, rebuke you! Is not this man a burning stick snatched from the fire?'

Joshua was standing before God as the high priest representing the nation of Israel. He was clothed in filthy garments, which was not a good thing. In the Old Testament, when the high priest came before God in the holy of holies on the Day of Atonement, he went through elaborate ceremonial washings so he would appear undefiled before God. The picture we have before us is of a man representing the sins of the people of Israel, and Satan is standing alongside to accuse him. But who does God rebuke? He rebukes Satan, proclaiming, 'Is not this man a burning stick snatched from the fire?' (Zech 3:2). Are we not children of God, snatched from the flames of hell?

What do you suppose God is doing today in the face of

Satan's accusations against the children of God? Let me construct a scene in the courts of heaven. Who is the judge? It is God the Father. Who are the accused? It is you and me. Who is the prosecuting attorney? It is Satan. Who is the defence attorney? It is Jesus. Can we lose this court case? There is *no way* we could, because 'He is able to save completely those who come to God through him, because he always lives to intercede for them' (Heb 7:25).

Jesus is standing at the right hand of the Father, saying, 'Look at my side that was pierced. Look at my hands and feet. My sacrifice is sufficient. I died once, for all.' What power does Satan have? Can he determine the verdict? Can he pronounce the sentence? No, all he can do is bring forth charges and accusations.

God builds us up

The entire thrust of the New Testament is to reestablish a fallen humanity and present us complete in Christ. God is trying to build us up and charges us to do the same for each other. So who is trying to destroy our relationship with God, tear us down, and accuse us day and night? Certainly not God!

The remaining question is, 'How can I know the difference between Satan's accusations and the Holy Spirit's conviction regarding sin in my life?' The answer, I believe, is in 2 Corinthians 7:9,10: 'Yet now I am happy, not because you were made sorry, but because your sorrow led you to repentance. For you became sorrowful as God intended and so were not harmed in any way by us. Godly sorrow brings repentance that leads to salvation and leaves no regret, but worldly sorrow brings death.' Paul is saying, 'I'm glad you are under the conviction of God, that you are feeling that sense of sorrow.' Why? Because it leads to repentance and to life with no regret. So as I confess my sins to God, there is never any lingering regret or condemnation. It is over and finished. But worldly sorrow brings death; it just tears you down.

Scripture uses the word 'sorrow' for the emotional result from the conviction of the Lord and the 'sorrow' of the world. The point is they may feel the same. The difference is in the result. One leads to life; the other leads to death. For instance, Judas betrayed Christ and probably came under conviction but responded to the sorrow of the world and committed suicide. Peter also betrayed Christ, felt the conviction of God, repented and became the spokesperson for the Church. I believe the Lord wants us free from Satan's condemning thoughts — free to love and serve Him.

Settle it once for all

Helping people find their freedom in Christ has been the thrust of my ministry for several years. When people are released from bondage, there is a peace of God that passes all understanding (see Philippians 4:7). Paul says, 'Examine yourselves to see whether you are in the faith; test yourselves. Do you not realise that Christ Jesus is in you — unless, of course, you fail the test?' (2 Cor 13:5).

Why don't you settle it once and for all. Where does your trust and confidence lie, in yourself or in God? Are you dependent upon yourself for your salvation, or are you dependent upon Christ's finished work on Calvary? Does God want you to know that you have an eternal relationship with Him? Of course He does. John says his words were written 'that you may believe that Jesus is the Christ, the Son of God, and that by believing you may have life in his name' (Jn 20:31). 'I write these things to you who believe in the name of the Son of God so that you may know that you have eternal life' (1 Jn 5:13).

Rather than close this chapter with a prayer, I am concluding with a declaration. Read it through, and if you find that it expresses the desire of your heart, then settle forever your relationship with God. Earnestly express the following declaration, then sign your name.

Declaration

Today, I call upon the name of the Lord for my salvation. I believe in my heart that God the Father raised Jesus from the dead in order that I might have eternal life. I now declare Him to be the Lord of my life. I renounce any effort on my part to save myself, and I renounce all the accusations of Satan that would rob me of my full assurance of eternal life. I have been transferred out of the kingdom of darkness and into the Kingdom of God's beloved Son. I declare myself to be a child of God forever because of the finished work of Christ.

Signed
_____

32
I Cannot Be Separated from the Love of God

'Who shall separate us from the love of Christ?
Shall trouble or hardship or persecution or famine
or nakedness or danger or sword? As it is written:
"For your sake we face death all day long; we are
considered as sheep to be slaughtered." No, in all
these things we are more than conquerors through
him who loved us. For I am convinced that neither
death nor life, neither angels nor demons, neither
the present nor the future, nor any powers, neither
height nor depth, nor anything else in all creation,
will be able to separate us from the love of God
that is in Christ Jesus our Lord.' ROMANS 8:35-39

The core issue of security is relationship. There is no greater assurance than that which is found in relationships built on trust and commitment. Likewise, there is no greater insecurity than when a significant relationship is threatened by desertion, danger or destruction.

The pain of separation

Driving in the mountains of Colorado, my wife and I happened upon an elk herd crossing the road. They leaped a barbed wire fence and started into the woods, but only for a short distance because one of the calves did not make it over the fence. It was caught trying to crawl through the barbed wire. The panic that overcame the young calf as it struggled to get through the barbed wire was a sickening sight. And the drama heightened as the mother emitted a haunting cry for her young, soon joined in anguished cries by the entire herd. The security of the close herd was suddenly threatened by danger and separation, and every animal seemed to feel the pain. Thankfully, the baby elk made it safely through the fence.

I recently watched a documentary on baby elephants that were orphaned because of ivory poachers. Their insecurity was so pronounced that they had to have constant attention just to survive.

I remember waking up from a nap to an empty house when I was a little boy. Insecurity turned to panic as I realised I was completely alone. Imagine how a child feels when he endures his parents' divorce. What might it be like to have hardships so severe that a father has to leave home to find work or the children are farmed out for their survival? One can hardly imagine the turmoil of families split because of persecution or the tremendous pain felt during times of slavery when mothers and fathers were sold separately.

The pain of deprivation

Then there is the peril of famine and nakedness. The anguish of not knowing where your next meal will come from or the devastating exposure of nakedness. The imminent danger associated with the ravages of war causes such fear that even the strongest of people are seen to faint.

Paul wrote of these temporal calamities under the inspiration of God, but also from the experience of his own life:

> Five times I received from the Jews the forty lashes minus one. Three times I was beaten with rods, once I was stoned, three times I was shipwrecked, I spent a night and a day in the open sea, I have been constantly on the move. I have been in danger from rivers, in danger from bandits, in danger from my own countrymen, in danger from Gentiles; in

danger in the city, in danger in the country, in danger at sea; and in danger from false brothers. I have laboured and toiled and have often gone without sleep; I have known hunger and thirst and have often gone without food; I have been cold and naked. Besides everything else, I face daily the pressure of my concern for all the churches. Who is weak, and I do not feel weak? Who is led into sin, and I do not inwardly burn? (2 Cor 11:24–29).

God's love in the midst of trials
Did all of Paul's hardships separate him from the love of God? No, the temporal insecurities of this world can do nothing to interfere with the eternal security we have in Christ. God's love was still operative in Paul's life and certainly in the lives of those whom Paul was seeking to reach for Christ. Paul addresses this when he quotes from Psalm 44:22: 'Ye for your sake we face death all day long; we are considered as sheep to be slaughtered.' Psalm 44 is a lament psalm of Israel and ends with verse 26: 'Rise up and help us; redeem us because of your unfailing love.'

The point is that God's chosen people have often had to face difficult trials and tribulations for His work to be accomplished. There will be suffering in this lifetime. We need to adopt the attitude of the early Church when the Sanhedrin (the ruling religious establishment of that time) had rejected and beaten them for proclaiming Christ. Acts 5:41 says, 'The apostles left the Sanhedrin, rejoicing because they had been counted worthy of suffering disgrace for the Name.' Paul writes in 2 Timothy 3:12, 'In fact, everyone who wants to live a godly life in Christ Jesus will be persecuted.'

God's love reaches into the future
Paul exclaimed that in all of these things we are more than conquerors through Him who loves us. But some may say, 'So because of our relationship with God we have an eter-

nal relationship that cannot be overcome by the temporal calamities of life, but what about the supernatural issues? What about uncontrollable things that seem to be looming ahead?' Paul's answer: 'I am convinced that neither death nor life, neither angels nor demons, neither the present nor the future, nor any powers, neither height nor depth, nor anything else in all creation, will be able to separate us from the love of God' (Rom 8:38,39).

Who has the power over life and death? Who has authority over the angelic realm? Who sovereignly governs the affairs of men and angels now and forever? Our heavenly Father is the Lord of eternity. We should have no fear of tomorrow, death, demons or eternity. The shepherd of our souls says, 'My sheep listen to my voice; I know them, and they follow me. I give them eternal life, and they shall never perish; no one can snatch them out of my hand. My Father, who has given them to me, is greater than all; no one can snatch them out of my Father's hand' (Jn 10:27–29). Our relationship with God is not a question of our ability to hang on to Him. It really isn't within our own personal power to do that anyway. The fact is, God holds on to us, and He has the power to keep us securely and safely in His hand.

Love beyond our ability to comprehend

Paul's reference to 'neither height nor depth' reminds one of his prayer in Ephesians 3:14–19:

> For this reason I kneel before the Father, from whom his whole family in heaven and on earth derives its name. I pray that out of his glorious riches he may strengthen you with power through his Spirit in your inner being, so that Christ may dwell in your hearts through faith. And I pray that you, being rooted and established in love, may have power, together with all the saints, to grasp how wide and long and

high and deep is the love of Christ, and to know this love that surpasses knowledge — that you may be filled to the measure of all the fullness of God.

The love of God surpasses knowledge. We can't fully comprehend how much He really loves us. The sceptic may ask, 'If God loves me, why is He allowing all of this persecution and hardship?' Suffering for righteousness' sake is a privilege we have, because we are left on earth for a purpose. In the midst of the harsh realities of life, we have the privilege to share that our security is not found in the temporal things of life but in the eternal relationship we have with our heavenly Father.

Nothing in all creation can separate us from the love of God that is in Christ Jesus, our Lord. Are you struggling through some temporal difficulties of life? Are you having difficulty fully understanding the nature of God's eternal relationship and love for you? Make Paul's prayer your prayer:

Dear heavenly Father, I kneel before You, for it is from You that Your whole family in heaven and on earth derived its name. I pray that out of Your glorious riches You may strengthen me with power through Your Spirit in my inner being so that Christ may dwell in my heart through faith. Since I am rooted and established in love, I pray that I may have power together with all the saints to grasp how wide and long and high and deep is Your love and to know this love that surpasses knowledge, so that I may be filled to the measure of all the fullness of God. In Jesus' precious name I pray. Amen.

33
I Have Been Established, Anointed and Sealed by God

'Now it is God who makes both us and you stand firm in Christ. He anointed us, set his seal of ownership on us, and put his Spirit in our hearts as a deposit, guaranteeing what is to come.'
2 CORINTHIANS 1:21,22

As a child, I was taught not to question authority. The battle cry was: 'Mine is not to reason why, mine is but to do or die.' Patriotism was based on 'my country, right or wrong.' Such is the basis for fanaticism and blind loyalty.

Credibility questioned
The Vietnam War brought the United States to its knees; leadership was questioned and patriotism was challenged. Watergate was the final straw as the credibility of leadership suffered a crushing blow. Politicians are no longer believed; many times for good reason. Some will say anything to get elected, as promises fall on deaf ears.

Today, because of that lack of integrity, everybody sits in judgement of authority figures. We go to church and critique the pastor and his message. Rather than sit in judgement of the message, shouldn't the message sit in judgement of us? Are we supposed to critique the worship service, or are we to enter into the experience and worship God?

Several years ago, while teaching worship at Talbot School of Theology, I found myself assuming the role of a critic as I visited various churches. One day, it hit me: 'What am I doing?' I realised I should be personally participating in the worship experience. I was there to worship God, not to be a critic.

God is true

We are living in a nation where authority is questioned and leaders are challenged — there is a lack of trust, a spirit of unbelief.

Does losing our faith in humanity have to alter our ability to trust God? 'What if some did not have faith? Will their lack of faith nullify God's faithfulness? Not at all! Let God be true, and every man a liar' (Rom 3:3,4).

Although questioning the credibility of leadership has intensified in our days, it is not a new problem. Paul addressed the issue of human leadership versus God's leadership in 2 Corinthians 1:17–20:

> When I planned this, did I do it lightly? Or do I make my plans in a worldly manner so that in the same breath I say, 'Yes, yes' and 'No, no'?
>
> But as surely as God is faithful, our message to you is not 'Yes' and 'No'. For the Son of God, Jesus Christ, who was preached among you by me and Silas and Timothy, was not 'Yes' and 'No', but in him it has always been 'Yes'. For no matter how many promises God has made, they are 'Yes' in Christ. And so through him the 'Amen' is spoken by us to the glory of God.

Numbers 23:19 says, 'God is not a man, that he should lie,' and Hebrews 6:18 says, 'It is impossible for God to lie.'

Man-made kingdoms come and go, human authorities rise and fall. However, the integrity of the Church is not based on the fickle nature of man or the credibility of human government; nor is our relationship based on that. Rather, it is based upon the faithfulness of God and the assurance of His Word because of His timeless, unchanging nature.

We are anointed by God

'Now it is God who makes both us and you stand firm in Christ' (2 Cor 1:21). God is the One who establishes us. How does He do this? First, He anoints us. *Cristos* is the Greek word for Christ, which means 'the anointed one.' In our passage, the word anointed is the Greek word *Chrio*, which is used in the Septuagint (a Greek translation of the Old Testament before the time of Christ) for kings, priests and prophets. This is kingdom terminology, meaning that someone is anointed for some regal position. Peter captures this idea when he declares, 'But you are a chosen people, a royal priesthood, a holy nation, a people belonging to God, that you may declare the praises of him who called you out of darkness into his wonderful light' (1 Pet 2:9). We are not speaking here of a temporal kingdom; this is God's *eternal* Kingdom, and *God Himself* has anointed us to be a part of it.

We have his seal of ownership

Not only that, God set His seal of ownership upon us. Historically, kings and other royalty used seals as a means of communicating integrity and the assurance of the authority of a message. They would pour melted wax upon a letter that was closed. Then they would seal it with an impression of their ring or another official insignia stamped into the wax. Once the letter was opened and the seal was broken, you could not ensure its contents any more.

We have in our country a seal that signifies the rights and privileges of citizenship, but Christians have a greater seal given by God that ensures much more. God demonstrated His seal upon the Israelites, protecting them from the plagues that the Egyptians would experience. Frequent references in Exodus (8:22; 9:4,26; 10:23; 11:7) attest that God dealt differently with those who were His covenant people. A graphic example of this is found in Exodus 12:12: 'On that same night I will pass through Egypt and strike down every firstborn — both men and animals — and I will bring judgement on all the gods of Egypt. I am the Lord. The blood will be a sign for you on the houses where you are; and when I see the blood, I will pass over you. No destructive plague will touch you when I strike Egypt.'

When the judgements of God come upon this earth, no eternal judgement will harm believers, because we have the blood of the Lord Jesus Christ to protect us. As we read in Revelation 9:4, 'They were told not to harm the grass of the earth or any plant or tree, but only those people who did not have the seal of God on their foreheads.' We have been bought and purchased by the blood of the lamb. God has placed His seal upon us ensuring that His protection will last through any enduring trials or judgement, both now and forever.

We are God's covenant people, and we are participants of a new covenant, not one written on stone tablets but on our hearts. 'This is the covenant I will make with them after that time, says the Lord. I will put my laws in their hearts, and I will write them on their minds.... Their sins and lawless acts I will remember no more' (Heb 10:16,17).

We have a guaranteed inheritance

Not only have we been sealed, but God has put His Spirit in our hearts as a deposit, guaranteeing what is to come. Paul says in Ephesians 1:13,14, 'And you also were included in Christ when you heard the word of truth, the gospel of your salvation. Having believed, you were marked in him with a seal, the promised Holy Spirit, who is a deposit guaranteeing our inheritance until the redemption of those who are God's possession — to the praise of his glory.' This guaran-

tee is not being made by some inflated politician or star-
struck entertainer or your pastor. God guarantees and
ensures it by placing His Holy Spirit within us as a down
payment. What an incredible promise!

Then we have the added assurance from Hebrews 13:5:
'Never will I leave you; never will I forsake you.' So while
the questionable promises of man and the destructive
tongues of others would tear down the very fabric of society, we would do well to pay heed to Ephesians 4:29,30: 'Do
not let any unwholesome talk come out of your mouths, but
only what is helpful for building others up according to
their needs, that it may benefit those who listen. And do not
grieve the Holy Spirit of God, with whom you were sealed
for the day of redemption.'

**Dear heavenly Father, I praise You for being a God who can-
not lie, whose promises are never No but always Yes. Forgive
me for believing the promise of man when I should have been
resting in Your promises. Forgive me for questioning Your
faithfulness because of the unfaithfulness of man. I renounce
the lies of Satan that would question Your word, and I submit
to the Holy Spirit, who guarantees my inheritance to come.
Thank You for establishing me, anointing me, placing Your
seal of ownership on me and putting Your Spirit in my heart.
In Jesus' name and by the authority of His Word I pray.
Amen.**

34
I Am Hidden
with Christ in God

*'For you died, and your life is now hidden with
Christ in God.'*   COLOSSIANS 3:3

Several years ago, a pastor made an appointment to see me.
He said he had heard of my ministry, and he needed to talk
with me. He had struggled for twenty-two years in his
Christian experience, going through one trial after another.
During his devotions one day, he read Colossians 3:3, and
he wanted to know how his life could be hidden in Christ.

I asked him to read the passage out loud and very slowly,
which he did. Again he asked me, 'That's what I wanted to
talk to you about. I think that is the secret. How do I do
that?' I asked him to read it again, even slower. 'For...you...
died,...and...your...life...is...now...hidden...with...Christ
...in...God.' Suddenly the light dawned and he realised he
had *already* died. For twenty-two years, this dear pastor
had been desperately trying to become something he
already was.

What is already true of us
Over the years, I have had several people try to convince me
that this is only a *positional* truth, implying that it describes
a relationship between us and God, but it is not something
we can experience in our daily lives. Is our position in Christ
only theological, just a nice thing to know but having no
practical relevance to our present lives? Nonsense! Our

position in Christ is the basis for our hope and the sole prerequisite to living by faith.

Colossians 3:1–10 contains several statements describing the believers' position in Christ. We are dead (v 3), have taken off the old self (v 9), have put on the new self (v 10), have been raised with Christ (v 1), and we are hidden with Christ who is now seated at the right hand of God (vs 1,3). All of this is *already* true because we are *in Christ*. We cannot *do* for ourselves what Christ has *already done* for us.

Many Christians are like the pastor who desperately tried to become something he already was. In order to live a fruitful Christian life by faith, we must first believe what Christ has already done for us and then walk accordingly. It's not our believing it that makes it true — that is New Age or magic thinking. The Christian says, 'It is true, *therefore*, I believe it .' When we do that, the reality of the truth works out in our experience, and we become what we already are by God's grace.

Things to do

Still, ours is not a passive role. For this truth to work out in our experience, there are things we must do. The same ten verses in Colossians 3 include several imperative statements indicating what we must do, now that we are in Christ. One is to set our hearts and minds on the things above (vs 1,2). This is analogous to fixing 'our eyes on Jesus, the author and perfecter of our faith' (Heb 12:2). This is not pie in the sky unreality. Jesus is the truth, and He is the only valid object of our faith. We are setting our minds on the truth from above, rather than the lies from the pit.

Colossians 2:8 warns us: 'See to it that no one takes you captive through hollow and deceptive philosophy, which depends on human tradition and the basic principles of this world rather than on Christ.' The world system we were raised in taught relative truth, self-reliance and that only that which can be perceived through the natural senses is real. Actually, the unseen world is more real than the seen world. That which is seen is only temporal, while that which is unseen is eternal. We must learn to walk by faith, not by sight.

Then we are to put to death the practices that belong to our earthly nature (see Colossians 3:5) and rid ourselves of behaviour that characterised who we were before Christ (see Colossians 3:9). Remember, death is the ending of relationship, not existence. The law of sin is still strong and appealing, but because of our position in Christ, we can rid ourselves of sinful behaviour and habits. 'Putting to death' is to render inoperative the power of sin — something we cannot do in the flesh, only through Christ.

In one sense, there is no painless way to die, and Paul endured tremendous hardship in making known the truth we are speaking about. So that we do not lose heart, he wrote in 2 Corinthians 4:7–11:

> But we have this treasure in jars of clay to show that this all-surpassing power is from God and not from us. We are hard pressed on every side, but not crushed; perplexed, but not in despair; persecuted, but not abandoned; struck down, but not destroyed. We always carry around in our body the death of Jesus, so that the life of Jesus may also be revealed in our body. For we who are alive are always being given over to death for Jesus' sake, so that his life may be revealed in our mortal body.

The total sufficiency and acceptance of God

The treasure is Christ in us, but our bodies are as jars of clay. In Paul's day, it was customary to conceal treasure in clay jars, which had little value or beauty and did not attract attention to their precious contents. The idea is that the insufficiency of man reveals the total sufficiency of

God. The frailty of the 'clay jars' of our humanity is plainly seen in the constant hardships and persecutions we face daily for the sake of the gospel. In that sense, we enter into Christ's sufferings, but the power of God is revealed in our lives. Truly, that is the treasure.

While I was a pastor, my son, Karl, had established quite a reputation as a football player. Other than our church involvement, most of our family's social life centred around his sports. When I accepted an invitation to teach at Talbot School of Theology, it necessitated a move that was very unsettling for Karl. He had to leave behind a team, friends, awards and recognition. However, his reputation preceded him to our new location. There, I was phoned by a football club inquiring whether Karl would care to be a part of their team. After checking out the coach, I felt it would be a good team to join. At the first practice, the coach expressed to me his delight at having Karl as a player, saying what a vital member of the team he was going to be.

Karl practised with reckless abandonment and afterward approached me with a long look on his face and a profound sense of insecurity that was baffling to me. Finally, he broke the silence: 'Well, am I on this team?'

I replied, 'Oh Karl, you were already on the team before we came. The coach had already made the necessary provisions, the roster had already been filled in, and your name was on it. The only thing that remains to be determined is the position you will play. That will be the coach's decision. He will put you where he needs you the most, and where you are best qualified. How well you play is up to you, but the coach promised you all the support you need to reach your potential.'

And play he did! He continued to practise diligently, to correct the bad habits developed on the school playground, and to develop new skills to become the best player possible for his coach and his team.

Over the years, I have been intrigued by the tremendous insecurity some people live with. I have seen five-talented, 'star' players on God's team who constantly struggle with insecurity. They fear the day when they will be cut from the team, often never sure they made it. Maybe they suspect that they got on the team because of how well they played. Now they think other younger, stronger, more gifted players will someday take their place.

On the other hand, I have seen single-talented, less gifted people excited about the game and thrilled that they are on the team. They look forward with great anticipation to the chance to play, even though they won't be the star. They know they are on the team not because of their great abilities but because the coach chose them, just as he has chosen every member. The coach exchanged their old, tattered uniform for a new one, and they are assured that they will play an important role on the team.

Dear Christian, you, too, are already on the team. Your name is on the roster: it's called the Lamb's Book of Life. 'Your life is now hidden with Christ in God. When Christ, who is your life, appears, then you also will appear with him in glory' (Col 3:3,4). Your God will determine where it is best for you to play, and when. How well you play will depend upon you. Would you like to thank Him?

Dear heavenly Father, thank You for choosing me and making it possible for me to be a member of Your team. I thank You for exchanging my dirty rags for Your uniform that will never wear out. I commit myself to practise daily, ridding myself of old habits and establishing new ones, so I can be the player that You want me to be. I pray for Your grace to sustain me during difficult times in the game of life, and I praise You for allowing me to play on Your winning team. In Jesus' name I pray. Amen.

35
I Am Confident that the Good Work God Has Begun in Me Will Be Perfected

'Being confident of this, that he who began a good work in you will carry it on to completion until the day of Christ Jesus.' PHILIPPIANS 1:6

In my early years of ministry, I served as an associate pastor having several interns working under me. The highlight of every week was my Wednesday night university Bible study. It was a tremendous group of young people who prayed and sang together with such joy and enthusiasm that I always looked forward to the meeting. In time, however, my responsibilities expanded, and I realised I needed to give up that special group and help with another ministry. I decided to turn over the university Bible study to one of my interns who had been asking for it for months. This seemed like a great opportunity for him, and I had full confidence in him. But after only three weeks the college ministry had withered to almost nothing.

Totally defeated, the intern came to my office and said, 'I suppose you want your ministry back after what I have done to it.' I was frustrated because he had taken a thriving ministry and all but destroyed it. But I knew if I took it back, it would probably severely affect the young man's whole career as a pastor. I said, 'No, I don't believe that's the right thing to do.' Together, we discussed what should be done, and out of it came another ministry. The new ministry broke down the university group into smaller groups, which the intern shepherded and managed in a way that was much more in keeping with his gifts. Within months, it was a far greater ministry than when I had it.

I imagine the former intern looks back on that experience as one of the greatest turning points in his life. As well, I am thankful I didn't give up on him, because he did go on to become a fine pastor. In the process, I learned some valuable lessons, one of which is that God never gives up on us either. God had a plan for that young man's life: to be fruitful in ministry. The work that Christ began in that intern's life would be completed, even though his gifts were different from mine.

What God begins, he completes

I have often been intrigued by Paul's statement in 2 Corinthians 7:4, 'Great is my confidence in you, great is my boasting on your behalf' (NASB). Then at the end of the chapter, in verse 16, he says: 'I am glad I can have complete confidence in you.'

Has Paul lost his mind? I could see where he would have confidence in the church at Ephesus, but the church in Corinth? It was a church wracked with dissension, immorality and carnality of every kind. Is this just some type of phony psychological hype? No, I believe Paul conveyed a very biblical principle: The work that God begins, He completes. This underscores the value to be gained by expressing confidence in others and encouraging one another to keep on keeping on.

I remember hearing about the famous guard for the American football team, the Green Bay Packers, Jerry Krammer, talking about his first year on the team. He was a rookie and the great coach, Vince Lombardi, was riding him constantly. Adding insult to injury, when the rest of the team was excused for the day, he was told to do another twenty minutes running through the tyre obstacle course! Frustrated and defeated, he went into the locker room and sat there contemplating quitting the team.

At Jerry's lowest moment, the coach walked by and thumped him on the back of the helmet and said, 'Someday, Krammer, you are going to be the greatest guard that football has ever known.' Vince Lombardi had the reputation of riding his people to perfection, but he was also a master of timing. Jerry's reflection at that moment sounded like this, 'I went from complete despair to total ecstasy, willing to do whatever the coach might have required of me, even another twenty minutes on the tyres.

Our boat won't sink

The point that Paul makes, however, goes far beyond any belief we have in others or a belief we have in ourselves. In Matthew 8:23–26, we read this account:

> Then he got into the boat and his disciples followed him. Without warning, a furious storm came up on the lake, so that the waves swept over the boat. But Jesus was sleeping. The disciples went and woke him, saying, 'Lord, save us! We're going to drown!'
>
> He replied, 'You of little faith, why are you so afraid?' Then he got up and rebuked the winds and the waves, and it was completely calm.

There is no way that boat would ever sink with Jesus in it; it was destined to make it to the other side. Though there are storms raging around us, we are destined to make it to the other side because Christ is in us — He is our hope of glory. It is He who has begun the work in us and will carry it on to completion.

A lady asked if I would see her husband, who was clinically depressed and hospitalised for six months. As he sat before me shaking because of the drugs, I asked when the depression began. He said six months ago, when he experienced serious financial difficulty. Though his financial condition was far better than most, he clearly recalled a day when a chilling thought came to his mind that he was going to 'lose it all,' he was going down, his boat was sinking. Then he believed the lie from the deceiver.

I had the privilege that afternoon to help him resolve his personal and spiritual conflicts, and he found freedom in Christ. Afterward, he sat calmly in front of me and expressed how unbelievably deceived he had been. He wondered why he had listened to that little lie when he knew God would meet his every need.

Don't rely on self

Another story involving Jesus and a boat is found in Mark 6:45–50:

> And immediately He made His disciples get into the boat and go ahead of Him to the other side of Bethsaida, while He Himself was sending the multitude away. And after bidding them farewell, He departed to the mountain to pray. And when it was evening, the boat was in the midst of the sea, and He was alone on the land. And seeing them straining at the oars, for the wind was against them, at about the fourth watch of the night, He came to them, walking on the sea; and He intended to pass by them. But when they saw Him walking on the sea, they supposed that it was a ghost, and cried out; for they all saw Him and were frightened. But immediately He spoke with them and said to them, 'Take courage; it is I, do not be afraid' (NASB).

My mind is riveted on the phrase, 'He intended to pass by them.' I believe that even today Jesus intends to pass by the self-sufficient. If we think getting to the other side is a question of how hard we row, we may never get there. We must never forget that it is He who began the work in us, and it is He who will carry it to completion.

Arriving late for a Little League game, a retired grand-father stopped to ask his grandchild how his team was doing. 'We are behind fifteen to nothing,' he said.

The grandfather asked, 'Are you discouraged?'

'Of course not,' the boy responded. 'We haven't been up to bat yet.'

That's the kind of confidence Christians can have because we know the Lord is working in us.

There's one more inning

I don't know what 'inning' of life you are in, but the odds are you have at least one more opportunity to come to the plate. Are you running against the wind? Is a storm about to swamp your boat? Have you failed in the past? Do you believe God has given up on you? I don't believe He has! In Philippians 3:12–14, Paul reflects the attitude I believe we ought to have:

> Not that I have already obtained all this, or have already been made perfect, but I press on to take hold of that for which Christ Jesus took hold of me. Brothers, I do not con-sider myself yet to have taken hold of it. But one thing I do: Forgetting what is behind and straining towards what is ahead, I press on towards the goal to win the prize for which God has called me heavenward in Christ Jesus.

Dear heavenly Father, I am thankful for the good work of sal-vation that You have begun in me. I know You are not finished with me yet, and I renounce the lies of Satan that would sug-gest that You are. Forgive me for the times I have lived in my own sufficiency. I renounce my self-sufficiency, and I choose to forget what lies behind. I now commit myself to press on to

I Am Confident 355

Your upward call and express with confidence that I shall see You face-to-face on the other side. I put no confidence in the flesh, for my confidence lies in You and that You will bring me to completion in Christ. In Jesus' precious name I pray. Amen.

36
I Am a Citizen of Heaven

*'But our citizenship is in heaven. And we eagerly
await a Saviour from there, the Lord Jesus Christ.'*
PHILIPPIANS 3:20

In the spring of 1992, I conducted a conference in Fresno, California. No sessions were planned for Thursday so I could drive back to Los Angeles to teach my classes at Talbot School of Theology.

The car radio caught me up on the news. The trial of the four policemen accused of beating Rodney King had reached completion, and tensions were already high in the city due to deteriorating race relations, gang wars and high unemployment. When the news hit that the policemen were acquitted, 'all hell broke loose' and for the next two days the world witnessed the total disintegration of society in Los Angeles. What greeted me early Thursday morning as I drove into the city was a ghostly sight! Smoke from thousands of fires filled the sky. It was like entering a war zone.

A Korean student was waiting for me at my first class, his jeans covered with soot and his hands smudged with charcoal. 'My family's business was burned to the ground,' he said.

I looked at the exhausted young man and said, 'What are you doing here? Go home to your family.'

Later, a black student shared his confrontation with a gang member who thrust a small automatic weapon in his face. 'Go ahead and shoot,' he told the gang members. Thankfully, the thugs walked away. I was supposed to have an evening class, but several students were missing because of a police curfew, so I let the rest of the students go. I was planning to spend the night in Los Angeles but reconsidered and thought it was best to leave. The stench of smoke was everywhere. The motorways were strangely empty, and the few of us still trying to get home were driving determinedly and defensively. When I was safely outside of the city limits, I stopped at a motel for the night and solemnly watched the telecasts.

What I saw was anarchy, a sickening demonstration of the depravity of man. I watched with horror as university students in expensive cars joined in the madness. Looters were grabbing all they could get. I wanted to cry as I watched the wanton destruction, yet I felt strangely detached.

The insecurity of earthly citizenship

I felt exactly like Paul when he wrote in Philippians 3:18–20, 'For, as I have often told you before and now say again even with tears, many live as enemies of the cross of Christ. Their destiny is destruction, their god is their stomach, and their glory is in their shame. Their mind is on earthly things. But our citizenship is in heaven.' We are in this world, but we are not of it. Paul continues, 'And we eagerly await a Saviour from there, the Lord Jesus Christ, who, by the power that enables him to bring everything under his control, will transform our lowly bodies so that they will be like his glorious body' (vs 20,21).

It is little wonder that the citizens of this world feel so insecure. Stress is a leading cause of physical illnesses. More money is spent on the temporary cures for anxiety than on any other consumer need. We mask our pain with prescription drugs or the escapes of alcohol, drugs, sex and food. Many people realise those habits are destructive, so they devote their lives to the preservation and glorification of their physical bodies. Someone handed me the following poem by Virginia Brasier, which seems to typify life in the fast lane:

> This is the age
> Of the half-read page
> And the quick hash
> And the mad dash
> The bright night
> With the nerves tight
> The plane hop
> With the brief stop
> The lamp tan
> In a short span
> The Big Shot
> In a big spot
> And the brain strain
> And the heart pain
> And the catnap
> Till the spring snaps
> And the fun's done![1]

We hope in the Resurrection

Our hope doesn't lie in a false assurance that we will never die but rather in the Resurrection, as Paul describes in Romans 8:23,24: 'Not only so, but we ourselves, who have the firstfruits of the Spirit, groan inwardly as we wait eagerly for our adoption as sons, the redemption of our bodies. For in this hope we were saved.' If we had only the security of this world, we would have little hope, but our citizenship is in heaven. We are subject to a different King, whose Kingdom is not of this world — His Kingdom is eternal. All this being true, have you ever wondered why God, who has the power to do so, doesn't just bring an end to all of this?

A black pastor in the inner city of Los Angeles gave me

the right perspective. He said twenty-five years ago, 'God looked into this kingdom of darkness, observed the citizens of this world, and saw they were without Christ. If He had shut the door twenty-five years ago, before I received Christ, I would have been forever locked out of the Kingdom of God.'

Peter talks about the days before the second coming of Christ. He warns us that there will be scoffers who will mock the possibility of a second coming. He talks about the sudden destruction that will come upon us. But in the midst of his warnings, we read, 'But do not forget this one thing, dear friends: With the Lord a day is like a thousand years, and a thousand years are like a day. The Lord is not slow in keeping his promise, as some understand slowness. He is patient with you, not wanting anyone to perish, but everyone to come to repentance' (2 Pet 3:8,9).

Left for a purpose

God is waiting for the gospel to be preached to all the nations; then the end will come. We are not of this world, but we are left here for a purpose: We are to fulfil His Great Commission. When the gospel has gone out to the ends of the world, He will return.

Please don't wear your citizenship in heaven as a badge of superiority. We are all saved by the grace of God. No matter how sick and depraved the fallen humanity around you may appear, always remember the sober reminder, 'There, but for the grace of God, go I.' Our heavenly citizenship is the basis for hope and security, which carries with it the responsibility to be servants of God and subservient to His will. We have been left on earth for a purpose, as Peter writes, 'Dear friends, I urge you, as aliens and strangers in the world, to abstain from sinful desires, which war against your soul. Live such good lives among the pagans that, though they accuse you of doing wrong, they

may see your good deeds and glorify God on the day he vis-
its us' (1 Pet 2:11,12).

**Dear heavenly Father, I thank You for my citizenship in
heaven. Forgive me for the times that I have sought my security in this world and lived as though I have no eternal relationship with You. I renounce the lies of Satan that my only
citizenship is on earth and not in heaven. I now claim my
rights and responsibilities as a citizen of heaven and declare
You to be my King. I commit myself to be Your servant and
to do Your will on earth as it is being done in heaven. My hope
is not in this present world but in the one to come. I will seek
to live a responsible life today so that, by Your grace, the
world may see my good deeds and thereby glorify You. In
Jesus' precious name I pray. Amen.**

NOTE

1. 'This Is the Age' by Virginia Brasier.

37

I Have Not Been Given a Spirit of Fear, but of Power, Love and a Sound Mind

'For God has not given us a spirit of fear, but of power and of love and of a sound mind.'
2 TIMOTHY 1:7 (NKJV)

We are living in a nation that is filled with anxiety. When people are anxious, it is usually because they don't know what is going to happen, and there's a sense of uncertainty. In fact, anxiety is usually understood as fear without an obvious cause.

In the Sermon on the Mount, Jesus admonished us not to worry about tomorrow and not to lay up treasures upon this earth. It's a question of trust. If God will take care of the birds of the sky and the lilies of the field, how much more will He care for us? So we are encouraged to seek first the Kingdom of God.

A fear object is always both potent and present

In contrast to anxiety, fear always has an object. People fear something known. We may fear heights, fire, small spaces, air travel or things that threaten us. In order for a fear object to be legitimate it must have two attributes: It must be potent as well as present. For instance, I have a healthy fear of snakes. As I sit here writing this, however, I don't sense that fear at all. The reason, of course, is that there are no snakes present. But if you were to open my study door and throw one towards my feet, my fear index would go from zero to ten immediately. That snake would be both present and potent! Suppose, though, that you threw a *dead* snake toward my feet. Well, provided I was *sure* it was dead, I wouldn't feel any fear. Even though it would be present, it would not be potent. To resolve the fear in your life, you must remove the fear object's presence or its potency.

No fear of man or death

Fear is a powerful controller, compelling us to do what is irresponsible or destructive. Two common fear objects in our lives are man and death, but we are told biblically not to fear either.

In Matthew 10:28, we read: 'Do not be afraid of those who kill the body but cannot kill the soul. Rather, be afraid of the one who can destroy both soul and body in hell.' Man is not a legitimate fear object for a Christian. Too many times we let people intimidate us to the point of losing self-control. The spirit of God no longer controls us, nor do we exercise self-control. We allow an unhealthy fear, instead of faith, to control our lives.

Suppose a secretary is intimidated by her boss. She works in fear of him all day because he is both present and potent to her. But what power does the boss have over the secretary? I suppose he could sack her. But could she overcome that power? Yes, she could quit or be willing to quit. By not allowing her boss to hold the job over her head she would free herself from his intimidation. I am not suggesting that you rebel against your boss: I am pointing out that the New Testament teaches we can live a responsible life without fearing intimidation from others.

Peter puts it this way: 'Who is going to harm you if you are eager to do good? But even if you should suffer for what is right, you are blessed. "Do not fear what they fear; do not be frightened." But in your hearts set apart Christ as Lord.

Always be prepared to give an answer to everyone who asks you to give the reason for the hope that you have. But do this with gentleness and respect' (1 Pet 3:13–15).

Even death is not a legitimate fear object. Hebrews 9:27 says, 'Man is destined to die once, and after that to face judgement.' Death is imminent, but God has removed its potency. It no longer has any power over us. As 1 Corinthians 15:54,55 says, 'Death has been swallowed up in victory. Where, O death, is your victory? Where, O death, is your sting?' The person who has been freed from the fear of death is free to live today.

The one legitimate and ultimate fear

There is, however, a legitimate and ultimate fear in our lives, and that is God. That's because He is *both* omnipresent and omnipotent. But the fear of God can expel all other fears. 'Do not call conspiracy everything that these people call conspiracy; do not fear what they fear, and do not dread it. The Lord Almighty is the one you are to regard as holy, he is the one you are to fear, he is the one you are to dread, and he will be a sanctuary' (Is 8:12–14).

When we, with reverence and awe, make God our ultimate fear object and sanctify Christ as the Lord of our lives, we will experience the freedom that Christ purchased for us on the cross. We need to understand that the fear of God does not involve punishment. I don't fear God because someday He will punish me — God the Father already punished His Son for my sins. 'There is no fear in love. But perfect love drives out fear, because fear has to do with punishment. The one who fears is not made perfect in love' (1 Jn 4:18). I reverentially fear God as the Lord of all the universe and Lord of my life, and I humbly bow before Him. To fear God is to ascribe to Him those attributes that become the basis for my sanctuary, my place of safety in this lifetime.

We don't have to fear Satan

Fear that has no object is usually referred to as a panic attack or an anxiety disorder. In my experience, when people have an overwhelming sense of fear and dread with no discernible reason, the cause is Satan, man's third fear object.

I have often been asked by people why I am not afraid in my line of ministry — spiritual warfare. I tell them, 'There is not a verse in the Bible where we are told to fear Satan.' His strategy is to roar like a hungry lion, seeking someone to devour. But why does the lion roar? The roar is to paralyse his prey in fear.

It has been my privilege to see hundreds of people freed from the fear of Satan. It is far more present than we would ever care to realise. A pastor who had used my material to help a person in his congregation received the following letter:

> Dear Pastor, For the past thirty-five years I have lived from one surge of adrenaline to the next. My entire life has been gripped by paralysing fears that seemed to come from nowhere and everywhere, fears that made very little sense to me or anyone else. I invested four years of my life obtaining a degree in psychology, hoping it would enable me to understand and conquer those fears. That only perpetuated my questions and insecurity. Six years of professional counselling offered little insight and no change in my level of anxiety. After two trips to the hospital and a battery of tests, my panic attacks only worsened. By the time I came to see you, full-blown panic attacks had become a daily feature. It has now been three weeks since I have experienced a panic attack, and I have been able to live a responsible life. I had no idea what freedom meant until now.
>
> When I came to see you, I hoped the truth would set me free, but now I *know* it has. When you live in a con-

stant state of anxiety, you are physically, emotionally, and mentally unable to focus on anything but the fear that is swallowing you. I could barely read a verse of Scripture at one sitting. It was as though someone snatched it away from my mind as soon as it entered. I could only hear the verses that talked about death and punishment. Scripture was such a fog to me, I had actually become afraid to open my Bible. These past weeks I have spent hours a day in the Word and it makes sense. The fog is gone. I am amazed at what I am able to hear, see, understand and retain.

Before going through *The Bondage Breaker*, I could not say 'Jesus Christ' without my metabolism going berserk. I could refer to the Lord with no ill effect, but whenever I said 'Jesus Christ', my insides went into orbit. I can now call upon the name of Jesus Christ with peace and confidence, and I do so regularly.

Psalm 118:5,6 says, 'In my anguish I cried to the Lord, and he answered by setting me free. The Lord is with me; I will not be afraid. What can man do to me?'

Dear heavenly Father, I acknowledge You as the only legitimate fear object in my life. You are omnipotent and omnipresent. Because of Your love and the finished work of Christ, I no longer fear punishment. I sanctify You as the Lord of my life and claim the spirit of power, love and a sound mind that comes from Your presence in my life. I renounce Satan as a fear object in my life, and I renounce all his lies that would hold me in fear. Show me how I have allowed the fear of man and the fear of death to control my life. I now commit myself to You and worship only You as my loving heavenly Father, that I may be guided by faith and not by fear. I ask this in the precious name of Jesus. Amen.

38
I Can Find Grace and Mercy in Time of Need

*'Let us then approach the throne of grace with
confidence, so that we may receive mercy and find
grace to help us in our time of need.'* HEBREWS 4:16

A dear friend of my wife, who attended our church, continuously struggled with severe depression. After many trips to
the doctor, several different medications and a few hospi-
talisations, this woman still was no better. Finally, my wife
said, 'Why don't you go see my husband?'

'Pastor Neil?' she exclaimed. 'Oh, I couldn't talk with
him, he's never down!'

It's true that I haven't struggled very much with depression — my down times are seldom and usually short-lived.
But for that very reason, you would think I would be the
first person she would want to see. If you wanted to get
healthy, would you search for a coughing, unkempt, out of
breath, exhausted person and ask for his secret? Wouldn't it
make more sense to inquire of one who is living a healthy
life? People often don't, though, and I believe the primary
reason is wrapped up in one attribute — mercy.

The sick and hurting search for comfort and compassion, and they question whether they can get it from a
healthy, exuberant person. So the problem drinker attends
Alcoholics Anonymous, and the overeater goes to Weight
Watchers. Why? Because they receive mercy there. Most of
the people in the recovery ministries are on one rung of a
ladder reaching down to the person on the rung below

them. They understand. They have been there themselves, perhaps on even lower rungs. They can relate, and they know from experience that the hurting person first needs acceptance and mercy.

Is that wrong? Of course not! In fact, it is a beautiful expression of Christian love. I used to require my seminary students to attend an Alcoholics Anonymous meeting as a part of one of my classes. For some, it was a cultural shock; they weren't used to the blue language and smoke-filled rooms. But every student expressed the same sentiment — they all wished they could get their Bible study groups to be as real, honest and caring as those people were. It is an embarrassing indictment when people receive more mercy from secular self-help groups than they do from churches.

To be merciful is *not giving people what they deserve in terms of judgement.* God has been merciful to us — if He gave us what we deserved, we would go to hell. 'But when the kindness and love of God our Saviour appeared, he saved us, not because of righteous things we had done, but because of his mercy' (Tit 3:4). And as Luke exhorts, 'Be merciful, just as your Father is merciful' (6:36).

Receiving mercy is the primary prerequisite to recovery. If hurting people don't sense that they can receive it from our churches, they will go elsewhere. But secular groups seldom have the capacity to offer the grace to help in time of need. Mercy is essential, but without grace, recovery groups can end up being little more than pity parties where everybody is swimming, and sometimes drowning, in a quagmire of unresolved problems and spiritual bondage. What they need along with mercy is Christ's freedom, and they need God's Word to drive out the lies. The mercy of God will accept you regardless of the rung you are on, and the grace of God will pull you up to the next one, and then the next.

But we are to go beyond not giving people what they deserve; we are to give them what they need. That's what grace is — *giving people what they don't deserve.* God didn't only save us from eternal damnation; He gave us life. 'For it is by grace you have been saved, through faith — and this not from yourselves, it is the gift of God — not by works, so that no one can boast' (Eph 2:8,9).

Can God understand?

So how can God possibly understand our struggles? He sits up there in the heavenlies, all powerful and all wise. He doesn't have any needs... He doesn't worry about putting the next meal on the table... He doesn't have an abusive parent or unfaithful spouse... He wasn't born on the wrong side of the tracks.

The answer is Jesus. His family suffered from the social rejection of an unexplainable birth... He was rejected by His countrymen... He took upon Himself the form of a man with no special privileges... He had no class status, no possessions... He carried the cross for His own crucifixion... He was cursed, beaten and spat upon. And to add final humiliation: 'One of the criminals who hung there hurled insults at him: "Aren't you the Christ? Save yourself and us!" But the other criminal rebuked him. "Don't you fear God," he said, "since you are under the same sentence? We are punished justly, for we are getting what our deeds deserve. But this man has done nothing wrong"' (Lk 23:39,40).

Jesus didn't deserve that punishment and death — we did! Do we actually think He lacks understanding, and is unmerciful? 'Let us fix our eyes on Jesus, the author and perfecter of our faith, who for the joy set before him endured the cross, scorning its shame, and sat down at the right hand of the throne of God. Consider him who endured such opposition from sinful men, so that you will not grow weary and lose heart' (Heb 12:2,3).

Our ultimate recovery source

Yes, you can turn to God for mercy and grace! If there's any doubt, Hebrews 4:14–16 settles it:

> Therefore, since we have a great high priest who has gone through the heavens, Jesus the Son of God, let us hold firmly to the faith we profess. For we do not have a high priest who is unable to sympathise with our weaknesses, but we have one who has been tempted in every way, just as we are — yet was without sin. Let us then approach the throne of grace with confidence, so that we may receive mercy and find grace to help us in our time of need.

One Christmas Eve, my wife, Joanne, and I received a special gift from a lady who had experienced unspeakable atrocities during her childhood. She had been so hurt by others that Joanne had to be present with me as I talked with her, just for her own personal sense of safety. The gift was a letter in the form of a parable that she wrote. It beautifully captures the message and ministry of the church. Let me share it with you:

> While on vacation as a child one year, I happened upon a gold watch that was lying facedown in the parking lot of our motel. It was covered with dirt and gravel. At first glance, it did not seem worth the effort to bend down and pick it up, but for some reason I found myself reaching for it anyway.
>
> The crystal was broken, the watchband was gone, and there was moisture on the dial. From all appearances, there was no logical reason to believe this watch would still work. Every indication was that its next stop would be the trash can.
>
> Those in my family who were with me at the time laughed at me for picking it up. My mother even

scolded me for holding such a dirty object that was so obviously destroyed. As I reached for the winding stem, my brother made a comment about my lack of intelligence.

'It's been run over by cars,' he chided. 'Nothing can endure that kind of treatment!'

As I turned the stem, the second hand of the watch began to move. My family was wrong. Truly, odds were against the watch working, but there was one thing no one thought of. No matter how broken the outside was, if the inside was not damaged, it would still run, and indeed it did keep perfect time. This watch was made to keep time. Its outside appearance had nothing to do with the purpose for which it was designed. Although the appearance was damaged, the inside was untouched and in perfect condition.

Twenty-five years later, I still have that watch. I take it out every once in a while and wind it up, and it still works. I think as long as the inside remains untouched, it always will. However, unless I had bothered to pick it up and tried to wind it years ago, I never would have known the part that really mattered was still in perfect condition. Although it looks like a piece of junk, it will always be a treasure to me, because I looked beyond the outside appearance and believed in what really mattered, its ability to function in the manner for which it was created.

Thank you, Neil and Joanne, for making the effort to 'pick up the watch,' and 'turn the stem.' You are helping me to see that my emotions may be damaged but my inner self is still in perfect condition, and that is what was created to be with Christ. The only permanent part. The part that really mattered. I know that deep within my heart, no matter what my feelings are telling me, this is true. I also believe that with the help of God's servants, even the 'casing' can be repaired, and maybe even that will become functional again.

There are people all over the world who have been 'run over by cars.' Damaged people. Desperate folk who are crying out for mercy and grace. We have the privilege to 'pick up the watch' and 'turn the stem.' We have to look beyond the casing and extend God's mercy and grace and connect these dear people to God. Perhaps you are one of those people. God has made a wonderful provision for your true recovery: Every hour of every day and for all eternity, we can go to our Great High Priest and receive mercy and grace in our time of need. Where does our confidence lie? 'Therefore, brothers, since we have confidence to enter the Most Holy Place by the blood of Jesus,…let us draw near to God with a sincere heart in full assurance of faith' (Heb 10:19,22).

Dear heavenly Father, forgive me for not coming first to You and for questioning whether You could really understand my needs. Thank You for Your mercy. I know I don't deserve it and neither do I deserve Your grace, but I praise You because You are a gracious God. I renounce the lies of Satan that distort the knowledge of who You really are. Teach me to be merciful to others as You have been merciful to me, and teach me to give people what they need, not what they deserve. I thank You for Jesus Christ, who made it possible for me to come before Your presence, and I resolve from this day forward to do just that. I praise You for Your mercy and grace and for Your open invitation for me to come to You. In Jesus' precious name I pray. Amen.

39
I Am Born of God and the Evil One Cannot Touch Me

> '*We know that anyone born of God does not continue to sin; the one who was born of God keeps him safe, and the evil one cannot harm him. We know that we are children of God, and that the whole world is under the control of the evil one. We know also that the Son of God has come and has given us understanding, so that we may know him who is true. And we are in him who is true — even in his Son Jesus Christ. He is the true God and eternal life.*'
>
> 1 JOHN 5:18–20

Several years ago, a Christian counsellor asked if I would sit in on one of his cases. He had been counselling a young woman for about four years, with little progress. Admitting that he had no experience in dealing with the demonic, he wondered if this might be the girl's problem. She had pentagrams cut into her skin, and many other physical evidences of satanic ritual abuse. I thought to myself, *That's a clue!*

After being with her for just a few minutes, I said, 'There is a battle going on for your mind.'

'Oh praise God,' she said, 'finally somebody understands.'

The next week she came into my office, and as we talked, this large lady suddenly became disoriented, started to get out of her chair and walked toward me. What would you do in that situation? I looked at her and said, 'I am a child of God; you can't touch me.' She stopped in her tracks. I told her to sit down, and she returned to her chair.

In situations like this, it is important to realise that authority does not increase with volume. We don't shout down the devil; we quietly take our authority in Christ. I shared this story with a group on the East Coast, and several weeks later a doctoral student approached me and thanked me for that illustration.

He said, 'Just the other morning I was down at the commuter station waiting for my ride, when three thugs approached me and demanded my money. Neil, it was like I could look right through them. So I said very confidently, "I am a child of God, and the evil one cannot touch me." The three thieves said, "What?" I said again, "I am a child of God, and the evil one cannot touch me." They said, "Oh," and walked away.' In this case his discernment detected the true source of his opposition, which was spiritual.

Know your identity in Christ

I have found that people with spiritual problems usually have a common problem — they don't have a true understanding of their identity in Christ. If the whole world is under the control of the evil one, then the *only* legitimate sanctuary we have is *in Christ*. In the other passage that began this chapter, John repeatedly says, 'We know...we know...we know.' In each case, he refers to the assurance we can have as children of God.

Our battle with the evil one cannot be won with ritualistic slogans or trite formulas, as some spiritual impostors found out in Acts 19:13–16:

> Some Jews who went around driving out evil spirits tried to invoke the name of the Lord Jesus over those who were demon-possessed. They would say, 'In the name of Jesus, whom Paul preaches, I command you to come out.' Seven sons of Sceva, a Jewish chief priest, were doing this. One day

the evil spirit answered them, 'Jesus I know, and I know about Paul, but who are you?' Then the man who had the evil spirit jumped on them and overpowered them all. He gave them such a beating that they ran out of the house naked and bleeding.

If you were confronted like that, how would you respond? I recall one particularly difficult case with a demon-possessed girl. In the middle of a counselling session, her countenance suddenly changed and a gruff voice said, 'Who the ___ do you think you are?' I looked straight at her and said, 'I am a child of God, so you shut up.' Immediately, the girl was back in her right mind, and we dealt with her problems.

Overcoming terror attacks

Have you ever awakened at night feeling terrorised? You may have felt a pressure on your chest or an evil presence in the room. Perhaps you tried to respond but couldn't. At virtually every conference I have led around the world, between one-third to one-half of the people have experienced such an attack. I have had several attacks like this. It is certainly no sin to be under attack, just as it is no sin to be tempted. But what should you do? First, remember what 2 Corinthians 10:4 says: 'The weapons we fight with are not the weapons of the world.'

Initially, you may feel powerless to respond physically. I believe God allows this for our testing. It is as though He is saying, 'Go ahead, try to get out of this by yourself; see what you can do.' But we can't. We absolutely need God. The Bible says that those who call upon the name of the Lord shall be saved. But how can you do that if you're speechless? The answer is in James 4:7: 'Submit yourselves, then, to God. Resist the devil, and he will flee from you.'

God knows the thoughts and intentions of your heart.

Regardless of what is happening around you, you can always inwardly direct your thoughts towards Him. As soon as you acknowledge His place in your life and His authority, you will be released to call upon the Lord. All you have to say is, 'Jesus.' But I believe you have to *say it*. Satan is under no obligation to obey your thoughts; he doesn't know them perfectly. Only God is omniscient. Never ascribe the divine attributes of God to Satan. He is a created being, not the Creator.

Our great deliverer

These attacks are not power encounters but truth encounters. The devil is the father of lies, and his power is in the lie. But the truth sets us free. If you expose the lie, you will break the power of it. For the Christian, power lies in the truth. Nowhere does the Bible tell us that we are to pursue power in this world. Why? Because we already possess it. We are told to pray so our eyes will be opened and we will know the power that we already have (see Ephesians 1:18,19).

That is essential. Because of our position in Christ, we have the authority and the responsibility to resist the devil. But trying to do so without first submitting to God will end in a power struggle, the error of many deliverance ministries. On the other hand, submitting to God without resisting the devil may leave you in bondage. Remember, James 4:7 says we should first submit to God, and then assume our responsibility to resist the devil.

Traditional approaches to deliverance have usually relied upon an outside agent — a pastor, missionary or counsellor who will often try to call up the evil one, maybe get its name or rank and try to cast it out. But if you examine that process, who is the deliverer? It would be the pastor, missionary or counsellor. And where are they getting their information? From demons! I wouldn't believe a word demons say. They are all liars, and they speak from their own nature.

I think there is a more biblical approach. I believe the deliverer has already come — He is Christ. I believe we ought to get our information from the Holy Spirit, who has promised to lead us into all truth. We are not to call upon the name of the pastor to set us free; we are to call upon the name of the Lord. A biblically balanced pastor or missionary should seek to maintain control, making sure that everything is done decently and in order, while recognising that Christ alone can bring freedom.

Safe in the arms of God

Habitual and unrepentant sin accumulates like rubbish, and rubbish attracts rats. The tendency is to want to drive off the rats but they would only come back. The key is to get rid of the rubbish; then the rats have no reason to return.

The one born of God does not continue in sin. He will be under the conviction of the Holy Spirit, who will always drive him back to God. Even if you are struggling in your Christian walk, you should know that you are safe in the arms of God. The evil one cannot touch those who are in Christ. We ought to have enough confidence in God and His Word to say, 'I know I am a child of God, that I have been bought and purchased by the blood of Jesus Christ, that I am in Christ, and that nothing can separate me from the love of God.'

This subject is so important that I encourage you to read my earlier books, *Victory over the Darkness*, *The Bondage Breaker* and *Released From Bondage*. In addition, Steve Russo and I wrote a book for parents and those who work with children called *The Seduction of Our Children*.

The critical thing is to know that our only sanctuary is in Christ. As 1 John 5:13 says, 'I write these things to you who believe in the name of the Son of God so that you may know that you have eternal life.' This is the confidence that God wants us to have, this is our sanctuary.

Dear heavenly Father, I thank You for my security in Christ. The evil one cannot touch me. I bring all the rubbish that I have accumulated in my life before You; I no longer desire to live in sin. I now choose to receive Your conviction and seek Your cleansing as I confess my sins. I will assume my responsibility to put on the armour of God and resist the devil. I renounce the lies of Satan that I am powerless and that I am under his control. I am in Christ and not subject to the god of this world. By Your grace I am Your child, and You will keep me safe. In Jesus' precious name I pray. Amen.

(See *Steps to Freedom* in Christ on page 453 to understand further.)

40
I Am Significant

'For we are God's fellow workers; you are God's
field, God's building.... So then, men ought to
regard us as servants of Christ and as those
entrusted with the secret things of God. Now it is
required that those who have been given a trust
must prove faithful.'   1 CORINTHIANS 3:9; 4:1,2

People often search for significance, but that can be elusive. What is significance? After much thought, I came to the conclusion that a significant event or person is something or someone who made a lasting impact on life. I initially thought that the key was on the immediate size of the impact, but now I know that significance is really measured by how long it lasts. What is forgotten in time is of little significance; what is remembered for eternity is of great significance.

I am amazed at what the world calls significant. Major sporting events, such as the Super Bowl and World Series in America, are of great significance in our society. I like sports, but I couldn't tell you who won the World Series ten years ago. And furthermore, I don't care. We try to immortalise such events by keeping records and building monuments, but every name will eventually be replaced in the record books. These are national pastimes that were originally developed for temporary enjoyment, but they have no eternal significance. Do you remember some years back when the World Series featured Oakland and San

Francisco? Talk about significant! This was a Bay Series, but how significant was it at 5.30 on a Tuesday afternoon when the big earthquake hit?

Not in people

Paul puts it all in perspective in 1 Corinthians 3:1 through 4:2. Open your Bible to this passage, and let's walk through Paul's argument. 'Brothers, I could not address you as spiritual but as worldly — mere infants in Christ' (v 1). They were children of God, but they were not acting like children of God. They weren't ready for solid meat, so he had to give them milk. Their carnality was evidenced by jealousy and quarrelling among them, and the fact that they were just following men. One said, 'I follow Paul,' and another said, 'I follow Apollos' (v 4). Verse 5 says, 'What, after all, is Apollos? And what is Paul? Only servants, through whom you came to believe — as the Lord has assigned to each his task.'

Many people today find their identity in following leaders or belonging to certain organisations, instead of finding it in Christ and being a part of the family of God. Paul had planted and Apollos had watered, but God caused the increase (see 2 Corinthians 3:6).

Not in self-effort

Considering what God wants to accomplish through the Church today, how much gets accomplished if man tries to do it all by himself? The answer is 'nothing'. And how much gets accomplished if we expect God to do it all? The answer is still 'nothing'. God operates through the Church — if no one waters and no one plants, nothing is going to grow. But even when Christians do plant and water, if God isn't in it, nothing will grow. 'The man who plants and the man who waters have one purpose, and each will be rewarded according to his own labour. For we are God's fellow workers; you are God's field, God's building' (1 Cor 3:8,9).

Also, it was by the grace of God that He laid the foundation, and He warns us to be careful how we build on that foundation. 'No one can lay any foundation other than the one already laid, which is Jesus Christ' (1 Cor 3:11). If we build on any other foundation our work will be tested. Someday, there will be a judgement, and the things we have built in total dependence upon the Lord our God will be as gold, silver and costly jewels. But the work we have done in the flesh — any attempt to build our own kingdom — will be as wood, hay and straw. 'It will be revealed with fire, and the fire will test the quality of each man's work. If what he has built survives, he will receive his reward' (1 Cor 3:13,14).

I have a little plaque I always keep near my work, which says, 'Only one life, 'twill soon be past, Only what's done for Christ will last.'[1] Only what we presently sow in God's Kingdom will last for eternity.

Not in our abilities

Paul then reminds us that we are God's temple; His spirit dwells within us. We are not to be deceived: 'If any one of you thinks he is wise by the standards of this age, he should become a "fool" so that he may become wise' (1 Cor 3:18).

There is always the dangerous tendency to think we can bring about God's Kingdom or accomplish something on our own. But Jesus said in John 15:5, 'Apart from me you can do nothing.' But the opposite is also true. 'I can do everything through him who gives me strength' (Phil 4:13). Because I am God's child, I have an entitlement: 'All things are yours, whether Paul or Apollos or Cephas or the world or life or death or the present or the future — all are yours, and you are of Christ, and Christ is of God' (1 Cor 3:21–23). So we are entitled to function as children of God, but we have also been given an entrustment.

Significance lies in stewardship

We will sense our significance when we become good stewards of what God has entrusted to us. As 1 Corinthians 4:1,2 says, 'So then, men ought to regard us as servants of Christ and as those entrusted with the secret things of God. Now it is required that those who have been given a trust must prove faithful.' God has not equally distributed gifts, intelligence or talents. Therefore, we will be judged only according to our use of what He has entrusted to us. He is a fair and just God. Our significance will not be measured by the greatness of our gifts, talents or intelligence, but how we have used what God has entrusted to us — because *whatever we sow*, by faith, in God's Kingdom, will last for eternity.

There are no insignificant children of God. A dear lady once said to me,. 'All I do is teach third grade boys in Sunday School.'

I said, 'What do you mean, that's all you do? You have the privilege of building scriptural principles into those third graders that will affect them for all eternity. You call that insignificant?'

One little seed sown in the Kingdom of God will reap eternal results. Sometimes we struggle because we do not see the lasting effect of our work. That's why Paul writes in Galatians 6:9, 'Let us not become weary in doing good, for at the proper time we will reap a harvest if we do not give up.'

Dear heavenly Father, help me to see the reality of life from Your eternal perspective. I confess the times I have sought immediate gratification. I renounce the lie of Satan that there is no eternal consequence to our stewardship. I claim no ownership of what You have entrusted to me, and to You I dedi-

cate my life, family, ministry and all my endowments. I commit myself to be a good steward of what You have entrusted
to me, and my search for significance is over. I no longer seek
to be wise by the standards of this age or seek the temporal
rewards and acclaim of living independently of You. I find my
significance in doing Your will, as my Saviour modelled for
me. I now commit myself to live a life dependent upon You
and trust You for the eternal dividends that come from a
faithful life today. In Jesus' precious name I pray. Amen.

NOTE

1. C. T. Studd, missionary to Africa.

41
I Am the Salt and Light
of the Earth

*'You are the salt of the earth. But if the salt loses
its saltiness, how can it be made salty again? It is
no longer good for anything, except to be thrown
out and trampled by men. You are the light of the
world. A city on a hill cannot be hidden. Neither do
people light a lamp and put it under a bowl.
Instead they put it on its stand, and it gives light to
everyone in the house. In the same way, let your
light shine before men, that they may see your good
deeds and praise your Father in heaven.'*

MATTHEW 5:13–16

The influence of the Church in our society has become
greatly diminished, and tragically, the Church in America is
only patronised. We have freedom of religion, but the message is clear: 'Don't interfere with the educational and political processes.' The accepted cultural religion in America is
fast becoming New Age, replacing humanism in our
schools and industries. New Agers have taken the lead on
the environment and holistic health, while the Church is
seen as a hospital where sick people go. But the Church is
not a hospital; it is a military outpost that has an infirmary.
    I have spent a lot of time working in the infirmary, but
the Church does not exist for that; the infirmary exists for
the Church. We have a lot of wounded people who need to
be healed so they can return to society and become the salt
and light that God has called them to be. But when the
Church becomes carnal, operating in the flesh, it is no

longer good for anything except to be thrown out and trampled by men, losing its purpose for being here.

The Church, as Israel in the Old Testament, has had
times of both great revival and great decline. Can it be made
salty again? Yes, of course it can. God says, 'If my people,
who are called by my name, will humble themselves and
pray and seek my face and turn from their wicked ways,
then will I hear from heaven and will forgive their sin and
will heal their land' (2 Chron 7:14).

Because we are children of God, we are salt and light.
And we will continue to be that as long as we operate in the
power of the Holy Spirit and don't hide our personal testimonies. What is the Lord saying when He refers to us as the
salt of the earth? Well, salt has two primary purposes — it
preserves and it flavours.

Salt preserves

I believe Christians are called to preserve God's truth whenever necessary. Paul says, 'The church of the living God, [is]
the pillar and foundation of the truth' (1 Tim 3:15).

In 1980, when I was finishing my first doctorate from
Pepperdine University, I took a class called 'Futures'. It was
a class for educators trying to construct realistic scenarios
for what the future might look like. The students were all
required to give a class presentation. A principal from the
inner city gave a presentation on what was nothing more
than the occult. He was excited as he talked about astral
projections and new frontiers of the mind. What astonished
me was how the educated people around me responded to
him. Curiosity rose and questions came from everyone. They
wanted to know more about this new frontier of the mind.

The concept of New Age wasn't yet fashionable, so
nobody quite understood what the principal was talking
about, but they were all curious. I just sat and listened,
astonished at what I was hearing. Finally, I asked the ques-

tion, 'As you were doing your research, did you ever consider whether this is right or wrong?' He said no, he wasn't concerned about that.

I told him I believe that's critical because what he was describing is not new — it's as old as biblical history. And God has very purposefully forbidden it as a practice.

The teacher thought that this was a good time to end the class, but as we dismissed, several people gathered around me and asked, 'What's wrong with what he was saying?' It gave me a tremendous opportunity to share God's perspective.

I believe that every child of God will be afforded such opportunities to be a witness. When the occasion arises — whether at work, play, school or church — we must choose to be the salt that will help preserve biblical standards. We must learn to speak the truth in love.

Salt flavours

We are also given the opportunity to be the salt that flavours life. Where the Church has flourished, there has been an elevation of social life. Our heavenly Father is a God of order and beauty, and whenever He is honoured, there is an appreciation for art, literature and music. In Christian cultures, women have equal status, children and the elderly are honoured, and all life is given dignity. God's people, filled with the Holy Spirit, bring peace in the midst of confusion, hope in the presence of despair, order when there is chaos, and light where there is darkness.

When I first became a Christian, I wanted to start a Bible study where I worked as an aerospace engineer. I really didn't have any idea how to do it, so I asked my pastor. He suggested that I put up a notice inviting people to come and begin by reading a few verses from the Gospel of Mark, asking questions and discussing them. Well, I could do that, so I put up a notice. But within the hour someone ripped it off the wall and brought it in to tell me that I could not bring Jesus into the company. I responded that I could not do otherwise, and he wanted to know why. I said that, 'Every day I come in, Jesus comes in with me.' He didn't like my answer, so he went to the personnel office. In a few minutes, they called me and said that it would be best for the company if I didn't have my Bible study. I asked if it would be acceptable to put up the notice and have the Bible study at the bowling alley next door. They said that would be fine, so that's what I did.

I was surprised at the number of 'secret service' Christians that came to the study. I had no idea they were Christians. I reflected on that later. To me, that would have to be the most embarrassing put-down a person could say to me — 'I wasn't aware that you are a Christian.'

Light dispels darkness

As a new believer, I chose to identify myself publicly as a Christian. I had learned from Colossians 3:23 that the one I really worked for was the Lord Jesus Christ, even though an aerospace company issued my pay cheque. My testimony brought light to those who were in darkness.

I also reasoned that being a Christian should make me a better engineer. My career took on a whole new meaning as I realised I was not only trying to earn a living; I had a ministry. Christians sought me out for prayer when they were discouraged, and I had the privilege of seeing many people come to Christ. One of the engineers I led to Christ took over the Bible study when I went to seminary. All of that was a result of the little Bible study we had at the bowling alley.

Jesus said, 'If anyone is ashamed of me and my words in this adulterous and sinful generation, the Son of Man will be ashamed of him when he comes in his Father's glory with the holy angels' (Mk 8:38). I don't want to use this verse to produce guilt, only to soberly remind us that we are to be salt and light. God may not ask you to start a Bible study, but He does want you to influence your world positively. As we take a stand, let it be done in the power of the Holy Spirit. We never have the right to violate the fruit of the Spirit. If what we do cannot be done in love, joy, peace, patience and kindness, then possibly it would be better left undone. Truth must be spoken in love. I came across this poem several years ago, and it still reminds me of the importance of being a positive influence.

10 Little Christians

10 little Christians came to church all the time;
   one fell out with the preacher, then there were nine.
9 little Christians stayed up late;
   one overslept on Sunday, then there were eight.
8 little Christians on their way to heaven;
   one took the low road, then there were seven.
7 little Christians, chirping like chicks;
   one didn't like the singing, then there were six.
6 little Christians seemed very much alive;
   one took a vacation, then there were five.
5 little Christians pulling for heaven's shore;
   one stopped to rest awhile, then there were four.
4 little Christians each as busy as a bee;
   one got his feelings hurt, then there were three.
3 little Christians couldn't decide what to do;
   one couldn't have his way, then there were two.
2 little Christians each won one more;
   now don't you see, two and two make four.
4 little Christians worked early and late,
   each brought one, now there were eight.
8 little Christians, if they double as before...
   in just seven Sundays we'd have 1,024.
In this little jingle there is a lesson true —
   you belong either to the building or to the
   wrecking crew![1]

Will you join me in choosing to let your light shine before men, that they may see your good deeds and praise your Father in heaven?

Dear heavenly Father, forgive me for the times that I have not taken a stand for righteousness sake, and forgive me for the times that I have responded in the flesh. Enable me to speak the truth in love and to be the salt and light that You have called me to be. I renounce the lies of Satan that my testimony and commitment to truth will have no value or will not count for eternity. I announce that my life is significant in Christ, that I have been called to be salt and light and that what I say and do in the power of the Holy Spirit will have eternal consequences. I now commit myself to be a part of the building crew. In Jesus' precious name I pray. Amen.

NOTE

1. Author and source unknown.

42
I Am a Branch of the True Vine, a Channel of His Life

*'I am the true vine, and My Father is the
vinedresser. Every branch in Me that does not bear
fruit, He takes away; and every branch that bears
fruit, He prunes it, that it may bear more fruit.
You are already clean because of the word which I
have spoken to you. Abide in Me, and I in you. As
the branch cannot bear fruit of itself, unless it
abides in the vine, so neither can you, unless you
abide in Me. I am the vine, you are the branches;
he who abides in Me, and I in him, he bears much
fruit; for apart from Me you can do nothing.'*

JOHN 15:1–5 (NASB)

Twice I have had the opportunity to tour and study in Israel. One of my most memorable experiences was travelling to the hill country where most of the vineyards are. As we walked among them, I was puzzled at what I saw. Being from California, I was used to seeing the vine directed upward to the poles and wires that would support the branches far above the ground. Not so in Israel. They follow the ancient custom of allowing the vine to simply grow along the ground. The branches also naturally rest upon the ground.

If the vines were left to grow wild in this condition, there would probably be no fruit. The vinedressers have to do two things: First, they raise up the vine and the branches by putting large stones under them. Second, they regularly prune the branches in order to get them to bear more fruit. Let's examine these two functions as they relate to us.

Picked up

Spiritually, Jesus is the true vine, the trunk that connects us to the roots. He is the source from which all growth begins. No vine, no branches. The branches cannot exist without being grafted into the vine. The opening text says, 'Every branch in Me that does not bear fruit, He takes away.' Some say that the non-fruitbearing branch represents someone who has lost his salvation. Others say that the Lord is simply taking to heaven the true believer because he is no longer bearing fruit. That would parallel the passage in 1 Corinthians 11:30, which implies that God will 'call home' the believer who fails to judge himself properly when participating in communion. The most common interpretation is that the vinedresser is just trimming off dead branches. They are not true believers. 'If anyone does not abide in Me, he is thrown away as a branch' (Jn 15:6, NASB).

The same verb — 'takes away' — is translated in John 8:59 as 'picked up.' This also fits the practice of the vinedresser in the days of Christ. There is no way that we are going to bear fruit mired in the clay, so the Lord picks us up. He puts a rock under us so that we are raised up with Christ. 'You are already clean [justified] because of the word I have spoken to you' (Jn 15:3, brackets added). That would have to apply to all those who are *in Christ*.

Pruned

We have to realise that apart from the vine (Christ), we can do nothing. We are in Christ — we have been grafted in — but if we attempt to operate independently of Him, we will not bear fruit. Operating in the flesh will produce no lasting fruit. As we have seen in previous chapters, every deed done in the flesh will produce only wood, hay and stubble, which will be burned up some day. Our *work* will be tested by fire, not us. We have already been justified.

A modern-day illustration would be to consider ourselves as light bulbs. Our light will not shine unless we are plugged in to the energy source. Someone has taken the first letters in the following words and formed an acrostic: Always Believing Indwelling Divine Energy (ABIDE). It is the Lord who energises my life. I try to maintain a constant awareness that God is always present in my life. I begin my day and start every ministry by declaring my dependency upon the Lord. My confidence isn't in my intellect, my degrees, my cleverness, techniques, strategies nor programmes. My confidence is in the Lord.

If God isn't in it, the best humanly designed programme *won't* work. If God is in it, almost any programme *will* work. This, then, is the second work of the vinedresser. the first is to lift us up in Christ; the second is to prune our lives so that we will bear more fruit.

Why does the grapevine need to be pruned? When left to grow wild, the leaves of the vine become the dominant feature. It may look good because the foliage is pretty, and it can have the appearance of being healthy. But the leaves sap the vine of its nutrients so that less goes to the grapes. Eventually, the foliage covers the grapes from the sun so that they never fully develop.

Where to seek approval

In ministry, there is always the temptation to *look* good rather than *be* good. Too much energy spent on looking good will take away from the energy needed to bear fruit. The moment we focus more on how we look than how we are, we have sown the seeds of our own destruction. We become man-centred rather than God-centred. King Saul lost his crown confessing, 'I have sinned. I violated the Lord's command and your instructions. I was afraid of the people and so I gave in to them' (1 Sam 15:24). The fear of the Lord, not the fear of man, is the beginning of wisdom.

Paul says in Galatians 1:10, 'Am I now trying to win the

approval of men, or of God? Or am I trying to please men? If I were still trying to please men, I would not be a servant of Christ.' If Paul were trying to please men, who would he be serving? Men! Seeking the approval of man rather than the approval of God is like playing for the grandstand instead of the coach. We must stay plugged in to the source of our life and make it our ambition to live in such a way as to please Him (see 2 Corinthians 5:9).

Don't damage the vine

Pruning is a delicate art. You can cut too soon, too fast and too much. The result will be injured branches and poor fruit. Our heavenly Father is the ultimate vinedresser. He trims (disciplines) us so we will bear more fruit. Discipline is not punishment. God does not punish us for doing something wrong. As 1 John 4:18 says, 'There is no fear in love. But perfect love drives out fear, because fear has to do with punishment.' Discipline is always future-oriented.

'Our fathers disciplined us for a little while as they thought best; but God disciplines us for our good, that we may share in his holiness. No discipline seems pleasant at the time, but painful. Later on, however, it produces a harvest of righteousness and peace for those who have been trained by it' (Heb 12:10,11).

Sometimes, when working with our children or other people, we can get ahead of God's timing. We can push too much, too fast, and try to accomplish the Holy Spirit's work. A lot of broken vine branches and damaged fruit are out there because of well-meaning ministries and people who don't practise gentleness. One such broken person came to me for help, and later shared the following poem that she had written. I still have trouble reading it without getting misty-eyed. It describes the need for compassion with one another while allowing God to do His work.

The Wreath

A friend of mine whose grapevine died, had put it
    out for trash.
I said to her, 'I'll take that vine and make something
    of that.'
At home the bag of dead, dry vines looked nothing
    but a mess, but as I gently bent one vine, entwining
    'round and 'round,
A rustic wreath began to form, potential did abound.
    One vine would not go where it should, and
    anxious as I was,
I forced it so to change its shape, it broke — and
    what the cause?
If I had taken precious time to slowly change
    its form,
It would have made a lovely wreath, not a dead
    vine, broken, torn.
    As I finished bending, adding blooms,
    applying trim,
I realised how that rustic wreath is like my life within.
    You see, so many in my life have tried to make
    me change.
They've forced my spirit anxiously, I tried to rearrange.
    But when the pain was far too great, they forced
    my fragile form,
I plunged far deeper in despair, my spirit broken, torn.
    Then God allowed a gentle one that knew of
    dying vines,
To kindly, patiently allow the Lord to take His time.
    And though the vine has not yet formed a
    decorative wreath,
I know that with God's servants' help one day when
    Christ I meet,
    He'll see a finished circle, a perfect gift to Him.

It will be a final product, a wreath with all the trim.
So as you look upon this gift, the vine round
and complete,
Remember God is using you to gently shape His wreath.[1]

Wherever you are on God's vine, commit yourself to bearing as much fruit as possible to glorify Him.

Dear heavenly Father, You are my vinedresser. I take Your discipline of me to be proof of Your love. I desire to bear much fruit to Your honour and glory. Forgive me for the times I have been more concerned about what people say than living my life to please You. Forgive me for being more concerned about how I look, rather than for being who I am, a channel of Your life. I renounce the lies of Satan that say You don't love me or that I can have power by any other means than abiding in You. I now choose to abide in Christ, and declare my dependency upon You. I confess that apart from You, I can do nothing. Teach me to be sensitive to other people's needs and to be gentle in dealing with them. I want to be a channel of Your love and be used of You to gently shape Your wreaths. In Jesus' precious name I pray. Amen.

NOTE

1. Unpublished poem by Kathleen Viaes, 'The Wreath'. Used by permission.

43
I Have Been Chosen and Appointed to Bear Fruit

'You did not choose me, but I chose you and
appointed you to go and bear fruit — fruit that will
last. Then the Father will give you whatever you
ask in my name. This is my command: Love each
other.'   JOHN 15:16,17

I love the fifteenth chapter of John. It tells us the source of our life and strength, why we are here, how to bear fruit, and gives us the goal for our ministry. Jesus is our life, and apart from Him we can do nothing. Many are waiting for God to choose them or appoint them to some ministry, not realising that they have already been called and appointed.

We have been called by God to be His children. We are all called and appointed to serve God full time. Being the mother, father, spouse, carpenter, engineer, homemaker, secretary, lawyer or politician that God has called us to be is full-time service. I don't think God is overly concerned whether His children are carpenters, plumbers or engineers. But He does care *what kind* of carpenter, plumber or engineer we may be. We don't need any ecclesiastical position to serve the Lord, although some have been called to those positions. The only person who can keep us from being what God wants is ourselves.

What God requires

Why are we here? To glorify God! How? 'This is to my Father's glory, that you bear much fruit, showing yourselves to be my disciples' (Jn 15:8). Some think that John 15 says we *must* bear fruit. This can lead to tremendous guilt and orient our ministry in the wrong direction.

John 15 is really about abiding in Christ. We aren't required to bear fruit; we are required to abide in Christ. The *result* of abiding in Christ is bearing fruit, and that is the proof of our discipleship. Failing to abide in Christ will lead to fruitless frustration, yet many ministries do just that. Annual reports recall all the activities of the previous year: 'We went here and we went there. We did this and we did that. What an exhausting year — just look at all the things we did!' All that sounds good, but how much fruit remains?

Is the fruit of the Spirit more evident in your life this year than last year? Are you more loving, patient, kind and self-controlled now than you were a year ago? Did you do something that will have lasting consequences? We have been called to bear fruit that remains.

Do you ever consider everything that happened in your life and ministry last year a result of your hard work and human ingenuity? If you do, then where was God, and how is He glorified by your self-effort? Remember, Jesus intends to pass by the self-sufficient. We can't measure our effectiveness in ministry by our activities; we must evaluate it on the basis of fruit that remains. I want nothing more than to have people say, 'You can't account for that man or his ministry apart from God's working through him.' Then, and only then, will our joy be made full (see John 15:11) and our heavenly Father be glorified.

Abiding is obedience

The error on the other extreme is to think that abiding in Christ is to sit around in some holy piety. Not so! 'If you keep My commandments, you will abide in My love' (Jn 15:10, NASB). What are His commandments? 'And this is His commandment, that we believe in the name of His Son

Jesus Christ, and love one another, just as He commanded us. And the one who keeps His commandments abides in Him, and He in him. And we know by this that He abides in us, by the Spirit whom He has given us' (1 Jn 3:23,24, NASB).

The Lord is not suggesting a legalistic walk with Him. We have a tendency to focus on behaviour and changing how people act. As I said earlier, we are not saved by how we behave; we are saved by how we believe. 'Not that we are competent in ourselves to claim anything for ourselves, but our competence comes from God. He has made us competent as ministers of a new covenant — not of the letter but of the Spirit; for the letter kills, but the Spirit gives life' (2 Cor 3:5,6). Belief always precedes behaviour. The commandment *is to believe* in the name of Jesus Christ. We are to do what we believe and become what we already are in Christ. It is the Holy Spirit who bears witness with our spirit that we are children of God (see Rom 8:16). And it is the Holy Spirit who enables us to walk by faith.

Doing God's will leads to answered prayer

Another motivation for abiding in God is the hope for answered prayer. 'If you abide in Me, and My words abide in you, ask whatever you wish, and it shall be done for you...that your fruit should remain, that whatever you ask of the Father in My name, He may give to you' (Jn 15:7,16, NASB). Effective prayer follows obedient living. Why? If you are a parent, would you honour all of your children's requests if they were disobedient to you? Would you want to give a rebel whatever he desires? Probably not, and neither would God!

When we choose to abide in Christ, we are seeking to do His will, which we understand to be good, acceptable and perfect (see Romans 12:2). 'Delight yourself in the Lord and he will give you the desires of your heart' (Ps 37:4). If we abide in Christ, our wishes will be God's wishes, and our desires will be God's desires. But we must first conform to His image. Then our desires and wishes will be in line with His, and whatever we ask will be granted because our desire is to do His will.

Entering into agape love

If we abide in Christ, what will be the result? We will love one another. The concept of *agape* (love) seems undefinable to many people. It is easy to understand if you realise that the word can be used as a noun or verb. When agape is used as a noun, it refers to the highest of Christian character. 'God is love' (1 Jn 4:8). 'Love is patient, love is kind' (1 Cor 13:4). According to 1 Timothy 1:5, 'The goal of this command is love, which comes from a pure heart and a good conscience and a sincere faith.'

Agape love is not dependent upon the object of love. God loves us because it is His nature to love us, not because we are lovable. If it were any other way, it would be conditional love. So when someone says they cannot love another person, they may be revealing more about their own character than the other person.

When *not* referring to the character of Christ, love is used as a verb. Then agape becomes an action word, something I would do on your behalf if I loved you. 'For God so loved the world that he *gave*' (Jn 3:16, emphasis added). The application of that verse for our lives is 1 John 3:16,17: 'This is how we know what love is: Jesus Christ laid down his life for us. And we ought to lay down our lives for our brothers. If anyone has material possessions and sees his brother in need but has no pity on him, how can the love of God be in him?'

This is not love and action based on feeling. We can't order our feelings towards anyone. But by the grace of God we can do what is right for the other person. We can love the unlovely and show mercy on the poor and suffering.

When I was a pastor, I used to greet people after church. One Sunday, a dear man in his seventies handed me a note. It said, 'Pastor, I have learned over the years that one of life's most enduring values is that no one can sincerely help another without helping himself in the process. It is more blessed to give than to receive.' As 1 John 4:7 says, 'Dear friends, let us love one another, for love comes from God. Everyone who loves has been born of God and knows God.' Let's pray towards that end:

Dear heavenly Father, I confess that I have tried to bear fruit without You. I have not always accepted my position in life, and have looked for, and waited for, a calling from You, not realising that You have already called and appointed me to bear fruit right where I am. I have petitioned You without first being submissive. I have not loved people as You have loved them. I renounce the lies of Satan that I can produce fruit without You if I just tried harder on my own. I don't want to be self-sufficient. I choose to find my significance in my relationship to You. Because my sufficiency is in You, I will trust You to use me to bear fruit that lasts. I want to love like You do. I have no greater desire than to abide in Christ. I now commit myself to a life of faith, believing in You, and by the power of the indwelling Holy Spirit, I commit myself to be obedient to Your will. In Jesus' precious name I pray. Amen.

44
I Am a Personal Witness of Christ

*'But you will receive power when the Holy Spirit
comes on you; and you will be my witnesses in
Jerusalem, and in all Judea and Samaria, and to
the ends of the earth.'* ACTS 1:8

Attending church has always been a vital part of my life,
primarily because of the way I was brought up. It was part
of my culture. We went to church every Sunday, because we
were expected to. Didn't everybody? It was the American
thing to do. I even told myself that I would be willing to die
rather than deny my belief in God. I don't remember a time
that I didn't believe in Him. Even as a husband, father and
aspiring young engineer, I continued my involvement in
church.

I had backed into the position of chairman of the board
in a struggling young church when an excited couple from a
sister church invited us to attend a Lay Institute for
Evangelism. For some reason, I didn't quite catch the purpose of the week-long conference, because the idea of evangelism was like a dirty word to me. I thought, *If you don't
knock on my door, I won't knock on your door!* I was content
with my religion, and I was quite content to let others
believe as they saw fit.

In the four years I worked as an engineer, I always
worked the day shift. But the week of the evangelism institute, I worked the night shift — the only time in four years
— because of a computer breakdown. I had no excuses, so

I went with my wife, father-in-law and our pastor to the daytime sessions. For some reason, it hadn't connected in my mind that they were going to train me to share my faith as a way of life!

By Wednesday, it finally dawned on me that I didn't have any faith to share. I had been playing church for twenty-plus years. In the middle of that week, I gave my heart to Christ. I didn't have any great personal needs, nor was I facing any kind of crisis. I just simply realised for the first time the simplicity of the gospel and that I didn't have a personal relationship with the living God.

That Friday, the conference leader said, 'Don't tell anyone you came to this conference if you don't complete it by going door-to-door with us on Saturday afternoon to share your faith.' I remember driving home thinking, *No way, José! I have come a long way since Wednesday but not far enough to go knock on somebody's door!*

I wrestled with the Lord most of Friday night and finally got some sleep after I told Him I would go. My wife wasn't excited about it either and agreed to go only if we would go together. But the first instruction we heard at the church the next day was, 'A husband and wife can't go together. We want you to be dependent upon the Lord, not each other.' So my father-in-law and I received our street assignments and we went together. 'You better let me go first,' I said, 'or I might chicken out.'

That Saturday, two days old in the Lord, I had the privilege to lead three people to Christ! God had to show me that 'the harvest is plentiful but the workers are few' (Mt 9:37). I have never been the same since.

What is a witness?

A witness is someone who has personally seen, heard or experienced something. The little band of apostles had seen the resurrected Jesus, but they hadn't yet experienced the power that brings new life in Christ. Just seeing the master wasn't enough. They were told to wait until they received power from above. When the Holy Spirit came at Pentecost, they were complete. The Church was born, and nothing could stop them — not the religious establishment of their day, not the power of the Roman government, not even the gates of hell.

Historically, the witness of the Church went out first in Jerusalem, then it spread to Judea, and now the gospel has been heard around the world. We are fast approaching the generation that will see the fulfilment of Matthew 24:14: 'And this gospel of the kingdom will be preached in the whole world as a testimony to all nations, and then the end will come.'

Roadblocks to evangelism

Every child of God has the privilege to be a part of God's eternal plan. We are all personal witnesses of the power of Christ within us. Why aren't we more effective?

First, I believe, is ignorance. Many are labouring under the wrong impression that eternal life is something we get when we die. Others are ignorant of their spiritual heritage and the power we already possess. That is why Paul prays in Ephesians 1:18,19, 'I pray also that the eyes of your heart may be enlightened in order that you may know the hope to which he has called you, the riches of his glorious inheritance in the saints, and his incomparably great power for us who believe.' We have no witness when we are living in the flesh. Trying to get defeated Christians to share their faith is counterproductive. What can they witness about? Only their defeat!

Second, I believe some people place too much emphasis on the temporal things of the world and not enough on the eternal relationships of life. Jesus said, 'Watch out! Be on your guard against all kinds of greed; a man's life does not consist in the abundance of his possessions' (Lk 12:15). He then tells a parable about a man who acquired great riches and reasoned that he had enough stored up so that he could eat, drink and be merry (see Luke 12:19). 'But God said to him, "You fool! This very night your life will be demanded from you. Then who will get what you have prepared for yourself?" This is how it will be with anyone who stores up things for himself but is not rich towards God' (Lk 12:20,21).

It seems to be the great ambition of man to seek happiness and comfort, with no thought for their souls. What would you exchange for love, joy, peace, patience, kindness, goodness, faithfulness, gentleness and self-control? A new car? Better social status? The lie of Satan is that social status, material possessions, appearance or other temporal rewards of this world will bring the lasting joy that only God can bring. That is exchanging the pleasures of the soul for the pleasures of things. Bad choice!

Third, I believe many people don't understand the urgency of evangelism. Who wouldn't drop whatever they were doing and immediately warn a blindfolded child walking towards the edge of a cliff? Yet every day, thousands of Christless feet march toward their eternal death. The loss of eternal life is far greater than the loss of our temporal physical life, which will ultimately be lost anyway.

Jesus appeals to our sense of compassion when He says in Luke 15:4–7:

> Suppose one of you has a hundred sheep and loses one of them. Does he not leave the ninety-nine in the open country and go after the lost sheep until he finds it? And when he finds it, he joyfully puts it on his shoulders and goes home. Then he calls his friends and neighbours together and says, 'Rejoice with me; I have found my lost sheep.' I tell you that in the same way there will be more rejoicing in heaven over

404 Part Three: Our Significance in Christ

one sinner who repents than over ninety-nine righteous persons who do not need to repent.

Seeing the significance of a soul

Nothing is more important than the salvation of one person, and we can have no greater significance than to be a witness.

While working as an engineer, I had my own encounter with this truth in what I now call the parable of the sunflower seed. I was acting as the lead engineer on an underwater fire control system. We had just built our first floor model, and I was assigned to get it up to specifications. I worked all day and most evenings, with a production engineer assigned to work with me on each shift.

The man who worked with me in the evenings was really no help at all. As I struggled late into the evening, he would sit and eat sunflower seeds. It was a most irritating habit, and it drove me nuts. As the hours increased, along with my fatigue, my tolerance to any distractions decreased. What's more, this man would call in sick more often than he seemed to be there. One night in sheer frustration, I asked him if he ever went to church. I was desperate for anything that would make him a better helper for me. Hardly the best motivation for good witnessing.

He said he didn't, but he and his wife had been thinking about it. I invited them to our church and was surprised when he and his wife came the following Sunday. Joanne and I escorted them to their proper Sunday School class and joined them later for the worship service.

The following Tuesday morning, I got a call from my pastor informing me that he had visited my co-worker and led him to Christ. I was overwhelmed with gratitude (and relief). My pastor also told me that my co-worker was an alcoholic! Suddenly, it all made sense. That was why he was absent so much. When my frustration factor had reached its limit, I finally did what I should have done from the beginning — be the witness that God had called me to be. That man's eternal life had far more value than the underwater fire control system I was working on, yet I had almost let that be more important.

I have had the privilege to be a pastor, seminary professor and now the founder of my own ministry, and I have determined that evangelism will always be on my front burner no matter what my place in life might be. There is no higher calling than evangelism. 'He who wins souls is wise' (Prov 11:30).

To this day, there is nothing more satisfying to me than leading someone to Christ or helping them find freedom in Him. We should follow Paul's instruction to Timothy: 'Keep your head in all situations, endure hardship, do the work of an evangelist, discharge all the duties of your ministry' (2 Tim 4:5). Evaluate your own life and witness, and then pray this prayer.

Dear heavenly Father, what a privilege it is to be a personal witness to Your resurrection power that is within me. Forgive me for the times that I have let other things overshadow the value of a lost sheep. And forgive me for placing a higher value on acquiring temporal things than on the value of life itself. I confess that I have sometimes focused on storing up treasures on earth rather than treasures in heaven.

I want to be a witness to the life of Christ that is within me. I renounce the lies of Satan that say I lack the power or ability to be a credible witness. I pray that You will enable me to be free in Christ so my life will be a witness to Your resurrection power. Open my eyes to the field that is ripe for harvest. Enable me to see the daily opportunities to witness and testify Your great love. I pray that I will never be a stumbling block to those who are blinded to the gospel. I ask all this in the wonderful name of Jesus my Lord. Amen.

45
I Am God's Temple

*'Don't you know that you yourselves are God's
temple and that God's Spirit lives in you? If anyone
destroys God's temple, God will destroy him; for
God's temple is sacred, and you are that temple.'*
1 CORINTHIANS 3:16,17

My wife and I have crisscrossed the United States in recent years, preferring to drive whenever possible on conference tours. We enjoy seeing our country and stopping at interesting places. Occasionally, we have come across a small town that would not have been noteworthy except it was the birthplace or residence of a celebrity. Small towns of America try to capitalise on the fact that somebody 'significant' was born there or has slept there. The place is then 'immortalised' by a historical marker, restored homestead or memorial. Some of our favourite stops have been the homes of presidents and the presidential libraries that are often located in their home towns.

Where God dwells
I don't want to take away those cities' claims to fame, but they all pale in significance compared to the places God has chosen to reside. How can any human celebrity compare to the Lord of the universe, who created all humans? In the Old Testament, the glory of God first took up residence in the holy of holies, which was in the Tabernacle. The high priest was the only person allowed to enter into that sacred place, and then only once a year on the great Day of Atonement.

When King Solomon's temple was built, it became the place of residence for the glory of God. The Shechinah glory was a manifestation of God's presence. When Solomon had the temple dedicated, the people 'raised their voices in praise to the Lord and sang: "He is good; his love endures forever." Then the temple of the Lord was filled with a cloud, and the priests could not perform their service because of the cloud, for the glory of the Lord filled the temple of God' (2 Chron 5:13,14).

I have often thought of that as one of the most beautiful pictures of what happens when we dedicate our temples (bodies) to the Lord. We are filled with the Holy Spirit so that our lives are controlled by the presence of God.

If it is significant to memorialise the dwelling place of a mortal, how much more significant to honour the present dwelling place of God. Today, the Old Testament tabernacle is nowhere to be found. 'The glory has departed from Israel, for the ark of God has been captured' (1 Sam 4:22). The temple site in Jerusalem is now under the control of Muslims. Where the temple once stood, there now stands the Dome of the Rock and an Arab mosque. The word *ichabod* (the glory has departed) is written all over the ancient sites. The dwelling place of God is no longer in structures made by human hands; instead, He resides in human hearts.

You are God's temple

When 1 Corinthians 3:16,17 refers to God's temple, the emphasis is not upon the individual but on the Church. The most definitive development of this thought is given in Ephesians 2:19–22: 'Consequently, you are no longer foreigners and aliens, but fellow citizens with God's people and members of God's household, built on the foundation of the apostles and prophets, with Christ Jesus himself as the chief cornerstone. *In him* the whole building is joined

Part Three: Our Significance in Christ

together and rises to become a holy temple in the Lord. And *in him* you too are being built together to become *a dwelling in which God lives by his Spirit'* (emphasis added).

Dear reader, *you* are no longer a foreigner nor an alien. *You* are, right now, a fellow citizen with God's people, and a member of God's household. You are not being prideful if you believe that; in fact, you will be defeated if you don't. You may not feel like a member of God's family sometimes, but you must believe it.

The true foundation that we build our lives upon is the revelation of God, the prophetic revelation of the Old Testament and the apostolic message of the New Testament. Jesus is the ultimate, perfect revelation of God. The glory of God has returned in Christ. 'The Word became flesh and made his dwelling among us. We have seen his glory, the glory of the One and Only, who came from the Father, full of grace and truth' (Jn 1:14).

God has a new blueprint, but it isn't for any physical structure. You and I are the dwelling places of God, and His divine blueprint is for the Church to become 'a holy temple.' 'You too are being built together to become a dwelling in which God lives' (Eph 2:22).

The heavens declare God's glory, so why don't we?

Unfortunately, many Christians don't live as though God dwells within them. The rest of creation seems to be doing what they were created to do. 'The heavens declare the glory of God; the skies proclaim the work of his hands' (Ps 19:1). The animal kingdom reflects the glory of God: the migratory birds know when to fly south for the winter; squirrels store up for the winter; bears hibernate. All living creatures operate by divine instinct, but they are not created in the image of God as is mankind. Awhile back, I ran across this poem, titled 'A Monkey's Observation', which humourously illustrates the differences between humans and animals:

> Three monkeys sat in a coconut tree;
> > and talked of things that were said to be.
> Said one to the others: 'See here, you two!
> > There's a rumour afloat that can't be true,
> That man descended from our lofty race,
> > To think of such is a great disgrace.
> No monkey ever beat his wife,
> > or starved her child or spoiled her life;
> And whoever heard of a mother monk
> > parking her babes for another to bunk,
> Or passing them on from one to another
> > till they couldn't tell who was their mother.
> And another thing you'll never see,
> > is a fence around a coconut tree.
> If a fence I should be 'round a coconut tree
> > starvation would force you to steal from me;
> And there is another thing a monk won't do,
> > that is to go out at night and get on a stew;
> Then use a gun, a club, or a butcher knife
> > to take another poor monkey's life.
> Man may have descended, the ornery cuss;
> > but brothers, he didn't descend from us!'[1]

Barriers to being the temples God wants us to be

Why is it that we often struggle to live as God's temple? First, we were never designed by God to operate independently of Him. The animal kingdom couldn't function without God either, but unlike us, they have no choice. When we become the dwelling place of God and function by the power of the Holy Spirit, then we glorify God.

Second, since we came into this world physically alive but spiritually dead, we learned during our formative years to live independently of God. We had neither the presence of God in our lives, nor the knowledge of His ways. When we were born again spiritually, nobody pushed the clear button. Our minds, like computers, were programmed to live independently of Him. That is why Paul says, 'Do not conform any longer to the pattern of this world, but be transformed by the renewing of your mind. Then you will be able to test and approve what God's will is — his good, pleasing and perfect will' (Rom 12:2).

Third, many Christians have been programmed to believe that they are worthless. Only mankind is created in the image of God, but we are often treated like animals or less. Our present world system has been known to place more value on whales and spotted owls than humans with eternal souls. Babies are slaughtered in mothers' wombs, simply because the little created being would be inconvenient or embarrassing.

Damaged temples being rebuilt

One of my former students has a prison ministry. He regularly tells the prisoners about the truth of God's freedom, sharing with them many of the statements and verses contained in this book. Somehow the message is getting through to them. They aren't just a bunch of thieves, thugs, derelicts, perverts, sex addicts or alcoholic bums. They are children of God, created in His image, but damaged by the worldly system in which they were raised. They are 'being built together to become a dwelling in which God lives by his Spirit' (Eph 2:22).

The monuments of earthly kings seem far more attractive and significant than these outcasts, but from God's perspective it isn't so. I pray that will be our perspective as well. The glory of earthly things will fade, and believers shall receive a glorified body. It's true that the men and women in our prisons are there because of choices they made, and they will have to assume their responsibility if they desire to be free, but be careful not to judge unless you fully understand the road they have travelled. The following poem conveys this powerful message:

> Pray, find no fault with the man who limps
>   or stumbles along the road,
> Unless you have worn the shoes he wears,
>   or struggled beneath the load.
> There may be tacks in his shoes that hurt,
>   though hidden away from view;
> Or the burden he bears, placed on your back,
>   might cause you to stumble too.
> Don't sneer at the man who's down today,
>   unless you have felt the blow
> That caused his fall, or felt the shame
>   that only the fallen know.
> You may be strong, but still the blows
>   that were his, if dealt to you
> In the selfsame way at the selfsame time,
>   might cause you to stagger too.
> Don't be too harsh with the man who sins,
>   or pelt him with words or stones,
> Unless you are sure, yes, doubly sure
>   that you have not sins of your own.
> For you know, perhaps, if the tempter's voice
>   Should whisper as soft to you
> As it did to him when he went astray,
>   'Twould cause you to falter too.[2]

In the early years of my ministry, I sometimes judged people by their performance, only to feel ashamed later when I heard their story. Over the years I have become more sensitive, realising that no one has had a perfect upbringing or background. And those previous hardships can cause

412 Part Three: Our Significance in Christ

great struggle. Today, I listen to horrendous stories of abuse. What a privilege to see God in action as He sets people free from their bondage and makes them temples of the Holy Spirit. What a privilege to have them read the verses that began this chapter and see their joy in discovering that they are the 'dwelling place of God.' That's significant! And so are you!

Dear heavenly Father, I thank You for Your presence in my life. Forgive me for the times I have lived as though You don't live within me. I submit myself to Your building process in my life. I desire to be a temple that glorifies God in my body. I renounce the lie of Satan that I am not a habitation of Yours. I accept by faith that I am Your temple, and I believe that there is nothing more significant than to manifest Your presence in my life. Teach me to take care of my temple properly and honour it as Your dwelling place. In Jesus' precious name I pray. Amen.

NOTES

1. Author and source unknown.
2. Author and source unknown.

46
I Am a Minister
of Reconciliation

*'Therefore, if anyone is in Christ, he is a new
creation; the old has gone, the new has come! All
this is from God, who reconciled us to himself
through Christ and gave us the ministry of
reconciliation: that God was reconciling the world
to himself in Christ, not counting men's sins
against them. And he has committed to us the
message of reconciliation. We are therefore
Christ's ambassadors, as though God were making
his appeal through us.'*   2 CORINTHIANS 5:17–20

Before the Vietnam War, I served a tour of duty in the
United States Navy. I was assigned to a destroyer in the
Pacific. In those days, we referred to the captain of the ship
as the 'old man'. The first captain I had was a mean old
man. He belittled his officers, drank with the chiefs (non-
commissioned officers) every opportunity he had and generally made life difficult aboard the ship. But if I was going
to survive on that ship, I had to learn to do it under his
authority. So I learned how to cope, succeed and defend
myself under his command. He was my 'old man'.

Then one day, he was transferred off the ship. I never
again had any relationship with him. I was no longer under
his authority. We got a new 'old man', and he was a good
one. But how do you think I continued to live on board that
ship? The way I was trained by the first old man, until I got
to know the new one.

The opening passage says, 'The old has gone, the new has come' (2 Cor 5:17). But often we will continue to live as we were trained before our salvation, until we obtain a true knowledge of God and our relationship with Him. Although the old man (self) is dead, the flesh is still present. We are no longer 'in Adam'; we are 'in Christ'. We are no longer under the authority of the god of this world; we are under the authority of God. 'All this is from God, who reconciled us to himself through Christ' (2 Cor 5:18).

Our ministry of reconciliation

Because we are a 'new creation' in Christ, we have a ministry of reconciliation. We are the bridge between a fallen humanity and a redeeming God. We are the peacemakers. 'Blessed are the peacemakers, for they will be called sons of God' (Mt 5:9). I can't think of anything I would rather be known for. Any fool can divide a fellowship; it takes the grace of God to unite. A simpleton can point out the character defects in another person; it takes the perspective of God to see the good. How can we justify tearing one another down, when the entire thrust of the New Testament is to restore a fallen humanity and build them up in the Lord?

I have been increasingly impressed by the fact that the heart of reconciliation is 'not counting men's sins against them' (2 Cor 5:19). Certainly our holy God cannot tolerate sin, and we are clearly instructed to discipline those who do sin. God does not turn His back on our sinning ways, thinking, *Well, I guess they are going to sin anyway so I may as well accept them.* But He did turn His back on His only Son and 'made him who had no sin to be sin for us, so that *in him* we might become the righteousness of God' (2 Cor 5:21, emphasis added).

Sin evidences a life separated from God

That is the heart of the gospel: Jesus has already done something about our sin so we can be reconciled to God. The heavenly Father doesn't count our sins against us, because He accounted them to Christ. Once we are reconciled to God, we have the power to live a righteous life because of His indwelling presence. Sin is just the evidence of a life lived separated from God. Dealing only with the sin is to deal only with the symptom; the disease is separation from God.

If we stop walking in the Spirit, the deeds of the flesh become evident. Galatians 5:19 clearly outlines what those deeds are. The problem is one of walking according to the old nature (flesh), instead of walking by the Spirit. The deeds of the flesh are only the evidence. Trying to correct the symptom is trying to *fix* the flesh when we are supposed to crucify it (see Galatians 5:24). It's like asking the question, 'What improvement have you seen in your old nature since you came to Christ?' You can't improve what is in opposition to God; you can only render it inoperative and overcome it by walking according to the Spirit.

Not counting sin against them

I care enough about those I have a relationship with to confront them concerning their sin. I know that as long as they are walking according to the flesh, they are living out of harmony with the Lord. There is no way they can experience the fruit of the Spirit as long as they continue in that condition. I'm not counting their sin against them, I just want them to get right with the Lord so they can live the abundant life. Some people expose others' sins not out of love but out of pride or maliciousness. But as Proverbs 10:11,12 says, 'The mouth of the righteous is a fountain of life, but violence overwhelms the mouth of the wicked. Hatred stirs up dissension, but *love covers over all wrongs*' (emphasis added). I don't know the author of the following poem, but I subscribe to it:

> If you see a tall fellow ahead of the crowd,
> A leader of music, marching fearless and proud,
> And you know of a tale whose mere telling aloud
> Would cause his proud head to in anguish be bowed,
>   It's a pretty good plan to forget it.
>
> If you know of a skeleton hidden away
> In a closet, and guarded and kept from the day
> In the dark; whose showing, whose sudden display
> Would cause grief and sorrow and lifelong dismay,
>   It's a pretty good plan to forget it.
>
> If you know of a spot in the life of a friend
> (We all have spots concealed, world without end)
> Whose touching his heartstrings would play or rend,
> Till the shame of its showing no grieving could mend,
>   It's a pretty good plan to forget it.
>
> If you know of a thing that will darken the joy
> Of a man or a woman, a girl or a boy,
> That will wipe out a smile or the least way annoy
> A fellow, or cause any gladness to cloy,
>   It's a pretty good plan to forget it.[1]

Saying only what is helpful

If we could see the good in people, not just the bad, we would be much more effective in our ministry of reconciliation. We need to catch our children doing something good, not just catch them doing something bad. As employers, we need to call in our employees when they do good work, not just when they need to be corrected. If we could memorise and put into practice Ephesians 4:29, we would see half of our problems in our homes and churches dissolve overnight: 'Do not let any unwholesome talk come out of your mouths, but only what is helpful for building others up according to their needs, that it may benefit those who listen.' Verse 30 says, 'And do not grieve the Holy Spirit of God, with whom you were sealed for the day of redemption.' It grieves God to see us put down one another. Our ministry of reconciliation will be curtailed by the degree that we use our tongues in any way other than that which edifies.

Our significance is found in our role as ambassadors. As amazing as it may seem, God makes His appeal to the world through us. An ambassador represents the kingdom (or country) in which he or she maintains citizenship. He speaks for the sovereign (king or president) and acts as a representative for the homeland.

I had my first taste of what an 'ugly American' is in my navy days. I saw my fellow sailors representing our country in ways that left me feeling ashamed. I wanted to tell all the foreigners we came in contact with, 'Don't judge America by our military.' It was one thing for them to get drunk and visit prostitutes, because, sadly enough, that was somewhat expected of sailors! It was still another thing for them to have an attitude of arrogance, selfishness and spitefulness. Before I joined the navy, I could never understand why so many foreigners hated Americans. But once I saw our 'ambassadors', I could see why.

We are Christ's ambassadors

The only Christ others see may be what they see in us. Jesus said, 'By this all men will know that you are my disciples, if you love one another' (Jn 13:35). I heard the story of an anxious executive who was rushing to catch his aeroplane flight. As he ran through the terminal, he brushed a little girl, knocking her and her packages to the ground. For a fleeting moment, he thought only of the plane he had to catch. Fighting the temptation to go on, he stopped and apologised. He helped the girl on to her feet and made sure she was all right. The little girl was overwhelmed by his care and concern. Looking up, she asked him, 'Are you Jesus?' What an ambassador!

I have been haunted by the words that Joan Deems penned:

> I saw no likeness to Him in you today.
> And since I shall not pass your way again,
> It matters not that yesterday His light shone in you,
> Or that tomorrow you may want to make amends.
> I passed your way today.[2]

As I read the Gospels, I notice that sinners loved to be around Jesus and that He waged war against the hypocrites. Today, we frequently hear the criticism that the Church is full of hypocrites, and that's why people stay away. This is not completely true, but there is enough truth in it to cause us to examine our hearts. We cannot be both ambassadors of Christ and hypocrites, nor will we see sinners reconciled to God as long as we keep counting their sins against them. We must deal with the cause, not the symptom. Let's be known for our ability to speak the truth in love and have a ministry of reconciliation.

Dear heavenly Father, I thank You for sending Jesus, who took my place so I could receive salvation. Thank You for making me a new creation in Christ. I want to be a good ambassador for You. I renounce the lies of Satan that I am unqualified and unworthy to represent You. I am worthy because of Your presence in my life. Teach me to see people as You see them. Guard my mouth so that it will only be used to edify. Forgive me for the times that I have used my mouth to hurt instead of heal. I want to have a ministry of reconcil-

iation so others can be reconciled to You as I have been. I ask this in the precious name of Christ Jesus. Amen.

NOTES

1. Author and source unknown.
2. Joan Deems.

47
I Am God's Co-worker

*'As God's fellow workers we urge you not to receive
God's grace in vain. For he says, "In the time of my
favour I heard you, and in the day of salvation I
helped you." I tell you, now is the time of God's
favour, now is the day of salvation.'*

2 CORINTHIANS 6:1,2

I served the Lord as a seminary 'prof' for ten years, helping
to equip God's co-workers. I was always frustrated by the
educational system, because it afforded very little time to
teach the way Jesus taught. His way was by example as He
walked with His disciples during the normal course of life.
The best learning takes place in the context of committed
relationships.

Fortunately, I did have the chance to get close to a few
students. One of them was Stu, who had the distinction of
being the only Caucasian pastor in a predominantly
Hispanic denomination. That's because he married the
bishop's daughter.

I was happy as I noticed Stu had signed up for a summer
class I was teaching; but he never showed up. When I saw
him at the beginning of the autumn semester, I asked about
his absence.

'Can we talk?' he asked. Straining to keep back the tears,
he said, 'I was in the hospital this summer, and they diag-
nosed me as having cancer. They say I have from six months
to two years to live.' He asked me not to share his illness
with anyone, saying that even his church family didn't know.

A month later, he asked me if I believed in prophecies. I

asked him what he was getting at, and he said, 'Well, ten years ago, a man stood up in our fellowship and prophesied that I was going to have a significant ministry. But I haven't had a significant ministry — at least not yet. Does that mean I'm going to be healed? I have led a few hundred people to Christ, but I'm not having a significant ministry in my little church.'

Knowing what's significant

I was flabbergasted! 'Stu,' I exclaimed, 'you have led a few hundred people to Christ! That's very significant! I know of some big-name people who can't come close to matching that.'

The next spring, he stopped me in the hall and said he was losing weight, and he knew it wasn't fat he was losing. He thought he was dying. I told him he ought to share his burden with our class, because God never intended for us to walk through trials alone. He did share his news that afternoon in what turned out to be the most incredible two-hour class in my seminary experience. He told of his pain and frustration in having to leave his wife alone. Suddenly, the issues of life and death and our work for the Lord were real to all of us.

'And all I want to do is graduate this spring,' he said. 'No one in my family has ever amounted to anything.' We gathered around him to pray, and he added, 'I totally forgot about that prophecy, but I have been telling every one of my fellow pastors, "Do you know what Dr Anderson said? He said there are some big-name people who can't say they have led a few hundred people to Christ."'

The most meaningful graduation I have ever attended was that spring when Stu walked forward to receive his diploma. There are no insignificant pastors, nor for that matter are there any insignificant children of God. Every one of us has the unfathomable privilege of being a co-worker with our Lord. God has extended to us the opportunity to participate with Him in His redeeming work here on earth.

I was in Philadelphia two years later when my wife phoned me with the news that Stu had died; he had asked me to conduct his funeral. He is now with the Lord and will spend eternity along with a few hundred people whom he led to Christ — and the Lord only knows how many others they touched as they continued on as co-workers with God. That's significant!

Who's the loser?

Let me contrast Stu's story with another pastor I knew years ago. He bemoaned the fact that our denominational leader had recommended him to the church he was in. 'They are nothing but a bunch of losers. I'm never going to get anywhere, stuck in this church. How does someone get a call from a more significant church? I keep sending my résumé out, but no one calls.' No wonder! His people weren't losers; they were children of God. His community was filled with people who didn't know the Lord. I don't know what he was waiting for — God had given him a great opportunity.

Consider the following poem:

> Father, where shall I work today?
> And my love flowed warm and free.
> Then He pointed out a tiny spot,
> And said, 'Tend that for Me.'
> I answered quickly, 'Oh no, not that.
> Why, no one would ever see,
> No matter how well my work was done,
> Not that little place for me!'
> And the word He spoke, it was not stern,
> He answered me tenderly,

'Ah little one, search that heart of thine;
Art thou working for them or me?
Nazareth was a little place,
And so was Galilee.'[1]

Be faithful in little things

Playing for the grandstand instead of the coach will always prove disastrous. Looking for approval from man instead of God will bring compromise and a diminished ministry. We have to show ourselves to be faithful co-workers in little things before He will put us in charge of greater things. Even then, be careful of motives. We should be willing to stay where we are for the rest of our lives if the Lord so wills. Looking at a present ministry as a stepping stone to a greater ministry will inevitably cause one to use people instead of *building* into them. And if they don't respond in a way that makes us look good, we conclude that they must be a bunch of losers. God forgive us for such an attitude.

I suppose most people would like to come alongside some esteemed person and be identified as their co-worker. I wouldn't wait for that opportunity, because you have the opportunity to be *God's* co-worker right now. As 2 Corinthians 6:2 says, 'Now is the time of God's favour.' You will receive grace to be what He has called you to be. Don't worry about the size of your ministry, because your significance is found in being Christ's co-worker. Size does not determine significance in the eyes of God. Labouring with Christ, doing what He wants you to do, is what will determine your lasting influence and, therefore, your significance.

The pursuit of significance in positions of power or renown is nothing new, of course. Listen to this mother's request and the Lord's response in Matthew 20:20–28:

> Then the mother of Zebedee's sons came to Jesus with her sons and, kneeling down, asked a favour of him.

'What is it you want?' he asked.

She said, 'Grant that one of these two sons of mine may sit at your right and the other at your left in your kingdom.'

'You don't know what you are asking,' Jesus said to them. 'Can you drink the cup I am going to drink?'

'We can,' they answered.

Jesus said to them, 'You will indeed drink from my cup, but to sit at my right or my left is not for me to grant. These places belong to those for whom they have been prepared by my Father.'

When the ten heard about this, they were indignant with the two brothers. Jesus called them together and said, 'You know that the rulers of the Gentiles lord it over them, and their high officials exercise authority over them. Not so with you. Instead, whoever wants to become great among you must be your servant, and whoever wants to be first must be your slave — just as the Son of Man did not come to be served, but to serve, and to give his life as a ransom for many.'

The potential for ministry does not lie in earthly positions but in godly character and a willingness to do God's will. Our example should be the servanthood chosen by Jesus. He didn't strive to become a member of the Sanhedrin or the Roman government. He had no title other than the Son of man. He held no positions of power. On earth, Jesus was not a king but a servant.

God's grace will sustain you

What if Jesus were to ask you, 'Can you drink the cup I am going to drink?' Would you be so quick to respond in the affirmative as James and John did? Being God's co-worker will include hardship and require God's grace to sustain you. Notice Paul's experiences in being God's co-worker in 2 Corinthians 6:3–10:

We put no stumbling block in anyone's path, so that our ministry will not be discredited. Rather, as servants of God we commend ourselves in every way: in great endurance; in troubles, hardships and distresses; in beatings, imprisonments and riots; in hard work, sleepless nights and hunger; in purity, understanding, patience and kindness; in the Holy Spirit and in sincere love; in truthful speech and in the power of God; with weapons of righteousness in the right hand and in the left; through glory and dishonour, bad report and good report; genuine, yet regarded as impostors; known, yet regarded as unknown; dying, and yet we live on; beaten, and yet not killed; sorrowful, yet always rejoicing; poor, yet making many rich; having nothing, and yet possessing everything.

Do you want to sign up? If you're a Christian, you already have! But don't be discouraged. God is with you! Remember, the will of God will never take you where the grace of God can't keep you. I'm sure Paul had no regrets at the end of his life. Though I haven't faced the degree of hardship that Paul did, I can say I have experienced much of the same in ministry, and I have no regrets. The joy of being God's co-worker and seeing the results of His grace far exceed the hardships that will inevitably accompany the journey. Furthermore, Paul contends, 'I consider that our present sufferings are not worth comparing with the glory that will be revealed in us' (Rom 8:18).

When I first entered ministry, I put the following poem in the cover of all my Bibles:

> I asked God for strength, that I might achieve;
> I was made weak, that I might learn humbly
> to obey.
> I asked for health, that I might do greater things;
> I was given infirmity, that I might do better
> things.

I asked for riches, that I might be happy;
   I was given poverty, that I might be wise.
I asked for power, that I might have the praise
   of men;
   I was given weakness, that I might feel the
      need for God.
I asked for all things, that I might enjoy life;
   I was given life, that I might enjoy all things.
I got nothing that I asked for;
   But everything I had hoped for.
Almost despite myself, my unspoken prayers
   were answered.
   I am, among all men, most richly blessed![2]

Let's pray and ask God to do what He must to make us His most effective co-workers.

Dear heavenly Father, I rejoice in being Your co-worker. I gladly accept whatever assignments You give me, knowing that I will only be fulfilled by being in Your will. Forgive me for the times I have searched for significance in temporal positions and expressed dissatisfaction with my present ministry. I renounce the lies of Satan that Your grace is not sufficient or that You will not see me through times of hardship. When I hear the lies of Satan saying, 'Where is your God now?' I will declare that You are with me and will be with me always. I wish not to presume upon You, Lord. If what I am doing right now in ministry is only my idea, done my way, I pray that You will reveal that to me. I am Your co-worker, You are not mine. I don't want to ask You to bless my ministry; I want to be blessed by Your ministry. I now commit my ministry to You and declare You to be the head of it. I ask all this in the precious name of Jesus. Amen.

NOTES

1. Author and source unknown.
2. Author and source unknown.

48
I Am Seated with Christ in the Heavenly Realm

'God raised us up with Christ and seated us with him in the heavenly realms in Christ Jesus, in order that in the coming ages he might show the incomparable riches of his grace, expressed in his kindness to us in Christ Jesus.' EPHESIANS 2:6,7

A few years ago, I was invited to speak at the Canadian Bookseller's Convention. There was a dinner preceding my talk, and those seated at the head table were asked to show up early so we could be instructed in how we were to march in. We did so to the tune of 'When the Saints Go Marching In'. We were all to stand until the master of ceremonies stated, 'Ladies and gentlemen, this is your head table.' The audience then politely applauded, and we were allowed to sit down. I had never been treated with such royal protocol before, and frankly, I felt rather foolish.

Seating arrangements have always been a part of protocol. Traditions vary from culture to culture, but seating position has always denoted some degree of honour — or lack of it. The peace talks for the Korean War were stalled by the choice and height of the tables for the respected delegations. The most exasperating negotiations at the Paris Peace Talks for the Vietnam War were over the shape of the table and who sat where.

Even the seating of dinner guests at social functions can be an honour or an insult. I have seen some people so insulted by their placement that they have become bitter. It may not always be a question of stature or recognition; sometimes you have to be careful how you seat people just to keep the peace. Try placing various members of a family at a wedding where the bride and groom come from divorced homes.

Can you possibly imagine the honour of being seated with Christ in the heavenly realm? The riches of His grace are incomparable. That He would give us such a privilege is beyond comprehension! Do you see the incredible kindness of our Lord in saying to a beggar who has known only rejection, 'Come, sit with me at my right hand'?

The place of authority

The right hand of God's throne is the centre of authority and power for the whole universe. That power was given to the ascended Lord. The elevation of His people with Him to the heavenlies means that we share His authority. We are made to sit with Him as heirs. 'The Spirit himself testifies with our spirit that we are God's children. Now if we are children, then we are heirs — heirs of God and co-heirs with Christ, if indeed we share in his sufferings in order that we may also share in his glory' (Rom 8:16,17).

The significance of this can't be overstated. Many people who don't experience freedom in Christ feel as though they are caught between two equal and opposite forces. Satan on one side and God on the other, and poor little me hanging between the two like a pawn. If that is what you believe, then you are defeated. The truth is that God is omniscient, omnipresent, omnipotent, kind and loving in all His ways. Satan is a defeated foe, and we are in Christ, seated with Him in the heavenlies. Notice the parallel account in Colossians 2:9–11,13–15:

For in Christ all the fullness of the Deity lives in bodily form, and you have been given fullness *in Christ*, who is the head over every power and authority. *In him* you were also circumcised, in the putting off of the sinful nature,... When you were dead in your sins and in the uncircumcision of your sinful nature, God made you alive with Christ. He forgave us all our sins, having cancelled the written code, with its regulations, that was against us and that stood opposed to us; he took it away, nailing it to the cross. And having disarmed the powers and authorities, he made a public spectacle of them, triumphing over them by the cross (emphasis added).

Testifying to God's greatness

The best way to show the 'incomparable riches of His grace' is through our testimony. As Revelation 12:10,11 says, 'Now have come the salvation and the power and the kingdom of our God, and the authority of his Christ. For the accuser of our brothers, who accuses them before our God day and night, has been hurled down. They overcame him by the blood of the Lamb and by the word of their testimony; they did not love their lives so much as to shrink from death.'

The Lord knows that responsibility can't be delegated without having the authority to carry it out. Because we are seated with Christ, we have authority over the kingdom of darkness. But our authority is not independent. We don't have the authority to do whatever we want. This is not an authority over each other either, because we are to 'Submit to one another out of reverence for Christ' (Eph 5:21). What we do have is the authority to do God's will.

The following testimony is from a pastor who attended my seminary class and also a conference I conducted:

It's Thanksgiving time, and do I ever have a lot to be thankful for! I'm free! I'm free! I'm free! I know that you will immediately credit the source of all your success, gifts, and abilities to our precious Lord and Saviour Jesus Christ. I'm thanking Him too, constantly!

Chalk up another pastor delivered from the terrible bondage of deception to freedom in Christ! Neil, I could match story for story, personal testimony for personal testimony, gross experience for gross experience the many letters that you share. I'm sparing you the vile details as you've heard enough, but if you can use a more detailed version to help other defeated pastors, I'd be happy to share my specific freedom from sexual sins, eating disorders, and inability to read and concentrate on the Word of God.

I now know what you must have been thinking as I stumbled into your Pastoral Counselling class this autumn. You knew what was going on in my life. I even want to thank you for reaching out and tapping me on the stomach as we chatted once. It was a loving yet symbolic gesture, pointing out an area where I was in bondage. When I read *Victory over the Darkness*, the light began to shine. I began to move towards freedom as the truth of God's Word began to enter my mind and drive out the lies! Then when I attended your conference, the light got even brighter and brighter. When we prayed through the *Steps to Freedom in Christ*, I knew I was free! Free from Satanic deception, free to enjoy my relationship with God, and free to think clearly again. Just a few days later I read *The Bondage Breaker*. What a blessing! What a glorious trip through the truth of God's Word.

Neil, how tragic it is that we in the Church are so deceived. What a number our cunning and wicked adversary has pulled. I reread Isaiah 14 and took note of these statements regarding Satan. 'You who weakened the nations! ...Is this the man who made the earth tremble, who shook kingdoms, who made the whole world as a wilderness and destroyed its cities, who did not open the house of his prisoners?' [Is 14:12,16,17, NKJV]. What mayhem, violence, and wickedness Satan has performed against God's people. Praise God that we have victory in Christ!

Neil, I was in such a fog when the semester began that it was difficult to read *Victory over the Darkness*. The voices kept saying, 'It's just another worthless book of pat answers on the Christian life, don't believe this junk, don't believe this approach.' But there was no hiding the truth and joy in the 'who I am' list.

After the conference, and right after going through the *Steps to Freedom in Christ*, I walked out of the auditorium and could hardly believe my eyes! The world around me had changed! Everything was more intensely in focus, and my mind was so clear! I prayed with joy and melody to the Lord in my car. I knew I was free.

I thank God for the freedom and authority that only Christ can give. He is the deliverer — I'm certainly not. I believe that God is showing in this age 'the incomparable riches of his grace, expressed in his kindness to us in *Christ Jesus*' (Eph 2:7, emphasis added).

Dear heavenly Father, I am overwhelmed by the thought that You will afford me such an honour as allowing me to sit with You. I know of no comparable position of honour. I thank You for Your kindness and grace that allows me to live freely in Christ. I renounce the lies of Satan that I have no authority over him. I acknowledge the authority that I have in Christ because I am seated with Him in the heavenly realm, and I assume my responsibility to live in a way that is a testimony to the incomparable riches of Your grace. In Jesus' precious name I pray. Amen.

49
I Am God's Workmanship

*'For we are God's workmanship, created in Christ
Jesus to do good works, which God prepared in
advance for us to do.'*   **EPHESIANS 2:10**

A former student brought a young lady named Beth to see
me who was emaciated by anorexia, plagued by condemning thoughts and secretively cutting herself. Her parents
were climb-the-ladder professionals who would do anything
for their child — so long as it would produce the type of
child that would make them proud.

Beth had the best swimming and gymnastics coaches,
and her parents were pressuring her to attend a top-rated
school and join the best sorority (which, of course, was the
one her mother had belonged to). She wanted to go to a
Christian school, but even though her parents professed to
be Christians, they wouldn't allow it. They wanted *more* for
their child!

As I helped her through the *Steps to Freedom*, Beth
struggled to forgive her parents from her heart. 'After all,
my folks are really good people, pillars of the community,'
she told me.

She hadn't cried in four years. Facing the need to forgive
her father, she said, 'I think *I* need to ask *his* forgiveness.'

'Maybe you do,' I responded, 'but we aren't dealing with
that right now. We are helping you find your freedom in
Christ by forgiving your father from your heart.'

For several agonising minutes, she stared at the list of
people she needed to forgive, then suddenly tears began to
form in her eyes. 'Lord, I forgive my father for never asking

me what I would like to become and for disregarding my thoughts and feelings.' The floodgate opened, and the freedom came.

Pressure to conform

The world puts a lot of pressure on us to conform to its image. Well-meaning parents often try to force their children to fit into their mould. Major companies have undone themselves with cookie-cutter mentalities, pressuring their employees to fit into their corporate image, as though everyone is the same. Performance-based acceptance and cloning mentalities often produce what J. K. Summerhill calls a 'loser's limp':

> 'Watch this,' chuckled an athletic coach as we watched his track team compete in a high school athletic meet. 'You see my boy there, coming in fourth? Limping! Chances are he just developed that limp to have an excuse for not doing better. I call it "loser's limp".'
>
> Some of the reasons why some men do not attain their goals — do not get one-tenth of the way to their goals — are no more convincing than the high school boy's suddenly developed limp. Worse yet, the loser's limp attitude may stop a man from even trying to lift his life above a subsistence level. When the gun goes off to start the race, he is licked before he starts.
>
> He may put it to you earnestly: 'You can see how badly I am handicapped by...' and what follows is something defined as a handicap. Very rarely is it actually a handicap. Over and over, when some man tells me he is handicapped, I see a built-in loser's limp.
>
> I am not talking about blind people, although one can still learn a wonderful lesson from Helen Keller. I am not talking about bedridden people, notwithstanding the fact that such men as James Royce, completely

immobilised by polio, have built thriving businesses from their beds. We should take off our hats to really handicapped people who still live constructive lives, but they are too exceptional for most of us to identify with.

I am talking, rather, about men who have the use of all their senses and all their limbs, surely the great majority of my readers.

And perhaps I speak directly to you — if you have never taken charge of your life-dynamics; if you know that many and many another man, who has nothing you haven't got, is building a grand career and a glorious future while you get pushed into some low-level corner. If you've lost a few of life's races, see if you're not assuming you're a loser forever, if you're not acquiring a loser's limp before you start.

Check yourself for loser's limp right now![1]

Part of what Summerhill addresses is not living up to our potential. The main reason people live at that level is they get caught up in a false failure-success syndrome. The world's definition of success is to come in first or never to fail. I saw a bumper sticker on a car that said, 'If at first you don't succeed, then erase all possible evidence that you ever tried in the first place!' To stumble and fall is not failure. To stumble and fall *again* is not failure. Failure is when you say, 'I got pushed!'

Don't fail to try

The greatest failure in life is never to try. The only difference between a winner and a loser is that the winner gets up one more time than the loser. As Proverbs 24:16 says, 'For though a righteous man falls seven times, he rises again, but the wicked are brought down by calamity.' The loser may also be the timid soul who knows neither victory nor defeat because he never enters the race. Remember, a mistake is never a failure, unless you fail to learn by it.

In the parable of the talents in Matthew 25:14–30, the slave was given only one talent, which he took and buried. His idea of duty, progress and stewardship was to slam on the brakes and throw the transmission into reverse! God considered him a wicked slave. He should have taken the talent entrusted to him and invested it in the Kingdom of God. The fearful person asks, 'What do I stand to lose if I do?' A person of faith is someone who asks, 'What do I stand to lose if I don't?'

Two types of people will never amount to anything: those who cannot do what they are told, and those who won't do anything unless they are told. In the parable, the slave with one talent had just as much responsibility as the one with five talents. Both were required to be submissive to the master. One took the risk of doing, while the other sought the security of hiding. I understand why people like to have the security of clinging to a tree trunk, but the fruit is always out on the end of the limb.

It's important to remember, however, that not everyone has the same level of giftedness. Maybe the young man in Summerhill's story had only the ability to come in fourth. Perhaps no matter what he did, or how hard he trained, the best he could ever do would be fourth place. What's wrong with that? In a four-man race, someone has to come in fourth.

We should seek to live up to our potential and not look for excuses, but not everybody's potential is the same. The Lord hasn't equally distributed gifts, talents or intelligence. But He has equally distributed Himself.

Whom do we please?
What constitutes success, and whose expectations are we to live up to? God uses parents, pastors and all the people we

rub shoulders with to mould us into the person He wants us to be. But we are *God's* workmanship: not our parents', not our pastor's, not society's.

Our children are not little lumps of clay that we can mould into our own image. They are gifts from God entrusted to us so we can train them in the Lord. The best gardener *cannot* take a tulip bulb and make it into a rose. He can plant, water, fertilise and trim it until it becomes a beautiful tulip. We each must discover the potential that God has put in us. The Greek word for workmanship carries the idea of a 'work of art.' In Christ Jesus we can become the masterpiece He intended from the foundation of the world. That is the good work to which God has called us.

Success is speaking words of praise,
In cheering other people's ways,
In doing just the best you can,
With every task and every plan.

It's silence when your speech would hurt,
Politeness when your neighbour's curt,
It's deafness when the scandal flows,
And sympathy with other's woes.

It's loyalty when duty calls,
It's courage when disaster falls,
It's patience when the hours are long,
It's found in laughter and in song.

It's in the silent time of prayer,
In happiness and in despair,
In all of life and nothing less,
We find the thing we call success.[2]

Dear heavenly Father, I praise You for knowing me and preparing me from the foundations of the world. I don't fully understand that, but I do know I want to be Your divine masterpiece. I want to be all that You created me to be. I know that the good work You have called me to do can only come from who I am in Christ. Forgive me for the times I have let others determine who I am and for the times I have tried to make others become what I wanted them to be.

I renounce the lies of Satan that would compare me with others who are more gifted or less gifted than I am. I refuse to believe the lies that say success is determined by the standards of this world. I renounce the lie that my success is found in my performance. I announce the truth that my success is found in being who You created me to be and doing what You called me to do. Forgive me for not taking the risk of stepping out in faith according to what I know to be true. I commit myself to making full use of the gifts, talents and other life endowments that You have entrusted to me. In Jesus' precious name I pray. Amen.

NOTES

1. J. K. Summerhill.

2. Author and source unknown.

50
I May Approach God with Freedom and Confidence

*'In him and through faith in him we may approach
God with freedom and confidence.'* EPHESIANS 3:12

Suppose you entered a contest that had an extraordinary
prize. The winner would get an all-expenses-paid trip to
Washington, D.C., including a fifteen-minute private session in the Oval Office of the White House with the president of the United States. You could ask him any question
and tell him whatever you wanted. You would have your
own private hearing with him. It would certainly be one of
the most significant days of your life.

I imagine that you would want to videotape the event, so
you could watch it over and over. The glory of the moment
would quickly fade, so you would want a picture of you
with the president to commemorate the occasion. You
could hang it on a wall in your home and show all your
friends and relatives who visit you. After all, how many
people have had such a privilege and honour? Millions of
influential leaders would pay handsomely to have a private
audience with the president.

You would undoubtedly have a few anxious moments as
you try to figure out what you want to say and ask. It
wouldn't take long to realise, however, that what you did say
would have little, if any, lasting impact on the course of history. I'm sure the president would be polite and treat you
cordially. After all, there is a little publicity value in this for
him also — the president of the United States rubbing

shoulders with an average citizen, showing that he is interested in what people have to say.

A far better prize

Are you aware that we have already won a far better prize? We have an all-expenses-paid trip to heaven, and we have a private audience with the one who *made* the president of the United States and all the other world leaders. What's more, we are assured that the encounter will have eternal and lasting consequences. Every child of God has received the same prize, yet few bother even to claim it!

I'm talking about free access to the God of the universe, twenty-four hours of every day. He has no office hours, and He never grows weary of our need for personal time with Him. How can this be? Because Jesus paid the price; He made the provision! 'For through him we both have access to the Father by one Spirit' (Eph 2:18).

We have a tendency to check in with God only during crises. In the ball game of life, prayer should be a first-down huddle asking for direction, not a fourth-down punting situation. When we pray according to the Holy Spirit's prompting, we may be assured that God the Father will answer in the affirmative. 'In the same way, the Spirit helps us in our weakness. We do not know what we ought to pray for, but the Spirit himself intercedes for us with groans that words cannot express. And he who searches our hearts knows the mind of the Spirit, because the Spirit intercedes for the saints in accordance with God's will' (Rom 8:26,27).

Wanting God's will

Primarily, what we try to determine in prayer is God's will. After addressing our Father in heaven, the Lord's prayer continues with, 'Your kingdom come, your will be done on earth as it is in heaven' (Mt 6:10). Sometimes the will of God includes suffering, so Paul said to the Ephesians, 'I ask

you, therefore, not to be discouraged because of my sufferings for you, which are your glory' (Eph 3:13). Sometimes
God's will appears to dash our hopes and dreams, as this
poem describes:

> 'Disappointment — His appointment,'
>   Change one letter, then I see
> That the thwarting of my purpose
>   Is God's better choice for me.
> His appointment must be blessing,
>   Tho' it may come in disguise,
> For the end from the beginning
>   Open to His wisdom lies.
>
> 'Disappointment — His appointment,'
>   No good will He withhold;
> From denials oft we gather
>   Treasures of His love untold.
> Well He knows each broken purpose
>   Leads to fuller, deeper trust,
> And the end of all His dealings
>   Proves our God is wise and just.
>
> 'Disappointment — His appointment,'
>   Lord, I take it, then, as such,
> Like clay in hands of a potter,
>   Yielding wholly to Thy touch.
> My life's plan is Thy moulding;
>   Not one single choice be mine;
> Let me answer, unrepining
>   'Father, not my will, but thine.'[1]

Be free to see

In prayer, we are also dependent upon the Holy Spirit to
open our eyes. The Holy Spirit will lead us into all truth and

keep us in God's will. In the first of two prayers recorded in the book of Ephesians, Paul says, 'I pray also that the eyes of your heart may be enlightened in order that you may know the hope to which he has called you, the riches of his glorious inheritance in the saints, and his incomparably great power for us who believe' (Eph 1:18,19).

It is not that we don't possess this inheritance; it's that we don't see it. Why not? That question has troubled me for years. The answer I found is that many, if not most, Christians aren't free — free from the abuses of the past, free from Satanic deception, free to be who God wants them to be. I have had the privilege to help many people find their freedom in Christ so that their eyes were opened to see the inheritance they have. The following letter I received from a dear lady beautifully attests to this truth:

> I am a sixty-six-year-old woman who has been under the 'bondage' of Satan's lies for fifty-seven years. I don't mean I haven't read, been taught, or learned the truth of what you have explained in your book; I have known intellectually who I am in Christ. I even knew that I had authority in Him. *But* I am writing you now, because at last I *know* the truth you speak. I've been enabled by the truth as set down in *The Bondage Breaker* to be set free. I'm very sure you understand what I am relating. It's one thing to 'know' — to be appraised of the fact and even agree with it. It's another thing to truly *know* — to be able at last to enter in and experience God's wonderful freedom.
>
> God revealed His Son to me at a Billy Graham Crusade forty years ago. I was thoroughly saved by Jesus' atoning work for me on the cross. Not only has He saved me, He has kept me as well. I have had the privilege of attending a Bible school, completing a Navigator Bible memory course, participating with Bible

Study Fellowship, and serving as a Precept leader. And
I have been ministered to by godly pastors.

In all that time I've carried with me the shame, the ill
feeling of inferiority, of not quite measuring up to other
people. I fought a continuous mental battle that I'm only
a 'Cinderella' in God's family and therefore not of much
use. I knew that wasn't the truth, for God shows no par-
tiality. His love is unconditional and perfect for each one
of His redeemed. Yet 'something' deep inside of me
always spoke those other lies that made me feel sort of
'outside'.

I am a child of alcoholic parents. I suffered the horrible experience of sexual abuse by three men. By
God's design, I heard of your book *The Bondage
Breaker* over Chuck Swindoll's radio programme. The
rest you know. You know how 'released' the woman in
the Bible with the 'issue of blood' must have felt. Now
you can rejoice with me at my release from bondage
after fifty-seven years.

God offers 'immeasurably more'

Paul's second prayer in Ephesians is followed by this bene-
diction: 'Now to him who is able to do immeasurably more
than all we ask or imagine, according to his power that is at
work within us, to him be glory in the church and in Christ
Jesus throughout all generations, for ever and ever! Amen'
(Eph 3:20,21). Remember that Jesus has provided you free
access to the heavenly Father; you can have a private audience with Him twenty-four hours of every day for the rest
of your life. Let's close this chapter by praying this prayer,
based on Ephesians 3:14–19. Make it your prayer by insert-
ing your name in it:

For this reason I, _____, kneel before You,
heavenly Father, from whom Your whole family in heaven and

on earth derives its name. I pray that out of Your glorious riches You may strengthen me, _____, with power through Your Spirit in my inner being, so that Christ may dwell in my heart through faith. And I pray that I, _____, may have power, together with all the saints, to grasp how wide and long and high and deep is the love of Christ, and to know this love that passes knowledge — that I, _____, may be filled to the measure of all Your fullness. Amen.

_____

NOTE

1. Author and source unknown.

51
I Can Do All Things Through Christ Who Strengthens Me

> *'I have learned to be content whatever the*
> *circumstances. I know what it is to be in need, and*
> *I know what it is to have plenty. I have learned the*
> *secret of being content in any and every situation,*
> *whether well fed or hungry, whether living in plenty*
> *or in want. I can do everything through him who*
> *gives me strength.'*   PHILIPPIANS 4:11–13

If God wants it done, can it be done? Does the Bible say, 'With God *most* things are possible?' No, it says, 'Everything is possible for him who believes' (Mk 9:23). If God tells us to do something, can we do it? I can't imagine God issuing a command that cannot be carried out. That would be like God saying, 'Son, this is what I want you to do. You won't really be able to do it, but give it your best shot anyway!' That's ludicrous! Even secular research and theory has ascertained that authority will be undermined if an order is given that cannot be obeyed.

Nothing can keep us from God's will
If we can do 'it', then what is the 'everything' that we can do? Certainly there are some limitations. The key, as in all biblical interpretation, is found in the context. Paul says he has learned to be content in all of life's situations. In other words, the circumstances of life do not determine who we are, nor do they keep us from being what God wants us to be. No person and no circumstances can keep us from

doing the will of God, which primarily is our sanctification (see 1 Thess 4:3). It is Christ who strengthens us.

We may not be able to rearrange the external events of life, nor have we been called to, but we have the assurance that God is rearranging our *internal* world and using the external world to do it. 'We also rejoice in our sufferings, because we know that suffering produces perseverance; perseverance, character; and character, hope. And hope does not disappoint us, because God has poured out his love into our hearts by the Holy Spirit, whom he has given us' (Rom 5:3–5). Our hope lies in proven character, not in favourable circumstances, and that is where Paul learned the secret of contentment. He stopped trying to change the world and allowed God to change him. If we all did that, the world would be radically changed.

Allow God to be the controller

The fruit of the Spirit is not spouse control, or child control, nor does it assure us of the ability to control the circumstances of life. The fruit of the Spirit is self-control. When we turn control of our lives over to God, we will move significantly closer to doing all things through Christ. We will stop trying to control our spouse, and start loving him or her. We will focus more on instructing our children instead of controlling them. As bosses and leaders, we will stop trying to manipulate our people and start caring for them. As employees and helpers, we will stop undermining authority and start serving with joy.

Our unbelief is the only obstacle keeping us from first being and then doing everything that God wants us to be and do. We are assured that all things are possible for those who believe. However, we can't determine for ourselves what it is we want to believe. We must believe the truth, and that's found in God's Word.

New Age versus Christianity

New Age philosophers say, 'If you believe something enough, it will become true.' They argue that we can create reality with our minds. In order to do that, we would have to be gods, which is precisely what they are saying. That lie goes all the way back to the garden. 'You will be like God' (Gen 3:5).

Christianity says, 'It is true, therefore I believe it.' Believing something doesn't make it true, and not believing something doesn't cause it to go away. Jesus prayed for us concerning this in His high priestly prayer in John 17:15,17: 'My prayer is not that you take them out of the world but that you protect them from the evil one.... Sanctify them by the truth; your word is truth.' We believe in God, and walk by faith according to His Word. In my book *Victory over the Darkness*, I shared the following:

If You Believe You Can, You Can

If you think you are beaten — you are.
If you think you dare not — you don't.
If you want to win but think you can't,
It is almost a cinch you won't
If you think you'll lose — you're lost.
For out of the world we find
That success begins with a fellow's will;
It's all in the state of mind.
Life's battles don't always go
To the stronger or the faster man;
But sooner or later the man that wins
Is the one who thinks he can.[1]

That poem has an element of truth and expresses the power of positive thinking. The Christian community has been somewhat reluctant to buy into this well-known axiom and for good reason. Thinking is a function of the mind and cannot exceed its inputs and attributes. Any attempt to push the mind beyond its limitations will only result in moving from the world of reality into fantasy. Believing something beyond what we know to be biblically true is not faith — it is presumption. And we dare not presume upon God.

Believe the truth

The Christian, however, has a far greater potential in the power of believing the truth. Belief incorporates the mind but is not limited by it. A lot of biblical truth I believe, but I don't fully understand. Belief, or faith, actually transcends the limitations of the mind and incorporates the world that is unseen but not unreal. With the infinite God of the universe as the object of Christian faith, what can stop the Christian if God wants something done? Couple that with the fact that it doesn't take any more effort to believe that one *can* than to believe that one *cannot*. The issue is choosing truth and taking every thought captive to the obedience of Christ, instead of believing the enemy's lies. Because you are God's child, you can confront doubts and unbelief:

> Why should I say I can't when the Bible says, 'I can do everything through him who gives me strength' (Phil 4:13)?
>
> Why should my needs not be met knowing that 'My God will meet all your needs according to his glorious riches in Christ Jesus' (Phil 4:19)?
>
> Why should I fear when the Bible says, 'God has not given us a spirit of fear, but of power and of love and of a sound mind' (2 Tim 1:7, NKJV)?
>
> Why should I lack the faith to serve God knowing that 'God has allotted to each a measure of faith' (Rom 12:3, NASB)?
>
> Why am I weak when the Bible says, 'The Lord is

the strength of my life' (Ps 27:1, NKJV) and 'People who know their God will display strength' (Dan 11:32, NASB)?

Why should I allow Satan to have supremacy over my life, for 'The one who is in you is greater than the one who is in the world' (1 Jn 4:4)?

Why should I accept defeat when the Bible says, 'Thanks be to God, who always leads us in triumphal procession in Christ' (2 Cor 2:14)?

Why should I lack wisdom when I am 'in Christ Jesus, who has become for us wisdom from God' (1 Cor 1:30) and 'If any of you lacks wisdom, he should ask God, who gives generously' (Jas 1:5)?

Why should I be depressed when I can recall to my mind and therefore have hope, 'Because of the Lord's great love we are not consumed, for his compassions never fail. They are new every morning; great is your faithfulness' (Lam 3:22,23)?

Why should I worry and fret when I can 'Cast all [my] anxiety on him [Christ], because he cares for [me]' (1 Pet 5:7)?

Why should I ever be in bondage, for 'Where the Spirit of the Lord is, there is freedom' (2 Cor 3:17) and 'It is for freedom that Christ has set us free' (Gal 5:1)?

Why should I feel condemned when the Bible says, 'There is…no condemnation for those who are in Christ Jesus' (Rom 8:1)?

Why should I ever feel alone when Jesus said, 'I am with you always, to the very end of the age' (Mt 28:20) and 'Never will I leave you; never will I forsake you' (Heb 13:5)?

Why should I feel accursed or the victim of bad luck when the Bible says, 'Christ has redeemed us from the curse of the law, having become a curse for us,...that we might receive the promise of the Spirit through faith' (Gal 3:13,14, NKJV)?

Why should I be discontented when I like Paul 'Have learned to be content whatever the circumstances' (Phil 4:11)?

Why should I feel worthless when 'He made Him who knew no sin to be sin on our behalf, that we might become the righteousness of God in Him' (2 Cor 5:21, NASB)?

Why should I ever have a persecution complex when the Bible says, 'If God is for us, who can be against us' (Rom 8:31)?

Why should I be confused since 'God is not the author of confusion but of peace' (1 Cor 14:33, NKJV)?

Why should I feel like a failure when 'In all these things we overwhelmingly conquer through Him who loved us' (Rom 8:37, NASB)?

Why should I let the world bother me when Jesus said, 'In the world you have tribulation, but take courage; I have overcome the world' (Jn 16:33, NASB)?[2]

Don't believe the lie

The biggest obstacle I encounter in helping people find their freedom in Christ are the lies people believe. Satan is the father of lies. Jesus is the truth. The Holy Spirit is first and foremost the Spirit of truth (see John 14:17), and He will lead us into all truth (see John 16:13). When I share my faith, people sometimes say, 'I just can't believe that.' And I respond, 'Of course you can; if I believe it, can you believe it? Belief is a choice.'

One of the most common lies I encounter is, 'I can't do that. I'm not good enough. I don't have the ability.' I always expose it for what it is, a lie from the pit. The truth is, 'I can do everything through him who gives me strength' (Phil 4:13). Here is a little poetic encouragement:

Someone said that it couldn't be done,
But he, with a chuckle, replied:
'That maybe it couldn't, but he would be one
Who wouldn't say so till he'd tried.'
So he buckled right in with the trace of a grin
On his face. If he worried he hid it.
He started to sing as he tackled the thing
That couldn't be done, and he did it!
Somebody scoffed, 'Oh, you'll never do that,
At least no one ever has done it.'
But he took off his coat and he took off his hat,
And the first thing we knew he'd begun it.
With the lift of his chin and a bit of a grin,
Without any doubting or quiddit,
He started to sing as he tackled the thing
That couldn't be done, and he did it!
There are thousands to tell you it cannot be done,
There are thousands to prophesy failure,
There are thousands to point out to you, one by one,
The dangers that wait to assail you.
But just buckle in with a bit of a grin,
Just take off your coat and go to it;
Just start to sing as you tackle the thing
That 'cannot be done,' and you'll do it.[3]

I started this chapter by asking, 'If God wants it done, can it be done?' and 'If God asks you to, can you do it?' The answer is, 'Absolutely!' And if God gives you grace, can you be content with His will in any situation? Yes, because He is there with you and you are in Him. You can say, 'I can do everything through Him who gives me strength' (Phil 4:13).

Dear heavenly Father, thank You for revealing my true identity in Christ. Thank You for showing me from Your Word how You are meeting my needs of acceptance, security and

significance in Christ. I feel like I need to say, 'Lord, I
believe, help me in my unbelief.' Teach me to take every
thought captive to the obedience of Christ. I want to be a child
of God who lives by faith. I renounce the lies of Satan that say
I can't, and I announce the truth that I can do all things
through Christ who strengthens me. I pray for the renewing of
my mind so that I can prove that the will of God is good,
acceptable and perfect for me. I love You with all my heart,
soul and strength. You are the Lord of the universe, and the
Lord of my life, now and forever. In Jesus' precious name I
pray. Amen.

NOTES

1. Neil T. Anderson, *Victory over the Darkness* (Ventura, CA: Regal Books, 1990), p 114. Used by permission.

2. Ibid., pp 115–117, adapted.

3. Author and source unknown.

Steps to Freedom in Christ

If you have received Christ as your personal Saviour, He has set you free through His victory over sin and death on the cross. If you are not experiencing freedom, it may be because you have not stood firm in the faith or actively taken your place in Christ. It is the Christian's responsibility to do whatever is necessary to maintain a right relationship with God. Your eternal destiny is not at stake; you are secure in Christ. But your daily victory is at stake if you fail to claim and maintain your position in Christ.

You are not the helpless victim caught between two nearly equal but opposite heavenly superpowers; Satan is a deceiver. Only God is omnipotent (all-powerful), omnipresent (always-present), and omniscient (all-knowing). Sometimes the reality of sin and the presence of evil may seem more real than the presence of God, but that is part of Satan's deception. Satan is a defeated foe, and we are in Christ. A true knowledge of God and our identity in Christ are the greatest determinants of our mental health. A false concept of God, a distorted understanding of who we are as children of God, and the misplaced deification of Satan (attributing God's attributes to Satan) are the greatest contributors to mental illness.

As you prepare to go through the *Steps to Freedom in Christ*, you need to remember that the only power Satan has is the power of the lie. As soon as we expose the lie, the power is broken. The battle is for your mind. If Satan can get you to believe a lie, he can control your life. But you don't have to let him control you. If you are going through the steps by yourself, don't pay attention to any lying, intimidating thoughts in your mind, such as, 'This isn't going to work,' 'God doesn't love me,' 'I'm just going to fall back into the same traps of sexual sin,' etc. Such thoughts are lies from the pit. They can only control you if you believe them, so don't.

If you are going through the steps with a pastor, counsellor,

453

or prayer partner (which we strongly recommend if there has been severe trauma in your life), share any thoughts you have which are in opposition to what you are attempting to do. You must co-operate with the person trying to help you by sharing what is going on inside.

Knowing the nature of the battle for our minds, we can pray authoritatively to stop any interference. The steps begin with a suggested prayer and declaration. If you are going through the steps by yourself, you will need to change some of the personal pronouns ('I' instead of 'we', etc.).

Prayer

Dear heavenly Father, we acknowledge Your presence in this room and in our lives. You are the only omniscient (all-knowing), omnipotent (all-powerful), and omnipresent (always-present) God. We are dependent upon You, for apart from Christ we can do nothing. We stand in the truth that all authority in heaven and on earth has been given to the resurrected Christ, and because we are in Christ, we share that authority in order to make disciples and set captives free. We ask You to fill us with Your Holy Spirit and lead us into all truth. We pray for Your complete protection and ask for Your guidance. In Jesus' name we pray. Amen.

Declaration

In the name and authority of the Lord Jesus Christ, we command Satan and all evil spirits to release (name) in order that (name) can be free to know and choose to do the will of God. As children of God seated with Christ in the heavenlies, we agree that every enemy of the Lord Jesus Christ is bound and gagged to silence. We say to Satan and all his evil workers that he cannot inflict any pain or in any way prevent God's will from being accomplished in (name).

The following seven specific steps will help you experience the full freedom and victory that Christ purchased for you on the cross. These steps will help you walk free of many areas of bondage, but in this book specific application is made to areas of sexual bondage. Realising your freedom will be the result of what you choose to believe, confess, forgive, renounce, and forsake. No one can do it for you. The battle for your mind can only be won as you personally choose truth.

As you go through these *Steps to Freedom*, remember that Satan will be defeated only if you confront him verbally. He cannot read your mind, and he is under no obligation to obey your thoughts. Only God has complete knowledge of your mind. As you take each step, it is important that you submit to God inwardly and resist the devil by reading aloud each prayer, verbally renouncing Satan, confessing sin, forgiving offenders, etc.

You will be taking a fierce moral inventory and making a rock-solid commitment to truth. If your problems stem from a source other than those covered in these steps, you have nothing to lose by going through them. If you are sincere, the only thing that can happen is that you will get right with God on these issues.

Step 1: Counterfeit Versus Real

Many roots of sexual perversion and bondage are found in false teaching and the occult. So the first step to freedom in Christ is to renounce your previous or current involvements with satanically inspired occult practices and false religions. You need to renounce any activity and group which denies Jesus Christ, offers guidance through any source other than the absolute authority of the written Word of God, or requires secret initiations, ceremonies, or covenants.

In order to help you assess your spiritual experiences, begin this step by asking God to reveal false guidance and counterfeit religious experiences.

Dear heavenly Father, I ask You to guard my heart and my mind and reveal to me any and all involvement I have had either knowingly or unknowingly with cultic or occult practices, false religions, and false teachers. In Jesus' name I pray. Amen.

Using the 'Non-Christian Spiritual Experience Inventory' shown below, circle any activities in which you have been involved in any way. This list is not exhaustive, but it will guide you in identifying non-Christian experiences. Add any other involvements you have had. Even if you 'innocently' participated in something or watched someone do it, you should write it on your list to renounce, just in case you unknowingly gave Satan a foothold.

Non-Christian
Spiritual Experience Inventory

Astral projection
Automatic writing
Bahaism
Black and white magic
Black Muslim
Blood pacts or cut yourself in a destructive way
Christian Science
Clairvoyance
Dungeons and Dragons
Eckankar
Father Divine
Fetishism (worship of objects)
Fortune-telling
Ghosts
Hare Krishna
Herbert W. Armstrong
Hinduism
Incubi and succubi (sexual spirits)
Islam
Jehovah's Witnesses
Magic eight ball
Masons
Materialisation
Mental suggestions or attempts to swap minds
Mormonism
New Age
Ouija board
Rod & pendulum (dowsing)
Rosicrucianism
Roy Masters
Science of Creative Intelligence
Science of the Mind
Seance
Self-hypnosis
Silva Mind Control
Speaking in trance
Spirit guides
Swedenborgianism
Table-lifting
Tarot cards
Telepathy
Theosophical Society
Transcendental Meditation
Unification Church
Unitarianism
The Way International
Yoga
Zen Buddhism
Other

Ask yourself

1. Have you ever been hypnotised, attended a New Age or parapsychology seminar, or consulted a medium, spiritist, or channeler? Explain.

2. Do you now have or have you ever had an imaginary friend or spirit guide offering you guidance or companionship? Explain.

3. Have you ever heard voices in your mind or had repeating and nagging thoughts condemning you or that were foreign to what you believe or feel, like there was a dialogue going on in your head? Explain.

4. What other spiritual experiences have you had that would be considered out of the ordinary?

5. Have you ever been involved in satanic ritual of any form? Explain.

When you are confident that your list is complete, confess and renounce each involvement, whether active or passive, by praying aloud the following prayer, repeating it separately for each item on your list:

Lord, I confess that I have participated in (activity). I ask your forgiveness, and I renounce (activity).

If you have had any involvement in satanic ritual or heavy occult activity (or you suspect past involvement because of blocked memories, severe nightmares, or sexual dysfunction or bondage), you need to state aloud the special renunciations which follow. Read across the page, renouncing first the item in the column for the Kingdom of Darkness and then affirming its counterpart in the Kingdom of Light. Continue down the page in this manner.

Renounce all satanic rituals, covenants, and assignments as the Lord allows you to remember them. Some people who have been subjected to satanic ritual abuse have developed multiple personalities in order to survive. Nevertheless, continue through the *Steps to Freedom* in order to resolve all you can remember. It is important that you resolve the demonic strongholds first. Eventually every personality must be accessed, and each one must resolve his or her issues and agree to come together in Christ. You may need someone who understands spiritual conflict to help you with this.

Special Renunciations
for Satanic Ritual Involvement

Kingdom of Darkness	Kingdom of Light
I renounce ever signing my name over to Satan	I announce that my name is now written in the Lamb's Book of Life.
I renounce any ceremony where I may have been wed to Satan.	I announce that I am the bride of Christ.
I renounce any and all covenants that I made with Satan.	I announce that I am a partaker of the New Covenant with Christ.
I renounce all satanic assignments for my life, including duties, marriage, and children.	I announce and commit myself to know and do only the will of God and accept only His guidance.
I renounce all spirit guides assigned to me.	I announce and accept only the leading of the Holy Spirit.
I renounce ever giving of my blood in the service of Satan.	I trust only in the shed blood of my Lord Jesus Christ.
I renounce ever eating of flesh or drinking of blood for satanic worship.	By faith I eat only the symbolic flesh and drink only the symbolic blood of Jesus in Holy Communion.
I renounce any and all guardians and Satanist parents that were assigned to me.	I announce that God is my Father and the Holy Spirit is my Guardian by whom I am sealed.
I renounce any baptism in blood or urine whereby I am identified with Satan.	I announce that I have been baptised into Christ Jesus and my identity is now in Christ.
I renounce any and all sacrifices that were made on my behalf by which Satan may claim ownership of me.	I announce that only the sacrifice of Christ has any hold on me. I belong to Him. I have been purchased by the blood of the Lamb.

Step 2: Deception Versus Truth

Truth is the revelation of God's Word, but we need to acknowledge the truth in the inner self (Ps 51:6). When David lived a lie after committing adultery and murder, he suffered greatly. When he finally found freedom by acknowledging the truth, he wrote, 'How blessed is the man…in whose spirit is no deceit' (Ps 32:2). We are to lay aside falsehood and speak the truth in love (Eph 4:15,25). A mentally healthy person is one who is in touch with reality and relatively free of anxiety. Both qualities should characterise the Christian who renounces deception and embraces the truth.

You doubtless became trapped in sexual bondage because you believed Satan's lies about sex and/or your sexuality. Begin this critical step by expressing aloud the following prayer regarding deceit and truth. Don't let the enemy accuse you with thoughts such as 'I wish I could believe this, but I can't' or any other lies in opposition to what you are proclaiming. Even if you have difficulty doing so, you need to pray the prayer and read the doctrinal affirmation which follows.

Dear heavenly Father, I know that You desire truth in the inner self and that facing this truth is the way of liberation (Jn 8:32). I acknowledge that I have been deceived by the father of lies (Jn 8:44) and that I have deceived myself (1 Jn 1:8). I pray in the name of the Lord Jesus Christ that You, heavenly Father, will rebuke all deceiving spirits by virtue of the shed blood and resurrection of the Lord Jesus Christ. By faith I have received You into my life and I am now seated with Christ in the heavenlies (Eph 2:6). I acknowledge that I have the responsibility and authority to resist the devil, and when I do so, he will flee from me. I now ask the Holy Spirit to guide me into all truth (Jn 16:13). I ask You to 'search me, O God, and know my heart; try me and know my anxious thoughts; and see if there be any hurtful way in me, and lead me in the everlasting way' (Ps 139:23,24 NASB). In Jesus' name I pray. Amen.

You may want to pause at this point to consider some of Satan's deceptive schemes. In addition to false teachers, false prophets, and deceiving spirits, you can deceive yourself. Now that you are alive in Christ and forgiven, you never have to live a lie or defend yourself. Christ is your defence. How have you deceived or attempted to defend yourself according to the following?

Self-deception

_____ Being a hearer and not a doer of the Word (James 1:22; 4:17).

_____ Saying you have no sin (1 Jn 1:8).

_____ Thinking you are something when you are not (Gal 6:3).

_____ Thinking you are wise in this age (1 Cor 3:18,19).

_____ Thinking you will not reap what you sow (Gal 6:7).

_____ Thinking the unrighteous will inherit the kingdom of God (1 Cor 6:9).

_____ Thinking you can associate with bad company and not be corrupted (1 Cor 15:33).

Self-defence (defending ourselves instead of trusting in Christ)

_____ Denial (conscious or subconscious).

_____ Fantasy (escape from the real world).

_____ Emotional insulation (withdrawal to avoid rejection).

_____ Regression (reverting back to a less threatening time).

_____ Displacement (taking out frustrations on others).

_____ Projection (blaming others).

_____ Rationalisation (defending self through verbal excursion).

For the self-deceiving attitudes and actions which have been true of you, pray aloud:

Lord, I agree that I have been deceived in the area of (attitude or action). Thank You for forgiving me. I commit myself to know and follow Your truth. Amen.

Choosing the truth may be difficult if you have been deceived and living a lie for many years. You may need to seek professional help to weed out the defence mechanisms you have depended upon to survive. Knowing that you are forgiven and accepted as God's child is what sets you free to face reality and declare your dependence on Him.

Faith is the biblical response to the truth, and believing the truth is a choice. When someone says, 'I want to believe God, but I just can't,' he is being deceived. Of course you can believe God! Faith is something you *decide to do*, not something you *feel like doing*. Believing the truth doesn't make it true. It's true; therefore we believe it. The New Age movement is distorting the truth by saying we create reality through what we believe. We can't create reality with our minds; we face reality. It's what or who you believe in that counts. Everybody believes in something, and everybody walks by faith according to what he or she believes. But if what you believe isn't true, then how you live won't be right.

Historically, the church has found great value in publicly declaring its beliefs. The Apostles' Creed and the Nicene Creed have been recited for centuries. Read aloud the following affirmation of faith, and do so again as often as necessary to renew your mind. Read it daily for several weeks.

Doctrinal Affirmation

I recognise that there is only one true and living God (Ex 20:2,3) who exists as the Father, Son, and Holy Spirit, and that He is worthy of all honour, praise, and glory as the Creator, Sustainer, and Beginning and End of all things (Rev 4:11; 5:9,10; Is 43:1,7,21).

I recognise Jesus Christ as the Messiah, the Word who became flesh and dwelt among us (Jn 1:1,14). I believe that He came to destroy the works of Satan (1 Jn 3:8), that He disarmed the rulers and authorities and made a public display of them, having triumphed over them (Col 2:15).

I believe that God has proved His love for me because when I was still a sinner, Christ died for me (Rom 5:8). I believe that He delivered me from the domain of darkness and transferred me to His kingdom, and in Him I have redemption, the forgiveness of sins (Col 1:13,14).

I believe that I am now a child of God (1 Jn 3:1–3) and that I am seated with Christ in the heavenlies (Eph 2:6). I believe that I was saved by the grace of God through faith, that it was a gift and not the result of any works on my part (Eph 2:8).

I choose to be strong in the Lord and in the strength of His might (Eph 6:10). I put no confidence in the flesh (Phil 3:3), for the weapons of our warfare are not of the flesh (2 Cor 10:4). I put on the whole armour of God (Eph 6:10–20), and I resolve to stand firm in my faith and resist the evil one.

I believe that apart from Christ I can do nothing (Jn 15:5), so I declare myself dependent on Him. I choose to abide in Christ in order to bear much fruit and glorify the Lord (Jn 15:8). I announce to Satan that Jesus is my Lord (1 Cor 12:3), and I reject any counterfeit gifts or works of Satan in my life.

I believe that the truth will set me free (Jn 8:32) and that walking in the light is the only path of fellowship (1 Jn 1:7). Therefore, I stand against Satan's deception by taking every thought captive in obedience to Christ (2 Cor 10:5).

I declare that the Bible is the only authoritative standard (2 Tim 3:15,16). I choose to speak the truth in love (Eph 4:15).

I choose to present my body as an instrument of righteousness, a living and holy sacrifice, and I renew my mind by the living Word of God in order that I may prove that the will of God is good, acceptable, and perfect (Rom 6:13; 12:1,2).

I put off the old self with its evil practices and put on the new self (Col 3:9,10), and I declare myself to be a new creature in Christ (2 Cor 5:17).

I ask You, heavenly Father, to fill me with Your Holy Spirit (Eph 5:18), lead me into all truth (Jn 16:13), and empower my life that I may live above sin and not carry out the desires of the flesh (Gal 5:16). I crucify the flesh (Gal 5:24) and choose to walk by the Spirit.

I renounce all selfish goals and choose the ultimate goal of love (1 Tim 1:5). I choose to obey the two greatest commandments: to love the Lord my God with all my heart, soul, and mind, and to love my neighbour as myself (Mt 22:37–39).

I believe that Jesus has all authority in heaven and on earth (Mt 28:18) and that He is the head over all rule and authority (Col 2:10). I believe that Satan and his demons are subject to me in Christ because I am a member of Christ's body (Eph 1:19–23). Therefore I obey the command to submit to God and to resist the devil (James 4:7), and I command Satan in the name of Christ to leave my presence.

Step 3: Bitterness Versus Forgiveness

You may have been mildly encouraged or strongly influenced into sexual sin and bondage by other persons. Perhaps a relative or neighbour sexually abused you as a child, or a sibling or schoolmate introduced you to pornography, or a boyfriend or girlfriend used you for sexual experimentation. You may harbour strong feelings against these people for their thoughtless, selfish, and sinful deeds — anger, hatred, bitterness, resentment.

You need to forgive others so that Satan cannot take advantage of you (2 Cor 2:10,11). As Christians, we are to be merciful just as our heavenly Father is merciful (Lk 6:36). We are to forgive as we have been forgiven (Eph 4:31,32). Use the following prayer to ask God to bring to your mind the names of people you need to forgive:

Dear heavenly Father, I thank You for the riches of Your kindness, forbearance, and patience, knowing that Your kindness has led me to repentance (Rom 2:4). I confess that I have not extended that same patience and kindness toward others who have offended me, but instead I have harboured bitterness and resentment. I pray that during this time of self-examination You will bring to my mind the people I have not forgiven in order that I may do so (Mt 18:35). I ask this in the precious name of Jesus. Amen.

As names come to mind, make a list of only the names. Include at the end of your list 'myself'. Forgiving yourself is accepting God's cleansing and forgiveness. Also, write 'thoughts against God'. Thoughts raised up against the knowledge of God will usually result in angry feelings toward Him. Technically, we don't forgive God because He cannot commit any sin. But you need to specifically renounce false expectations and thoughts about God and agree to release any anger you have toward Him.

Before you pray to forgive the people on your list, stop and consider what forgiveness is, what it is not, what decision you will be making, and what the consequences will be.

Forgiveness is not forgetting. People who try to forget find that they cannot. God says He will remember our sins no more (Heb 10:17), but God, being omniscient, cannot forget. 'Remember our sins no more' means that God will never use the past against us (Ps 103:12). Forgetting may be the result of forgiveness, but it is never the means of forgiveness. When we bring up the past against others, we are saying we haven't forgiven them.

Forgiveness is a choice, a crisis of the will. Since God requires us to forgive, it is something we can do. But forgiveness is difficult for us because it pulls against our concept of justice. We want revenge for offences suffered. However, we are told never to take our own revenge (Rom 12:19). You say, 'Why should I let these people off the hook?' That is precisely the problem. You are still hooked to them, still bound by your past. You will let them off your hook, but they are never off God's hook. He will deal with them fairly, something we cannot do.

You say, 'You don't understand how much these people hurt me!' By not forgiving them, you are still being hurt by them. How do you stop the pain? Forgive. You don't forgive others for their sake; you do it for your sake, so you can be free. Your need to forgive isn't an issue between you and the offender; it's between you and God.

Forgiveness is agreeing to live with the consequences of another person's sin. Forgiveness is costly. You pay the price of the evil you forgive. You're going to live with those consequences whether you want to or not; your only choice is whether you will do so in the bitterness of unforgiveness or the freedom of forgiveness. Jesus took the consequences of your sin upon Himself. All true forgiveness is substitutionary, because no one really forgives without bearing the consequences of the other person's sin. God the Father 'made Him who had no sin to be sin for us, so that in him we might become the righteousness of God' (2 Cor 5:21).

Where is the justice? It is the cross of Christ that makes forgiveness legally and morally right: 'The death he died, he died to sin once for all' (Rom 6:10).

How do you forgive from your heart? You acknowledge the hurt and the hate. If your forgiveness doesn't visit the emotional core of your life, it will be incomplete. Many people feel the pain of interpersonal offences, but they won't or don't know how to acknowledge it. Let God bring the pain to the surface so He can deal with it. This is where the healing takes place.

Decide that you will bear the burdens of their offences by not using the past against them in the future. This doesn't mean you must tolerate sin; you must always take a stand against sin.

Don't wait to forgive until you feel like forgiving; you will never get there. Feelings take time to heal after the choice to forgive is made and Satan has lost his place (Eph 4:26,27). Freedom is what will be gained, not a feeling.

As you pray, God may bring to mind offending people and experiences you have totally forgotten. Let Him do it even if it is painful. Remember, you are doing this for your sake. God wants you to be free. Don't rationalise or explain the offender's behaviour. Forgiveness is dealing with your pain and leaving the other person to God. Positive feelings will follow in time; freeing yourself from the past is the critical issue right now.

Don't say, 'Lord, please help me to forgive,' because He is already helping you. Don't say, 'Lord, I want to forgive,' because you are bypassing the hard-core choice to forgive, which is your responsibility. Stay with each individual until you are sure you have dealt with all the remembered pain — what the offender did, how he or she hurt you, how he or she made you feel (rejected, unloved, unworthy, dirty, etc.).

You are now ready to forgive the people on your list so that you can be free in Christ, with those people no longer having any control over you. For each person on your list, pray aloud:

Lord, I forgive (name) for (specifically identify all offences and painful memories or feelings).

Step 4: Rebellion Versus Submission

We live in a rebellious generation. Many people believe it is their right to sit in judgement of those in authority over them. But rebelling against God and His authority gives Satan an opportunity to attack. As our General, the Lord commands us to get into ranks and follow Him. He will not lead us into temptation, but He will deliver us from evil (Mt 6:13).

You may have a problem with authority figures because someone you looked up to or followed was instrumental in your moral downfall. Perhaps a teacher or coach abused you. Perhaps an employer or spiritual leader took advantage of you sexually. You may not trust or want to submit to other leaders because of what happened to you.

We have two biblical responsibilities in regard to authority figures: Pray for them and submit to them. The only time God permits us to disobey earthly leaders is when they require us to do something morally wrong before God or attempt to rule outside the realm of their authority.

Pray the following prayer:

Dear heavenly Father, You have said that rebellion is as the sin of witchcraft and insubordination is as iniquity and idolatry (1 Sam 15:23). I know that in action and attitude I have sinned against You with a rebellious heart. I ask Your forgiveness for my rebellion and pray that by the shed blood of the Lord Jesus Christ all ground gained by evil spirits because of my rebelliousness will be cancelled. I pray that You will shed light on all my ways that I may know the full extent of my rebelliousness. I now choose to adopt a submissive spirit and a servant's heart. In the name of Christ Jesus, my Lord, I pray. Amen.

Being under authority is an act of faith. You are trusting God to work through His established lines of authority. There are times when employers, parents, and husbands violate the laws of civil government which are ordained by God to protect innocent people against abuse. In those cases you need to appeal to the state for your protection. In many states, the law requires such abuse to be reported.

In difficult cases, such as continuing abuse at home, you may need further counsel. In some cases, when earthly authorities have abused their position and require disobedience to God or a compromise in your commitment to Him, you need to obey God rather than man.

We are all admonished to submit to one another as equals in Christ (Eph 5:21). However, there are specific lines of authority in Scripture for the purpose of accomplishing common goals:

- Civil government (Rom 13:1–7; 1 Tim 2:1–4; 1 Pet 2:13–17);
- Parents (Eph 6:1–3);
- Husband (1 Pet 3:1–4);
- Employer (1 Pet 2:18–23);
- Church leaders (Heb 13:17);
- God (Daniel 9:5,9).

Examine each area and ask God to forgive you for those times you have not been submissive:

Lord, I agree I have been rebellious toward (name or position). Please forgive me for this rebellion. I choose to be submissive and obedient to Your Word. In Jesus' name I pray. Amen.

Step 5: Pride Versus Humility

Pride is a killer. Pride says, 'I can do it! I can get myself out of this mess of immorality without God or anyone else's help.' But we can't! We absolutely need God, and we desperately need each other. Paul wrote, 'We...worship in the Spirit of God and glory in Christ Jesus and put no confidence in the flesh' (Phil 3:3 NASB). Humility is confidence properly placed. We are to be 'strong in the Lord and in His mighty power' (Eph 6:10). James

4:6–10 and 1 Peter 5:1–10 reveal that spiritual conflict follows pride.

Use the following prayer to express your commitment to live humbly before God:

Dear heavenly Father, You have said that pride goes before destruction and an arrogant spirit before stumbling (Prov 16:18). I confess that I have lived independently and have not denied myself, picked up my cross daily, and followed You (Mt 16:24). In so doing, I have given ground to the enemy in my life. I have believed that I could be successful and live victoriously by my own strength and resources. I now confess that I have sinned against You by placing my will before Yours and by centring my life around self instead of You. I now renounce the self-life and by so doing cancel all the ground that has been gained in my members by the enemies of the Lord Jesus Christ. I pray that You will guide me so that I will do nothing from selfishness or empty conceit, but with humility of mind I will regard others as more important than myself (Phil 2:3). Enable me through love to serve others and in honour prefer others (Rom 12:10). I ask this in the name of Christ Jesus my Lord. Amen.

Having made that commitment, now allow God to show you any specific areas of your life where you have been prideful, such as:

____ Stronger desire to do my will than God's will.

____ More dependent upon my strengths and resources than God's.

____ Sometimes believe that my ideas and opinions are better than others'.

____ More concerned about controlling others than developing self-control.

____ Sometimes consider myself more important than others.

____ Tendency to think I have no needs.

____ Find it difficult to admit I was wrong.

____ Tendency to be more of a people-pleaser than a God-pleaser.

____ Overly concerned about getting the credit I deserve.

____ Driven to obtain the recognition that comes from degrees, titles, positions.

____ Often think I am more humble than others.

____ Other ways that you may have thought more highly of yourself than you should.

For each of these that has been true in your life, pray aloud:

Lord, I agree I have been prideful in the area of _____ _____. Please forgive me for this pridefulness. I choose to humble myself and place all my confidence in You. Amen.

Step 6: Bondage Versus Freedom

The next step to freedom deals with habitual sin. People who have been caught in the trap of sin-confess-sin-confess may need to follow the instructions of James 5.16: 'Confess your sins to each other and pray for each other so that you may be healed. The prayer of a righteous man is powerful and effective.' Seek out a righteous person who will hold you up in prayer and to whom you can be accountable. Others may need only the assurance of 1 John 1:9: 'If we confess our sins, he is faithful and just and will forgive us our sins and purify us from all unrighteousness.' Confession is not saying 'I'm sorry'; it's saying 'I did it.' Whether you need the help of others or just the accountability of God, pray the following prayer:

Dear heavenly Father, You have told us to put on the Lord Jesus Christ and make no provision for the flesh in regard to its lust (Rom 13:14). I acknowledge that I have given in to fleshly lusts which wage war against my soul (1 Pet 2:11). I thank You that in

Christ my sins are forgiven, but I have transgressed Your holy law
and given the enemy an opportunity to wage war in my members
(Rom 6:12,13; Eph 4:27; James 4:1; 1 Pet 5:8). I come before Your
presence to acknowledge these sins and to seek Your cleansing (1
Jn 1:9) that I may be freed from the bondage of sin. I now ask You
to reveal to my mind the ways that I have transgressed Your moral
law and grieved the Holy Spirit. In Jesus' precious name I pray.
Amen.

The deeds of the flesh are numerous. You may want to open
your Bible to Galatians 5:19–21 and pray through the verses,
asking the Lord to reveal the ways you have specifically sinned.

It is our responsibility not to allow sin to reign in our mortal
bodies by not using our bodies as an instrument of unrighteousness (Rom 6:12,13). If you are struggling with habitual sexual sins (pornography, masturbation, sexual promiscuity) or
experiencing sexual difficulty and lack of intimacy in your marriage, pray as follows:

Lord, I ask You to reveal to my mind every sexual use of my body
as an instrument of unrighteousness. In Jesus' precious name I
pray. Amen.

As the Lord brings to your mind every sexual use of your
body, whether it was done to you (rape, incest, or any sexual
molestation) or willingly by you, renounce every occasion:

Lord, I renounce (name the specific use of your body) with (name
the person) and ask You to break that bond.

Now commit your body to the Lord by praying:

Lord, I renounce all these uses of my body as an instrument of
unrighteousness and by so doing ask You to break all bondages
Satan has brought into my life through that involvement. I confess
my participation. I now present my body to You as a living sacrifice, holy and acceptable unto You, and I reserve the sexual use of
my body only for marriage. I renounce the lie of Satan that my

body is not clean, that it is dirty or in any way unacceptable as a result of my past sexual experiences. Lord, I thank You that You have totally cleansed and forgiven me, that You love and accept me unconditionally. Therefore, I can accept myself. And I choose to do so, to accept myself and my body as cleansed. In Jesus' name I pray. Amen.

Special prayers for specific needs

Homosexuality

Lord, I renounce the lie that You have created me or anyone else to be homosexual, and I affirm that You clearly forbid homosexual behaviour. I accept myself as a child of God and declare that You created me to be a (your sex). I renounce any bondages of Satan that have perverted my relationships with others. I announce that I am free to relate to the opposite sex in the way that You intended. In Jesus' name I pray. Amen.

Abortion

Lord, I confess that I did not assume stewardship of the life You entrusted to me, and I ask Your forgiveness. I choose to accept Your forgiveness by forgiving myself, and I now commit that child to You for Your care in eternity. In Jesus' name I pray. Amen.

Suicidal tendencies

I renounce the lie that I can find peace and freedom by taking my own life. Satan is a thief, and he comes to steal, kill, and destroy. I choose life in Christ, who said He came to give me life and to give it abundantly.

Eating disorders or cutting yourself

I renounce the lie that my worthiness is dependent upon my appearance or performance. I renounce cutting myself, purging, or defecating as a means of cleansing myself of evil, and I announce that only the blood of the Lord Jesus Christ can cleanse me from my sin. I accept the reality that there may be sin present in me because of the lies I have believed and the wrongful use of my body, but I renounce the lie that I am evil or that any part of my body is evil. I announce the truth that I am totally accepted by Christ just as I am.

Substance abuse

Lord, I confess that I have misused substances (alcohol, tobacco, food, prescription or street drugs) for the purpose of pleasure, to escape reality, or to cope with difficult situations. The result has been the abuse of my body, the harmful programming of my mind, and the quenching of the Holy Spirit. I ask Your forgiveness, and I renounce any satanic connection or influence in my life through my misuse of chemicals or food. I cast my anxiety onto Christ, who loves me, and I commit myself to no longer yield to substance abuse but to the Holy Spirit. I ask You, heavenly Father, to fill me with Your Holy Spirit. In Jesus' name I pray. Amen.

After you have confessed all known sin, pray:

I now confess these sins to You and claim through the blood of the Lord Jesus Christ my forgiveness and cleansing. I cancel all ground that evil spirits have gained through my wilful involvement in sin. I ask this in the wonderful name of my Lord and Saviour Jesus Christ. Amen.

Step 7: Acquiescence Versus Renunciation

Acquiescence is passively agreeing with or giving in to something or someone without conscious consent. For example, to some extent your sexual bondage may be the result of tendencies or curses passed on to you from your ancestors. You did not have a vote in the matter, and likely you have little or no knowledge of such activities. You only reaped the sad results.

The last step to freedom is to renounce the sins of your ancestors and any curses which may have been placed on you. In giving the Ten Commandments God said: 'I, the Lord your God, am a jealous God, visiting the iniquity of the fathers on the children, on the third and fourth generations of those who hate Me' (Ex 20:4,5 NASB).

Familiar spirits can be passed on from one generation to the next if they are not renounced and if your new spiritual heritage in Christ is not proclaimed. You are not guilty for the sin of any ancestor, but because of their sin, Satan may have gained access to your family. This is not to deny that many problems are transmitted genetically or acquired from an immoral atmosphere. All three conditions can predispose an individual to a particular sin. In addition, deceived people may try to curse you, or satanic groups may try to target you. You have all the authority and protection you need in Christ to stand against such curses and assignments.

In order to walk free from past influences, read the following declaration and prayer to yourself first so that you know exactly what you are declaring and asking. Then claim your position and protection in Christ by humbling yourself before God in prayer and making the declaration aloud.

Declaration

I here and now reject and disown all the sins of my ancestors. As one who has been delivered from the power of darkness and translated into the kingdom of God's dear Son, I cancel out all demonic working that has been passed on to me from my ancestors. As one who has been crucified and raised with Jesus Christ and who sits with Him in heavenly places, I renounce all satanic assignments that are directed toward me and my ministry, and I cancel every curse that Satan and his workers have put on me.

I announce to Satan and all his forces that Christ became a curse for me (Gal 3:13) when He died for my sins on the cross. I reject any and every way in which Satan may claim ownership of me. I belong to the Lord Jesus Christ, who purchased me with His own blood. I reject all other blood sacrifices whereby Satan may claim ownership of me. I declare myself to be eternally and completely signed over and committed to the Lord Jesus Christ. By the authority that I have in Jesus Christ, I now command every familiar spirit and every enemy of the Lord Jesus Christ that is in or around me to leave my presence. I commit myself to my heavenly Father to do His will from this day forward.

Prayer

Dear heavenly Father, I come to You as Your child purchased by the blood of the Lord Jesus Christ. You are the Lord of the universe and the Lord of my life. I submit my body to You as an instrument of righteousness, a living sacrifice, that I may glorify You in my body. I now ask You to fill me with Your Holy Spirit. I commit myself to the renewing of my mind in order to prove that Your will is good, perfect, and acceptable for me. All this I do in the name and authority of the Lord Jesus Christ. Amen.

Once you have secured your freedom by going through these seven steps, you may find demonic influences attempting re-entry days or even months later. One person shared that she heard a spirit say to her mind 'I'm back' two days after she had been set free. 'No, you're not!' she proclaimed aloud. The attack ceased immediately.

One victory does not constitute winning the war. Freedom must be maintained. After completing these steps, one jubilant lady asked, 'Will I always be like this?' I told her that she would stay free as long as she remained in right relationship with God. 'Even if you slip and fall,' I encouraged, 'you know how to get right with God again.'

One victim of incredible atrocities shared this illustration: 'It's like being forced to play a game with an ugly stranger in my own home. I kept losing and wanted to quit, but the ugly stranger wouldn't let me. Finally I called the police (a higher authority), and they came and escorted the stranger out. He knocked on the door trying to regain entry, but this time I recognised his voice and didn't let him in.'

What a beautiful illustration of gaining freedom in Christ! We call upon Jesus, the ultimate authority, and He escorts the enemy out of our lives. Know the truth, stand firm, and resist the evil one. Seek out good Christian fellowship, and commit yourself to regular times of Bible study and prayer. God loves you and will never leave or forsake you.

After Care

Freedom must be maintained. You have won a very important battle in an ongoing war. Freedom is yours as long as you keep choosing truth and standing firm in the strength of the Lord. If new memories should surface or if you become aware of lies that you have believed or other non-Christian experiences you have had, renounce them and choose the truth. Some people have found it helpful to go through the steps again. As you do, read the instructions carefully.

For your encouragement and further study, read *Victory Over the Darkness* (or the youth version, *Stomping Out the Darkness*), and *The Bondage Breaker* (or *The Bondage Breaker: Youth Edition*). If you are a parent, read *The Seduction of Our Children*. *Walking in the Light* (formerly *Walking through the Darkness*) was written to help people understand God's guidance and discern counterfeit guidance.

Also, to maintain your freedom, we suggest the following:

1. Seek legitimate Christian fellowship where you can walk in the light and speak the truth in love.

2. Study your Bible daily. Memorise key verses. You may want to express the Doctrinal Affirmation daily and look up the verses.

3. Take every thought captive to the obedience of Christ. Assume responsibility for your thought life, reject the lie, choose the truth, and stand firm in your position in Christ.

4. Don't drift away! It is very easy to get lazy in your thoughts and revert back to old habit patterns of thinking. Share your struggles openly with a trusted friend. You need at least one friend who will stand with you.

5. Don't expect another person to fight your battle for you. Others can help but they can't think, pray, read the Bible, or choose the truth for you.

6. Continue to seek your identity and sense of worth in Christ. Read *Living Free in Christ* and the devotional *Daily in Christ*.

Renew your mind with the truth that your acceptance, security, and significance is in Christ by saturating your mind with the statements at the end of this chapter. Read the entire list aloud morning and evening over the next several weeks.

7. Commit yourself to daily prayer. You can pray the following suggested prayers often and with confidence:

Daily Prayer

Dear heavenly Father, I honour You as my sovereign Lord. I acknowledge that You are always present with me. You are the only all powerful and only wise God. You are kind and loving in all Your ways. I love You and I thank You that I am united with Christ and spiritually alive in Him. I choose not to love the world, and I crucify the flesh and all its passions.

I thank You for the life that I now have in Christ, and I ask You to fill me with Your Holy Spirit that I may live my life free from sin. I declare my dependence upon You, and I take my stand against Satan and all his lying ways. I choose to believe the truth, and I refuse to be discouraged. You are the God of all hope, and I am confident that You will meet my needs as I seek to live according to Your Word. I express with confidence that I can live a responsible life through Christ, who strengthens me.

I now take my stand against Satan and command him and all his evil spirits to depart from me. I put on the whole armour of God. I submit my body as a living sacrifice and renew my mind by the living Word of God in order that I may prove that the will of God is good, acceptable, and perfect. I ask these things in the precious name of my Lord and Saviour Jesus Christ. Amen.

Bedtime Prayer

Thank You, Lord, that You have brought me into Your family and have blessed me with every spiritual blessing in the heavenly realms in Christ. Thank You for providing this time of renewal through sleep. I accept it as part of Your perfect plan for Your children, and I trust You to guard my mind and my body during my sleep. As I have meditated on You and Your truth during this day, I choose to let these thoughts continue in my mind while I am

asleep. I commit myself to You for Your protection from every attempt of Satan or his emissaries to attack me during sleep. I commit myself to You as my rock, my fortress, and my resting place. I pray in the strong name of the Lord Jesus Christ. Amen.

Cleansing Home

After removing all articles of false worship from your home, pray aloud in every room if necessary.

Heavenly Father, we acknowledge that You are Lord of heaven and earth. In Your sovereign power and love, You have given us all things richly to enjoy. Thank You for this place to live. We claim this home for our family as a place of spiritual safety and protection from all attacks of the enemy. As children of God seated with Christ in the heavenly realm, we command every evil spirit that claims ground in the structures and furnishings of this place based on the activities of previous occupants to leave and never to return. We renounce all curses and spells utilised against this place. We ask You, heavenly Father, to post guardian angels around this home (flat, room, etc.) to guard it from attempts of the enemy to enter and disturb Your purposes for us. We thank You, Lord, for doing this, and pray in the name of the Lord Jesus Christ. Amen.

Living in a Non-Christian Environment

After removing all articles of false worship from your room, pray aloud in the space allotted to you.

Thank You, heavenly Father, for my place to live and to be renewed by sleep. I ask You to set aside my room (my part of the room) as a place of spiritual safety for me. I renounce any allegiance given to false gods or spirits by other occupants, and I renounce any claim to this room (space) by Satan based on activities of past occupants or myself. On the basis of my position as a child of God and a joint-heir with Christ who has all authority in heaven and on earth, I command all evil spirits to leave this place and never to return. I ask You, heavenly Father, to appoint guardian angels to protect me while I live here. I pray this in the name of the Lord Jesus Christ. Amen.

In Christ I am accepted

- I am God's child (Jn 1:12).
- I am Christ's friend (Jn 15:15).
- I have been justified (Rom 5:1).
- I am united with the Lord, and I am one spirit with Him (1 Cor 6:17).
- I have been bought with a price. I belong to God (1 Cor 6:19,20).
- I am a member of Christ's body (1 Cor 12:27).
- I am a saint (Eph 1:1).
- I have been adopted as God's child (Eph 1:5).
- I have direct access to God through the Holy Spirit (Eph 2:18).
- I have been redeemed and forgiven of all my sins (Col 1:14).
- I am complete in Christ (Col 2:10).

In Christ I am secure

- I am free forever from condemnation (Rom 8:1,2).
- I am assured that all things work together for good (Rom 8:28).
- I am free from any condemning charges against me (Rom 8:33–34).
- I cannot be separated from the love of God (Rom 8:35–39).
- I have been established, anointed, and sealed by God (2 Cor 1:21,22).
- I am hidden with Christ in God (Col 3:3).
- I am confident that the good work that God has begun in me will be perfected (Phil 1:6).
- I am a citizen of heaven (Phil 3:20).
- I have not been given a spirit of fear but of power, love, and a sound mind (2 Tim 1:7).
- I can find grace and mercy in time of need (Heb 4:16).
- I am born of God, and the evil one cannot touch me (1 Jn 5:18).

In Christ I am significant

- I am the salt and light of the earth (Mt 5:13,14).
- I am a branch of the true vine, a channel of His life (Jn 15:1,5).
- I have been chosen and appointed to bear fruit (Jn 15:16).
- I am a personal witness of Christ (Acts 1:8).
- I am God's temple (1 Cor 3:16).
- I am a minister of reconciliation for God (2 Cor 5:17–21).
- I am God's co-worker (1 Cor 3:9; 2 Cor 6:1).

- I am seated with Christ in the heavenly realm (Eph 2:6).
- I am God's workmanship (Eph 2:10).
- I may approach God with freedom and confidence (Eph 3:12).
- I can do all things through Christ, who strengthens me (Phil 4:13).

Taken from *Living Free in Christ* by Neil T. Anderson, published by Regal Books.